AF574893

Pre-Modernism

J. M. Mancini

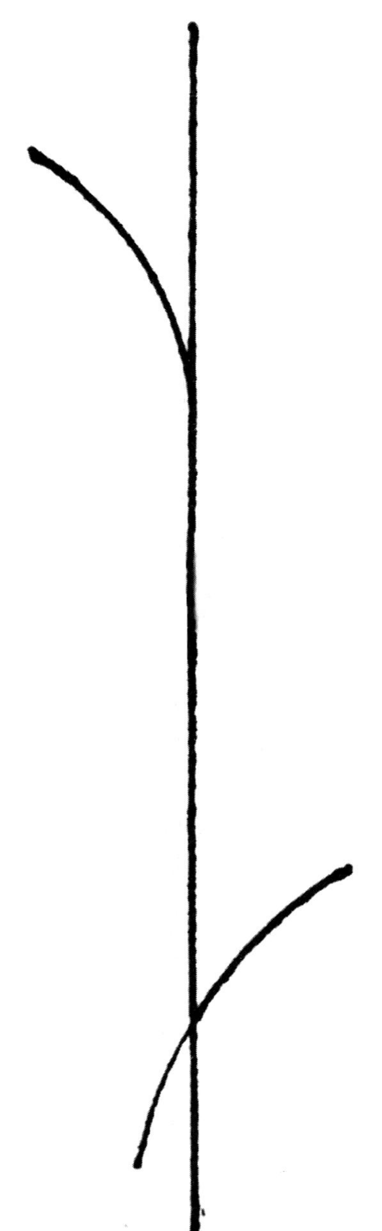

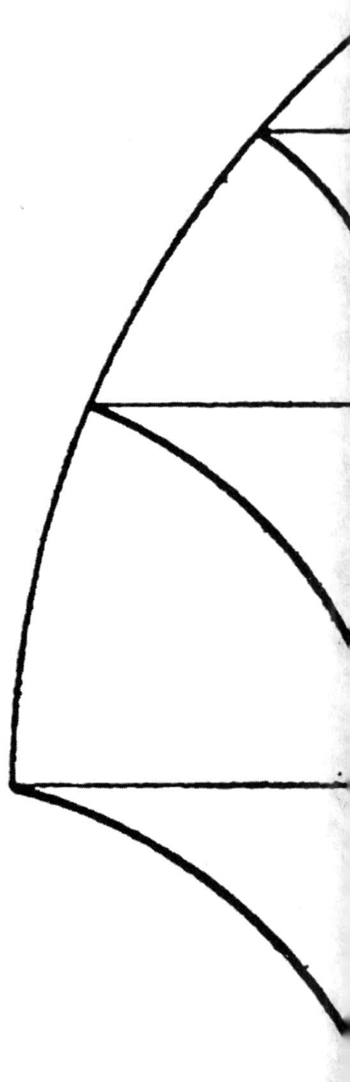

Princeton University Press
Princeton and Oxford

Pre-Modernism

Art-World Change and American Culture from the Civil War to the Armory Show

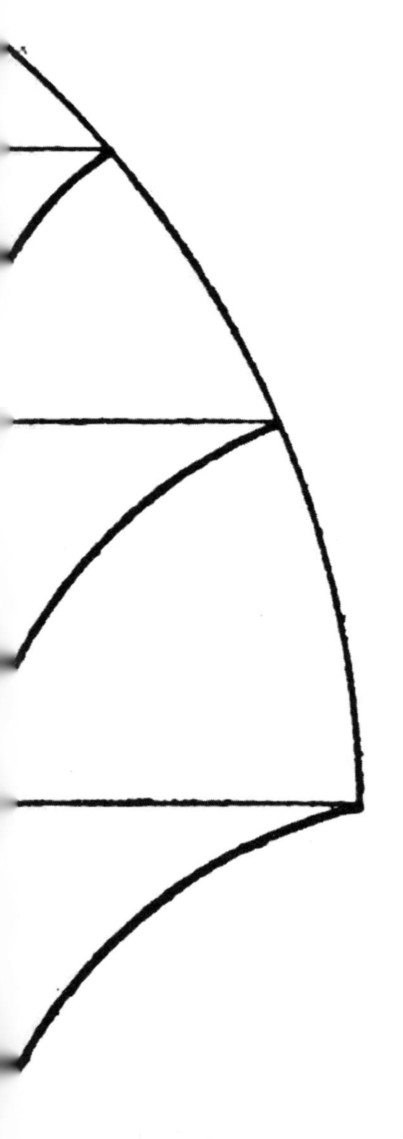

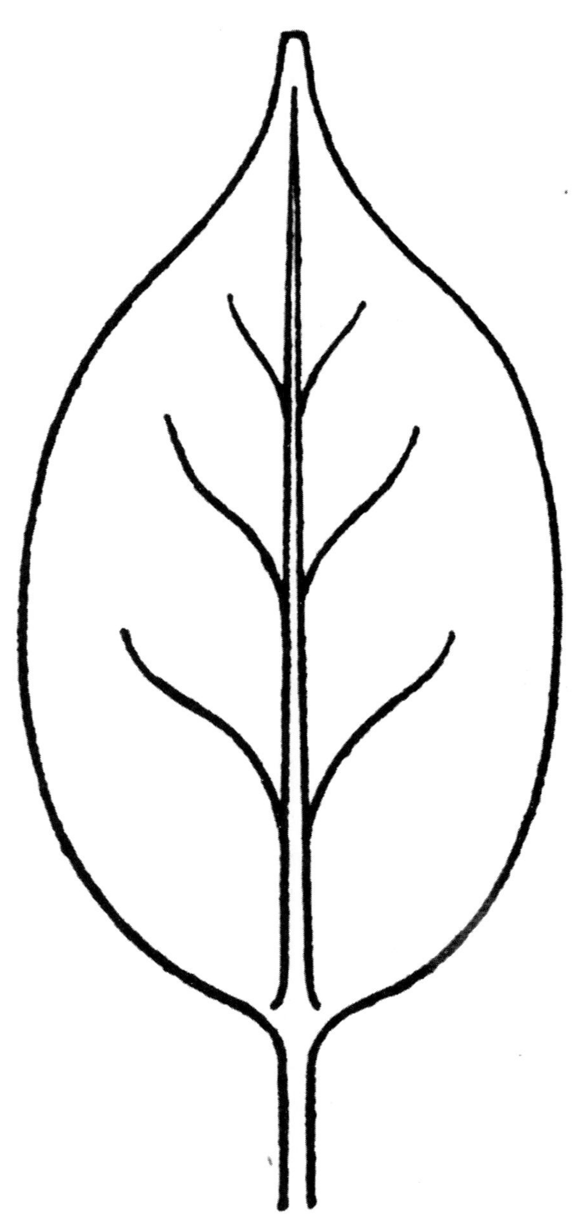

To my parents

And in memory of my grandparents

Published by Princeton University Press,
41 William Street, Princeton,
New Jersey 08540

In the United Kingdom: Princeton
University Press, 3 Market Place,
Woodstock, Oxfordshire OX20 1SY
pup.princeton.edu

Designed and composed by
Misha Beletsky
Printed by Maple-Vail, Binghamton,
New York

10 9 8 7 6 5 4 3 2 1

Library of Congress Cataloging-
in-Publication Data

Mancini, JoAnne Marie, 1968–
Pre-Modernism : art-world change and
American culture from the Civil War to
the Armory Show / J. M. Mancini.
p. cm.
Includes bibliographic references and
index.
ISBN: 0-691-11813-2 (cl : alk. paper)
1. Art, American–19th century. 2. Art,
American–20th century. 3. Modernism
(Art)–United States. I. Title.
N6510.M35 2005
306.4–dc 22 2004044530

Cover: Interior, *Munsell Crayons No. 3 Box, 22 Colors* (detail). Korzenik Art Education Ephemera Collection, Box 71, Set 4. The Huntington Library, San Marino, California

Frontispiece: detail of fig. 31

Contents

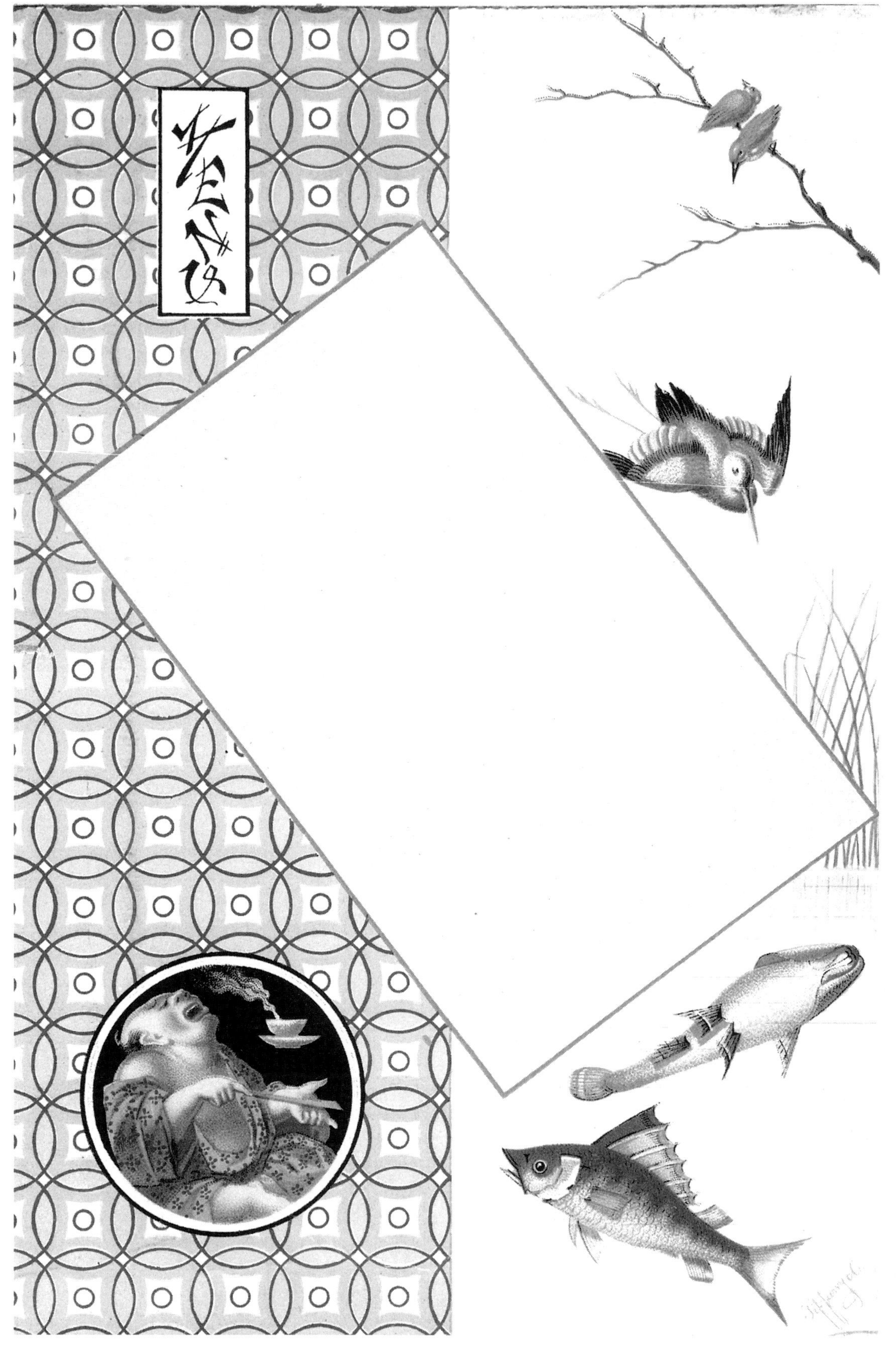
MENU

Introduction Interrogating Modernism

What distinguishes modern art
from the art of other ages is criticism.
—Octavio Paz, 1967

At the 1913 International Exhibition of Modern Art, better known as the Armory Show, thousands of Americans lined up to see what was billed as the first major exhibition of modern art in the United States. Even before the show opened, the art world was alive with anticipation. In a letter to her friend Gertrude Stein, the wealthy Greenwich Village salonist and patron of modern art Mabel Dodge set down a breathless account of what the show would mean to American culture. "There is an exhibition coming," she wrote, "which is the most important public event that has ever come off since the signing of the Declaration of Independence, & it is of the same nature. . . . The academy are frantic. Most of them are left out of it. . . . I am *all* for it . . . there will be a riot & a revolution & things will never be quite the same afterwards."[1] In these brief comments, Dodge provided a template that defined American modernism in its own time and dominated its historical interpretation for

1. Tiffany and Co., *Menu Card*, c. 1879. Published in *The Art Amateur* 1–2 (1879–80). Fine Arts Department, Boston Public Library

nearly a century: modernism as a riot, modernism as a revolution against existing institutions, modernism as a break in history.

This is a book about one of the most unyielding questions in the history of culture: the issue of how and why the course of art can appear to suddenly and dramatically change, in seemingly revolutionary fashion, from one dominant style to another. Under study here is one particular change, the emergence of modern art in the United States, and one very important aspect of that change: the roles that art criticism, art critics, and art publishing played in fostering not only a new aesthetic but also an altered mode of cultural production between the end of the Civil War and the second decade of the twentieth century.

From the outset, participants and scholars have devoted extensive effort to explaining the modernist revolution. As Dodge's comments indicate, modernists themselves were self-conscious about their own role as iconoclastic creators of a revolutionary upheaval in American art and culture. Many of modernism's early defenders not only described their activities as a challenge to outmoded artistic fashions, but also linked themselves to the loosening of moral strictures, the budding of radical politics, and the wholesale rejection of a stifling Victorian society in the years before the First World War. Over time, these self-creating gestures have become part of the historical fabric, so that it is sometimes impossible to separate performance from practice. This is not in itself surprising—historical figures always have a hand in their own self-fashioning. The difference is that modernists, unlike their peers the Progressives or their predecessors in the Gilded Age, still speak largely for themselves. Despite what seems like constitutional skepticism toward virtually everything anyone said at the turn of the century, once historians move out of the settlement house and the White City (see fig. 40) and into the bohemian quarters of the Village, they seem inclined to believe, along with Virginia Woolf, that "on or about December 1910, human character changed," and are content to direct their skepticism toward fiddling with the dates.[2]

While the revolution against outmoded standards of art and behavior unquestionably played a part in the transformation of American art, I believe that the roots of the modernist revolution were deeper and more tangled than acknowledged by participants or scholars. Modern art was neither an isolated collection of works and makers nor the mere byproduct of social and political radicalism, but a mutually constitutive set of institutional practices and aesthetic beliefs, deeply rooted in the immediate context of the American art world. More than that, it was a historical movement, with historical antecedents. As in the case of political revolutions, which historians convincingly have shown to be the product of multigenerational developments in political culture and language rather than immediate catalytic ruptures in the political order, the artistic revolution called "modernism" did not happen overnight but was made during the course of a generation or more by people who were not even necessarily modernists themselves.[3]

My primary objective here is to challenge the mythical history of American visual modernism as a sudden, revolutionary rupture with the past. My aim is to demonstrate that late-nineteenth-century art criticism and publishing contributed significantly to the emergence of modern art by fostering the aesthetic principles, like abstraction, that would underpin modernist artworks, and by establishing the institutional and professional framework that would allow American art and the avant-garde to flourish after the turn of the century. Specifically, this book makes three arguments. The first and most general one is that turn-of-the-century transformations in American art must be understood within the context of a broader and earlier boom in art publishing that included new mass visual media like magazines, chromolithography, and art education materials for the public schools. The second is that the drive by Gilded Age criticism to promote an integrated, national infrastructure of museums, schools, and associations—and to construct art publishing as a portable branch of the art world—provided not only the organizational topography of the "mainstream" twentieth-century American art world, but also the framework for avant-garde organizers like Alfred Stieglitz. And finally, I argue that a push toward professionalization in criticism that began as early as the end of the Civil War led writers to embrace the principle of abstraction even before artists did, a move that provided an aesthetic platform for modernism even as it strengthened the authority of professional criticism.

This book also seeks to reframe another key transformation in turn-of-the-century American culture: the emergence, in Lawrence Levine's famous phrase, of "cultural hierarchy."[4] Particularly among historians and sociologists, there has been little effort to challenge the hugely influential thesis, set forth by Levine and Paul DiMaggio, that the post–Civil War art world was predicated upon the establishment of "sacralized," nonprofit, metropolitan museums meant to house only original and unique art objects.[5] According to Levine and DiMaggio, this development (and parallel developments in music and theater) triggered the emergence of sharp divisions between "high art" and "popular culture" for the first time in the nation's history. In examining this issue, I will argue that the many interconnections between the "fine arts" and its institutions, including museums, and "popular" media such as the graphic, decorative, and industrial arts, militate against this view. I will not suggest that museum builders and their allies in publishing did not contribute to the stratification of art, particularly as the nineteenth century neared its end. Contrary to prevailing interpretations, however, I will contend that the key villains in this tale were not primarily entrepreneurs in either the nonprofit sector or the commercial world of image publishing, but the critics who sought to wrest professional control over the interpretation of art from both of them—and from their audiences.

This study rests upon a few basic premises. The first and most basic of these is that all art derives from and is defined by a multilayered process of cultural production, deeply rooted in the art world.[6] The most important implication of this is that in the art world, a complex nexus of interlocking constituencies including critics and publishers, museums, the public, patrons, art schools, the market, and artists, all play productive as well as supporting roles in the definition, creation, distribution, and consumption of art. Many people who were not artists at all—or who are considered to be "minor" artists—shaped the future of American art. In insisting on the importance of the art world, however, I do not wish to diminish the ingenuity or the work of artists. The choices available to artists were conditioned by the contexts in which they lived and worked, and their creativity was both fostered and limited by those contexts. Nonetheless, artists did not lack agency. Like publishers and museum builders, many turn-of-the-century artists were canny entrepreneurs whose *strategic* resourcefulness facilitated and enhanced their ability to pursue *creative* goals. If I emphasize this entrepreneurial aspect of artists' careers, it is not because of a lack of interest in their works or in artistic creativity. Rather, it is because many others are able to read and analyze it with far more eloquence than I. And, if I emphasize the significance of non-artists, it is not in order to denigrate the contributions of artists. Rather, it is because the very real roles these people played in making art—and in making art possible—are all too rarely acknowledged. This book is meant, then, as a companion to the many fine studies of the individual artists and artworks of the period, rather than as a polemic against them.

The second premise is that art worlds, and art-world practice, are historically specific. Like the styles that emerge from within art worlds, the latter change over time and develop in response to specific cultural conditions that vary with time and place. As a result, entire ways of making, understanding, and seeing art can be forgotten, lost, and rendered invisible with the passage of time, even when the works produced and consumed by those art worlds remain. Although art worlds and art-world practice are always the products of social conditions and social experience, neither they nor their constituencies are sociological universals. Like art, art worlds have histories that require historical interpretation.

The third supposition is that criticism, as both a discourse and an interlocking series of institutions and practices, is richer, more varied, and more important than is generally recognized. Perhaps more than any other art-world agent, criticism sets the art world's boundaries, not only shaping the modes of viewing and making that will be available at a given time and place, but also defining an art world's purpose, its personnel, and its aesthetics. What I mean by this is that even before a work is conceived, made, viewed, or interpreted, it has been fostered, directed, and limited by the critical context into which it is born. Aesthetics do not just proceed from artworks; they also precede them.

It is thus my intention to focus on something that has not generally received much attention: the importance of criticism and publishing in creating the parameters that define what kind of art will or will not be made, that determine who will or will not make art, and that delimit how and by whom art will or will not be seen. Sociologists of art have pioneered the study of how "organization and process" influence "how artists work and how their creations . . . are disseminated or marketed in relation to the broader socio-political-economic context."[7] And yet, even they often unnecessarily limit the history of criticism to purely the history of *taste*, and too narrowly describe the function of criticism as solely the legitimization of artworks that are *already made*. From the groundbreaking work of Howard Becker to the more recent efforts of Vera Zolberg and David Halle, the sociology of art often assumes that "artists produce works, some of which critics ratify."[8] But criticism also directly shapes what modes of "organization and process" are available to artists even *before* their works are made—and even *before they have become artists*. It is certainly true, as Malcolm Gee argues, that critics "have been central to the process by which twentieth-century artworks have been promoted, viewed, and understood."[9] It is crucial, however, to understand that critics both produce judgments and build systems.[10] To fail to ask what drives critics to promote entire art worlds as well as individual artists or artworks is to fail to understand one of the driving forces behind artistic change.

A related point that must be made here is that the history of American art and criticism in this period is inseparable from either the history of print culture or the history of art-world institutions—local, as well as international. European painting, training, and criticism undoubtedly had an immeasurable impact on American modernism;[11] Americans *were* insecure about their culture in the nineteenth and early twentieth centuries, and they *did* look outward not just for what was old, but also for what was new. It is true, as Johanna Drucker writes, that "Clive Bell and Roger Fry were read by Alfred Barr and Clement Greenberg who were read by Michael Fried and Rosalind Krauss, by Tim Clark and Victor Burgin."[12] And it is true that expatriate painters like James Abbott McNeill Whistler absorbed both European and Asian influences in their art and relayed them to fellow Americans abroad through their artworks, their critical commentary, and their personal relationships.[13] At the same time, however, many of the architects of American modernism, from the time of Manet to the time of Greenberg and at all points in between, were American: they went to American schools and museums; they read American books, magazines, and newspapers; and they worked in the American art world. The result was that foreign and expatriate influences, important as they were, were mediated through the institutions of the art world, including the media itself.

Take, for example, the case of Whistler, who (alongside Frank Lloyd Wright in architecture and Alfred Stieglitz in photography) is perhaps the only American painter before the middle of the twentieth century to be considered significant in the international development of modernism. In part, this is on account of Whistler's novel incorporation of Japanese design, which helped him to achieve the flat, decorative effects that became his trademark—and which would also be important to the work of other early American modernists like Mary Cassatt. To put in context Whistler's role as an importer of Japanese influences, however, it should also be noted that one of the most popular art sections of the massively attended 1876 Philadelphia Centennial was the Japanese display. This event gave many thousands of American men, women, and children their own firsthand glimpses of the prints, ceramics, and other works that had influenced Whistler. Following the success of this display, in 1879 the new magazine *The Art Amateur* presented a series of full-color *japoniste* "Menu Cards Presented to Subscribers . . . with Compliments of [its editor] Montague Marks," designed by Tiffany and Co. (fig. 1); Boston chromolithographer Louis Prang began selling sets of "Japanesque Floral Designs," priced at twelve cards for sixty cents; and *The American Art Review* published an illustrated article called "Notes on Hokusai, The Founder of the Modern Japanese School of Drawing" (fig. 2).[14] Its author was the collector of Japanese art, Edward Sylvester Morse of Salem, Massachusetts. Morse was also mentor to the first curator of Asian art at the Museum of Fine Arts, Boston, Ernest Fenollosa, who, in turn, was a major influence both on the artist and teacher Arthur Wesley Dow and on Ezra Pound, Fenollosa's literary executor.[15] Whistler's art (and personal contact with artists) was certainly important in bringing Japanese art to Americans, but it was not unique.

It is also notable that Whistler was himself shaped by his early experiences in the American art world, as well as by his expatriation. Born in Lowell, Massachusetts, Whistler began his artistic training in the Drawing Department of the United States Naval Academy under Robert Weir, father of artists Julian Alden Weir and John Ferguson Weir; the latter Weir also became the first Director of the Yale Art School.[16] Once again, this is not to make an argument for American exceptionalism, or to discount either foreign influences or the two-way experience of expatriation on Americans. Rather, it is to suggest that art-world institutions also

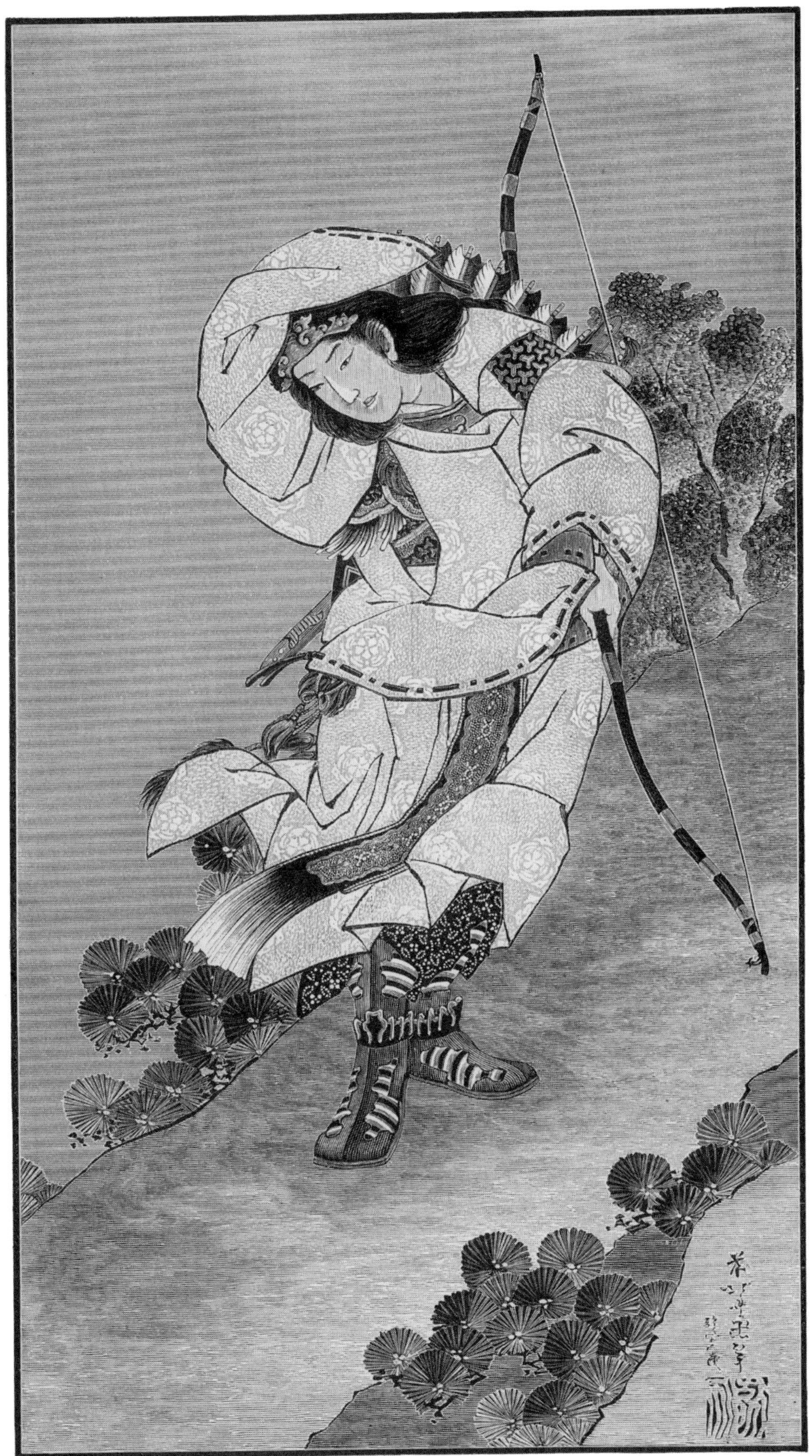

2. Unidentified artist after Hokusai (1760–1849), *Yamato-Daké No Mikoto*. Published in *The American Art Review* 1, div. 1 (1880). The Huntington Library, San Marino, California

played a formative but little-understood role in shaping American art, and provided an important context for the reception and translation of international influences.

Finally, it is necessary to say a few words about some of the terms that appear frequently in this book: "avant-garde," "vanguardism," "modernism," and "modern." The focus of this work is historical, rather than theoretical. As such, I do not aim to offer new definitions for these fraught and much-debated terms. Instead, I have tried to employ these expressions in ways that reflect what I have observed from my own research and the historical research of other scholars, without straying too far from definitions already in use elsewhere. It is hoped that a greater understanding of the historical context for the cultural changes in this period will help others to refine the "theory of the avant-garde" and the definition of modernism, particularly as they relate to American art and culture. This would be especially welcome because so much of the current theoretical literature for this period is based on European rather than American examples.

Definitions of the avant-garde vary widely.[17] Despite these differences, two aspects do link a number of descriptions of the avant-garde: its revolutionary intention, as Matei Calinescu writes, "to overthrow all the binding formal traditions of art and to enjoy the exhilarating freedom of exploring completely new, previously forbidden, horizons of creativity"; and its metaphorical origin in the military concept of the "advanced guard."[18] Drawing upon both themes—the "overthrow of traditions" and the use of military organization to attain it—I use the terms "avant-garde" or "vanguardism" primarily to describe the *organizational* efforts, employed largely but not exclusively by artists, to create institutions and fields for "progressive" art. Contrary to many other observers, however, I do not use "progressive" in a normative sense: it is not my aim to pass that kind of critical judgment on artworks, and I believe that the vanguard was only one among many locations in which "exhilarating" explorations of creativity occurred. What this definition does reflect, though, is the tendency of a number of turn-of-the-century artists (and artists' associations) to define their *own* work as "progressive," and to pursue rhetorical, organizational, and exhibition strategies that emphasized their newness and difference from older art and artists. It is for this reason, for example, that I have described both the 1877 Society of American Artists and Alfred Stieglitz's Photo-Secession as "vanguardist"—rather than because of similarities in the aesthetic character of their works.

The term "modernism" is somewhat more complicated because it must fulfill two distinct roles. First, it must describe a multifaceted *aesthetic* phenomenon: the movement in both art criticism and the visual arts away from representation and toward abstraction; the idealization of authentic, irreducible, art objects; the search for unique formal methods distinctive to individual artistic media; the effort to depict new conceptions of time and space within the visual arts; and so on. But "modernism" is also the most appropriate term for the broader overall artistic milieu I am describing, which includes both art and the art world. This is further complicated by the fact that modernism also cannot be entirely separated from vanguardism. Although it is useful, for analytical purposes, to distinguish between modernist aesthetics and avant-garde organizational strategies, they were often overlapping and mutually reinforcing phenomena. At times I have tried to overcome this difficulty by employing the hybrid phrases "vanguardist modernism" or "American visual modernism" to connote the general milieu (rather than aesthetics), but these expressions are too cumbersome to use with great frequency.

"Modern," on the other hand, will denote social, economic, or cultural phenomena (except when it is used to modify "art"). Like "modernism," this is a broad term, which refers not only to the self-consciously "modern" milieu populated by social nonconformists, but also to the wider cultural environment wrought by industrialization and its attendant social changes. Indeed, one of my aims here is to suggest how the relationship between "modernism" and "modernity" might be reformulated slightly to include more of an emphasis on how participants in the art world grappled with "modernity" in its broader aspects: how artists and artisans responded to de-skilling and obsolescence in the industrializing economy; how critics emulated the strategies of other professionals in order to capitalize on the post–Civil War crisis of authority; and how these social trends within the art world contributed to aesthetic change. These relationships were exceedingly complex, and I do not pretend to exhaust this line of analysis. Instead, I hope that this study will present future scholars with further avenues of inquiry.

In the end, the problem presented by these definitions mirrors the central difficulty posed by the research itself: how to relate social, cultural, or economic change to the question of aesthetic transformation. In order to untangle the history of modern art, it is also necessary to untangle the history of cultural hierarchy. That is the aim of this book.

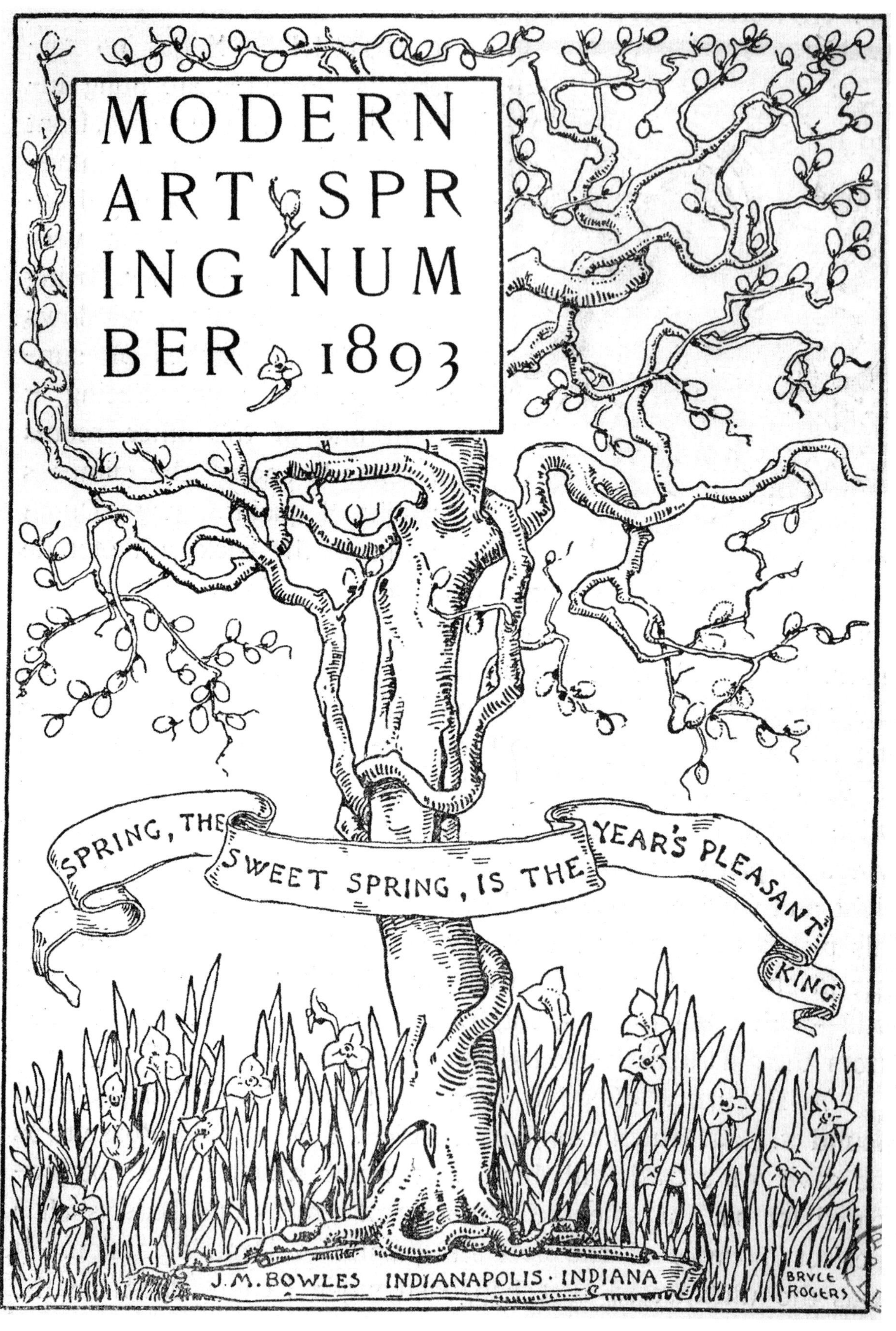
MODERN ART SPRING NUMBER 1893
SPRING, THE SWEET SPRING, IS THE YEAR'S PLEASANT KING
J. M. BOWLES INDIANAPOLIS · INDIANA
BRUCE ROGERS

Chapter 1

Modern Art and Modern Art: From the Christmas Card to the Avant-Garde

All this clamor and confusion of new movements is but the prelude to a new and grand expression in modern art.
—William Forsyth, 1894

In 1895, an Indianapolis editor, printer, and sometime gallery owner named Joseph Moore Bowles moved his magazine, *Modern Art* (fig. 3), from his home city to Boston.[1] This event and the journal itself were an instant hit in the local papers. As a page in the magazine entitled "Recent Comments on Modern Art" proudly reported, the *Boston Transcript* "confess[ed] that it is so beautiful we tremble for its fate"; to the *Boston Commonwealth*, "Modern Art [was] much the best thing published in America."[2] The journal also made a positive impression on the national press. The *New York Times* declared "The Spring Number" to be "admirable both in its makeup and in the quality of its reproductions," and suggested that "[t]hree of Raffaelli's pictures," reproduced in the journal, would be "much prized by art lovers." Even the tough-minded *Nation*, whose editor and founder Edwin Lawrence Godkin had once waged war against "the chromo-civilization," admitted that the magazine's

3. Cover of *Modern Art* 1, no. 2 (spring 1893), by Bruce Rogers. Fine Arts Department, Boston Public Library

"illustrations are on a higher level."[3] This was despite the fact that *Modern Art*'s new publisher was none other than Louis Prang, the "father of the Christmas card" and the chief purveyor of chromolithography in nineteenth-century America.[4]

The mere existence of *Modern Art*, then, immediately presents a number of questions. Why would the editor of a journal called *Modern Art* knowingly place it in the hands of an entrepreneur like Prang, whose images are synonymous with the sentimental and the sweet (fig. 4), the popular and the commercial (fig. 5)? What was a man so far from the reputed centers of the art world doing publishing an art magazine in the first place, let alone a journal called *Modern Art*? And, given these unlikely origins, how modernist, really, could *Modern Art* have been?

As it turns out, there was a lot that *was* modernist about *Modern Art*, beginning with the journal's overlap in personnel with the Stieglitz circle. Below Prang and Bowles on the masthead, the tables of contents in-

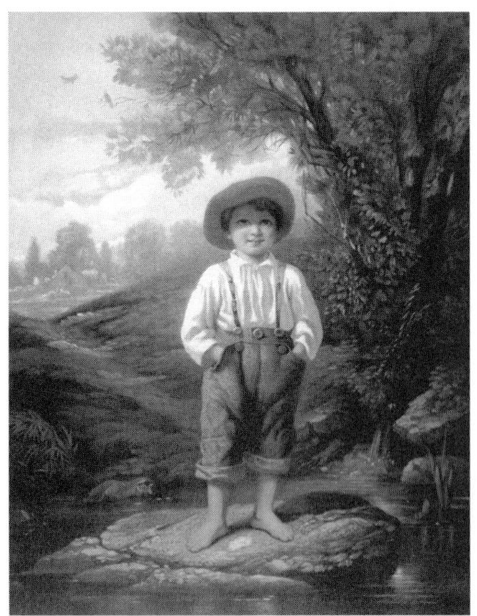

Above:
4. Unidentified artist after Eastman Johnson (1824–1906), *The Barefoot Boy*, 1867. Chromolithograph, 13 × 10 in. (33 × 25.4 cm). Printed by L. Prang & Co. Boston Public Library, Print Department

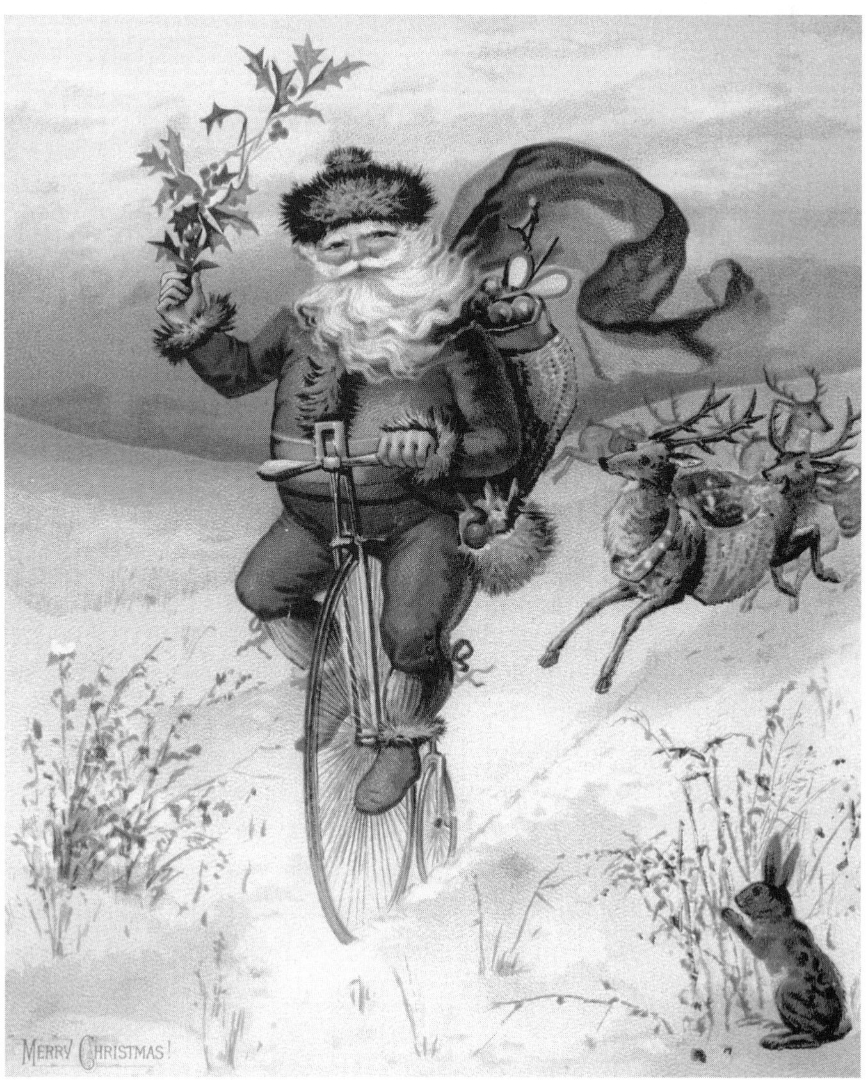

Right:
5. L. Prang & Co., *"Santa Claus" on Bicycle (Merry Christmas)*, 1886–87. Chromolithograph, 5 3/8 × 6 3/8 in. (13.7 × 16.2 cm). Boston Public Library, Print Department

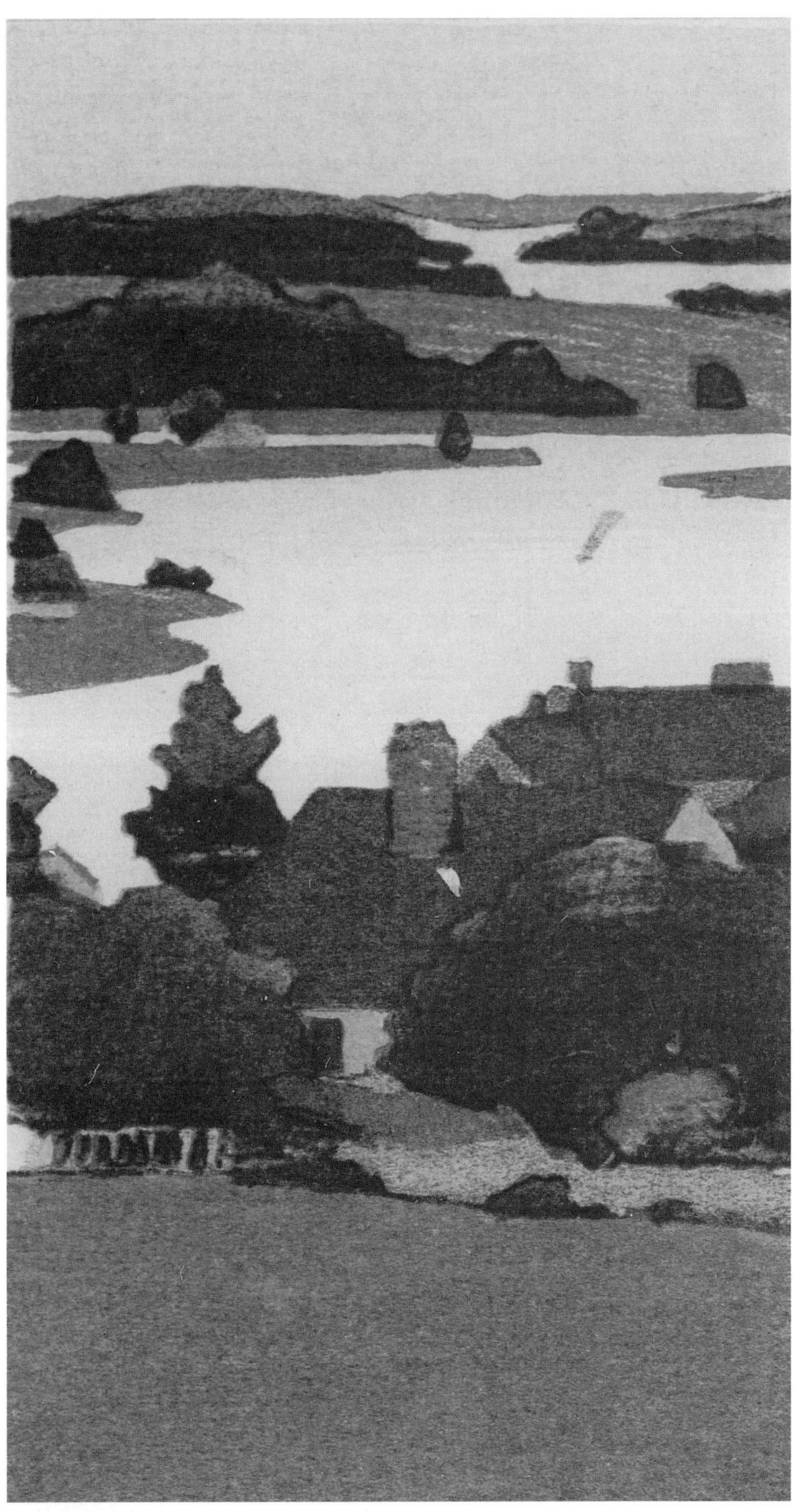

6. Arthur Wesley Dow (1857–1922), "Illustration, 'Along Ipswich River,' Fac-simile by Chromolithography of a Print from Wooden Blocks." *Modern Art* 4, no. 3 (summer 1896). The Huntington Library, San Marino, California

7. Arthur Wesley Dow, *Composition*, title page (Boston: J. M. Bowles, 1899). Fine Arts Library, Harvard College Library, Cambridge, Massachusetts

COMPOSITION

A SERIES OF EXERCISES SELECTED
FROM A NEW SYSTEM OF
ART EDUCATION
BY

ARTHUR W. DOW

Curator of the Japanese Paintings and Prints
Boston Museum of Fine Arts
Instructor in Composition at Pratt Institute
and at Art Students' League of New York

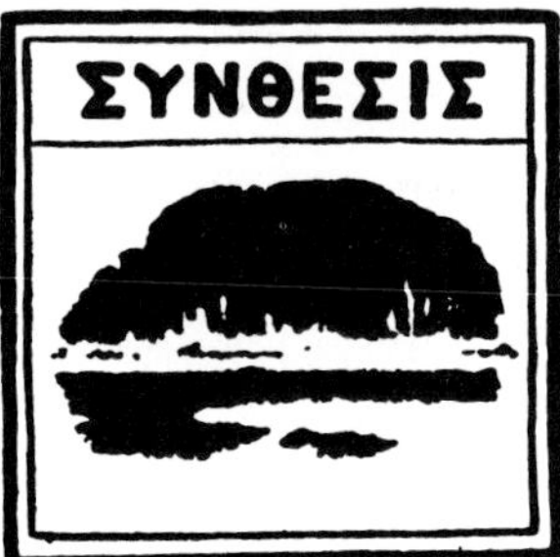

PART I

PUBLISHED BY J. M. BOWLES

No. 234 Congress Street
BOSTON
1899

cluded Arthur Wesley Dow, who taught Georgia O'Keeffe, Max Weber, and Alvin Langdon Coburn; and critic Sadakichi Hartmann, who, like Dow, was a proponent of modernism and a conduit for Japanese art in America.[5] After moving to New York in 1902 with his wife, arts and crafts metalworker Janet Payne Bowles, Bowles would himself go on to write for *Camera Work*.[6]

As the presence of these contributors suggests, *Modern Art* was a key site for the elaboration and circulation of an emerging modernist aesthetics in the 1890s. This can be seen in Dow's contributions. In 1896, *Modern Art* included an image from Dow's 1893 book of woodcuts, *Along Ipswich River* (fig. 6), reproduced as a "Fac-simile by Chromolithography." This was accompanied by Dow's explanation of the increasingly abstract, experimental approach that underpinned his work. In an article entitled "Painting with Wooden Blocks," Dow explained that his images did *not* "represent any place, or any time of day, or season." Rather, the "beautiful groupings of lines and shapes, chosen from the scenery of the old New England town," had simply provided "a groundwork for different color-schemes, for a mosaic of hues and shades." By keeping the design (the "lines and shapes") constant, but altering the colors he used in "successive inking of the blocks," Dow produced a series of very different compositions based upon the same scene. The result was "a purely imaginative treatment as brilliant and unreal as stained glass."[7] Three years later, Dow made this point even more clearly in another work published by Bowles, the teaching manual *Composition* (fig. 7).[8] Dow exhorted his students: "[T]hink of a picture first as pure design, secondly and subordinately as Representation."[9] The lesson proved popular, and *Composition* was reprinted over a dozen times by 1920.

Modern Art was also a kind of modern art in its own right. Visually and materially, the journal integrated many of the elements that would become staples of "little magazines" like Stone & Kimball's *Chap-Book*, published in Chicago in the 1890s, and Stieglitz's *Camera Work*, which began publication in 1902. With its self-described "artistic" typeface, "luxurious margins" and "imported, rough-edge, French hand-made paper," *Modern Art* advertised both its debt to William Morris and its difference from earlier art magazines like the visually dense *Art Amateur* (fig. 8).[10] While it may not have been "unique among periodicals," as its subscription page promised, it was quite unlike many of the art journals of the 1870s and 1880s, whose tiny fonts, multiple-column layout, and cramped margins show an overriding desire to squeeze in as much subject matter as possible. In contrast to "the many publications whose contents must surely have been collected to fill up space," as another of *Modern Art*'s testimonials put it, *Modern Art*'s design was simultaneously sparse and opulent. As such, it contributed to visual modernism's significant redefinition of "economy of design" in minimalist terms (fig. 9).[11]

Modern Art also reflected the rising generation's fondness for vanguardist enthusiasm. In 1894 Bowles's fellow Indianan, the painter William Forsyth, declared his sympathies with the "Secession: The New Movement in the Art of Germany." Himself a former student at Munich's Royal Academy and a contributor of images, as well as criticism, to the journal, Forsyth wrote that "the present art centers of the world are just now very much alive, and as a consequence revolutions, or at least rebellions, of more or less magnitude, are of frequent occurrence; so frequent, in fact, that many who love the calm, unruffled peace of settled opinion predict the smash of all standards of established taste, with chaos at the end of it all. Possibly their view of things may be the true one, but to those of more hopeful spirit, all this clamor and confusion of new movements is but the prelude to a new and grand expression in modern art."[12] Fusing sympathy with the new to impatience with "exploded bogey-criticisms," *Modern Art* thus became a voice for a newly emergent, newly self-conscious vanguardism in the 1890s.

If *Modern Art*'s new look and its talk of revolution signified a self-conscious desire to break from the past, however, it is absolutely essential to understand the degree to which it also belonged to, and was sustained by, an art world that was passing. In a crucial sense, *Modern Art*—and the 1890s themselves—were *pivotal* rather than *revolutionary*, joining the postwar art world to the modernist art world that would emerge after the turn of the century. Even before he took over as publisher, Prang's presence could be seen in articles like Katherine M. Ball's lengthy and admiring discussion of his contribution to color theory. "The world has long known standards of weights and measures," she declared, "but to Mr. Louis Prang, of the Prang Educational Company . . . are we indebted for

8. "Fancy Work." Typical page from *The Art Amateur* 1 (June 1879). Fine Arts Department, Boston Public Library

WOOD-CARVING FOR WOMEN.

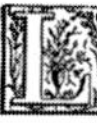ATELY our schools of design have run strongly to some one branch. The course of instruction includes, no doubt, a liberal number of studies, but the tendency of the day toward specialties apparently invades the school, and the best work is to be found in some one department.

Thus, in New York, much wood engraving is done; in the St. Louis school the specialty has been porcelain decoration, and in Cincinnati the one thing which has been most talked of is the "Cincinnati wood-carving." This is due to the individual enthusiasm and energy of Mr. Benn Pitman, to whose national reputation as a phonographer was added years of practical interest in all matters pertaining to art, and especially to industrial art. About four years ago, Mr. Pitman fitted up, at his own expense, a room for a class in wood-carving, to which he gave free instruction. Very soon there were not less than seventy-five ladies at work, and the experiment was so palpable a hit that the wood-carving class was made a permanent department in the School of Design. During the first year there were begun, finished and taken in hand several hundred pieces of work, large and small, and at the close of the year a most creditable exhibition was made. The work shown at the Centennial was the result of the training of two years, and, in beauty of design and good mechanical execution, attracted universal praise. It was then, and is yet comparatively so new a thing for women to work with tools, that a description in detail of the carving-room on a working morning may be interesting.

The tools which were used during the first two years were small tools, chisels, gouges and stamps, exactly like professional carving tools, in miniature. Probably much of the first success of the women of the class was due to use of these tools, which were so short that they required merely a motion of the hand and wrist, to which women were already accustomed. Though there was no compulsion in the matter, a small wall-pocket was usually the first piece of work undertaken. That was alpha, and there was no perceptible omega. With the assurance born of success, girls sat down to carve a cabinet that they knew it would take them weeks to accomplish. The first lesson consists in simply sketching on a panel some simple design, either natural or conventional. This was outlined by the tool, and the design either molded slightly, and left as "concised work," or cut away in relief. The background was stamped, breaking the grain of the wood, which then more readily absorbed the oil, and formed a soft, rich background that was most effective. When finished, the panel was oiled, and was a piece of work which was a thing of beauty and a joy to the pupil until the sight of better work imbued her with a divine discontent. The one thing insisted on was faithfulness and truth of design, and so, no matter how crude the execution, the work had a certain artistic value. It meant something. The leaves and flowers were studied from the life. The pupil followed copy faithfully, and though you might miss the purple and gold of her fancies, they would certainly escape the possible humiliation of being mistaken for roses. Every possible article of household furniture fell under the chisel of the school of design girl. The exhibition room was crowded with tables, with triple gothic standard, and elaborately carved; mirror frames, picture frames, brackets, caskets, cabinets—standing and hanging, chairs, "prie-dieus," every article of use or ornament, and all decorated in appropriate designs. That is the beauty of this hand carving. If an article demands individual decoration, it may receive it, and designs need never be duplicated. Are we not all very tired of the stereotyped carved leaves of the furniture stores? And is it not worth something that the carved convolvuli on the panel at the head of a bedstead should be sleepy and shut, while those at the foot, which salute one's first morning glance, are wide open? It gratifies that fine sense of the eternal fitness of things which we are beginning to carry about with us, that poppies should be carved in the Spanish mahogany of the baby's crib, and water lilies float on the panels of the washstand. Many will remember the decoration of the cabinet organ at the Centennial, done by Miss Banks, of the School of Design, and the bedstead so elaborately carved by the Misses Johnson. The pupils have, for some time, used the regular professional carving tools, though still retaining the smaller ones for work of delicacy. If this wood carving resulted simply in the making of pretty things to decorate the homes of women already rich in luxuries, it would, though desirable, hardly be a matter of any serious consideration. But it does much more than this. It is one of the vigorous beginnings of our industrial art. It is creating a market demand for itself, and unemployed women are glad to work to supply the demand. For the vast number of women who occupy the debatable land between housework and teaching, who will not do the one and who cannot do the other, this, or any other branch of artistic handwork is really the ideal work.

The best carving tools manufactured are the Addis tools, of English make. There are, of course, a large number of tools, but a well-selected assortment of thirteen gouges, chisels and stamps, will do any work which an amateur would be apt to undertake in wood-carving.

The first thing for the pupil to do is to learn to handle the tools and manage the grain of the wood. For a first lesson, then, take a block of inch black walnut, 10 x 6 inches, free from knots and cross grain, and dressed on both sides. Any other wood will of course answer the purpose, if black walnut is inaccessible, or, as it is in some localities, too expensive to be cut to pieces in first exercises. Fasten the block to your carving bench—if not a regularly made bench, it must be a solid table—with a hand-screw or a common carriage clamp, which can be bought at any hardware store. This clamp is smaller, more easily handled, and sufficient to hold firmly any but the largest pieces of work.

Clamp the block to the bench, then, with gouge No. 4 of the Addis tools, cut a concave chamber straight across the block, cutting with the grain. Take care to keep the tool in the same position, and aim to make a clean, straight, even cut. Most beginners spend an unnecessary amount of strength in trying to cut deep. That is useless. In these chambers a light cut is as good as a deep one, only let it be of uniform depth and width. Fill the block with these concave chambers, running parallel to each other and $\frac{1}{16}$ inch apart. Then take off the edge of each of the four sides in a concave chamber. This will be more difficult. Now one side of your block is full. If the cutting is good and clean and satisfies you, consider that exercise finished. If not, repeat it on the other side of this block and on other blocks until you can carry the gouge with a firm, free sweep, just where you want it.

Take another block like the first. Rule a pencil line $\frac{1}{4}$ inch from the edge all around. Cut a concave chamber straight across the block, exactly as before, but stop short at the pencil line. Set a chisel at the end of the chamber on the pencil line, cut straight down. Turn the block, and carry the gouge back, finishing up the other end of the chamber in the same way. This is a concave chamber cut short, and is an excellent bit of practice, as a beginner finds it much more difficult to stop a tool than to set it or help it going. The above exercise is a practical first lesson in wood-carving. CALISTA HALSEY.

SPATTER-WORK.

AMONG the many ways of utilizing the fern-leaf for decorative purposes none, we think, produces such beautiful results as spatter-work. To one who does not know the secret, it seems little short of a miracle that the fern forms, in all their grace, can be so literally transformed to such common-place objects as table-tops, work-boxes, and card-receivers. The first impression is that the work is done by photography, which seems the only way to account for the delicate gradations of shade which can be so skillfully contrived as to make the designs appear to stand out in bold relief from the background. Yet the process is quite simple. Before attempting to apply it to wood-work, the novice had better begin on Bristol board, which, lined with silk and bound with narrow ribbons, can be used for a variety of such objects as wall brackets, cigar-stands, portfolios, glove boxes, and handkerchief cases.

The pattern need not be confined to fern designs. Well pressed sprays of ivy, maiden's-hair, bits of strawberry-vine, and tiny leaves will furnish a variety of graceful patterns. In addition to the Bristol board there will be needed India-ink, a fine-toothed comb, a tooth-brush with long stiff bristles, a few drawing pins, a tack hammer, some small ordinary pins, and a drawing-board, on which to fasten the work. The Bristol board having been well secured with drawing pins, place your leaves and ferns in position to form the pattern you have previously determined on, and be careful to pin down the leaves so firmly that when you begin to use the ink it will not spatter under them.

The ink should be rubbed from the cake into a small saucer containing a little water until the mixture is about the consistency of cream. Dip the tooth-brush into it and, holding it over the paper, rub it against the comb so as to spatter the ink; or you may dip the comb into the ink, if you please, and rub the brush against the comb. This is repeated until the background is the desired shade. Some parts will have to be darker than the others to give the idea of perspective; but in darkening these it must be borne in mind that the ink will appear blacker when dry.

When the ink is dry, take the pins out carefully and remove the leaves, the forms of which will now appear on the Bristol board as white on a gray background. The details of the design, such as veining the leaves, must be filled in with a camel-hair brush, and the general effect produced will depend a good deal on the skill shown in the shading, which must be done with delicacy and taste. When the work is quite dry, a hot iron is pressed on the wrong side of the Bristol board.

In applying spatter-work to wood, perfectly smooth white holly wood should be used, and burnt umber, which produces a beautiful brown, should be substituted for the India-ink. The artistic effect is greatly enhanced in results achieved by this kind of spatter-work by the judicious use of fine varnish, which changes the light parts of the wood to a pale yellow, making them harmonize beautifully with the rich brown of the background of the object.

A CHEAP SUBSTITUTE FOR STAINED GLASS.

PAINTED glass fire-screens have been much used during the past winter, their opaque surface being usually adorned by a central medallion and pretty corner designs. The ruddy glare of the flames behind, lighting up all the colors with a brilliant glow, produces a beautiful effect. An ingenious and very cheap substitute for painted glass, not only for fire-screens, but for window blinds, which at this season of the year is more to the purpose, has been devised by Charles H. Chapin, the artist. It is in use at his studio at the corner of Broadway and Twenty-first street, and we do not doubt that he would be pleased to receive a visit from any one who wanted to copy the idea. He takes a yard or two of bleached muslin, of good quality, and stretches it on such a frame as is used for mosquito netting. First, a preparation of light colored varnish and turpentine, mixed in about equal parts, is applied with a varnish brush. This makes the material transparent. It is placed so that a current of air will pass through it, and then it will dry in about two hours. When it is dry, the design is traced with a lead pencil, it being transferred from a rough drawing on paper, by holding the copy against the window, so that the light passes through both paper and cloth, on the same principle as a child's drawing slate. The outline being filled in, he takes some ordinary tube color, thins it with drying-oil, and applies it, not with a brush, but with a cloth. But as the texture of the muslin would otherwise show through now, he takes a dry rag, without color, and rubs the other side of the cloth. After the broad tints are put in, the details are finished in oil color with a brush in the ordinary way. The colors, of course, cannot be made as brilliant as those generally used for stained glass. But for the purpose to which they are applied, they are the better for that; for the effect of their somberness is to give a pleasant subdued light to the apartment. Mr. Chapin has had to put two or three thicknesses of heavy paper behind the blinds he has made for his studio, so as to reduce the volume of light.

FRET-SAWING.

THE illustration at the top of this page will give the amateur wood-worker an idea for a motto and frame, and perhaps a suggestion for other designs. Fret-sawing will receive especial attention in our next number.

standards of color."[13] After *Modern Art*'s move to Boston, Prang's influence became more pronounced. The full-page spread of admiring reviews with which Bowles celebrated the transition closely resembled similar sheets Prang had used to sell chromos. A page in *Kaufmann's American Painting Book* of 1871 entitled "What Is Said About Prang's Chromos," for example, proffered glowing reviews from the *Boston Traveller*, the *New York Evening Mail*, the *Zeitschrift für Bildende Kunst*, and the *North British Daily Mail*, as well as the acclaim of the painter Frederic Edwin Church, Ralph Waldo Emerson, and the art-collecting senator from Massachusetts, Charles Sumner.[14]

Bowles's affiliation with Prang provided him with more than just the

MODERN SYMBOLISM

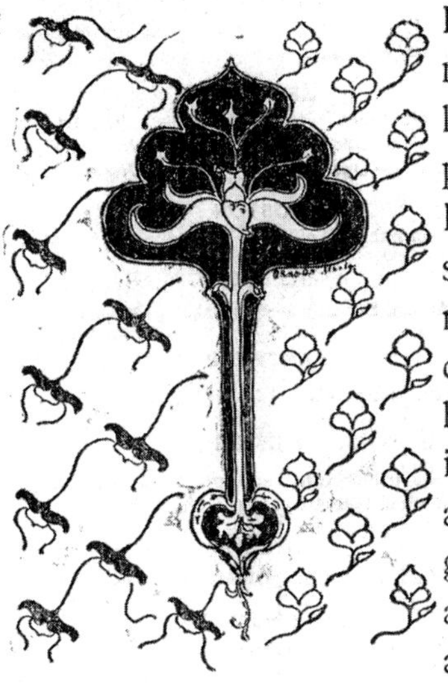

HE revival of symbolism is one of the marked tendencies of the times in at least two or three of the great art producing countries of the world. In Paris, where every phase of art is strong and there is always room for a new sensation, the followers of this cult are well organized and hold exhibitions open to the uninitiated; which is a mistake, as the Philistine is more amused than benefited. In England the great school of decorative artists there are strongly tinged with this influence, almost mediæval, in spite of the very modern way in which it is sometimes expressed. In Belgium are several names well known to students of the restless, ever-changing world of art as dreamers of strange phantasies. In Holland, to quote again from the letter from The Hague, "there is a whole 'school' of symbolists. * * We were astonished at Beardsley's eccentricity, you know, but Beardsley is tame and prosaic—an exact copyist of nature's forms—a realist, compared to some of these vague imaginations. I don't know the artists' names, I was not interested enough to notice, but the things surely have a weird fascination."

In Germany, as will be seen by the curious plate reproduced on the opposite page, they have symbolism with a vengeance. But I will leave it to my readers to guess the significance of the grief of the gentleman in checked trousers. One might almost start another prize competition with regard to it. The question is, what is the motive power that causes such waves of thought? Is it the necessary reaction from extreme, merciless realism—one more revolution of the wheel of time?

9. "Modern Symbolism." Typical page from *Modern Art* 2, no. 4 (autumn 1894). Fine Arts Department, Boston Public Library

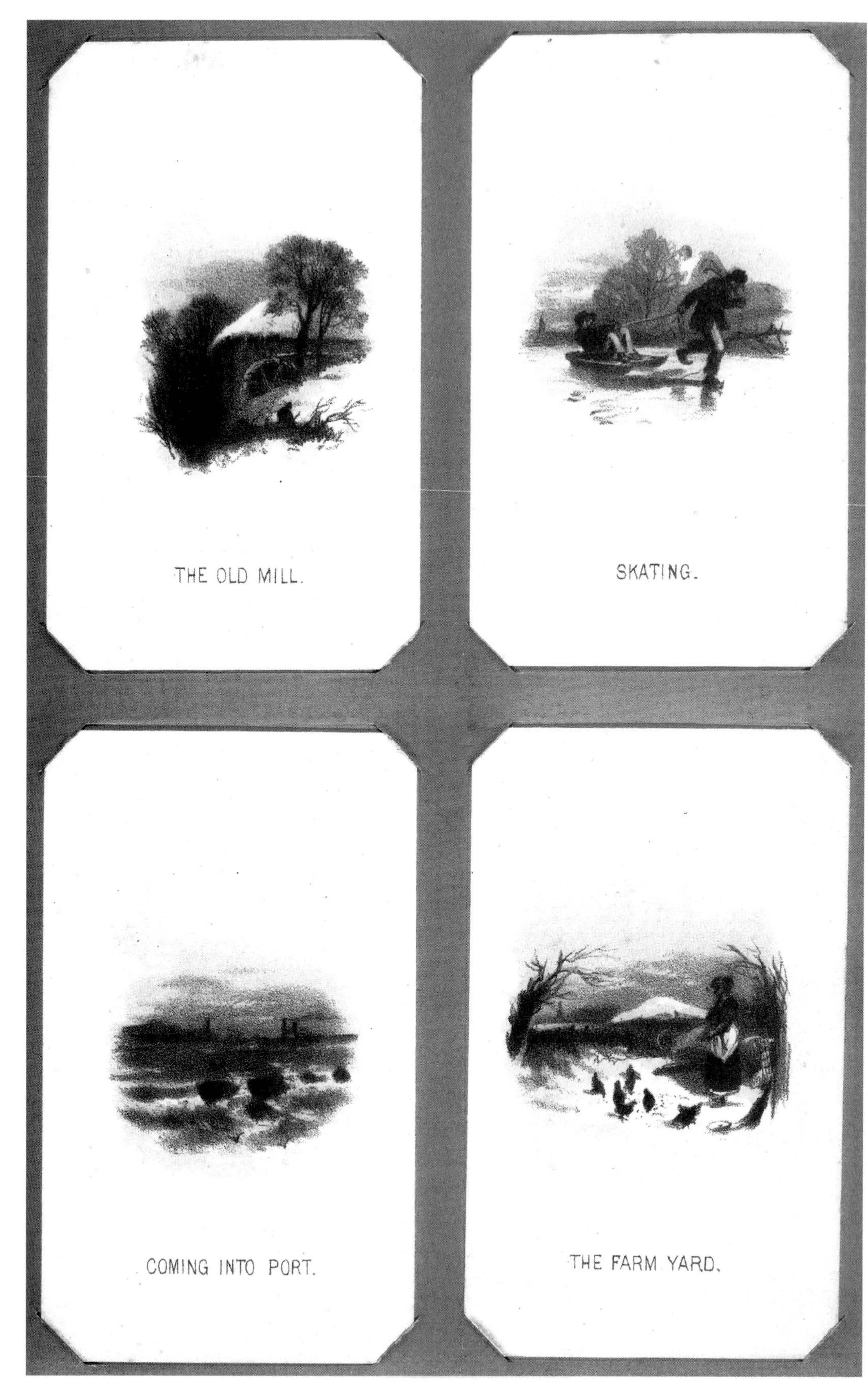
THE OLD MILL.
SKATING.
COMING INTO PORT.
THE FARM YARD.

publisher's sales techniques. It also gave him access to the chromolithographic process itself, which allowed *Modern Art* to incorporate full-color illustrations. Since the 1860s, Prang had sold hundreds of thousands—perhaps millions—of color images to consumers across the United States and Europe. These ranged from inexpensive images of flora, fauna, and outdoor scenes (fig. 10) "in oil colors . . . put up in envelopes containing 12 cards," to luxurious replicas of the brilliantly colored Western landscapes of Church, Albert Bierstadt, and Thomas Moran (fig. 11).[15] By the 1890s, audiences had lost the taste for these grand views of Colorado and California. As can be seen from Dow's work, however, American artists

Opposite:
10. L. Prang & Co., *Outdoor Scenes.* Chromolithographs. From *American Album* (Boston: L. Prang & Co., 1864). The Huntington Library, San Marino, California

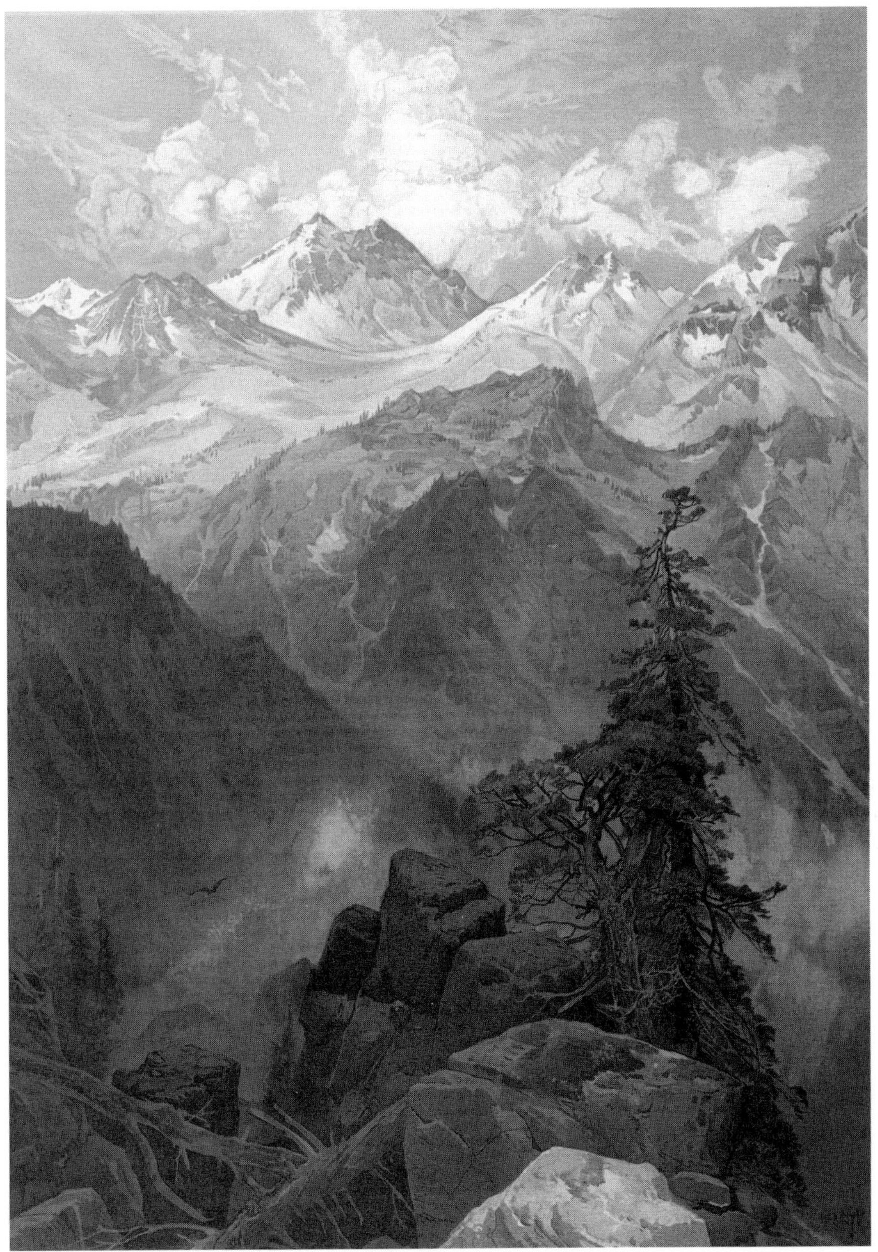

11. Thomas Moran (1837–1926), *Summit of the Sierra Nevada.* Chromolithograph. Published in Ferdinand V. Hayden and Thomas Moran, *The Yellowstone National Park* (Boston: L. Prang & Co., 1876). The Huntington Library, San Marino, California

continued to join experimentation with color to the depiction of the landscape, and Prang continued to support this process by publishing their results—even when the end product was a very different kind of art than is normally associated with the "chromo-civilization."

Modern Art's debt to the past extended well beyond Prang to an entire generation of publications whose content and techniques, if not whose overall design, Bowles appropriated. One area in which the journal emulated its predecessors was in its multiple focus on painting alongside the decorative arts, the graphic arts, and printing.[16] This mirrored the content of general-interest monthlies such as *Harper's* and *Scribner's*, and of art magazines like the *American Art Review*, which commonly featured articles on painting alongside writings on architecture, ceramics, metalwork, textiles, and even "points of taste in rural ornamentation." In a not-atypical table of contents for the *Art Amateur*, "Whistler as an Etcher" was followed directly by "Wood Carving for Women."[17] It is not surprising that Bowles would have emulated this aspect of postwar publishing. Like Dow, who advocated "synthesis" (see fig. 7) or the pursuit of virtuosity in fields of art ranging from printmaking to ceramics to metalwork, Bowles was active in promoting the arts and crafts from the 1880s onward. From 1892 to 1895 he was a member of the board of directors of the Indianapolis Art Association (1883), which held a display of textiles by William Morris in 1892.[18]

Modern Art appropriated the methods of the postwar art media in two of its other regular features, the "Table of Art Exhibits" and the "Table of Art Reading." Both of these features provided exactly what their titles promised: voluminous lists of recent and forthcoming art events and publications that introduced readers to a broad section of events and publications "for present study and future reference."[19] Significantly, these "Tables" were offered without distinction as to each entry's relative merit. Unlike the journal's authored essays (Hartmann's commentary on Aubrey Beardsley, for example), which encouraged readers to approach art from a particular aesthetic perspective, the "Tables" encouraged readers to follow their own inclinations. As such, they closely resembled features like *Harper's Monthly*'s "Editor's Literary Record," the *Art Amateur*'s "Art Publications," and the *American Art Review*'s "Bibliography," which aimed (among other things) to provide a comprehensive list of "Articles on Art Contained in American Periodicals."[20]

Instead of convincing readers of the merits or defects of particular artists, artworks, or schools of criticism, the "Tables" presented a wide range of art-world options to be sampled. If readers followed *Modern Art*'s bibliographical suggestions, they would have encountered many of the rising generation of artists and critics, including Photo-Secession cofounder Gertrude Käsebier and writer Henry McBride, who as art critic

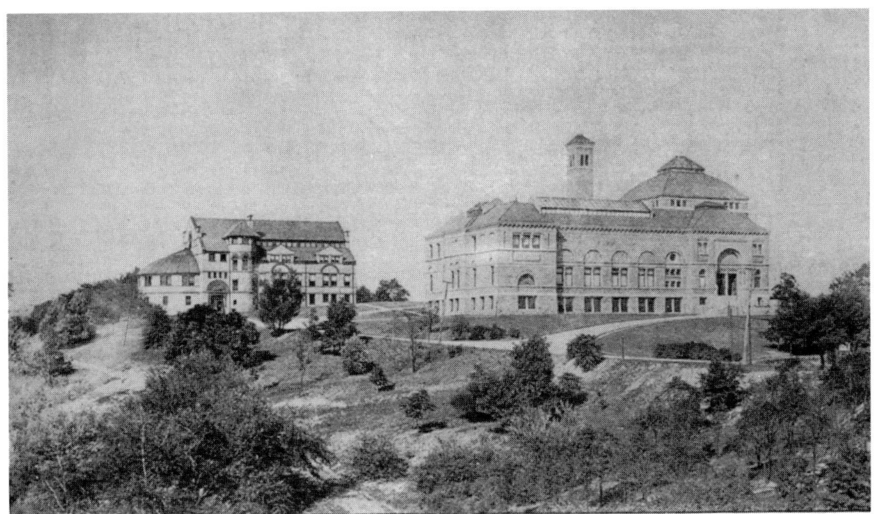

The Cincinnati Museum of Art

The Cincinnati Museum Association maintains an Art Museum and an Art Academy in Eden Park. It was incorporated in 1881; opened the Museum building in May, 1886, and the Academy building in November, 1887. The Association is the result of private enterprise, having received no financial assistance from the city. The city did, however, grant it the exclusive use of about twenty acres of park land as a building site. ◆ The Museum is comprehensive in the scope of its collections, embracing the fine arts, the applied arts, and what might be called an historical department, in which are collections relating to ethnology and prehistoric anthropology. The collections emphasize the unity of art—its universal application. The building contains seven picture galleries with oil paintings, water colors, pastels, drawings and prints of various kinds; a loggia filled with ceramics, and one containing ivory carvings and about one thousand casts of important ivories in European collections. In the large entrance hall and in a long gallery on the main floor is sculpture, including original marbles and bronzes, and a collection of casts. The textile section occupies a room on this floor. In it are Cashmere shawls, Japanese embroidered brocades, and some six hundred pieces of lace illustrating that art from the Fifteenth Century in Italy to the Eighteenth Century in France and Belgium. In another room is a collection of arms and armor. In another, about six hundred examples of gold and silversmiths' work, mostly reproductions. Here are also several cases of old Chinese and Japanese bronzes. In another room are musical instruments. Two rooms on this floor contain the interesting Bookwalter Collection of oriental art—ceramics, textiles and metal work, and also examples of modern Italian wood carving. The lower floor of the building is devoted to ethnology and prehistoric anthropology—perhaps forty thousand specimens. ◆ The Art Academy of Cincinnati is the successor of the School of Design, which was founded in 1869, and was transferred to the Cincinnati Museum Association in 1884. It is a well equipped Art School with thirteen teachers. There are daily classes in drawing and painting from the figure. Life models are freely used. Among other classes may be mentioned those in composition, illustrating, modeling, wood carving, decorative design, architectural drawing and china painting. ◆ The museum has an endowment of $251,078, a building that cost $334,416, has objects of art, etc., valued at about $250,000, and contains loans of perhaps equal value. The Academy has an endowment of $383,002, and a building that cost $97,175, besides its equipment of casts, etc. These funds have been given by citizens, among whom are to be mentioned Charles W. West, Joseph Longworth, Reuben Springer and David Sinton. On Saturday and Sunday the admission fee to the Museum is ten cents, and on other days, twenty-five cents.

A. T. GOSHORN, DIRECTOR

12. "American Museums.–III. The Art Museum of Cincinnati, with Descriptive Notes." *Modern Art* 2, no. 3 (summer 1894). Fine Arts Department, Boston Public Library

for the *Dial* became one of the best-known defenders of modern art in the United States. At the same time, they would have been introduced to many of the most prominent voices in nineteenth-century American art criticism, including Ruskin adherent William James Stillman, who published the first American art journal, the *Crayon*, in the 1850s; Mariana Griswold Van Rensselaer, the nation's first professional woman art critic; and Sylvester Rosa Koehler, the editor of Boston's *American Art Review* and a prolific organizer of art exhibitions in the decades following the Civil War. *Modern Art*'s appropriation of the postwar art bibliography allowed it to bridge other gaps, too, most importantly the emerging divide between "mass" and "elite" culture in publishing and (presumably) among the magazines' readerships. Together with contributions from the "genteel" general-interest magazines that flourished after the war, such as *Harper's*, *Scribner's*, and the *Century*, and art journals like the *Art Amateur*, *Modern Art* also recommended articles from the then-new ten-cent mass-circulation magazines, like *Cosmopolitan*'s "The Cathedrals of France" and "The Beautiful Models of Paris." Indeed, Bowles must have been impressed with these new magazines; by 1902, he was managing the art department at *McClure's*, one of *Cosmopolitan*'s biggest rivals.[21]

Similarly, the "Table of Art Exhibitions" reflects *Modern Art*'s continued embrace of another common feature of art publishing in the 1870s and 1880s: the conscious desire to include cities and towns outside the art world's national and international centers. In the decade or so before the emergence in the 1890s of regional journals like *Modern Art*, Chicago's *Brush and Pencil* (1897), and the *Western Graphic* (1893; later *Los Angeles Graphic*), editors in the eastern cities worked hard to keep places like Bowles's Indianapolis within their purview by seeking out contributors and content from across the country. In Boston's *American Art Review*, Koehler deliberately noted the place of residence of his original "List of Contributors," including "Prof. Halsey C. Ives, Director St. Louis School of Fine Arts, Washington University, St. Louis," "Major J[ohn] W[esley] Powell, Geographical and Geological Survey of the Rocky Mountain Region, Washington," and "Mr. P. B. Wight, Chicago," an architect and critic. Particularly in its "American Art Chronicle," the *American Art Review* also offered regular coverage of the nation's disparate regional art museums, associations, and schools like the "San Francisco Etching Club," the "Trenton, New Jersey, School for Potters," and the "St. Louis Museum of Fine Art."[22] From its first issue, New York's *Art Amateur*, too, committed itself to a national scope, combining features on the National Academy of Design with entries for museums, exhibitions, and decorative arts associations in Cincinnati, Washington, and Boston, as well as "Correspondence" from Boston, Providence, St. Louis, and San Francisco.[23]

Modern Art continued in this vein, including a range of regional and national material that encouraged readers from across the country to participate in local arts events. In the "Table of Art Exhibits," announcements of goings-on in New York, Paris, and London jostled alongside listings for events in Chicago, San Francisco, Detroit, St. Louis, and, of course, Indianapolis.[24] These notices were paired with another regular feature in *Modern Art*, "American Art Museums," which profiled both powerful, eastern, metropolitan institutions like the Museum of Fine Arts, Boston, and more far-flung, regional museums in Cincinnati (fig. 12), Detroit, and Springfield, Massachusetts.[25] The journal's advertising, moreover, featured notices for Stone & Kimball and for Thomas B. Mosher's *The Bibelot*, of Portland, Maine (whose work Stieglitz ally Charles Caffin admired), as well as for local Indianapolis organizations like the Indiana School of Art.

One such promotion for the Indianapolis Art Association (fig. 13) gives a sense of the confidence of advertisers well outside New York or Boston. This ad lured readers to its spring 1893 exhibition with promises of "Twenty-five paintings from the Cincinnati Art Club" and "Pictures loaned by New York and Western Artists, etc. etc.," shown at the grandly titled Propylaeum.[26] As has frequently been argued regarding the late-nineteenth-century art worlds of New York and Boston, this title, signifying the monumental entrance to a temple, indicates a desire to cast art in sacred terms. The fact that the art organizers of Indianapolis could have devised such a pretentious name for their exhibition hall (and that their publicity ranked pictures by New Yorkers somewhere between those of Cincinnati and the West), however, suggests an additional interpretation. It is that the art organizers of Indianapolis—including the personnel of *Modern Art*—wished to represent their city and other regional art communities as important parts of an interlocking national

MODERN ART April 1, 1893. Vol. 1. No. 2.

Entered at the Post-Office at Indianapolis as second-class matter. Modern Art is a quarterly magazine published in Spring, Summer, Autumn and Winter numbers at $2.00 a year. Single or sample copies, 50c.

Subscriptions *commencing with the first number*, $3.00. No *single copies* of the first number are for sale, the few remaining being held for yearly subscribers. The magazine will be found at the following newsdealers:

New York,	Brentano's, 31 East Seventeenth Street.
Chicago,	Brentano's, 204-206 Wabash Avenue.
Washington,	Brentano's, 1015 Pennsylvania Avenue.
Boston,	Damrell & Upham, "The Old Corner Book Store."
Hartford,	E. W. Sill.
Louisville,	Flexner Brothers.
Cincinnati,	Robt. Clarke & Co.
Minneapolis,	The Beard Art and Stationery Co.
Omaha,	Chase & Eddy.
Kansas City,	Osborne & Pitrats.

And at all the book stores and leading news stands in Indianapolis. Sample page mailed free.

J. M. BOWLES, 23 North Meridian Street, Indianapolis, Indiana.

INDIANAPOLIS

ART ASSOCIATION

SPRING EXHIBIT

AT THE PROPYLAEUM, APRIL 11TH to 27TH.

Oil Paintings and Water Colors by well-known Artists.

Twenty-five paintings from the Cincinnati Art Club —Pictures loaned by New York and Western Artists, etc., etc.

Mrs. Frances M. Haberly's Lectures, illustrated with the stereopticon, on the "Italian Old Masters," are being given twice a month until May 2d. Admission, 25c. Members Free.

MEMBERSHIP

Members' tickets admit you free to all the entertainments and exhibits of the Association. $5.00 a year. Send for one to the Secretary, Mrs. A. C. Harris, 744 North Meridian Street, before the Spring exhibit opens.

CANDIES

PURE AND FRESH BON BONS AND CHOCOLATES

NOT HOW CHEAP—

HOW GOOD!

CRAIG

No. 20 East Washington Street

13. Advertisement for Indianapolis Art Association exhibition at the Propylaeum. *Modern Art* 1, no. 2 (spring 1893). Fine Arts Department, Boston Public Library

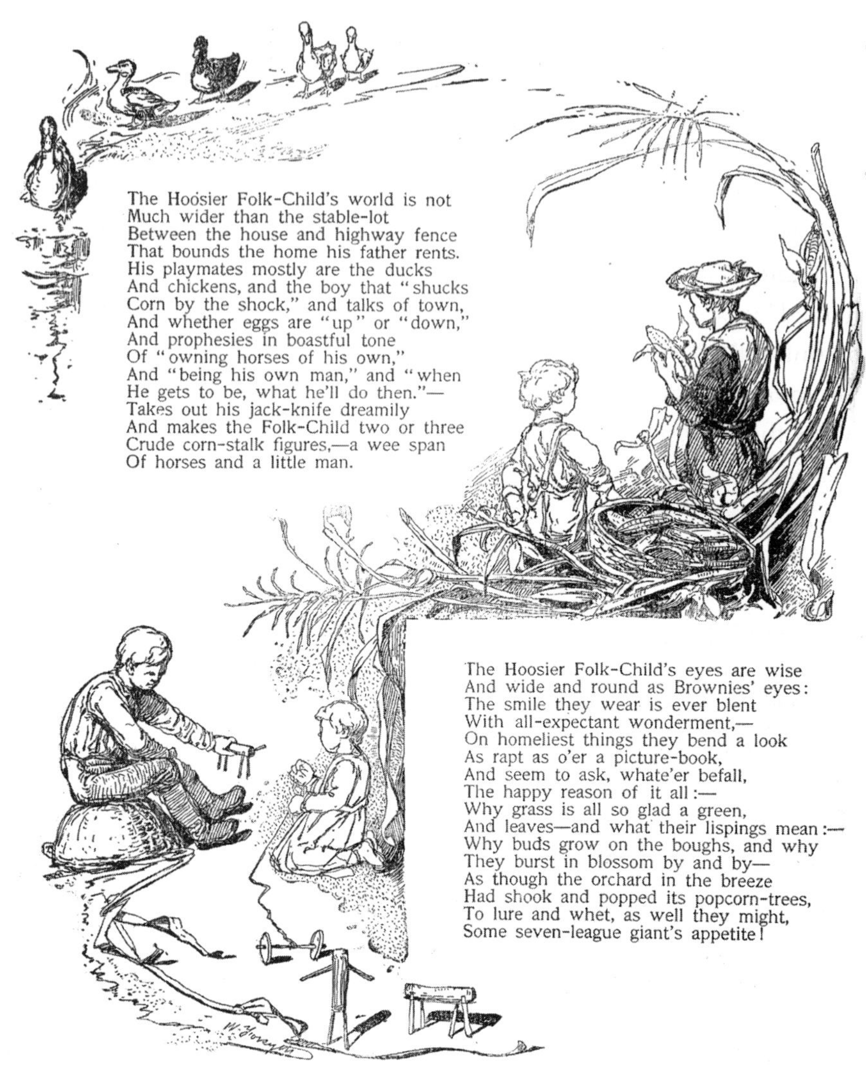
The Hoosier Folk-Child's world is not
Much wider than the stable-lot
Between the house and highway fence
That bounds the home his father rents.
His playmates mostly are the ducks
And chickens, and the boy that "shucks
Corn by the shock," and talks of town,
And whether eggs are "up" or "down,"
And prophesies in boastful tone
Of "owning horses of his own,"
And "being his own man," and "when
He gets to be, what he'll do then."—
Takes out his jack-knife dreamily
And makes the Folk-Child two or three
Crude corn-stalk figures,—a wee span
Of horses and a little man.

The Hoosier Folk-Child's eyes are wise
And wide and round as Brownies' eyes:
The smile they wear is ever blent
With all-expectant wonderment,—
On homeliest things they bend a look
As rapt as o'er a picture-book,
And seem to ask, whate'er befall,
The happy reason of it all:—
Why grass is all so glad a green,
And leaves—and what their lispings mean:—
Why buds grow on the boughs, and why
They burst in blossom by and by—
As though the orchard in the breeze
Had shook and popped its popcorn-trees,
To lure and whet, as well they might,
Some seven-league giant's appetite!

14. William Forsyth (1854–1935), decorations for James Whitcomb Riley, "The Hoosier Folk-Child." Published in *Modern Art* 1, no. 1 (winter 1893). Fine Arts Department, Boston Public Library

(and international) whole, instead of as the periphery of an eastern artistic center. If art was the new religion in late-nineteenth-century America, it was an art of the circuit-riding, evangelical sort.

Some unlikely juxtapositions arose from *Modern Art*'s dual commitment to both the establishment of a national network of local American arts communities *and* to an emerging, often European-influenced, vanguardist modernism. William Forsyth's admiring report on the Secession was just one among many contributions he made to the journal. It also printed his illustrations for James Whitcomb Riley's poem "The Hoosier Folk-Child" (fig. 14). Complete with ducks, crude whittled animals, and covered wagons, these images convey Forsyth's commitment to a sentimental vocabulary of rural life that flourished in nineteenth-century visual culture.[27] More specifically, their location as illustrations for a self-consciously "Hoosier" poem, within an Indiana publication, marks them as elaborations of a regional identity that drew upon this rural mythology—even as it also incorporated the very real modernity of both *Modern Art* and Indianapolis itself.

The contrast between these two features jars the sensibilities of present-day readers. In part, this is because we are accustomed to thinking of modernism as a short, sharp break from the sentimentalism of nineteenth-century culture. It is also because the frequent expatriation of artists in the 1880s and 1890s corresponded to a decline in the depiction of "American-themed" landscapes in favor of figure painting. This has made it tempting to think of the "cosmopolitanism" of the last two decades of the century as the opposite of the "nationalism" that preceded it.[28] If "nationalism" is recast as the search for and development of native *institutions* rather than American subject matter or an American "style," however, it becomes possible to see "cosmopolitanism" and "nationalism" as two sides of the same coin.

Recent work on Forsyth's fellow Munich expatriates, William Merritt Chase and John White Alexander, suggests the extent to which the European training of artists born at mid-century interconnected with institutional development in the American art world. Both Chase, from Indiana and St. Louis, and Alexander, from near Pittsburgh, were important art-world leaders, as well as artists.[29] As Annette Blaugrund demonstrates, Chase's innovative transformation of his studio in the Tenth Street Studio Building into an extravagantly decorated, ongoing "event" for prospective clients was a model of cultural entrepreneurship (fig. 15).[30] He was also a highly influential teacher who, in addition to working at the Art Students' League, the Brooklyn Art Association, the Pennsylvania Academy of the Fine Arts, the Art Institute of Chicago, and in the artists' colony in Carmel, California, also established his own schools at Shinnecock, on Long Island, and in New York City.[31] He was involved in associations that ranged from the vanguardist Society of American Artists, to the charitable 1883 Pedestal Fund Art Loan Exhibition,[32] to the whimsical Tile Club, whose purpose was as much to enjoy the sunshine and the pleasure of artistic fellowship as to produce artworks.

Modern Art contributor Alexander, too, was deeply enmeshed in the institutions that made New York an art-world center.[33] His ongoing relationship with the print media, most significantly his long-term career as an illustrator for *Harper's Weekly* and the *Century*, directly facilitated his employment as a portraitist and figure painter. As Sarah Moore explains, Alexander frequently turned his magazine commissions to produce likenesses of noted public figures like Confederate Vice-President Alexander Hamilton Stephens into opportunities to secure private contracts with the sitters for portraits in oil.[34] The artist was then able to use these paintings as the basis for drawings that could be reproduced easily in the press, effectively making two sales out of one job.[35] Like that of Chase,

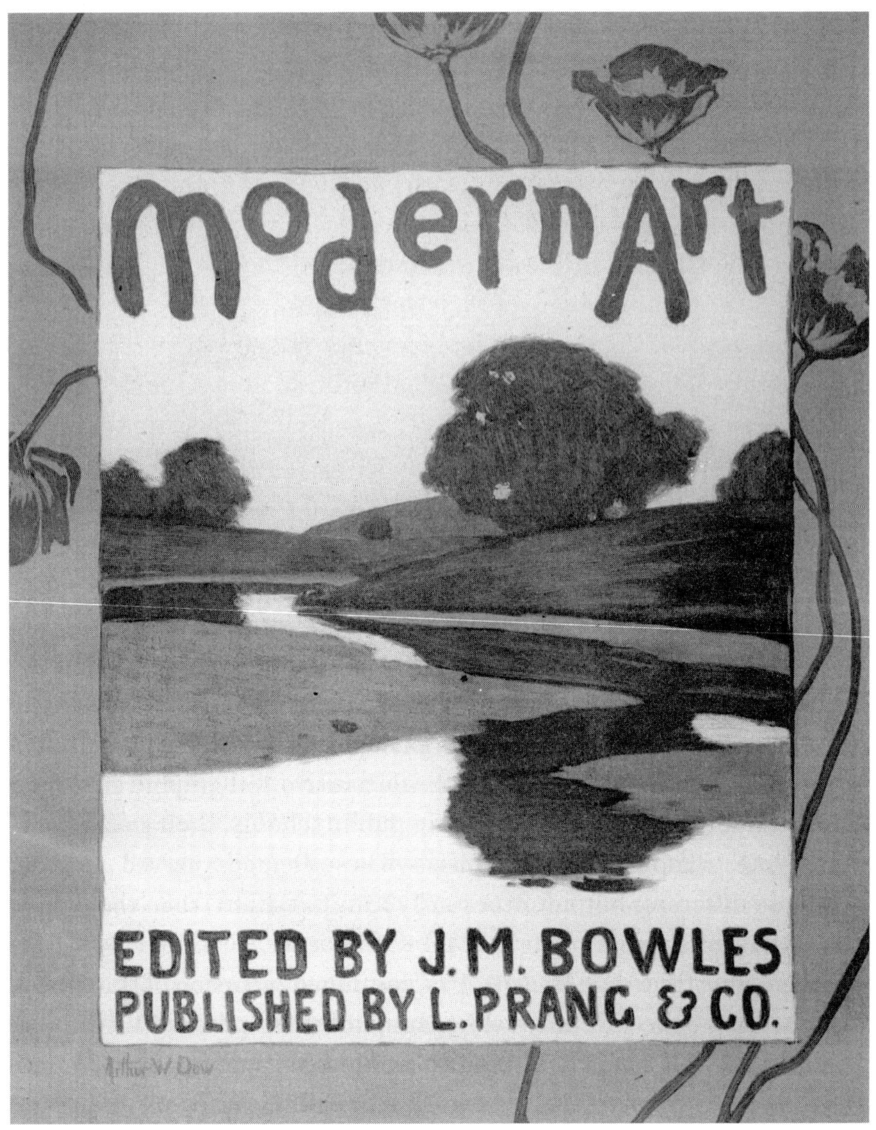

16. Arthur Wesley Dow, *Modern Art*, 1895. Color lithograph, 17¾ × 13¹¹⁄₁₆ in. (45.1 × 34.7 cm). Boston Public Library, Print Department

project, and the more general issue of the scope and definition of art publishing, it is necessary to make a further point. It is that *Modern Art* and the journals that preceded it were more than just windows onto external art events. They were also extensions of the art world in their own right. When Bowles declared that the goal of *Modern Art* was to "give expression to the spirit of the art of to-day," he was not just referring to its critical content—evaluative or otherwise. As a circulating compendium of images and advertisements, as a work of design itself, and as the host of contests like the "Modern Art Prize Competitions," *Modern Art* both told readers about what was happening in the art world *and* brought it directly to national and international readers in a form they could possess and influence.

The journal's subscription page specifically promised readers "four full-page illustrations" in each number, which were intended as accom-

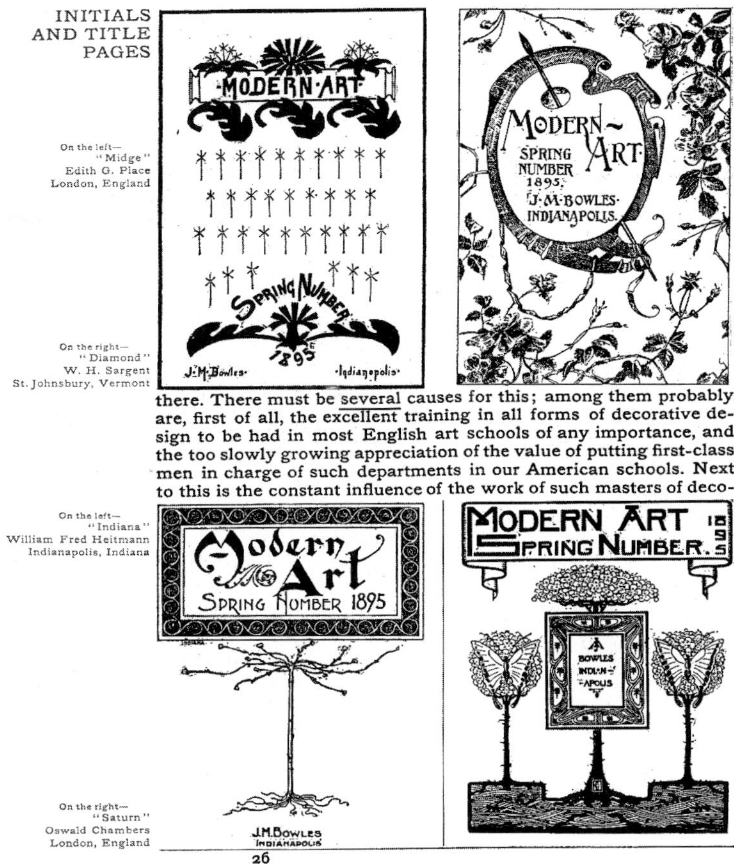
INITIALS AND TITLE PAGES

On the left—
"Midge"
Edith G. Place
London, England

On the right—
"Diamond"
W. H. Sargent
St. Johnsbury, Vermont

there. There must be several causes for this; among them probably are, first of all, the excellent training in all forms of decorative design to be had in most English art schools of any importance, and the too slowly growing appreciation of the value of putting first-class men in charge of such departments in our American schools. Next to this is the constant influence of the work of such masters of deco-

On the left—
"Indiana"
William Fred Heitmann
Indianapolis, Indiana

On the right—
"Saturn"
Oswald Chambers
London, England

26

17. "Initials and Title Pages: The Record of the First Modern Art Competition in Decorative Drawings." *Modern Art* 3, no. 1 (winter 1895). The Huntington Library, San Marino, California

paniments to the journal's writings and as works to be kept and admired. In some cases, *Modern Art* specifically invited readers to do just that: for a price of one dollar, and later as a free bonus to subscribers, Bowles offered "50 proofs on Japan paper" of Dow's lithograph, *Modern Art* (fig. 16), "signed by Mr. Dow and Mounted on mats, ready for framing."[40] These and other color images were much prized by nineteenth-century consumers. The art posters that publishing houses distributed in the 1890s to sell magazines, for example, often sold out well before the magazines themselves; color advertisements were so cherished that collectors assembled them into albums specifically devoted to the purpose.[41] Within this context, Prang and Bowles must have hoped that *Modern Art*'s images would be as highly prized by readers as the *New York Times* promised they would be.

There is evidence to suggest that Bowles conceived of art publishing as more than just a circulating venue for the *display* of art, but as an institution that could encourage artistic *production*, as well. The "Modern Art Prize Competitions for Art Students!" solicited entries from "students at public and private art schools and . . . bona fide amateurs," promising prizes and the possibility that entrants' work could, like the winning cover of the Spring 1895 number, be circulated throughout *Modern Art*'s entire readership.[42] Like Prang, who funded a series of lucrative contests for the design of Christmas cards in the 1880s and who often bought losing, as well as winning entries, Bowles devoted several pages of this number to some of the many designs he received (fig. 17).[43] Bowles's disappointment that many of the readers who entered the contest were English suggests his commitment not only to "good design," but also to the goal of increasing the numbers of Americans involved in its creation.

As in the case of many of *Modern Art*'s individual features, this conception of art publishing as a portable branch of the art world itself had significant roots in the publishing environment of the 1870s and 1880s. Like *Modern Art*'s design contest, the *Art Amateur*—devoted to "the cultivation of art in the household"—provided lessons and patterns that called upon readers to transform their homes into studios. Correspondingly, Koehler's campaign to bring the graphic arts before the eyes of the American public gave interdependent roles to exhibitions, catalogues and books, and the periodical press. This multifront approach to the circulation of art can be seen in Koehler's efforts on behalf of one of his special enthusiasms, American etching. Koehler organized several exhibitions in this medium at the Museum of Fine Arts, Boston, where he was curator of prints. These included the *Exhibition of American Etchings* (1881) and *Women Etchers of America* (1887). As Phyllis Peet notes, the latter show represented "the first time that [Mary] Cassatt's etchings, drypoints, and aquatints were exhibited in the United States."[44] But Koehler also used the *American Art Review* to display and circulate work in this medium, running an illustrated series that profiled more than two dozen American etchers during the magazine's run. That Koehler saw the museum and the periodical press as mutually supporting sites for the display of contemporary art can be seen from the fact that he exhibited some of the same works in multiple venues. Mary Nimmo Moran's *Solitude* of 1880 (fig. 18), for example, appeared in both the 1881 and 1887 exhibitions and in the *American Art Review*, where the table of contents listed it as an "original etching."

Similarly, both the *Art Amateur* and the *Art Union*, a journal published out of the Tenth Street Studio Building, offered supplemental images that were meant to be kept and displayed.[45] In 1884, the *Art Union* presented an etching by Walter Shirlaw after Eastman Johnson's *The Reprimand* (c. 1880; Graphic Arts Collection, National Museum of American History, Smithsonian Institution, Washington, D.C.), claiming it had "been characterized by a competent authority as the finest figure etching thus far produced in this country, and one of the finest that has been published in the whole history of etching."[46] As the *Art Union*'s hyperbolic description of the work indicates—it also promised that "this etching alone is worth several times the cost of the Annual Subscription to the American Art Union"—there was a distinct commercial element to the circulation of images, both in the 1870s and 1880s and at the time Bowles produced *Modern Art*. Then, as now, publishers knew that images sold copies. Certainly, there were few figures that understood this more than Prang, whose own empire was built upon the circulation of images, including the extravagantly successful chromolithograph after Johnson's own *Barefoot Boy* (1860; Louis Prang Roewer, Auburn, Maine) and *The Boyhood of Lincoln* (1868; University of Michigan Museum of Art).[47]

The fact that there was a distinctly commercial cast to the art world's appropriation of print culture in the decades following the Civil War does not detract from its importance. Rather, this commercialism is in itself highly significant, for it suggests that what Michele Bogart has described as "the ideological borders of fine art"—the boundaries between "high" and "low," "mass" and "unique," "commercial" and "sacred," and, I would add, "decorative" and "fine"—were more permeable in the last third of the nineteenth century than is usually recognized.[48] Bogart's work has convincingly shown that "the rise of mass-market periodicals," among other factors, worked to blur these divisions in the 1890s. Similarly, the work of art historian Sarah Burns suggests the high degree of

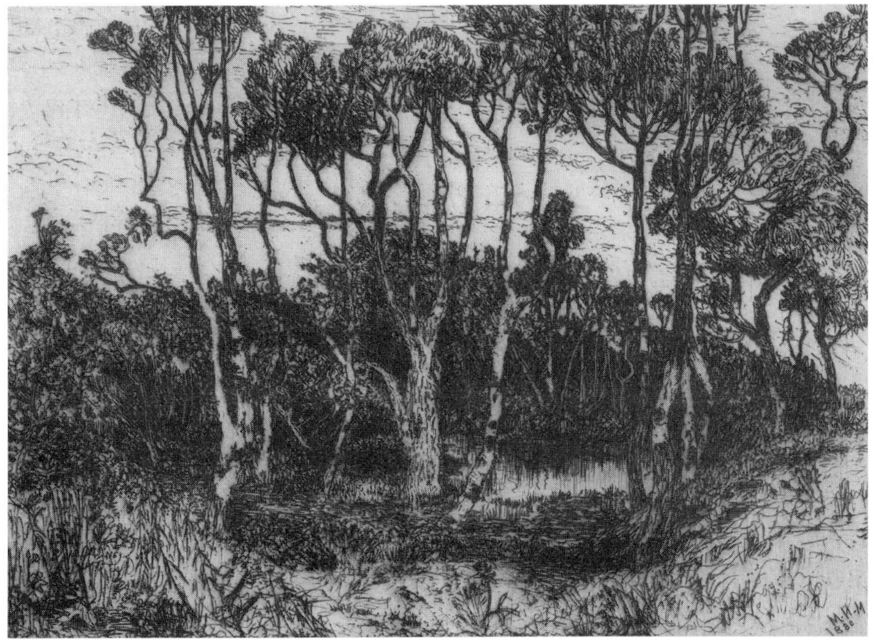

18. Mary Nimmo Moran (1842–1899), *Solitude*, 1880. Etching, 7 7/16 × 5 3/8 in. (19 × 13.7 cm). Published in *The American Art Review* 2, div. 1 (1881). The Huntington Library, San Marino, California

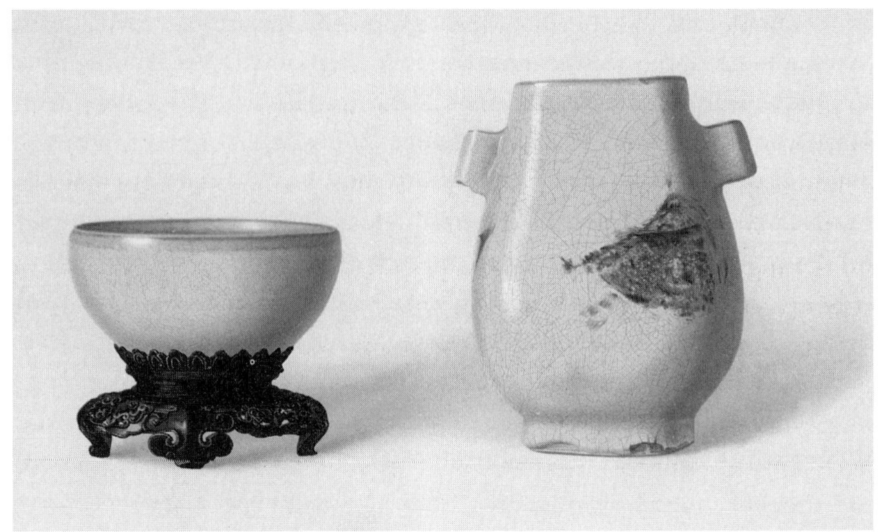

19. L. Prang & Co., *Two Primitive Pieces: Teacup and Vase for Flowers*. Lithograph, 7×10 5/16 in. (17.8×26.2 cm). Published in S. W. Bushell, *Oriental Ceramic Art* (New York: D. Appleton and Co., 1897). Private collection

overlap between painting, the press, and "popular" media such as chromolithography, both at mid-century and in the Gilded Age.[49] Following Levine and DiMaggio's influential work, however, scholars outside the history of art have generally been reluctant to dwell upon the intersections between these categories, focusing instead on the distinctions and hierarchies that separated them.

In the world of art publishing, however, there was no strict divide between the commercial and the ideological. As a commercial publisher, Prang pursued goals that have normally been associated only with nonprofit "cultural entrepreneurs" like the Brahmins Charles Callahan Perkins and Henry Lee Higginson, founders of the Museum of Fine Arts (MFA) and the Boston Symphony Orchestra, respectively. Alongside Christmas cards, business stationery, and advertisements, Prang also produced the 116 color plates for one of the most luxurious, rare art volumes of the day, *Oriental Ceramic Art, Collection of William T. Walters* (fig. 19), for the Baltimore collector.[50] This book, which required more than two thousand lithographic stones and took eight years to produce (Walters himself died before it was finished), is surely the equivalent in print of the museum as Propylaeum. Prang also published dozens of volumes devoted to art education, including the series written by Walter Smith to accompany the introduction of art education into the public schools following the Massachusetts Drawing Act of 1870. Notably, this initiative was itself instigated by Perkins, who as a member of the Boston School Committee brought Smith in to supervise the new program in 1871.[51]

This blend of uplift and commercialism within art publishing can also be seen in the career of publisher and manufacturer Milton Bradley, of Springfield, Massachusetts. Bradley (fig. 20) wrote and published numerous art-educational books, such as *Water Colors in the Schoolroom* and *Elementary Color*.[52] These books were designed to introduce the study of color into early education, in order to develop children's perception of its scientific and aesthetic properties. As the introduction to Bradley's *Elementary Color* argued, "The principles of chromatic harmony are perhaps not simple, but a child, before whom right standards of color combinations are constantly presented, will acquire a correct aesthetic judgment that may become intuitive. The effect of such a training on the higher development of our people and on their appreciation of true art would be of the highest value."[53] This call for training in the "appreciation of true art"—and the use of materials that appealed to multiple skills and senses to achieve it—was only one aspect of a wide and long-running campaign Bradley waged for art on behalf of the kindergarten movement.[54] Bradley was also the first American manufacturer of the Froebel "gifts"—the colored cards and three-dimensional objects designed to develop children's cognitive and spiritual sense named after the movement's founder.

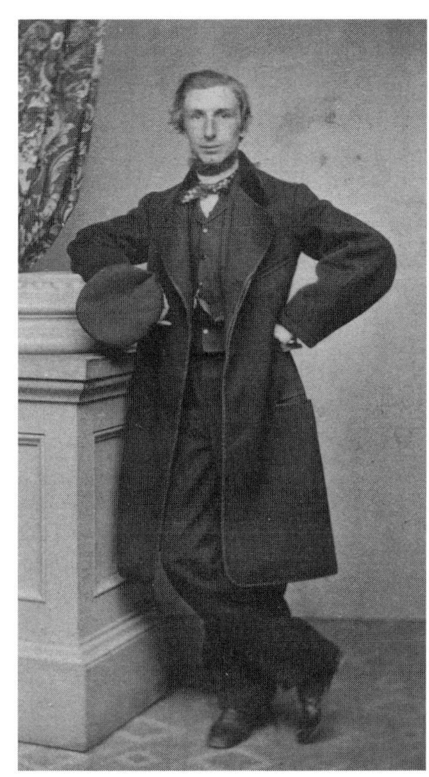

20. Milton Bradley (1836–1911). Connecticut Valley Historical Museum, Springfield, Massachusetts

It might be tempting to assume that Bradley, like Perkins and Higginson, was the product of a privileged Brahmin upbringing, and that it was this social background that led him to embrace cultural entrepreneurship and the "appreciation of true art." This was not the case. His father was a small producer of potato starch, who was driven by the blight of the 1840s to seek employment in the mills of Lowell; Bradley began his own career as a draftsman and lithographer. Like Prang, his early productions included advertisements like the *Knowles' Patent Steam Pump* (c. 1861; American Antiquarian Society), technical drawings, and an 1860 lithograph of the clean-shaven Abraham Lincoln that rapidly stopped selling after Lincoln grew a beard.[55] And, like Prang, Bradley never completely left the shop floor. Long after he could have abandoned such labor to others, Bradley developed "new tools and machines" in his plant, "specially for the work" of manufacturing the "gifts." He also promoted art and manual education in the primary and secondary schools, working with Luella Fay, Springfield's supervisor of drawing, to develop new art materials for the public schools and helping to found the city's Manual Arts High School.[56] Bradley was rewarded for these efforts. His *Paradise of Childhood, a Practical Guide to Kindergartners* received an honorable mention at the 1876 Philadelphia Centennial, and his watercolors became standard in thousands of public schools.[57] And, although the aesthetic impact of Bradley's foray into cultural entrepreneurship is difficult to gauge, his Froebel "gifts" provided a key early influence on at least one pupil: the young Frank Lloyd Wright, whose autobiography mentions not only Froebel, but also Bradley, by name.[58]

Milton Bradley is best known not for his nonprofit activities, however, but for his part in the newly commercialized pursuit of leisure. By 1860, he was already lithographing invitations for a traveling stereopticon show;

Bradley's invitation, which included a portrait of a haughty-looking woman in classical dress, claimed that the medium was "one of the Highest Efforts of Art."[59] Soon Bradley decided not just to advertise games and amusements, but to turn his lithographic skills to their manufacture. His first effort was *The Checkered Game of Life* (fig. 21), which he printed, cut, and boxed himself. Nearly 40,000 copies sold in the first winter alone.[60] By the early 1870s, Bradley was publishing *Work and Play*, "the only original juvenile," and "The first Magazine Ever Illustrated With Oil Chromos in This Country," which published hundreds of "indoor and out-door games, parlor tricks, acting charades, &c., with A Collection of Illustrated Rebuses, Puzzles, Riddles, Enigmas, Charades, and Bible Questions."[61] This magazine and its annual also marketed dozens of games, puzzles, and amusements manufactured by Milton Bradley & Co., including the flagship *Checkered Game of Life*, a thirty-cent *Puzzle Map of North America*, and various prototypes of the moving image. These included *The Zoetrope or Wheel of Life* and *The Myriopticon—An Historical Panorama of the Rebellion*, whose backlit, scrolled color lithographs of Civil War scenes could be unfurled to the accompaniment of a rousing historical commentary.

It was within this context that Bradley began selling both geometrical

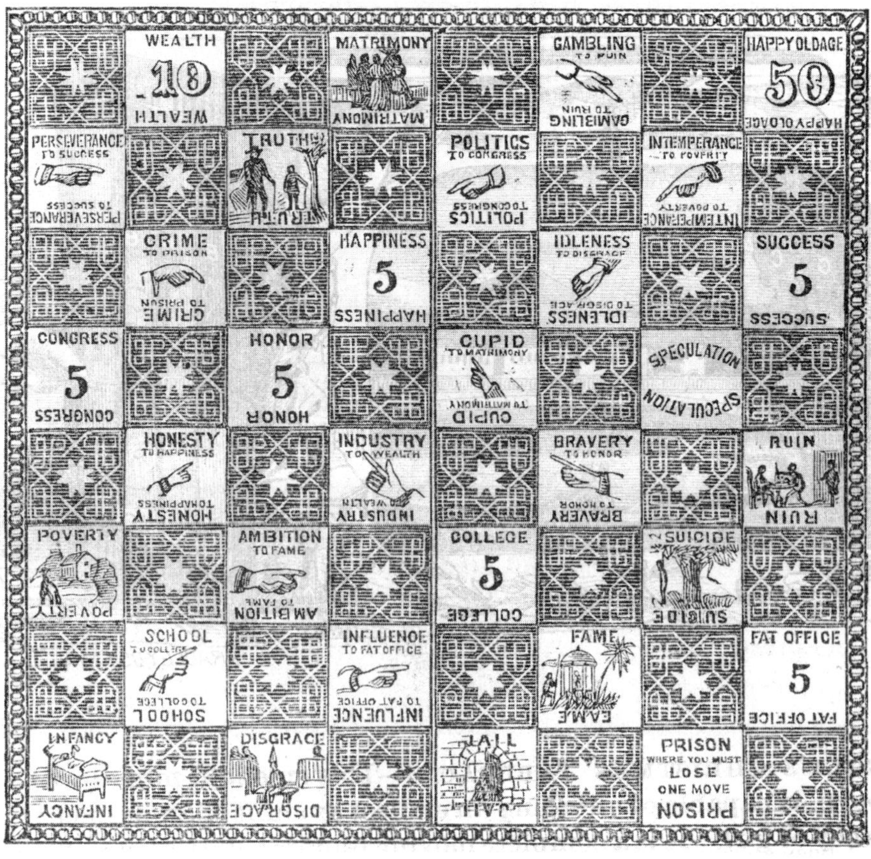

21. Milton Bradley, *The Checkered Game of Life*, 1860–61. From *Work and Play Annual of Home Amusements and Social Sports* (Springfield, Mass.: Milton Bradley & Co., 1872). Widener Library of the Harvard College Library, Cambridge, Massachusetts

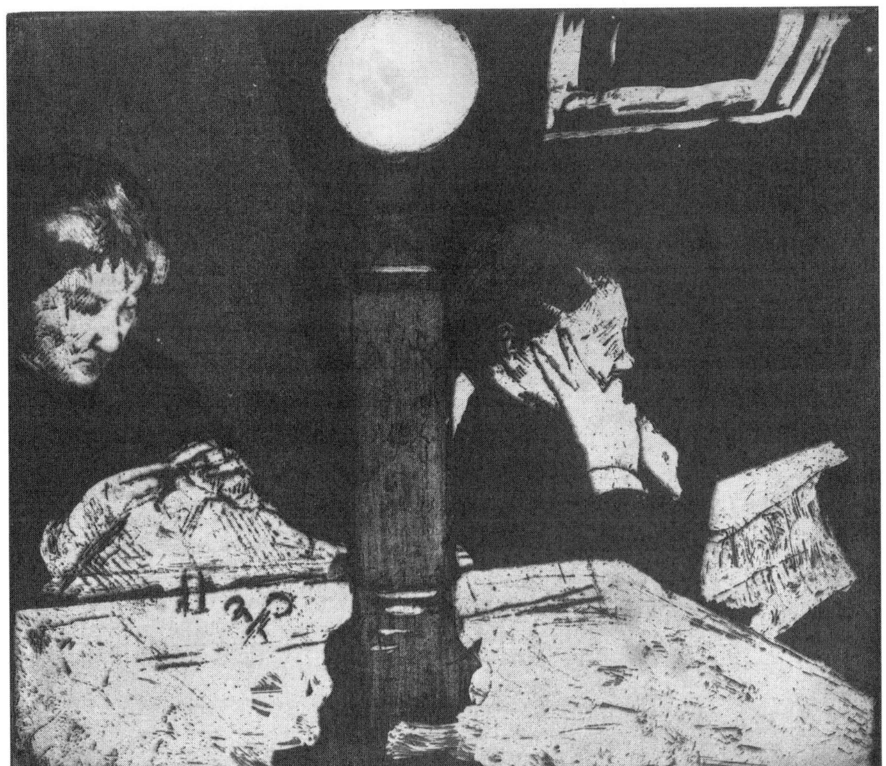

22. Mary Cassatt (1844–1926), *Under the Lamp*, c. 1883. Soft ground etching and aquatint, 7¾ × 8¹¹⁄₁₆ in. (19.7 × 22 cm). S. P. Avery Collection, Miriam and Ira D. Wallach Division of Art, Prints and Photographs, The New York Public Library, Astor, Lenox, and Tilden Foundations. *Under the Lamp* was exhibited at Sylvester Rosa Koehler's 1887 *Women Etchers of America* exhibition at the Museum of Fine Arts, Boston.

puzzles and *The Kindergarten Alphabet and Building Blocks*: although Froebel's system gave specific shape to his faith in kindergarten arts, crafts, and games, Bradley believed that commercially distributed amusements could keep children out of the "traps of Satan" even as they "exercis[ed] the inventive faculties of the mind."[62] Bradley's salesmanship complemented, rather than undercut, his support for public initiatives like universal art education, the development of well-crafted educational materials, and the encouragement within his factory of skilled workers and workmanship.[63]

This is not to say that all nineteenth-century art publishers embraced commercialism equally. Sylvester Rosa Koehler downplayed this aspect of his ventures, preferring (like Dow) to focus on the uplifting qualities of art. Nonetheless, it should be remembered that Koehler's career as a publisher and as a curator at the Museum of Fine Arts was preceded by more than ten years as Prang's technical director.[64] This collaboration resulted in a number of joint projects, including a translation of Wilhelm von Bezold's *Theory of Color in Its Relation to Art and Art-Industry* in 1876 and an art historical "Atlas," *Illustrations of the History of Art*.[65] Later on, Koehler gave space in his *American Art Review* to Prang's Christmas card contests—even though he was not satisfied with the results—as did the MFA. Moreover, Koehler continued to publish the work of artists whose creations Prang also circulated, including William Merritt Chase and Chase's student, Dora Wheeler.[66]

In the 1890s, *Modern Art*'s use of Prang-style testimonials alongside full-page illustrations reminiscent of the *American Art Review*—including, for example, works by Mary Cassatt (fig. 22)—suggests that Bowles, at least, was comfortable with and influenced by both nonprofit and profit (Koehler's and Prang's) approaches to the circulation of images.[67] While Bowles did not, like Prang, send out salesmen with sample books, his desire to circulate *Modern Art* to the farthest corners of the continent is plainly written on its subscription page. It proudly and regularly listed the names and addresses of booksellers who carried *Modern Art* in Pittsburgh, St. Louis, San Francisco, Louisville, Cincinnati, Minneapolis, Kansas City, New Orleans, and Cleveland, and promised that "orders may be sent through book stores, news dealers or subscription agencies anywhere in the United States and Canada."[68] Bowles's career after *Modern Art* suggests his continued ability to reconcile commercial with aesthetic goals, even well into the twentieth century. After his stint at *McClure's*, Bowles pursued a number of ventures in the world of advertising, including the publication in 1918 of a trade book of paper samples, *Some Examples of the Work of American Designers*.[69] In it he wrote, "Good printing makes its appeal to two senses—sight and touch, and neither may be left out of consideration. The 'feel' of the paper, its solidity, its firmness, and its attraction for the eye, are certainly as essential a part of good printing as cleanliness, fine color, good composition and competent presswork."[70] While in the 1890s Bowles used commercial strategies to "sell" modern art, in the 1910s he used aesthetics to sell commercial products.

This continued interrelationship between art and commerce, and between profit and nonprofit entrepreneurship, was not limited to publishing alone in the postwar decades. As can be seen from the careers of Chase and Alexander, it also marked the careers of individual artists, including decorative artists such as Candace Wheeler. Wheeler was a commercially successful textile artist and founder, along with Louis Comfort Tiffany, of the Associated Artists firm (1879). Wheeler later turned Associated Artists, which received extensive coverage in the press, into a manufacturing outfit run by women.[71] But she was also the instigator of two extremely important charitable organizations, the New York Society of Decorative Art (1877 [NYSDA]) and the New York Exchange for Woman's Work (1878), which provided spheres for women to sell their work outside the conventional labor or art market.[72] She was also the publisher of a journal, the *Art Interchange* (1878). As historian Mary Blanchard has shown, this journal promoted the decorative arts while attacking misogyny, and combined these two positions in "an aggressive defense of the woman artist."[73] And finally, Candace Wheeler was also the mother of Dora Wheeler (fig. 23), herself a student of Chase, a contribu-

23. William Merritt Chase, *Dora Wheeler*, c. 1882. Oil on canvas, 62 5/8 × 65 1/2 in. (159 × 165.5 cm). The Cleveland Museum of Art, gift of Mrs. Boudinot Keith in memory of Mr. and Mrs. J. H. Wade (1921.1239)

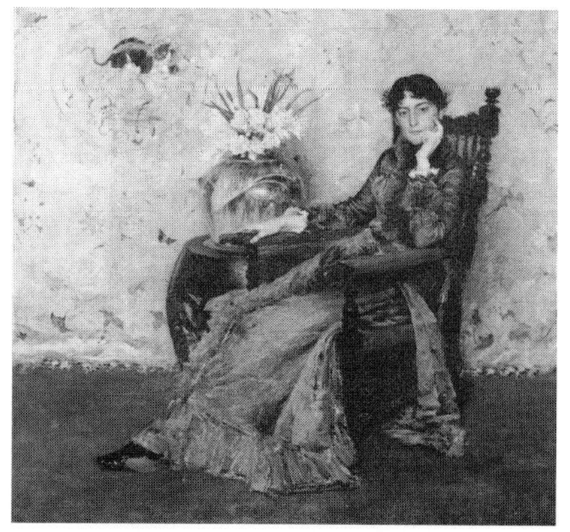

tor to the *American Art Review* (fig. 24), the winner of Prang's 1882 Christmas card contest, and a designer for her mother's firm.[74]

The fusion of both fine art and commercialism, and profit and nonprofit entrepreneurship, also persisted in the institutions in which art was made, displayed, and sold, including the Tenth Street Studio Building (1858–1956), where Chase—like the entrepreneurial Bierstadt and Church before him—set up shop. Commissioned in 1857 by James Boorman Johnston and built in the vernacular style by Richard Morris Hunt, the Studio Building was, as Annette Blaugrund writes, the first known structure to have been "built specifically and exclusively as commercial space for artists."[75] As both Chase's residence and the presence of the *American Art Union* in the Studio Building show, the antebellum commercialism that motivated the building did not leave with Church and Bierstadt. At the same time, the Tenth Street Studio Building was intimately connected to the art world that is supposed, after the Civil War, to have supplanted the vernacular and the entrepreneurial with the palatial and the "highbrow." Many of the artworks produced in the building ended up in the Metropolitan Museum of Art; by 1881, the building itself was in the hands of Johnston's older brother, the Metropolitan cofounder and first president, John Taylor Johnston.

There was, as historians have frequently lamented, no P. T. Barnum in the Gilded Age. Like their antebellum peers, however, late-nineteenth-century cultural entrepreneurs nonetheless created a complex, multivalent art world in which categories that are often seen as unmixable opposites—"commercial" and "nonprofit"; "decorative" and "fine"; "national" and "cosmopolitan"; "center" and "periphery"; "popular" and "elite"; "avant-garde" and "sentimental"; and "naturalistic" and "abstract"—overlapped and fused in unpredictable ways. What the case of *Modern Art* suggests is that the print media—as images and texts, and as an art-world institution in its own right—was one of the threads that tied these allegedly immutable opposites. It is the multiplicity of this art world on the eve of modernism that this research aims to capture.

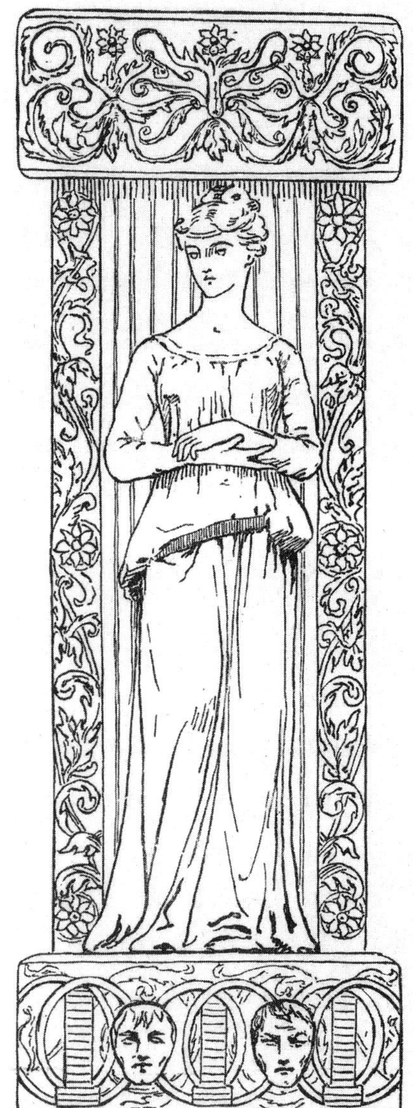

24. Dora Wheeler (1856–1940), *Initial I.* Published in *The American Art Review* 2, div. 2 (1881). The Huntington Library, San Marino, California

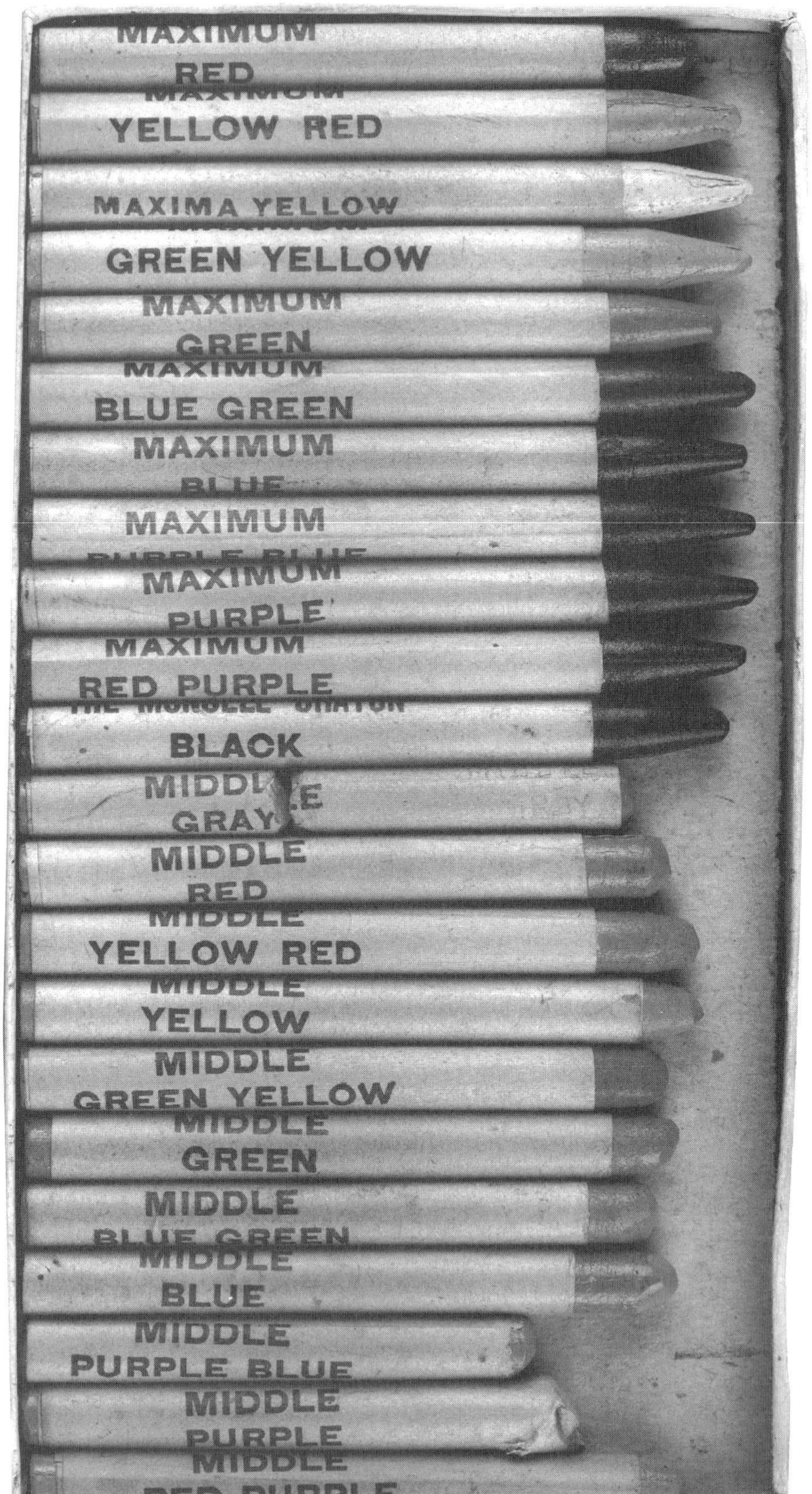

MAXIMUM
RED
YELLOW RED
MAXIMA YELLOW
GREEN YELLOW
MAXIMUM
GREEN
MAXIMUM
BLUE GREEN
MAXIMUM
MAXIMUM
MAXIMUM
PURPLE
MAXIMUM
RED PURPLE
BLACK
MIDDLE
GRAY
MIDDLE
RED
MIDDLE
YELLOW RED
MIDDLE
YELLOW
MIDDLE
GREEN YELLOW
MIDDLE
GREEN
MIDDLE
BLUE GREEN
MIDDLE
BLUE
MIDDLE
PURPLE BLUE
MIDDLE
PURPLE
MIDDLE
RED PURPLE

Chapter 2

Building an American Art World

All children who can be taught to read, write, and cipher, can be taught to draw.
—Walter Smith, 1880

In the years following the Civil War, a difficult situation confronted American art admirers. Observers agreed that an abundance of native talent and a receptive attitude toward art blessed the nation. Yet, somehow, American art had not fulfilled its promise. Despite important achievements in governance, trade, and industry, American visual culture seemed to lag behind that of other nations. One commentator who expressed this view was the poet, novelist, and critic, George Parsons Lathrop.[1] As Parsons lamented in 1879, "We have it fairly well established that there is both a positive bias in our national character toward productivity in the arts, and an innate cordiality about encouraging those who produce. Nevertheless, painters find existence hard and precarious among us."[2] The absence of a supportive climate for art, he wrote, forced artists to waste "that fine superfluity of inspiration" worrying about "starvation."[3]

25. Interior, *Munsell Crayons No. 3 Box, 22 Colors*. Korzenik Art Education Ephemera Collection, Box 71, Set 4. The Huntington Library, San Marino, California

Lathrop's mood was not entirely gloomy, though, for he believed it was possible to make art stand its own ground within the "whirlpool of energy wherein we exist."[4] What he proposed was that art-world institutions—particularly the development of art education in schools and museums—would guarantee the steady attention art needed in order to flourish. As associate editor of the *Atlantic Monthly* in the mid-1870s, Lathrop would have been well placed to watch the emergence and growth of a range of initiatives in the Boston art world, including the Museum of Fine Arts (MFA) and the Massachusetts Drawing Act, both established in 1870. From his observations, Lathrop was happy to report that significant progress was being made, particularly with regard to the Drawing Act, which made art "a part of the regular education of all embryo citizens who should attend the public schools at all."[5]

Institutional Solutions: Nonprofit and Commercial Development in the Art World

As both complaint and recommendation, Lathrop's comments captured a prevailing sentiment in the decades following the Civil War. Despite the frequent glorification of the individual artist as a uniquely creative genius, many nineteenth-century Americans seem to have believed that individual talent alone was insufficient to guarantee artistic progress and that institutional solutions were required to ensure it. This was not a new idea. Since the beginning of the nineteenth century, with the creation of the American Academy of the Fine Arts, Americans had established nonprofit organizations devoted to artistic display, fellowship, and education. This included the establishment of such successful ventures as the Cooper Union for the Advancement of Science and Art, founded in 1859, and the Philadelphia School of Design for Women (1848), which as the Moore College of Art and Design is still dedicated to providing lifelong opportunities in art education for women.[6] In addition to their educational role, these institutions also provided an important source of employment to artists, like R. Swain Gifford and Wyatt Eaton, who taught in Cooper Union's School of Design for Women (fig. 26).[7]

After the Civil War, this enthusiasm for institutional development flourished, resulting in a period of intense organizational effort in the cultural sphere. The most visible result of this campaign was the establishment of public, metropolitan museums designed to collect and display art and to educate both artists and the general public. Among the earliest such institutions were Boston's Museum of Fine Arts and New York's Metropolitan Museum of Art, also founded in 1870.[8] As in the case of art publishing, however, this was not strictly an eastern phenomenon. By the 1880s and 1890s, the creation of the Art Institute of Chicago (1879), the

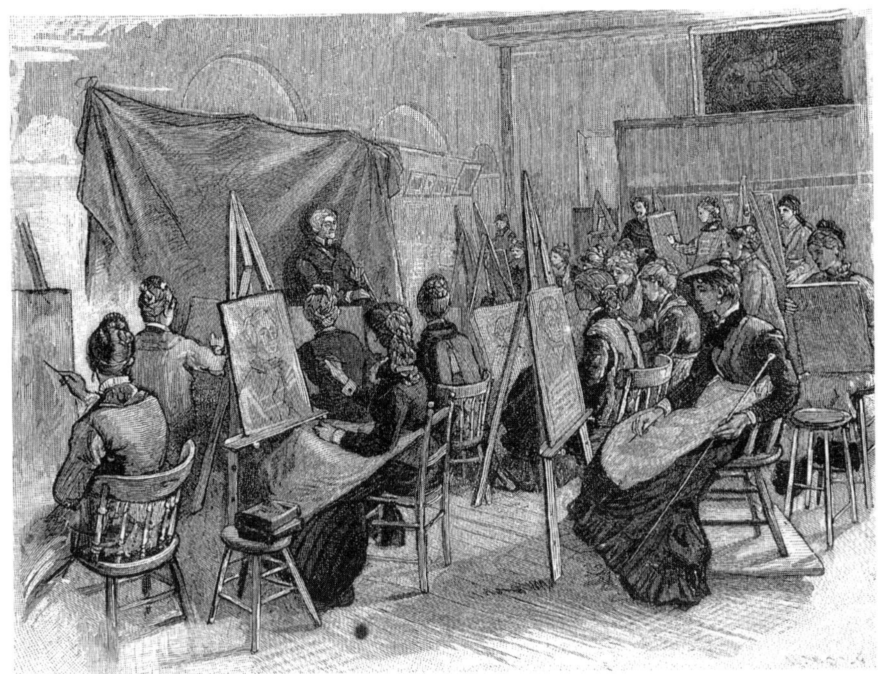

26. F. Lathrop, "Portrait Class, School of Design for Women, Cooper Union; Wyatt Eaton, Teacher." Published in *Scribner's Monthly* 16 (Oct. 1878). The Huntington Library, San Marino, California. F. Lathrop was most likely the artist Francis Lathrop (1849–1909), brother of George Parsons Lathrop.

Cincinnati Art Museum (1881), and the Portland (Oregon) Art Museum (1892) signaled the rise of a national movement.

One of the primary goals of these institutions was to collect and display art. A glance at their early collections suggests, however, that this activity had multiple dimensions, including the public maintenance of local collections, the exhibition of contemporary art, and the representative display of the history of art—including, importantly, the decorative, graphic, and industrial arts. In its first decades, the MFA's collections mostly consisted of loans and donations, including the 5500-strong Gray Collection of Engravings, "Egyptian antiquities . . . casts from Assyrian, Greek, and Roman sculptures . . . vessels of earthen and glass ware . . . a complete set of the electrotypes from ancient coins published by the South Kensington Museum . . . architectural casts . . . the sculpture of the Renaissance, and its industrial arts, and the industrial arts of the East and of mediaeval Europe, in ceramics, enamels, textiles, carvings, metal work, etc. . . . and a small beginning . . . towards a collection illustrating the art of the aborigines of America."[9] In its first decade, the museum also collected work by the living American sculptors Harriet Hosmer, Augustus Saint-Gaudens, and Olin Levi Warner, and it held numerous exhibitions of works by contemporary American artists, including shows to which "no picture will be accepted which has been publicly shown in Boston."[10]

The heterogeneity of the MFA's early collection was mirrored in the Cincinnati Museum Association, whose first displays centered on donations from private benefactors, the Women's Art Museum Association, and the Ninth Cincinnati Exposition. They included "the

'Studiorum' of Turner; a ceramic display exhibiting the progress of the art in Cincinnati, from the first experiments by Miss McLaughlin to the latest work of the Ro[o]kwood Pottery; and a loan collection of painting, bric-à-brac, etc." Indeed, the association's initial mandate extended well beyond art to collection and education in science and natural history.[11] Even the Metropolitan Museum of Art, which as Steven Conn notes became a treasure house for masterpieces within a few decades of its founding, originally emphasized "completeness and symmetry" as much as "value and rarity" in its collections, and its first constitution declared that "the proposed Museum should be comprehensive in its scope and purpose." Toward these ends, the Metropolitan's early collections included engravings, architectural models, and "specimens illustrating the application of art to manufactures," as well as drawings, paintings, and sculptures.[12]

The early municipal museums also placed a high priority on education. The Milwaukee Museum of Fine Arts for the State of Wisconsin (1882), whose first slate of officers included two women, proposed "to cultivate and advance art in all its branches" by establishing "a public collection of works of art and a School of Design." This initiative reflected the high esteem in which Americans held London's South Kensington Museum and School (now the Victoria and Albert Museum). Founded in the wake of the Crystal Palace Exhibition of 1851, South Kensington had been established as a unique complex of schools and display spaces intended to improve Britain's production of high-quality, well-designed consumer goods such as textiles and wallpaper. As an institution, it mixed education and display, the decorative and fine arts, and pragmatism and uplift. Many American museums specifically cast themselves in this mold, including the Cincinnati Museum Association and the Pennsylvania Museum and School of Industrial Art.[13]

Education was also a prominent goal even within those institutions, such as the Museum of Fine Arts, Boston, and the Metropolitan Museum of Art, which were not explicitly modeled after South Kensington. The Metropolitan's school, which had an enrollment of more than three hundred male and female pupils in 1882, offered day and night courses ranging from "Fresco Decoration" to "Carriage Drafting and Construction."[14] Similarly, the floor plan of the MFA in 1880 shows that a large proportion of the building was dedicated to educational purposes (fig. 27). The entire basement was devoted to classrooms, and a significant number of rooms on the upper floors had designations such as "architectural & mechanical room," "antique room," "still life room," "life room," "drawing from the round," "head master's business room," "lecture theatre," and "assistants meeting room."[15] This was in keeping with the museum's Act of Incorporation, which had declared an intention to

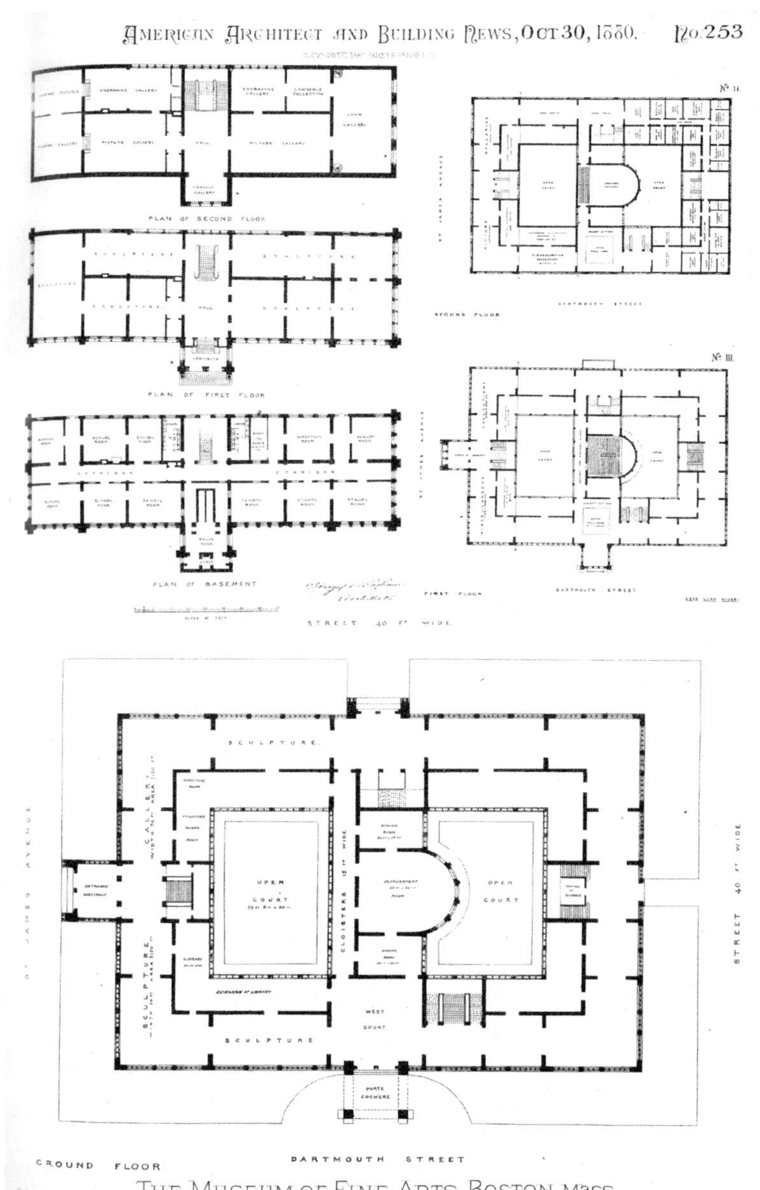

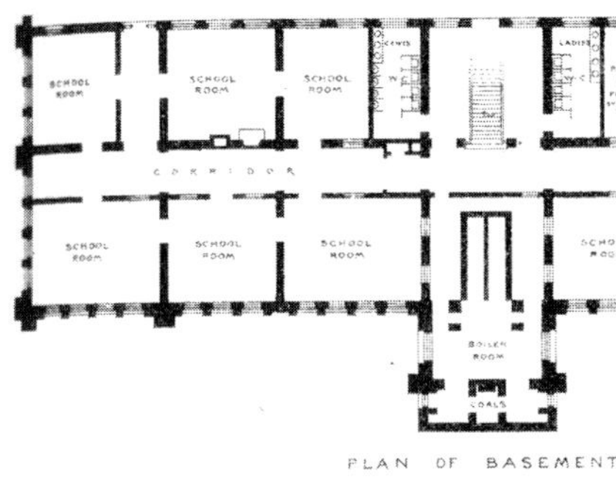

Left and detail above:
27. Floor plan of the Museum of Fine Arts, Boston. From *The American Architect and Building News* 8, no. 253 (30 Oct. 1880). The Huntington Library, San Marino, California

"provide opportunities and means for giving instruction in Drawing, Painting, Modelling and Designing, with their industrial applications, through lectures, practical schools, and a special library."[16]

Museums were important, but they were only the most visible organizations in the cultural field. The campaign to foster American art by creating an American art world also found expression in a wide range of other institutions devoted to artistic fellowship, the circulation and display of images, art education, and art criticism. A wide range of social and professional organizations emerged at this time, through which American artists and art admirers sought strength and advocacy. Perhaps the most prominent artists' association to appear in the postwar decades was the Society of American Artists (SAA).[17] Founded in New York in 1877, the

SAA represented a self-conscious, vanguardist challenge to the National Academy of Design. This was largely driven by the Academy's decision, as critic George William Sheldon reported, to reserve the choicest part of the display space at its annual exhibition—"eight feet on the line"—for members.[18] It was never the case, however, that SAA members were excluded from the older institution. In fact, as Trudie Grace observes, fully twenty-one of the original twenty-two members of the SAA had exhibited at the Academy, and nine were members; in 1906, the two organizations merged.[19] Rather, members of this splinter group mainly seem to have objected to the fact that their work was made to hang alongside work they considered weak and inferior, and to the Academy's persistent use of a crowded, floor-to-ceiling style of display (fig. 28). For both its lesser-known members and for the many prominent artists, like Saint-Gaudens and Warner, and like Frederick Dielman, R. Swain Gifford, John La Farge, Louis Comfort Tiffany, and A. H. Wyant, who were also Associates or full members of the Academy, the SAA offered a prominent and selective venue in which to forge alliances and display their work.[20]

Although its prominent membership and vanguardist stance has guaranteed the SAA a place in history, it was only one among many art associations that emerged in the postwar decades. Some of these organizations, like the American Water-Color Society (New York, 1868, initiation fee $25 as of 1882), paralleled the SAA in scope, outlook, and membership. The American Water-Color Society's main purpose, like that of the SAA, was to provide fellowship and prominent exhibition opportunities, in this case for artists working in a particular medium. What is perhaps most striking about the period, however, is the heterogeneity, geographical di-

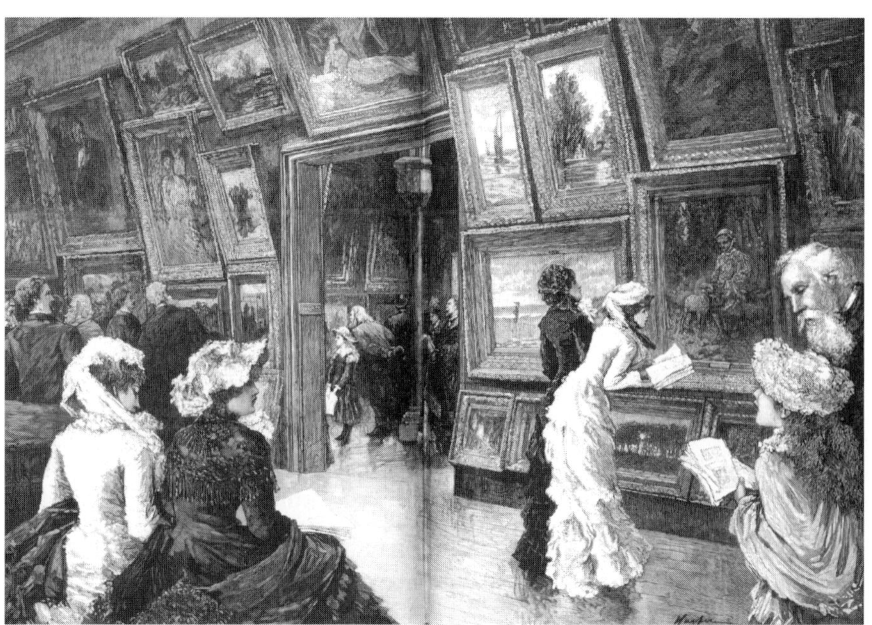

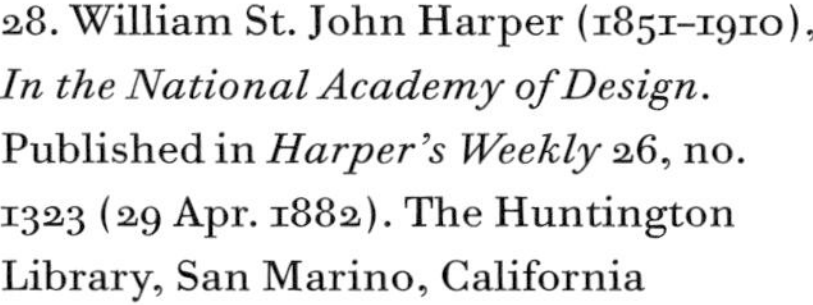

28. William St. John Harper (1851–1910), *In the National Academy of Design*. Published in *Harper's Weekly* 26, no. 1323 (29 Apr. 1882). The Huntington Library, San Marino, California

versity, and sheer volume of organizations devoted to art. Some associations aimed directly to train artists and help them make a living. The Ladies' Art Association of Pittsfield, Massachusetts (1880), asked members to contribute one dollar per year to "raise the standard of woman's work" and "to establish free classes, that may help to direct many [women] into desirable ways of earning a livelihood." Others focused on the aesthetic and social benefits of art appreciation. Boston's exclusive St. Botolph Club (1880) charged a twenty-dollar initiation and a thirty-dollar annual assessment so that "Members (males only)" could enjoy "social intercourse among authors and artists, and other gentlemen connected with or interested in literature and art."[21] Reflecting its elite membership, its first officers included the historian Francis Parkman and the publisher James R. Osgood.[22]

Neither the gender restrictions nor the high fees of the St. Botolph Club were typical. More representative was the Jacksonville, Illinois, Art Association, founded by art teacher Ella O. Browne "in the parlor of the Illinois Female College." This organization dedicated itself to "the study and appreciation of the Fine Arts, especially of the arts of design, by the formation of a public collection of art treatises, pictures, engravings, photographs, casts, models, and such other material as may aid in this; and furthermore by lectures, essays, and discussions on art subjects." It raised money by mounting an Annual Loan Exhibition, "made up of works owned by citizens, productions of pupils and teachers in the four art schools in the city, drawings by pupils in the Public Schools, and paintings, engravings, etc. loaned by artists and dealers in St. Louis, Chicago, New York, and elsewhere." Its membership included men as well as women, who paid an annual fee of one dollar.[23] And, while the St. Botolph Club's membership policy toward non-artists was certainly restrictive, its exhibitions were much less so. From the very beginning, it exhibited the work of contemporary American artists, regardless of social background; although most of the artists it featured were men, as early as the 1880s it also showed the work of women artists such as Ellen Day Hale and Dora Wheeler. By early in the twentieth century, it was also exhibiting the work of urban realists like George Bellows, William Glackens, Robert Henri, and George Luks.[24]

The rapid growth of nonprofit art associations was matched by, and intertwined with, developments in the commercial sector. Driven in part by the staggering multiplication of wealth in the decades following the Civil War, dealing and collecting underwent a process of formalization and intensification during the last third of the nineteenth century. A three-part art market arose, characterized by the emergence and proliferation of full-time art dealers, the gradual integration of the United States into the international art market, and the appearance in the 1890s of dealers who specialized in the trade in American art.[25] One of the most important dealers at this time was Frederick Keppel, an immigrant from Tullow, County Carlow, Ireland. Keppel began as a bookseller, but soon extended his trade to prints, holding frequent exhibitions at his New York gallery from the 1870s onward; he is perhaps best known as Whistler's primary dealer in the United States, a relationship that ended in public acrimony. Keppel also gave tips on collecting to the *Art Amateur* and published extensively, producing exhibition catalogues and books like *The Golden Age of Engraving*, culled from his writings in *Harper's*, *Scribner's*, and the *Outlook*.[26]

Like Sylvester Rosa Koehler, Keppel combined an abiding interest in the history of printmaking and in canonical figures like Rembrandt and Dürer with an admiration for contemporary printmakers such as Whistler and Peter Moran, brother of Thomas Moran (and brother-in-law of Mary Nimmo Moran). Both men expressed this admiration by exhibiting and publishing the work of these artists; the first volume of the *American Art Review* included an "original etching" by each brother—Peter Moran's *Noonday Rest* and Thomas Moran's *The Passaic Meadows*—as well as Peter Moran's etching after Van Marcke's *Landscape and Cattle* and an engraving after Thomas Moran's *Walls of the Grand Cañon*.[27] Unlike Koehler, however, who seems to have donated most of the works in his possession to museums, Keppel turned both historical and contemporary prints into a lucrative business.

Keppel was also highly influential as a mentor. Another emigrant, William Macbeth, left Ireland in the 1880s to work for Keppel in New York. After ten years with Keppel, Macbeth struck out on his own to start the Macbeth Gallery (1892), the first gallery devoted to American art.[28] This gallery was the site for the landmark 1908 exhibition of works by The Eight, the group of painters led by Robert Henri, which Henri organized to protest the Academy's exclusion of "non-traditional" art.[29] Following Keppel's example, Macbeth also soon started a journal, *Art Notes*, which educated the public even as it helped to sell art.

Among Keppel's other protégés were his two sons, New York art dealer David Keppel and Frederick Paul Keppel.[30] As President of the Carnegie Corporation from 1923 to 1941, Frederick Paul Keppel was instrumental in securing more than $13 million in funding for American museums. Underlining these philanthropic efforts was the younger Keppel's understanding of the purposes of the museum: he believed, as Paul DiMaggio describes it, "that the arts, defined broadly after the fashion of the reformers, were essential elements in the good life and that with proper planning, infusions of expertise, and enlightened leadership, art museums could become as vital to public education as libraries."[31] DiMaggio argues that this belief jarred with "the traditional [museum] model's focus on insulating art and its patrons from nonart, the market, and the larger public," and he attributes Keppel's reformism to the influence of the "professional vanguard of museum work" in the 1920s.[32] What I would propose is that Keppel's father also provided a powerful example of how art and commerce could join to foster "the good life," and that, at least in this instance, the break between nineteenth- and twentieth-century models of organizing the art world was not as sharp as DiMaggio's account suggests.

As the success of print dealers like Keppel indicates, the expanding postwar art trade was not limited to dealers in original, unique works of painting and sculpture. It was not limited to men either, but was marked by the rise of a number of successful women entrepreneurs in the decorative arts. As in other areas of the art world, women art entrepreneurs often combined careers as successful artists with ventures into writing, publishing, organizing, and teaching. As Candace Wheeler's career suggests, New York's art world provided fertile ground for some ambitious women. Yet, many of the women who were most successful in the decorative arts—and who had the most varied careers—lived and worked outside New York or, like Janet Payne Bowles, lived in New York only for a short time. Milwaukee's Susan Stuart Goodrich Frackelton was a prize-winning ceramicist and inventor of a gas kiln, an officer of the Milwaukee Industrial Exposition Association, and the author of an instructional manual, *Tried by Fire: A Work on China Painting*.[33] Similarly, Cincinnati's M. Louise McLaughlin began writing instructional books almost as soon as she started making and selling her own works in the mid-1870s, publishing *China Painting*, *Pottery Decoration*, *Painting in Oil*, and *Suggestions to China Painters*, a compendium of articles she wrote for the *Art Amateur*.[34] At least nineteen thousand copies of *China Painting* alone were printed by the mid-1890s. McLaughlin was also much lauded for her art, winning prizes at the 1889 Paris Exposition and the 1893 World's Columbian Exposition.[35] And, at the very end of the century, the ceramicist and teacher Adelaide Alsop-Robineau—a student of Dow's—began publishing the *Keramic Studio: A Monthly Magazine for the Designer, Potter, Decorator, Firer* (1899–1924) out of Syracuse and New York (fig. 29). Echoing the words of the journal's masthead—"Keep the Fire Alive"—this journal lasted almost until the end of Robineau's life.

Art Education: Theory into Practice

Alongside the growth of museums, voluntary associations, and the market, one of the most significant developments in the postwar art world was the campaign to improve and expand American art education. Like these other schemes, initiatives on behalf of art education were not isolated within one set of homogeneous institutions, but cut across many different

29. Adelaide Alsop-Robineau (1865–1929), *Treatment of Cup and Saucer*. Published in *Keramic Studio: A Monthly Magazine for the Designer, Potter, Decorator, Firer* 1, no. 5 (Sept. 1899). Fine Arts Library, Harvard College Library, Cambridge, Massachusetts

KERAMIC STUDIO 107

you will find that the entire design has been preserved, if directions have been followed.

For second fire make the dark blue enamel by adding a trifle of Deep Purple and Brunswick Black to Dark Blue. Use only turpentine, and add one-eighth of Dresden Aufsetzweis (in tubes). Use a long-haired tracer, No. 1 or 2, fill the brush with the enamel, made quite thin with turpentine, and fill in each petal at one stroke: no touching up, or the enamel will look patchy. If the enamel is just right it will flow to the outline and look smooth and dull when dry. For the broader washes of blue in the border, work in the same way, using enamel even thinner, and work rapidly in order that one brush full may melt into the one before, for as turpentine is the only medium used, it dries rapidly. This blue should fire a beautiful dark blue, highly glazed, but only slightly raised from the dish. For the green enamel leaves and background above panels, use Apple Green with a little Silver Yellow added, and a touch of Chrome Green B, adding one-fourth Aufsetzweis, and turpentine only. Make the smaller leaves a lighter green by using Mixing Yellow instead of Silver. Outline *all* the gold bands and little patterns with a clear fine black line (leaving the gold on edge of dish, of course), made from Brunswick Black with touch of Dark Blue added. Also outline the red bands with the same.

Now all rests with the fires. Do not fire too hot, or too long, and the enamel will never flake off, blister, or do anything but prove a joy forever. A test of these enamel mixtures would be advisable before using them in this design.

A new decoration has been introduced by the Rookwood Pottery. The firm has artists scouring the country in the vicinity of Cincinnati for views, historical and otherwise, to decorate their ware. Some exquisite productions are promised.

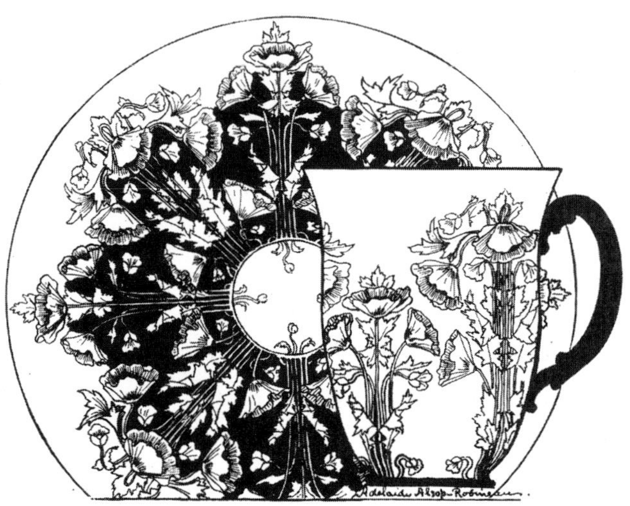

TREATMENT OF CUP AND SAUCER

DRAW on your design carefully with India ink. Dust the upper light background with Pearl Grey, the lower portion with Copenhagen Grey. Take a mixture of Dresden Aufsetzweis and best English Enamel, half of each, and model the flowers as you would raised paste. For leaves and stems, mix a very little Copenhagen with your enamel, remembering that it fires darker, and your enamel must be lighter than your ground. Use a little Copenhagen to shade centers of flowers. Or treat the design with lustres: tint the background with steel blue used thin; clean out flowers, leaves and stems. Dry thoroughly in oven, being careful not to dry too much or it will rub off. Now go over stems and leaves with Light Green. The center flower shade with Orange, the side ones with ruby, and the buds and lower flowers with Rose.

For second fire, go over lower portion of background with Dark Green. Dry. Shade leaves and stems with Light Green. Go over the orange poppy with Yellow, the ruby ones with Orange, and the rose with Orange also. The ruby ones will come out scarlet, and the rose mahogany. Now outline carefully with black.

For the third fire, strengthen any needed shading and go over any weak spots in your outlining.

The handle should be Ruby for first fire, Dark Green for second. No gold.

sectors of the art world. Museums, public and private art institutes and academies, public schools and universities, critics and publishers, and art associations all participated. Like art associations, these other organizations did not all define "art education" in exactly the same terms. Some institutions, such as the Denver Academy of Fine Arts (1882), emphasized the training of professional artists. Others conceived of art education in more holistic terms, as a source of "fundamental principles" that would enhance the pursuit of a range of occupations. Cornell University (1865), for example, required all of its students in agriculture, architecture, civil engineering, mechanic arts, mathematics, and natural history to take "Free-Hand Drawing," including outline drawing, perspective, model and object drawing, drawing from casts, and sketching from nature.[36]

These institutions offered extremely wide-ranging curricula, reflecting the diversity of the organizations themselves. Even within individual schools, however, it was often possible to gain instruction in a range of fields, including both traditional "fine arts" disciplines like drawing, painting, and sculpture and the decorative, industrial, and graphic arts. The Denver Academy of Fine Arts offered "Perspective, Chiaro-scuro . . . Study from the Life, [and] Composition" alongside courses in "Engraving on Wood and Metal, Etching, China Painting, etc." The Columbus (Ohio) Art School (1878), which was maintained by the Columbus Art Association, presented a similarly diverse curriculum. Admitting only women as full members of the Association, but accepting both men and women as associates and students, it offered classes in "Drawing, Decorative Design, Landscape Sketching from Nature, Elementary Life Sketch Class, Advanced Life Sketch Class, Water-Color, Oil Painting, China Painting, Wood Carving, Art Needlework" and, in its evening school, "Architectural and Machine Drawing."[37]

Perhaps the most interesting development was the move to introduce art education into the nation's public schools, exemplified by Massachusetts' landmark "Act Relating to Free Instruction in Drawing," passed in 1870. This legislation was based on a radical proposition: "all children who can be taught to read, write, and cipher, can be taught to draw."[38] It made drawing a compulsory part of the public school curriculum.[39] It also mandated that free instruction in industrial and mechanical drawing be made available to adults in all towns with a population of 10,000 or more. In both respects, the Act was a first: before its passage, art had never been a compulsory subject in the common schools of an American state, although as Boston's School Committee noted, the subject had been offered since the 1860s in Cincinnati and in two of three of Boston's own high schools.[40]

Educators had high hopes for drawing. As the School Committee put it, drawing "is connected with habits of correct observation. It opens the eye to nature. It is in itself a language. It becomes to the possessor, forever, a pleasant resource. . . . its pursuit is, in nearly all cases, so delightful as to be a joy rather than a task."[41] The committee was careful to emphasize, however, that drawing was not merely "an ornamental branch of education, superfluous unless as a matter of show."[42] Drawing was, the committee maintained, "a most desirable discipline both for the eye and the hand. . . . There is hardly an artisan who would not be a better workman, if he knew how to handle a pencil; and neither a merchant nor a professional man, would be the less qualified for his duties if he knew how to draw a plan, or sketch a landscape."[43] Moreover, defenders of art education insisted that the individual aesthetic and personal benefits of art education were matched by the economic potential of good design. As Lathrop argued, "So much value does ornament add."[44]

While proponents of the Drawing Act believed that art education would lead some pupils to pursue artistic careers, their primary intention was never to produce a professional class of artists or art teachers. Rather, they hoped that art would so permeate the curriculum that all students would gain a fundamental virtuosity in the field, and that teachers would learn to teach drawing as they did other key subjects like writing and arithmetic. As Walter Smith put it, "Specialties in education must end somewhere, and in the common schools the right place for them to end is before they begin, or like the man and camel in the fable, we shall have specialties in the tent, and education outside."[45] The only exception to this was the Free Evening Schools for Mechanical Drawing, in which teachers were expected to have a specialized, professional knowledge that would facilitate the teaching of "Botanical analysis/applied design," "Machine or Build[ing]. Con[struction]. Or Ship-Draughting," and other courses in industrial design.[46] These specialist teachers were rewarded for their expertise; evening drawing instructors were paid better than their counterparts in the regular evening schools, earning five dollars versus three dollars per night, respectively, as principal teachers, and four dollars versus one dollar per night as assistant teachers in 1871. Unlike in the regular evening schools, moreover, positions in the Free Evening Schools for Mechanical Drawing do not appear to have been specifically limited to men.[47]

Despite its proponents' resistance to specialization, one immediate effect of the Drawing Act was to spark a sudden demand for art teachers. To respond to its pressing need for competent drawing instructors, Massachusetts followed up the Drawing Act with another landmark provision: the establishment in 1873 of the first state-sponsored higher education institution for the training of art teachers, the Massachusetts State Normal Art School (now Massachusetts College of Art).[48] In the spirit of the Drawing Act, the Normal Art School was free to all citizens of Massachusetts, male or female, who expressed an intention to teach drawing in the state.[49] Unlike the Free Evening Schools, the Normal Art School offered a blend of instruction in both the industrial and fine arts.[50] It still provided industrial art courses, such as an elective "Class in the Art Industries and Reproducing Arts."[51] However, the Normal Art School also gave instruction in "Free-Hand, Light and Shade Drawing . . . Painting in Water-Color . . . Painting in Oil," and "Sculpture and Design in the Round," and examined students on their ability "to model a relief from the bust or entire figure, from the antique, or life, or shaded copy."[52] The diverse interests of its faculty can also be seen from the weekly papers they presented to each other, which covered subjects in both the fine and industrial arts.[53]

Without devoting an entire study to the art education movement, it is hard to gauge its full impact on either the art or the citizens of Massachusetts, Cincinnati, or New York, which also enacted similar legislation in the postwar period. At the very least, though, it can be said that Massachusetts's program did have a wide reach: at the time of its passage, fully 247,000 out of 270,000 of the people in the state between the ages of five and fifteen attended school for at least part of the year, and the average attendance in the public schools in winter was 200,000.[54] The Drawing Act also can be seen to have opened employment opportunities for both men and women. In 1907, the Normal Art School published "Some of the Positions Filled by Past Pupils of the Massachusetts Normal Art School," along with a full "List of Students who have performed the work of one or more classes."[55] These included Anson K. Cross (Class C, 1883), who became "Instructor, Massachusetts Normal Art School, and School of Drawing and Painting, Museum of Fine Arts, Boston"; Laura E. Palmer (1876), "Artist; photograph librarian, Pratt Institute, Brooklyn, N.Y."; and Robert W. Vonnoh (1879), "Portrait Artist."[56] And it seems to have sparked a national campaign on behalf of art education, accelerated by the migration of Normal Art School graduates to cities like Pittsburgh, Wichita, and Chicago; and to institutions like Pasadena's Throop Polytechnic Institute (now California Institute of Technology); Newcomb College in New Orleans; and the "Manual Training School, University of Chicago."[57]

By the 1890s, enough school districts had introduced art into their curricula to support a range of professional art teachers' associations, including the Western Drawing Teachers' Association, the Southern Art Teachers' Association, and at least one journal, *Art Education: Devoted to Art and Manual Training as Essential Elements of Education, Industry and General Culture* (1894–1901).[58] Like the curriculum of the Normal Art School itself (and like the *Art Amateur*), this journal blended articles on exhibitions and artists like the Union League Club's display of "the pictures of George Inness and Winslow Homer" and "John W. Alexander: His Paintings" with dissertations on "Bamboo Flower Holders" and on "Historic Ornament and Its Application to Design by Fred H. Daniels," the "Director of Drawing, Public Schools, Buffalo, N. Y." Daniels was a former student at the Normal Art School, where he completed both an art degree and a diploma in its "Public School Class."[59] *Art Education* also provided extensive coverage of art-educational institutions and programs, such as the "Experiment with Applied Art in Newcomb College, New Orleans" and the "large normal class" at Throop, "ten of whom will receive sloyd (wood-carving) diplomas in June. Eight of these have just subscribed for *Art Education*."[60]

A sense of the broader possibilities offered by the Massachusetts Drawing Act can also be gleaned by looking at the career of one student who

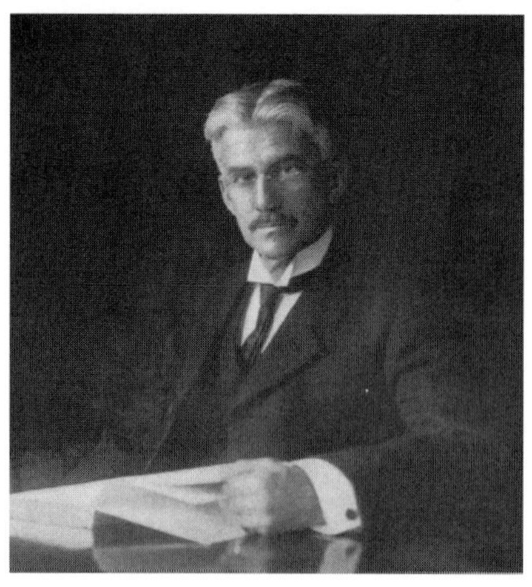

Above:
30. Albert Henry Munsell (1858–1918). Processed digital image provided by Munsell Color Science Laboratory, Rochester Institute of Technology

Below:
31. "Union of Lines." From *The American Text-Books of Art Education. Drawing Cards, to Be Used in Conjunction with the Teacher's Manual for Teaching Drawing in Primary Schools* (Boston: L. Prang & Co., 1881). Fine Arts Department, Boston Public Library

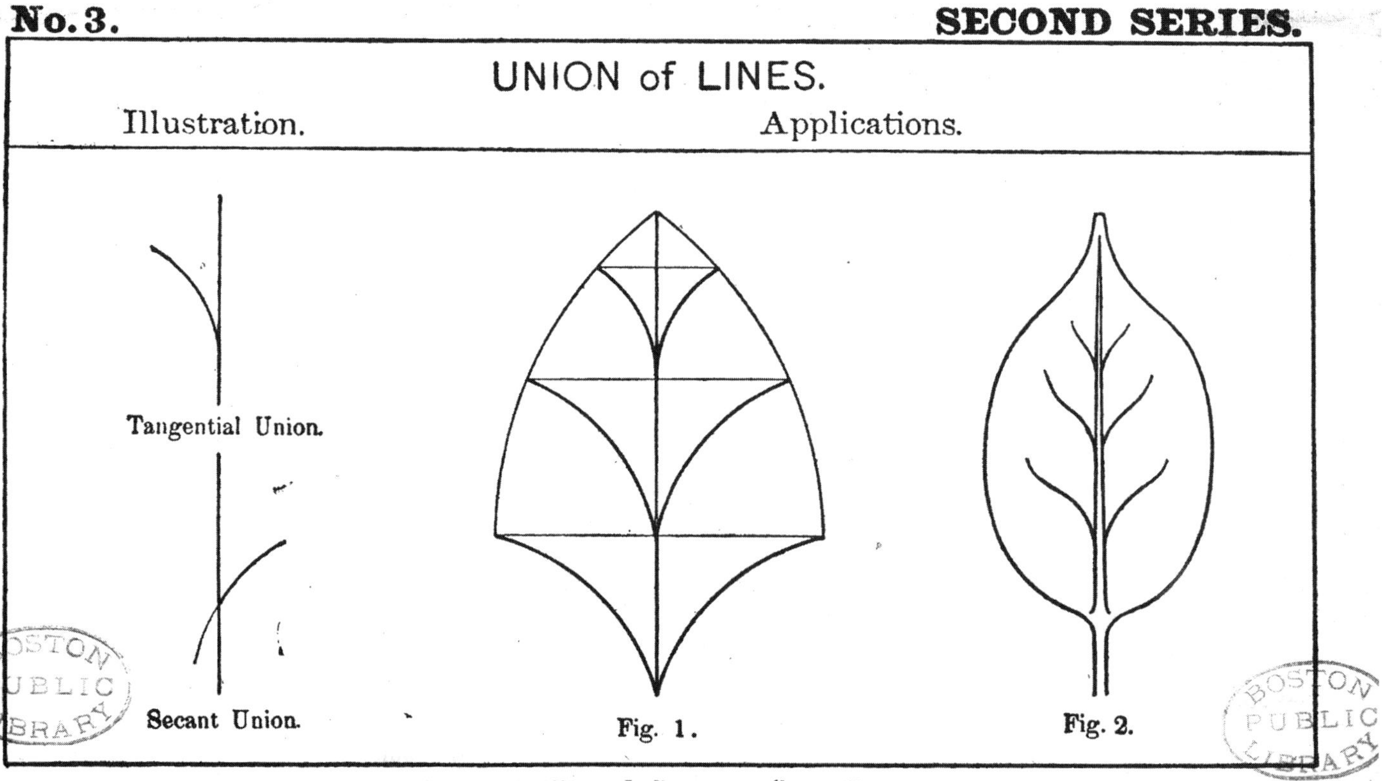

thrived under its influence, Albert Henry Munsell, listed as "Portrait painter; instructor, Massachusetts Normal Art School, Boston" in the 1907 circular.[61] Munsell (fig. 30) first appears in the records of the new art schools in 1874, with the note that an "Albert H. Mansoll," of the Appleton Street Evening Class, had been awarded the mark of "excellent" for his "flat copy" work.[62] Munsell went on to enroll in the Normal Art School, where he completed Grade C in 1880.[63] He appears to have excelled in his new environment and was elected in the next year to the position of student "Curator," which paid $500 per year.[64] In the same year, Munsell also gained a foothold as an instructor in the Normal Art School, offering courses in "Sculpture and Advanced Perspective," anatomy, and "Charcoal Time Sketch. Figure."[65] At this time he also became active in the Massachusetts Art Teachers' Association, serving as its secretary.[66]

In the most general sense, Munsell's experience under the Massachusetts Drawing Act and the Normal Art School suggests that these provisions provided the Commonwealth's citizens with new access to careers in the art world. As significant, though, is the influence that the curriculum itself—in particular, its fusion of industrial or technical pedagogy *and* instruction in traditional fine arts subjects—seems to have had on Munsell's career. This dual provision has sometimes been represented as a two-tiered, discriminatory system in which the children of the poor received an inferior artistic education to those wealthy enough to seek out instruc-

No. 3. **SECOND SERIES.**

UNION of LINES.

Illustration. Applications.

Tangential Union.

Secant Union.

Fig. 1.

Fig. 2.

tion in private academies or in museum schools. In Munsell's case, however, education in the free schools did prepare him for conventional artistic success. In the 1890s, he exhibited his paintings at least three times at the St. Botolph Club, alongside the works of Dow, Whistler, John Singer Sargent, and his fellow student and teacher at the Normal Art School, the impressionist painter (and *Modern Art* contributor) Robert Vonnoh.[67] Some of Munsell's paintings are still in public collections.[68]

Munsell also put the technical side of his training to good use. In addition to teaching and painting, he invented the daylight photometer and, after the turn of the century, published *A Color Notation* and the *Atlas of the Munsell Color System*.[69] This system, which classifies color according to the attributes of value (the scale from black to white), chroma (intensity of color), and hue (the relationship of a given color to other colors in the spectrum), is still an international standard in the field of color science. Munsell's understanding of color, based on perception rather than the chemical or physical qualities of pigment or light, emerged from decades as a practicing artist and art teacher. His extensive observations as a painter, for example, enabled him to propose significant changes to current conceptions of hue, describing it in terms of five principal hues (Red, Yellow, Green, Blue, and Purple) and five intermediate hues (Yellow-Red, Green-Yellow, Blue-Green, Purple-Blue, and Red-Purple).

Munsell's conceptualization and display of this system, which plotted all remaining hues in relation to these ten, also owed a significant debt to his technical instruction in the Free Evening Schools for Mechanical Drawing and at the Normal Art School. From the primary school to the evening class, training in industrial and mechanical drawing taught, above all, how to translate increasingly complex, three-dimensional objects, like leaves and flowers (fig. 31), buildings, and machines into legible, two-dimensional schema based on monochrome line drawings. In the hands of a polymath like Munsell, it also allowed for the conceptualization and representation of more abstract notions, like color, as three-dimensional objects that could then be re-translated into schematic line drawings. Most notably, Munsell conceptualized color as a sphere, which allowed him to integrate value, chroma, and hue into one model (fig. 32). Within this framework, Munsell depicted hue as points on a 360-degree grid, formed by drawing ten equidistant axes from a central point to represent the five principal (R, Y, G, B, and P) and the five intermediate (YR, GY, BG, PB, and RP) hues. Munsell then plotted hue as a "slice" of the sphere, so that the other attributes could also be accounted for (fig. 33).

Munsell's ability to join artistic and technical knowledge was not unusual among other Normal Art School graduates, like Charles L. Adams (1879), "Professor, Massachusetts Institute of Technology; principal,

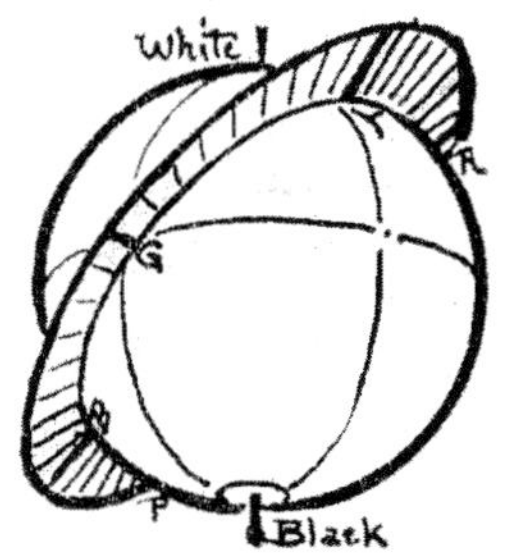

Below and detail above:
32. Exterior, *Munsell Crayons No. 3 Box, 22 Colors*. Korzenik Art Education Ephemera Collection, Box 71, Set 4. The Huntington Library, San Marino, California

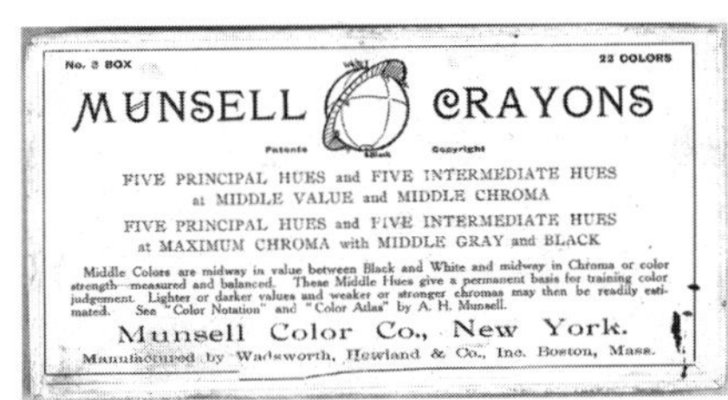

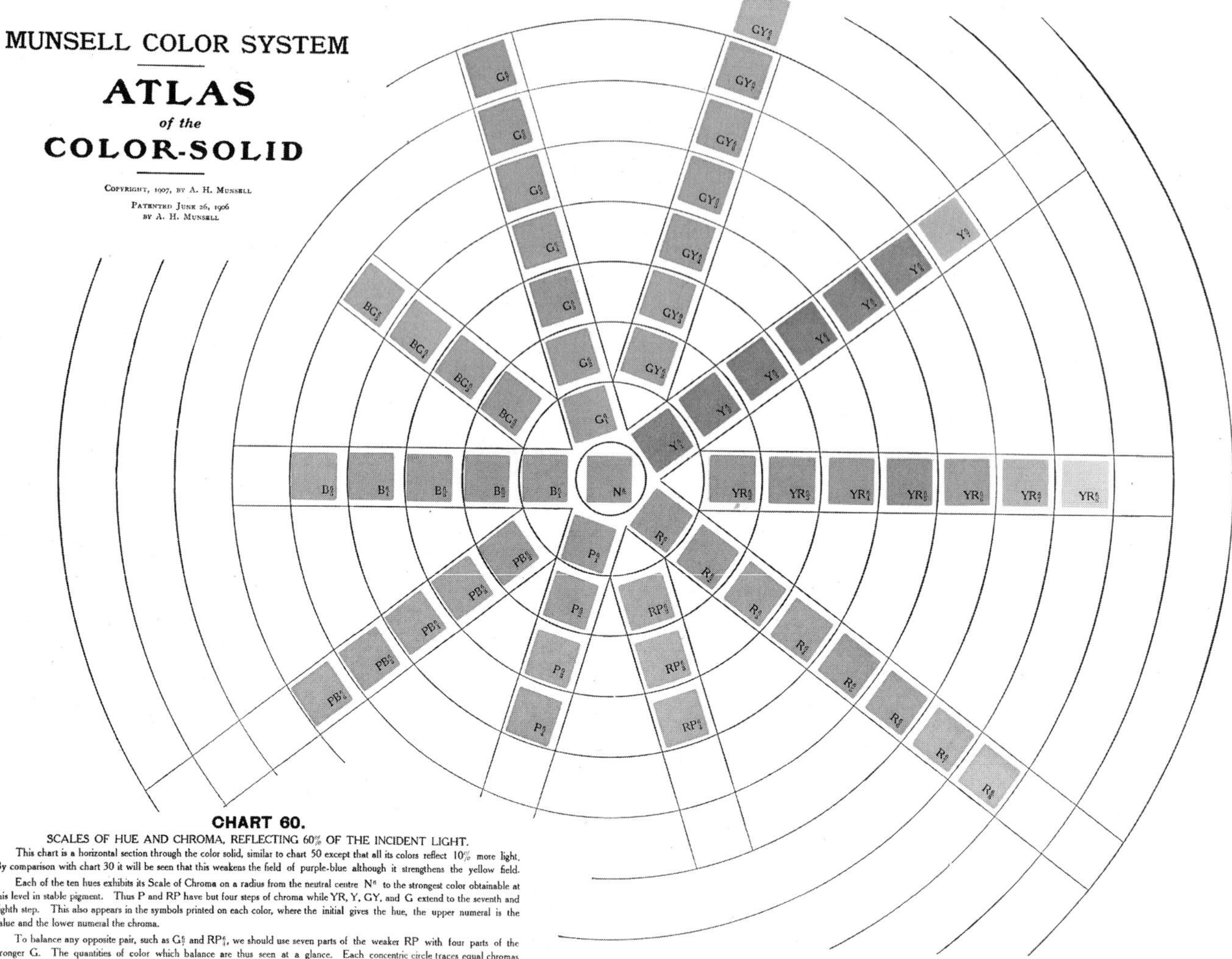

33. "Chart 60, Scales of Hue and Chroma, Reflecting 60% of the Incident Light," 1906. From A. H. Munsell, *Atlas of the Munsell Color System* (Malden, Mass.: Wadsworth, Howland & Co., 1915). Widener Library of the Harvard College Library, Cambridge, Massachusetts

evening drawing school, Roxbury."[70] It did, however, distinguish them from many of their peers in the art world. In the decades surrounding the publication of *A Color Notation*, a number of Americans developed color systems, including Prang (see fig. 69), Bradley, and the modernist painter and proponent of Synchromism, Stanton Macdonald-Wright, who published a *Treatise on Color* in 1924. Yet, none of these authors used schematic drawings to represent their findings. And, while Prang's and Macdonald-Wright's color systems were each influential in their own way, neither had Munsell's scientific impact.[71]

Like the Drawing Act itself (and like the efforts of Bradley and Prang, who also sold art supplies), Munsell's foray into the science of color matched education to entrepreneurship. In conjunction with *A Color Notation*, Munsell marketed a line of "Materials for the Munsell Color System" (fig. 34). Like Prang, Munsell promoted this system with testimonials, in this case from "Mr. Leslie W. Miller of the Museum and School of Industrial Art in Philadelphia," "Miss Haven of the Kindergarten In-

MATERIALS FOR THE

Munsell Color System

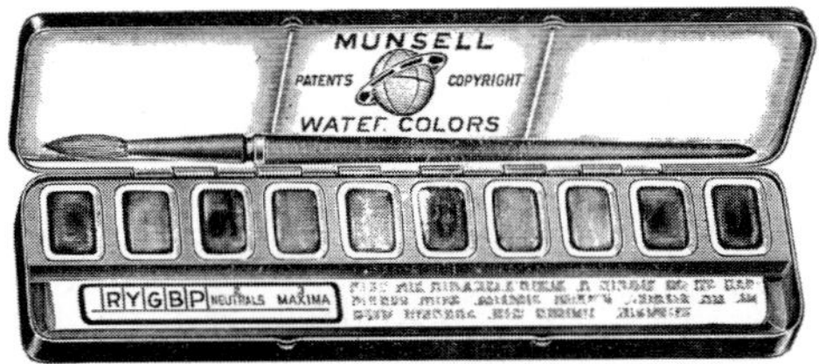

Munsell No. 2 Water Color Box. Containing the five middle colors, with Gray, Black, and the maxima of Red, Yellow, and Blue. Per box, $ .50

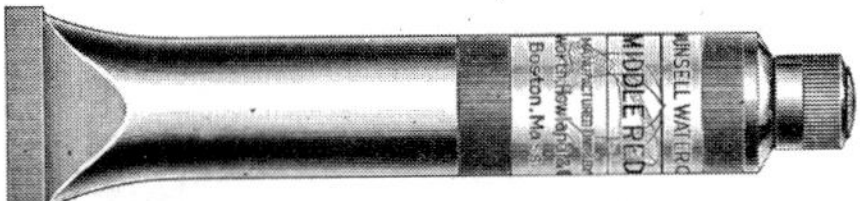

Munsell Water Colors in Tubes. Set of five middle hues, with Gray and Black.	Per set,	$ 60
Munsell Water Colors in Tubes.	Per doz.,	1.00
Munsell Water Colors in Tubes. Maxima Colors,	Per doz.,	1.00
Enamel Cards, 1¼ x 1½ in., set of 15,		.10
Enamel Cards, 4 x 6 in., set of 15,		.50
Balls, set of 5,		.10

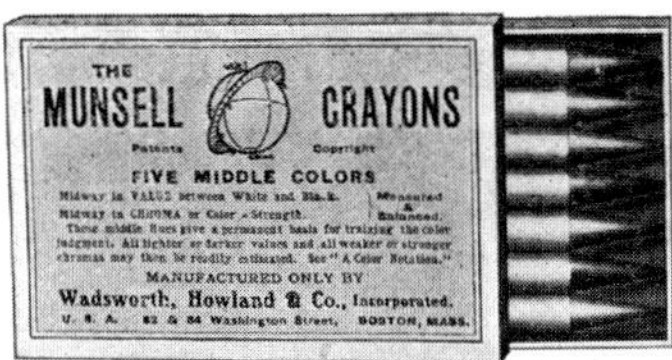

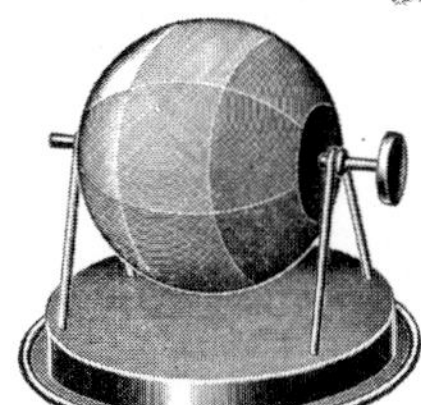

Munsell Crayons in box containing the five middle hues, with Gray and Black. Per box, $ .10
Per dozen boxes, .96

Munsell Color Sphere. Two Sizes of the Color Sphere are Made.
A 2-inch size for children shows five middle hues around the equator, with five lighter and five darker values of each, 1.00
A 5-inch size for the teacher's use shows the same color steps, but is large enough to be seen by all the class at once, 2.50

Manufactured only by

WADSWORTH, HOWLAND & CO., Incorporated,

82 and 84 Washington Street. BOSTON, MASS. 222 Clarendon Street.

34. Advertisement for "Materials for the Munsell Color System." From A. H. Munsell, *Atlas of the Munsell Color System* (Malden, Mass.: Wadsworth, Howland & Co., 1915). Widener Library of the Harvard College Library, Cambridge, Massachusetts

stitute in Chicago," and Arthur Wesley Dow, whose efforts on behalf of art education had earned the artist a prominent position on the faculty at Columbia Teachers College.[72] This "system" included pedagogical devices like spheres that represented his three-dimensional color system, colored enamel cards, and balls of "measured" colors. It also included materials for making art, such as watercolor paints and crayons (see fig. 25). Like Munsell's other products, his crayons could be had more cheaply by the dozen or by the gross.[73]

And yet, unlike today's crayons—whose colors seem to conform mostly to the market-research-derived names on their labels—Munsell's crayons were not just commodities. They also embodied both the science of color *and* his aesthetic beliefs. The No. 3 Box (see figs. 25, 32) contained "five principal hues and five intermediate hues at middle value and middle chroma," "five principle hues and five intermediate hues at maximum chroma" and "middle gray and black."[74] Just by opening the box, pupils could begin to see how the system worked. And, by turning "These Middle

Hues" into images, Munsell hoped, students would develop a preference for the "Middle Colors," which "are midway in value between Black and White and midway in Chroma or color strength—measured and balanced." By studying his system and turning his materials into art, the nation's youth, he believed, would gain "a permanent basis for training in color judgment."

It is impossible to tell whether Munsell's plan worked, although the fact that the Maximum Colors in this box are virtually untouched, while his preferred "Middle Colors" are worn down with use (see fig. 25), suggests that at least some students followed his advice. And, whether or not Munsell managed to convert the nation's youth to middle colors, his career was marked by phenomenal and broad-ranging success. Indeed, Lathrop could not have asked for better proof that institutional development would bear fruit in the art world and beyond. By learning the discipline of art in the free schools of Massachusetts, Munsell avoided "starvation." More than that, he became a successful teacher and artist, a scientist whose system is still recognized as a standard in its field, and an entrepreneur whose company eventually became rich enough to endow, after his death, a color science laboratory at the Rochester Institute of Technology. Seen in this light, the Boston School Committee's utopian vision of drawing as a "language" that would bring a "great addition of power" to its possessors—and its eager defense by Lathrop—was more than just a dream.[75]

Art Publishing: Creating an Organizational Field

American art criticism and publishing also grew and expanded dramatically after the Civil War. Neither art writing nor art magazines were new in this period. At least since the 1850s, Americans had had access to periodicals such as the *Cosmopolitan Art Journal* (New York, 1856-61), the *Philadelphia Art-Union Reporter* (1851-52), and the *Crayon* (1855-61), as well as less-regularly published commentary on art in newspapers, books, magazines, and poems.[76] But with the more generalized boom in magazine publishing in the 1870s, the number of journals devoted wholly or partly to art exploded.[77] In addition to *The American Art Review*, *The Art Amateur*, and *Modern Art*, these included *The Aldine* (New York, 1868), *The Workshop, a Monthly Journal Devoted to Progress of the Useful Arts* (New York, 1868), *The Art Review* (Chicago, 1870), *Fine Arts* (New York, 1872), *The Art Journal* (New York, 1875), *The Art Interchange* (New York, 1878), *The Art Worker: A Journal of Design* (New York, 1878), *The Critic* (New York, 1881), *The Art Student* (New York, 1882), *The Art Age* (New York, 1883), *The Art Folio* (Providence, 1883), *American Art* (Boston, 1886), *The Connoisseur* (Philadelphia, 1886), *The American Art Printer*

(New York, 1887), *The Art Critic* (Boston, 1894), *The Arts* (Chicago, 1893), *Western Graphic* (Los Angeles, 1893), and *Brush and Pencil* (Chicago, 1897). Art writing also emerged as a staple within middle-class monthlies such as the *North American Review*, *Harper's Monthly* and *Scribner's Monthly*, and in daily newspapers. Taken alongside the hundreds of exhibition catalogues and illustrated books published at this time, art publishing came to represent a significant element of American print culture in the 1870s and 1880s.

Art publishing owed its importance in the emerging postwar art world not merely to its new and wider reach, but to its unusual focus and approach. As in the present day, much of the writing of the 1870s and 1880s aimed to analyze and evaluate artworks, often through articles that explored the lives and works of individual artists or through exhibition reviews. In addition to the Academy, publishers provided illustrated coverage of a wide range of public exhibitions, including the American Water-Color Society and the Boston Society of Architects' Decorative Arts Exhibition, and fairs like the Centennial at Philadelphia in 1876 (fig. 35) and Cincinnati's Ohio Valley Centennial in 1888.[78]

At the same time, both art periodicals and general-interest magazines contained much more within their covers than assessments of exhibitions, artists, and artworks. These publications also burst with information and opinions on art-world events, people, and institutions; news from local art clubs; art lessons and tips; and bibliographic guides to art history, theory, and practice.[79] *Scribner's*, for example, often pointed readers outward to further images, further theories on art, or further instruction, by copiously noting the other art publications of the day.[80] Some of these notices undoubtedly were intended to sell the publisher's

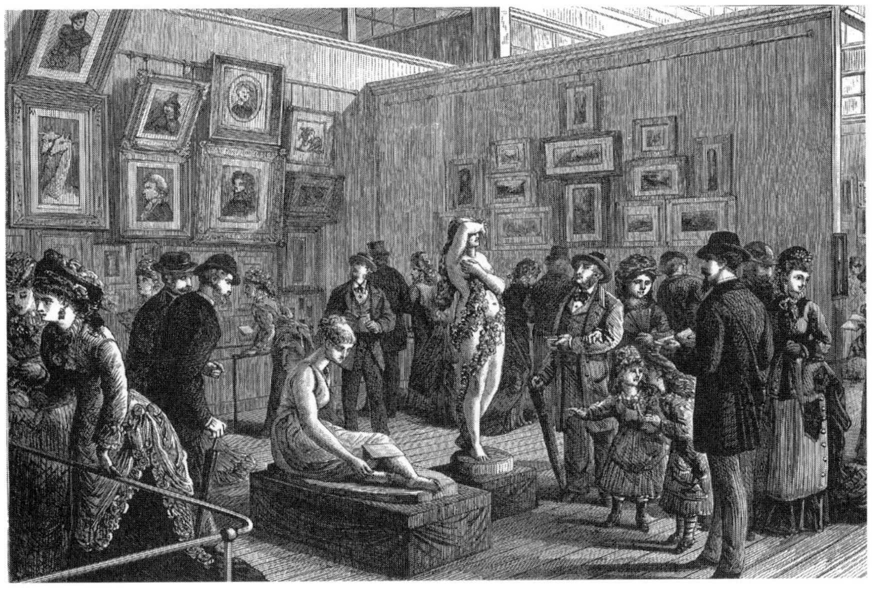

35. "The Art Department in the Woman's Pavilion." From *Frank Leslie's Historical Register of the United States Centennial Exposition, 1876* (New York: Frank Leslie, 1877). The Huntington Library, San Marino, California. Note that the pictures displayed on the right wall are "Mrs. Greatorex's pen and ink drawings."

Pacific Monthly. Yet, Wood remained an amateur in the art world, making his living as an Army officer and lawyer.[86]

One institution, which attracted considerable attention from critics from the 1860s onward, was the museum.[87] Critical discussions of museums explored virtually every aspect of their conception, planning, and management, including how to expand museums into new regions, their educational role, the appropriateness of various European models, and the pressing issue of fees and access.[88] As might be expected, some of this commentary focused on collections and how to display them. One writer in the *Art Union*, for example, provided a detailed itinerary of Carl A. Brandt's European trip to build a collection of originals and casts for Savannah's new Telfair Academy in 1884, concluding enthusiastically that "without spending the total amount of money at his command, he bought enough to more than fill the present . . . building."[89] Others offered very specific suggestions about the lighting and wall color of interiors, and the size and construction of display cases.[90]

The art press also addressed the difficult question of museum architecture, printing both critical commentary and proposed and actual designs. In William H. Beard's fanciful plans, published in *Scribner's Monthly* in 1871 (fig. 38), it was proposed that patrons would pass through a tunnel-like entrance graced by cavemen and wild beasts. For Beard and for a number of his contemporaries, the creation of the museum meant the construction of grand, imposing edifices—"ceremonial monuments," as Carol Duncan describes them—whose bulk would attest to the magnitude of art and whose temple-like architecture would inspire worship and ac-

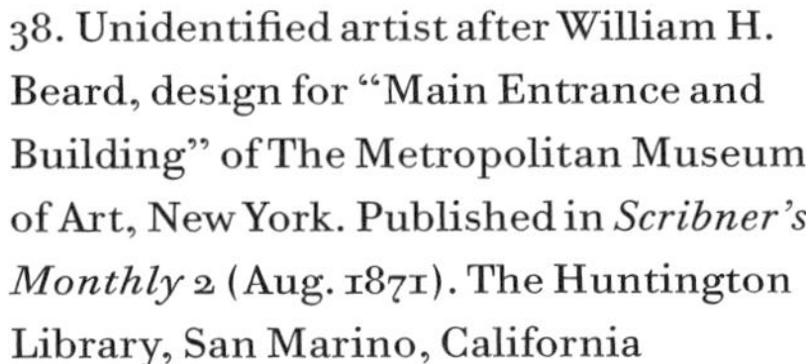

38. Unidentified artist after William H. Beard, design for "Main Entrance and Building" of The Metropolitan Museum of Art, New York. Published in *Scribner's Monthly* 2 (Aug. 1871). The Huntington Library, San Marino, California

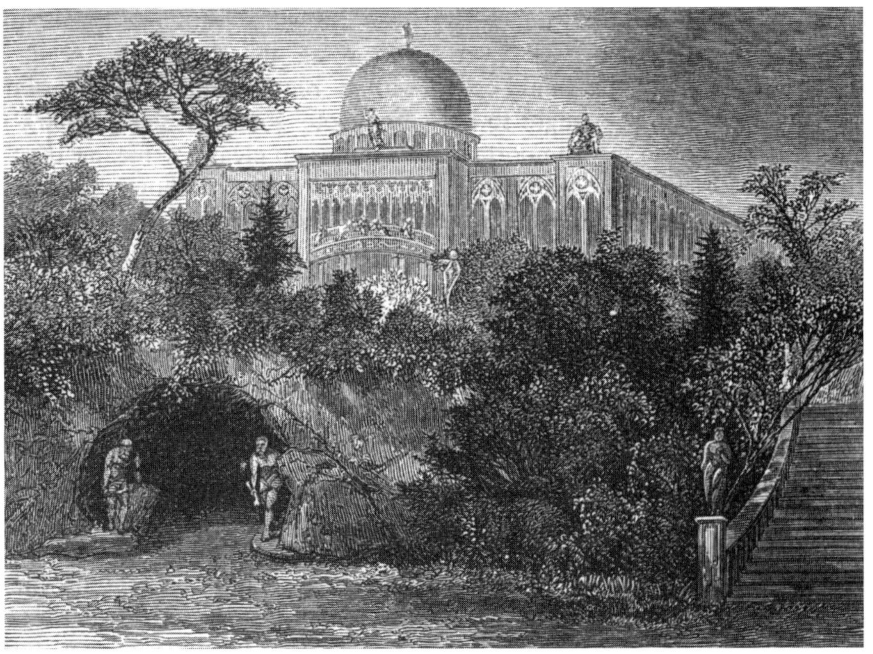

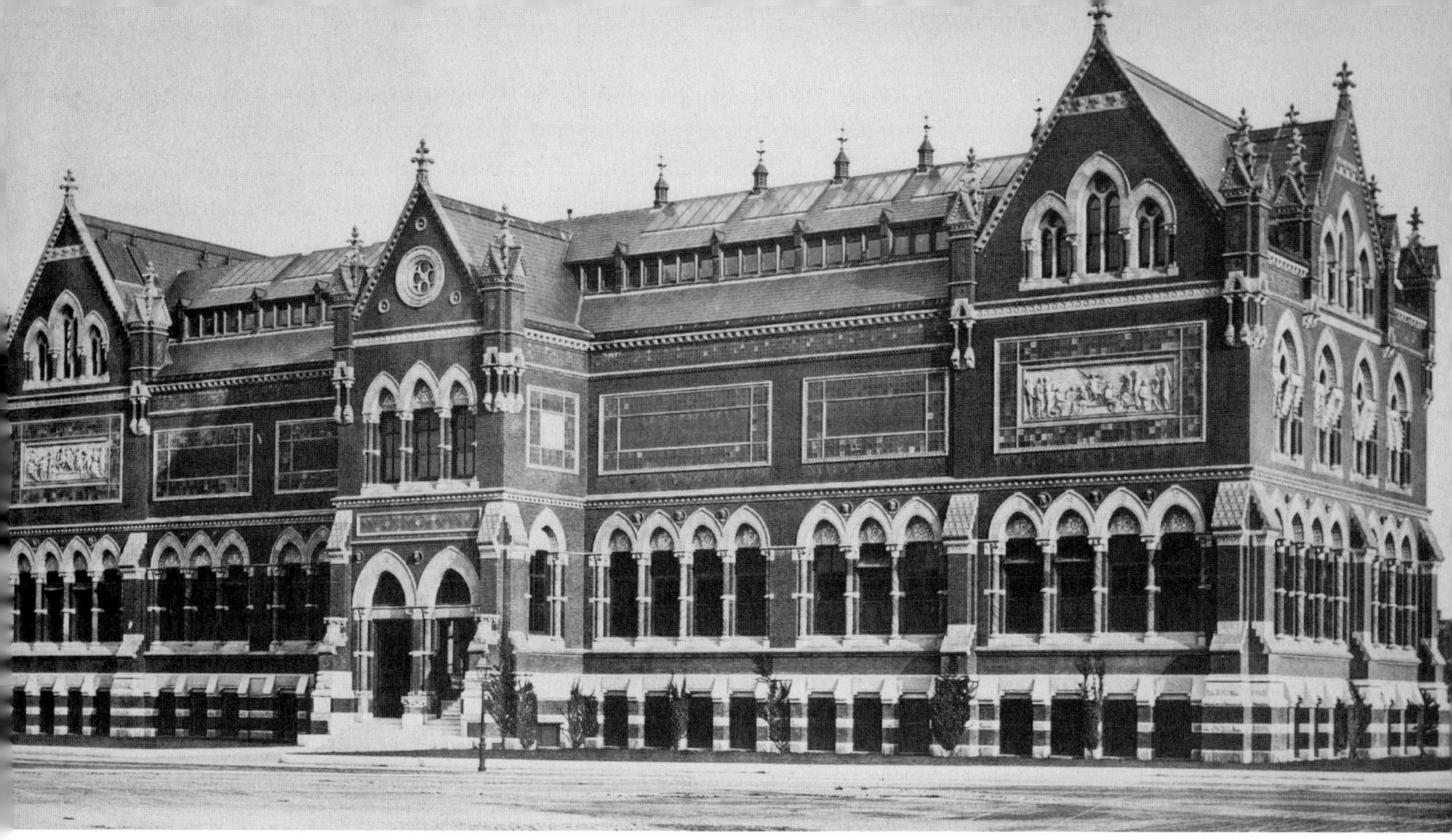

39. Museum of Fine Arts, Boston, 1880. Published in *American Architect and Building News* 8, no. 253 (30 Oct. 1880). The Huntington Library, San Marino, California

quiescence among audiences.[91] Others embraced palatial architecture not for ideological reasons, but as a kind of fancy packaging that would draw tourists to their cities. In his commentary on Beard's fanciful designs, J. R. G. Hassard eagerly quoted critic James Jackson Jarves's maxim that "Central Parks pay. So do National Museums, as that city will discover which is the first to found one on a Central Park scale of organization and administration."[92]

Neither museum founders nor critics wholly embraced the model of the museum as palace or temple, however. An anonymous "Companion to the Catalogue" (1877) of the MFA called upon visitors to inspect the exterior of the building at Copley Square (fig. 39) for exactly its lack of unusual expense: "Notice how rich-looking it is, incrusted with squares of harmonious color, and large and well-executed *relievi* of figures suitable to such a building. These are from England, are in terra-cotta, very permanent, very effective, and not dear. They serve as a link with the great Museum of Kensington, to which they are related. You will guess at once that it is not a church or a court-room, and already might suppose it a building for Fine Art."[93] Some critics could be quite explicit in their rejection of palatial architecture, particularly for the many small, regional museums being established. M. G. Humphreys admired the Portland (Maine) Art League's $2200 building, warning that museums designed to look like "miniature temple(s)" or "clipped editions of the Parthenon" were ill suited to the American landscape and customs. Instead, Humphreys suggested that art museums be built in a vernacular style, upon pleasant, accessible, and spacious parcels of land. As Humphreys indicated, this last provision was meant as a safeguard against fire, reflecting pervasive fears following Boston's devastating 1872 conflagration, which had destroyed many works of art.[94]

Even in the 1890s, as the appetite for overblown, neo-classical pastiche assumed epic proportions in the form of the "White City" (fig. 40) and the presidential monument, some critics derided trustees and building committees who erected grandiose temples when simple, fireproof buildings would have sufficed.[95] One such critic hinted that exaggerated temples to art reflected the egotism of large donors such as Andrew Carnegie, rather than the best interest of visitors. "While it is nice to talk about the elevating and educating influence of art with a big A," he noted cynically, "it is much surer to trust to a big pile of masonry with Doric columns in front and marble staircases approached over roman mosaic, etc., to perpetuate your memory."[96]

Like the exhibition reviews of the 1870s and 1880s, which tell us so much about the art and artists of the postwar years, writing about museums (and schools, associations, and other institutions) represents an invaluable source of information about the many organizations that emerged in this crucial period of art-world development. As significant as these writings are as a record of individual institutions, however, together they represent more than the sum of their parts. Thus, it is also important to try to understand how they fit together, as features joined within a single publication, and as publications within a body of works produced by one figure or cohort of interconnected figures. Seen in this way, American art criticism and publishing have the potential to reveal a great deal about not only how Americans envisioned particular institutions, but also how they imagined the art world as a whole.

The sociologist Paul DiMaggio offers an intriguing model for conceptualizing art publishing in this way. DiMaggio has written extensively about American art museums, including the Museum of Fine Arts, Boston, and the Philadelphia (formerly Pennsylvania) Museum of Art. One of the most interesting aspects of DiMaggio's approach is that it situates a detailed analysis of individual museums within the context of the emergence of a national network—in DiMaggio's phrase, an "organizational field"—of similar institutions. DiMaggio argues that this kind of analysis is necessary because the direction taken by individual museums depended to a great extent on developments at the level of the organizational field. He writes: "To understand the institutionalization of organizational *forms*, we must first understand the institutionalization and structuring of organizational *fields*."[97] Moreover, he suggests that the de-

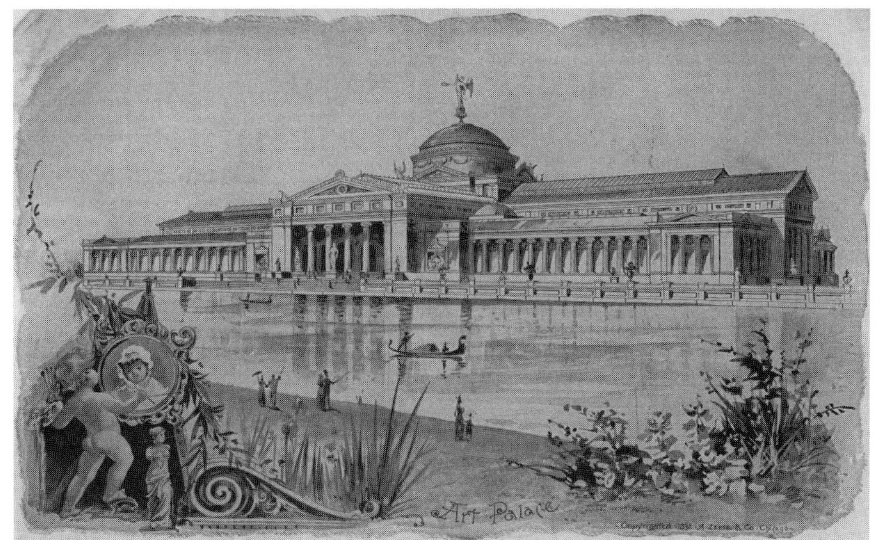

40. "The 'Art Palace' of the 'White City' at the World's Columbian Exposition, 1893." Frontispiece to Halsey C. Ives, *Official Catalogue. Part X, Art Galleries and Annexes: Department K. Fine Arts, Painting, Sculpture, Architecture, Decoration,* ed. M. P. Handy (Chicago: W. B. Conkey, 1893). Massachusetts Historical Society, Boston

velopment of an "organizational [field] for high culture," like the emergence of "industries" in the corporate sector, was not a random process, but resulted from deliberate actions on the part of those working in the field. As DiMaggio argues, organizational "fields are not simply investigators' aggregative constructs, but are meaningful to participants."[98]

There is one significant point on which my analysis diverges from DiMaggio's. His research very profitably considers the interactions between museums and the philanthropic agencies upon which they came to depend for support in the early twentieth century. Yet, he generally defines museums as a unitary organizational field, and attributes to them a uniquely vital role in defining and purveying art in the late nineteenth century.[99] What I would like to emphasize, instead, is the presence of many institutions, organizational initiatives, and constituencies of participants that grew and developed alongside museums—including, but not limited to, education, voluntary associations, criticism and publishing, and, of course, artists themselves. In each of these areas, individuals and groups of individuals worked to shape their own institutions and their own organizational fields, to influence the parallel institutions with which they were so frequently intertwined, and also to shape the art world as a whole.

Participants in the art media certainly worked to shape the "field of art," perhaps because critics and publishers so frequently had multiple affiliations within the art world. The personal correspondence of Alexander Wilson Drake, superintendent of the art department at the *Century*, gives a good sense of the interrelationships between figures in the art media and other sectors of the art world. Drake was responsible for acquiring the journal's images, but he was more than just a gatherer of illustrations. In one week in 1886, as he described it to his friend C. E. S. Wood, Drake went to "the opening of the water-color exhibition," to tea with the painter J. Alden Weir, and to a master printer's dinner at Delmonico's where he spoke to Mark Twain about Wood.[100] In the same letter, Drake also commented on "Mrs. Morgan's collection," which was about to be put on exhibition and reproduced in an "edition de-luxe" but was "not . . . worth buying"; on the vagaries of the hot-headed illustrator Alfred Laurens Brennan; on the high price of a recent work by painter Will H. Low; and on the "beautiful" architecture of the *Century*'s new printing house. As well, he revealed that his young son Frank "is taking to drawing and is . . . making a drawing of a tiger's head from a water-color sketch that I have," and urged Wood to try and reconstruct a portière Drake had seen "made of pieces of bamboo and glass beads," which was reproduced "on page 183 of Morse's book, fig. 165."[101] In one week, Drake managed to step into every corner of New York's art world—exhibitions, the print trade, the market, education and the development of youth interest, and home art production—and to relay it by letter to his friend, who was himself trying to develop similar institutions in the West.

Sylvester Rosa Koehler

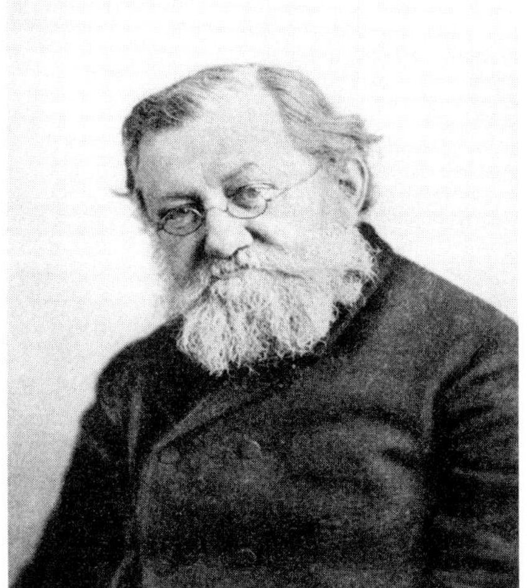

41. Sylvester Rosa Koehler (1837–1900). Graphic Arts Collection, National Museum of American History, Smithsonian Institution, Washington, D.C.

In some cases, it seems that critics and publishers deliberately and self-consciously worked toward the goal of defining an organizational field for art. Sylvester Rosa Koehler (fig. 41) was one such figure. As has already been noted, Koehler was the editor of the *American Art Review*, the first curator of prints at the MFA, and the senior technical advisor to Louis Prang & Co. in the 1870s. Koehler was also the curator of graphic arts and photography at the National Museum of History and Technology (now National Museum of American History), a position he held jointly with his post at the MFA from 1886 until his death in 1900. In these capacities, Koehler was the curator of dozens of exhibitions, and the author, editor, or translator of as many catalogues and books. Most of these productions centered on his main interest: prints and printmaking.[102] Within this broad category, however, his efforts were extraordinarily diverse, encompassing American, European, and Asian art; contemporary and historical figures, works and techniques; and art made by men and women.

Many of these exhibitions focused on the practice of printmaking and its history, rather than a single artist or school of artists. The catalogue for the *Exhibition of American Etchings*, which displayed a case of "tools and materials employed in etching," contained an eleven-page explanatory section signed by Koehler; his 1893 show at the MFA was "Arranged Chronologically to Illustrate The Various Processes of Engraving Invented from the 15th to the End of the 18th Century."[103] This fascination with the tools and techniques of artistic practice—common in publications from Frackelton's *Tried by Fire* (see fig. 58) to Dow's *Composition*—can also be seen in the landmark 1892 exhibition and catalogue of woodcut printmaking Koehler organized in cooperation with T. Tokuno, Chief of the Bureau of Engraving and Printing of the Japanese Ministry of Finance, which included illustrations of woodcut tools and instructions on how to use them.[104] Koehler was also a voracious collector and a generous donor; he lent images to the Society of American Artists and the Pennsylvania Academy of the Fine Arts, and donated thousands of prints and books to the Smithsonian, the Boston Public Library, the Museum of Fine Arts, and other developing institutions.[105]

One of Koehler's most ambitious projects was the *American Art Review: A Journal Devoted to the Practice, Theory, History, and Archaeology of Art* (1880–81). As in Koehler's repertory as a whole, the *American Art Review* defined "art" in broad terms. It combined reviews of the paintings exhibited at the Society of American Artists and the National Academy of Design with extensive, illustrated coverage of the works and careers of contemporary artists, including SAA members Chase, Mary Nimmo Moran, and R. Swain Gifford.[106] Within this framework, Koehler paid extra attention to artists working in graphic media, from whom he commissioned new works especially for the journal. Gifford, for example, "had the kindness to execute" *The Path to the Shore* "especially for the American Art Review" (fig. 42).[107] The journal also assessed the history of printmaking, in articles like W. J. Linton's multi-part "History of Wood-Engraving in America," and considered the decorative and industrial arts in articles on "Venetian Enamel," "Pueblo Pottery," and "American Stained Glass."[108] In addition to these features, the *American Art Review* also included regular articles on the institutions of the art world, such as "The Public and Private Collections of the United States" and "The Keramic Museum of Sèvres."

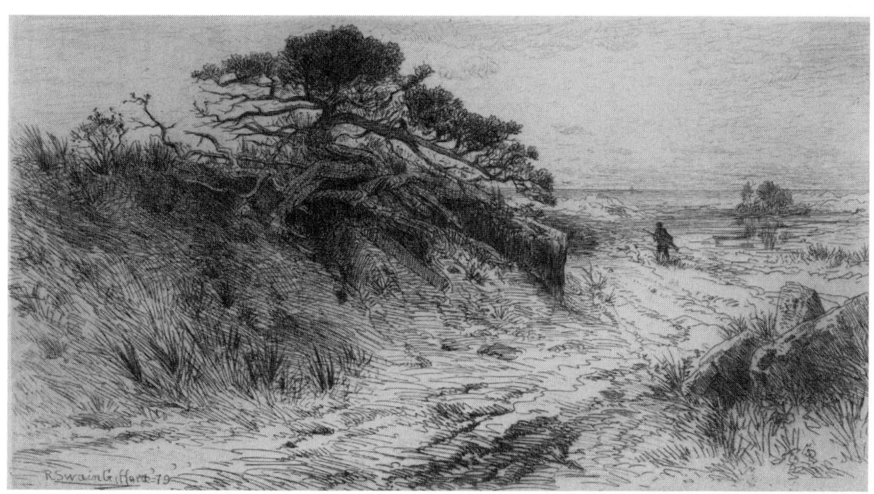

42. R. Swain Gifford (1840–1905), *The Path to the Shore*, 1880. Etching, 7⅝ × 4⅛ in. (19.4 × 10.5 cm). Published in *The American Art Review* 1, div. 1 (1880). The Huntington Library, San Marino, California

Koehler also set aside a significant portion of the journal for an "American Art Chronicle," which provided an extensive, ongoing commentary on the institutions of the art world in sections titled "Archaeology and History," "Museums and Collections," "Art Education," "Exhibitions and Sales," and "Clubs and Societies." As mentioned previously, these notices covered the activities not only of institutions in large eastern cities like Koehler's own Boston, but in San Francisco and Zanesville, Ohio, whose "art club . . . holds receptions that do great credit to its members."[109] Like the other features in the journal, the "American Art Chronicle" presented amateurs and professionals, women and men, and the fine, the graphic, and the decorative arts, as linked elements within a common art world. Alongside notices of the National Academy of Design, the "American Art Chronicle" remarked upon the "exhibition of 15,000 pencil drawings" by the 6-to-17-year-olds of the public schools of New York.[110] It also noted the 1880 "exhibition of works by the pupils of the Massachusetts State Normal Art School, and of the free evening drawing schools in Boston and other cities of the State," describing the show as "even more worthy of commendation" than the previous year's.[111] And, it reported with pride that the women of the NYSDA had filled "about 5,000 orders . . . for needle-work," could count receipts of $29,501 for 1879, and had sent "632 books on art and sheets of design . . . as loans, to nearly all parts of the country."[112] For Koehler, initiatives like the NYSDA and the Providence Art Club, which "made its first exhibition to comprise exclusively the original work of *local* professional and amateur artists," were neither separate from nor inferior to those who catered exclusively to established fine-arts professionals. Rather, they formed integral parts of an interlocking whole whose purpose was to enable and increase the making of art for all Americans, even those "in the spheres of industrial art or in humbler spheres still."[113]

The appearance of this material in the *American Art Review* was not an accident. Koehler's letters show that he devoted immense labor to obtaining current, comprehensive information on the state of the art world's organizations. He maintained a vast correspondence with personalities as distinct as the photographer F. Holland Day and the tycoon August Belmont, and with countless publishers, museums, and related institutions. He wrote hundreds—thousands—of individual letters in order to discover tiny scraps of information, such as the details of the University of Minnesota's fine arts course or the correct name of the Buffalo Academy of Fine Arts.[114] It was only through this almost incomprehensibly laborious and time-consuming effort that Koehler was able to glean the information that allowed him to publish the accounts of the art world that appeared in the *American Art Review*, and to work toward what seems to have been his ultimate goal: to furnish a complete and ongoing database of the nation's entire organized arts activity. In the age of the Internet, the *Art Index*, and the *Official Museum Directory*, this kind of project may seem simple enough. Even in Koehler's day, some European models did exist, such as *L'Année Artistique* and the *Statistisches Handbuch für Kunst u. Kunstgewerbe im deutschen Reich*, which Koehler reviewed in 1880.[115] In the United States, however, such a project had never been undertaken—or, one suspects, even imagined.

Although the *American Art Review* folded after two years, Koehler did succeed in producing a published record of the art world as he conceived it, *The United States Art Directory and Year-Book: A Guide for Artists, Art Students, Travellers, Etc.*[116] This volume contained detailed descriptions of the missions, activities, structure, and personnel of "Academies, Art Schools, Museums, Collections, Exhibitions, Decorative Art Societies, Art Clubs, Etc." in more than eighty cities in the United States. It also included a "Statistical Table of Exhibitions," which outlined the opening and closing dates, the number of works and artists represented, and the number of works sold, plus the dollar value of sales, for the twenty or so biggest exhibitions of 1881 and 1882, plus a list of coming exhibitions for the next year. It had comprehensive lists of both the books on art and the art journals published in the United States in the previous year (not including Koehler's own *American Art Review*). And finally, it contained an "Art Teachers' Directory," complete with addresses, and an "Artists' Directory" in which nearly 2000 American artists were listed, again with addresses. This list was indexed according to membership in the National Academy of Design, the Society of American Artists, the American Water-Color Society, the Ladies' Art Association, New York, and a number of other organizations, and also by whether the artists had exhibited at recent exhibitions ranging from the New York Etching Club Exhibition and the Philadelphia Society of Artists to Chicago's Interstate Industrial Exhibition. As such, the *Art Directory* is one of the single most important sources of information about the organizational makeup of the art world in the early 1880s, offering both specific information about many individual institutions and practitioners and a broad overall picture of the teaching practices, the cost of art education, and the level and kinds of participation in voluntary associations at this time.

Koehler's inclusion of this kind of information also tells us a great deal about his goals as a critic and publisher, and the ways he defined the "field of art." The most salient fact about the *Art Directory* is its consistent emphasis on the institutional substructure of the art world, revealed even in his index of artists by affiliation. That Koehler organized his writing in this way—and that he undertook the effort in the first place—suggests that he conceived of art not merely as art and artists, but organizations and fields. More specifically, the fact that the majority of the entries spell out whether women were participants, and in what numbers, suggests that Koehler specifically demanded this information. The book's inclusion of numerous societies and schools devoted to the decorative and industrial arts, and to architecture, suggests that Koehler believed these fields to be important, as does his placement of the decorative arts and art education on the title page. His attempt to cover the activities of organizations in all parts of the country, and in peripheral parts of more populated regions, suggests that Koehler wished very strongly to build a national, rather than a Boston- or New York–based art world. And, the regular inclusion of information about entry fees to museums, schools, and organizations suggests that the issue of art-world access was very much on Koehler's mind. Indeed, despite the laconic style of the *Art Directory*, it is possible to detect Koehler's pleasure in reporting that the MFA offered free admission on Saturdays and Sundays, a policy which resulted in the entry, between 1877 and 1881, of "779,270 persons, of whom 89,000 paid an admission fee," plus an indeterminate number of "students who are entitled to the privileges of the Museum" and would also have been admitted without charge.[117]

Louis Prang

Few art publishers promoted art-world development as deliberately as Koehler, few left as complete a record of how they imagined the "field of art," and few constructed an art world that looked *exactly* like Koehler's. In key respects, Louis Prang defined the art world differently from his fellow Bostonian. Most importantly, Prang saw the market, rather than nonprofit institutions, as the primary engine of artistic development. Prang made no apologies for this position. He clearly loved selling and had absolute confidence in what he was doing: in 1868, *Prang's Chromo* proudly featured an illustrated feature on "Our New Publishing-House" (fig. 43),

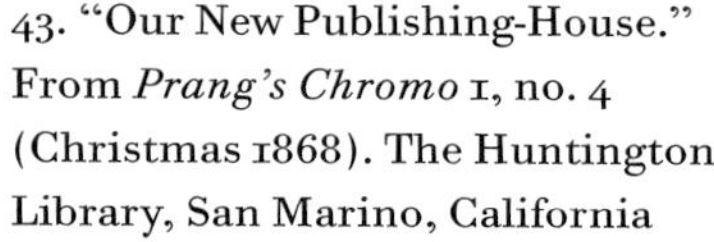

43. "Our New Publishing-House." From *Prang's Chromo* 1, no. 4 (Christmas 1868). The Huntington Library, San Marino, California

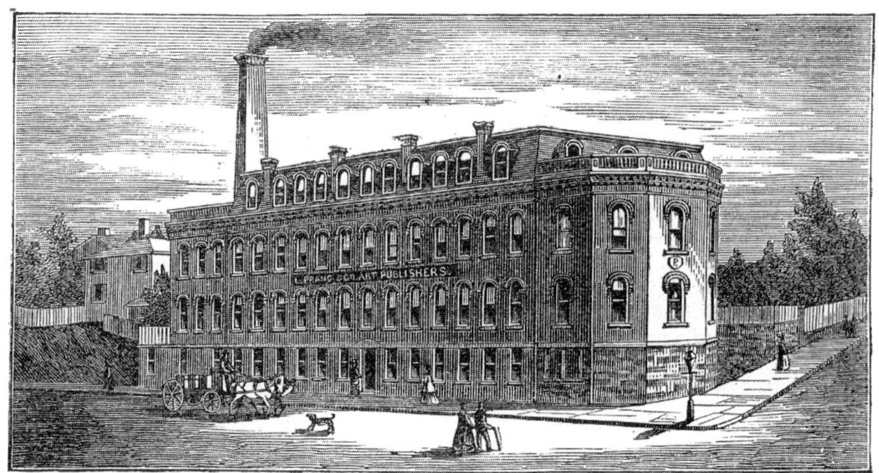

which bragged that "our Picture Gallery, situated in the front addition of the building . . . serves as a show-room, and to tempt courageous tradesmen who visit the Hub to provide themselves with Yankee notions and Prang's American chromos to order a larger bill."[118]

Prang's placement of the market at the center of the art world differentiated him from Koehler. Nonetheless, the two men had a lot in common. In addition to their shared work history, both men were German immigrants born into the art world—Prang's father was a printer of textiles, Koehler's was an artist. They also moved in some of the same circles. Prang was friendly with the *American Art Review* contributor and collector of Japanese art, Edward S. Morse. In 1887, Prang gave Morse a color print of a peach blow vase, which Morse described as a "beautiful present." It was, Morse exclaimed, an example of "the most wonderful color work ever done," and wished the two could "find a publisher willing to" put out "a handsome volume of Japanese pottery."[119] Even before Prang began work on Walters's book, and even as he produced large volumes of inexpensive "Japonesque" designs, Prang clearly saw the depiction in color lithography of Japanese ceramics as a subject for his most personal artistic efforts.

Prang also had private and business connections with a range of other prominent figures, both within Boston and beyond. His work was sold not only through outlets like the American Baptist Publishing Society and the Western Tract and Book Society, but also the New York art dealers William Schaus and M. Knoedler. Prang was able to solicit testimonials for his work not only from Emerson and Sumner (one of the first donors to the MFA), but also from Bayard Taylor, Harriet Beecher Stowe, Henry Wadsworth Longfellow, and the abolitionist, poet, and cousin of Boston Symphony Orchestra founder Henry Lee Higginson, Thomas Wentworth Higginson.[120] Prang convinced architect Richard Morris Hunt, creator of the Statue of Liberty Pedestal and the Tenth Street Studio Building, to be one of his contest judges. And both Prang and Koehler were sufficiently admired by the print and book collector, Metropolitan Museum of Art trustee, and printing press manufacturer, Robert Hoe, to organize exhibitions at Hoe's Grolier Club—Prang on lithography, in 1896, and Koehler on the black-and-white work of Dürer, a year later.[121]

Prang was able to build these links not only because of his personal charm, but because his work really was admired in its day. It won prizes, including a medal at the 1889 Paris Exposition. It also found favor among the cultural and social elite. The abolitionist and "Great Agnostic," Robert Green Ingersoll, thanked Prang effusively for sending his wife a set of chromos in 1880. "The designs, coloring and execution—all wonderful. You have made thousands upon thousands of homes beautiful with your art. . . . I have confidence in the idea of Schiller that the world would be regenerated through the beautiful."[122]

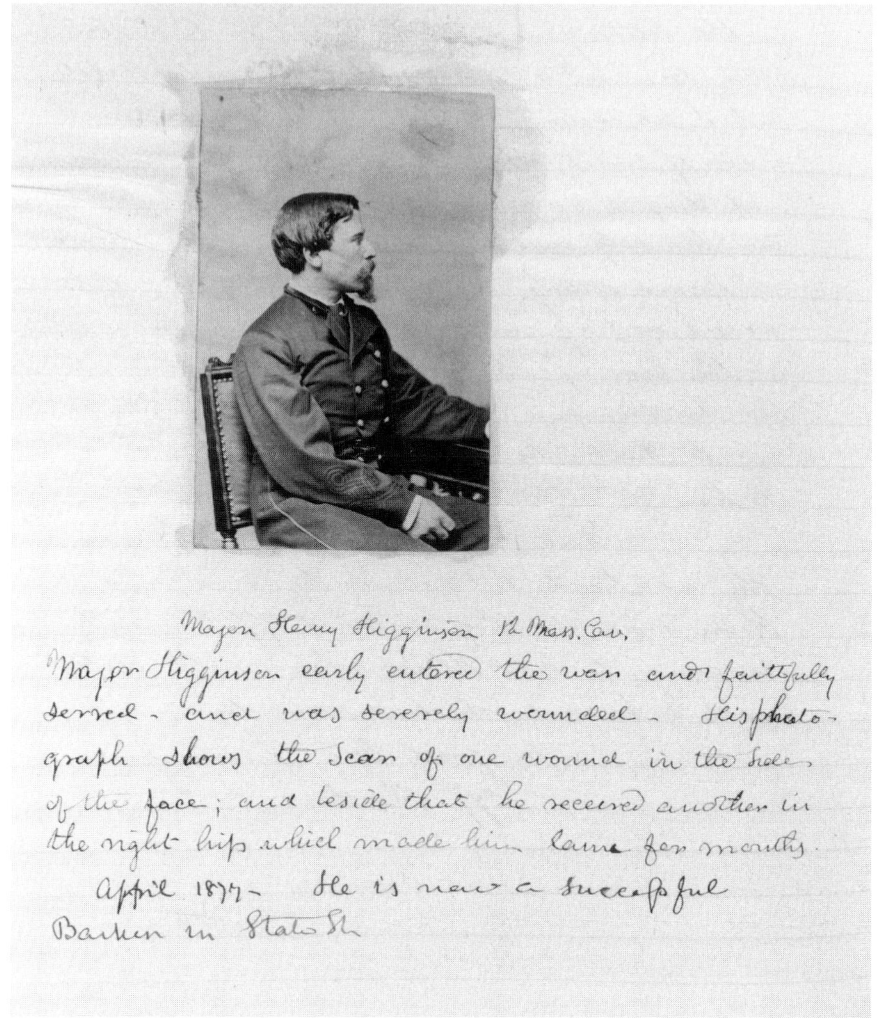

44. Major Henry Lee Higginson (1834–1919). This photograph is pasted into Henry Ingersoll Bowditch's scrapbook, "A Memorial of Lieut. Nathaniel Bowditch, A.A.G., 1st Cavalry Brigade, 2nd Division, Army of the Potomac," 1864. Massachusetts Historical Society, Boston

Prang's less luxurious products also gained the admiration of elite consumers. One of the customers for his album cards was the prominent abolitionist doctor Henry Ingersoll Bowditch, son of the mathematician, astronomer, and navigator Nathaniel Bowditch. The physician made a scrapbook commemorating the life of his son Nathaniel Bowditch of the First Massachusetts Cavalry, killed "at Potomac Creek at 10 p.m. March 18 1863; aged 23 years; 3 mos., 12 ds."[123] This highly personal testament to the intense grief of Bowditch's father contained letters, as well as images of Lincoln and illustrious military men like Henry Lee Higginson (fig. 44), a family friend. And, on the page immediately following Higginson's picture, Bowditch's father pasted a full set of Winslow Homer's Prang Album Cards, *Campaign Sketches* (fig. 45).

Prang's art world also overlapped with Koehler's in other ways. Like Koehler, Prang was interested in both the history of art and of printmaking, as well as in the contemporary generation of artists. Many of the artists whose work appeared in the *American Art Review* or Koehler's

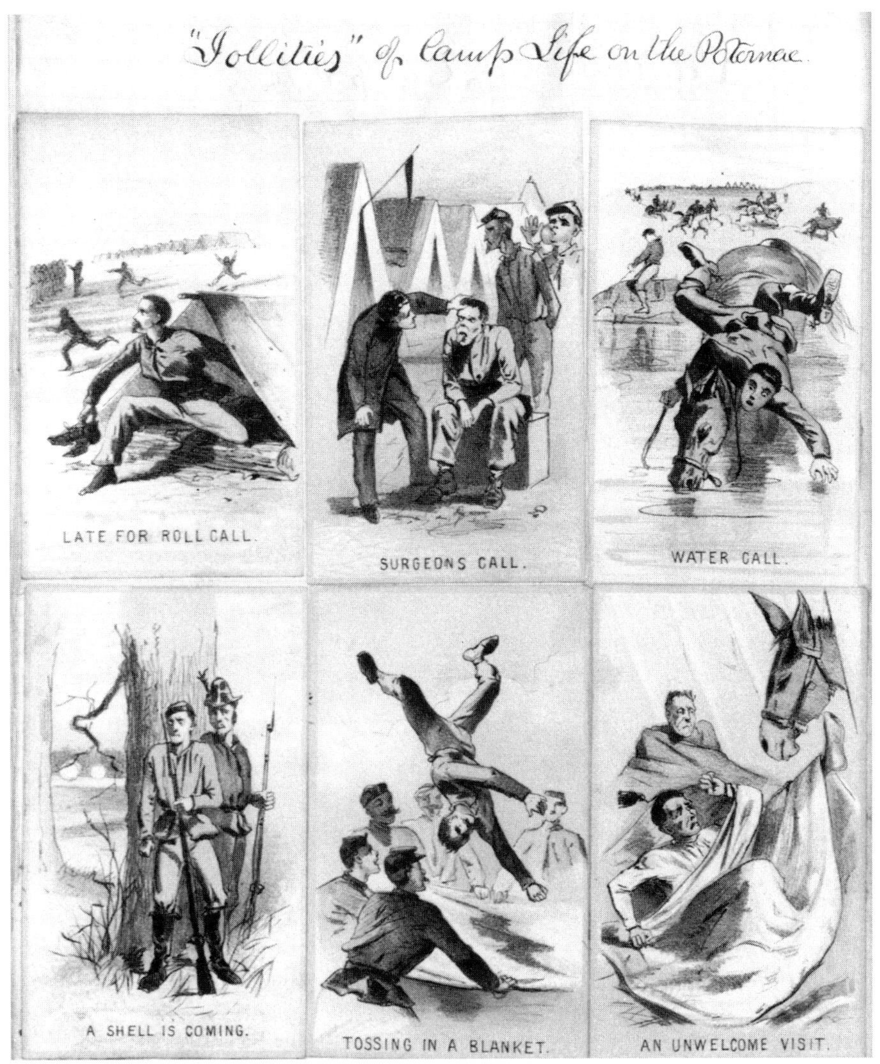

45. Winslow Homer (1836–1910), *Campaign Sketches ("Jollities" of Camp Life on the Potomac)*, 1864. Chromolithographs, 4 × 2 3/8 in. (10.2 × 6 cm) each. Printed by L. Prang & Co., Boston. Massachusetts Historical Society, Boston. These album cards are pasted into Henry Ingersoll Bowditch's scrapbook, "A Memorial of Lieut. Nathaniel Bowditch, A.A.G., 1st Cavalry Brigade, 2nd Division, Army of the Potomac," 1864. The scrapbook also contains a set of Prang's outdoor scenes.

exhibitions, like the expatriate Elihu Vedder, whose *The Sea Serpent* appeared in the former in 1881, or the engraver G. Kruell, who exhibited a woodcut after Vedder at the *Exhibition of American Etchings*, also worked for or sold works to Prang.[124] A number of SAA members, including J. Carroll Beckwith, Thomas Wilmer Dewing, Frederick Dielman, and J. Alden Weir, entered Prang's Christmas card contests, as did Rosina Emmet, who exhibited in the SAA annual and in the *American Art Review* after her card design won first prize in 1880.[125] And, by the 1890s, Prang was actively supporting modernism, not only as the publisher of *Modern Art*, but also in his Grolier Club exhibition. Alongside works by Francisco Goya, Eugène Delacroix, and Gustave Courbet, this exhibition featured works by Whistler, Cassatt, and Édouard Manet—even though Prang himself admitted, in the catalogue, to having some reservations about the newest European art. Prang's exhibition was also the first American show to include the work of Odilon Redon, a feat for which the Armory Show is mistakenly credited.[126]

Like Koehler's exhibitions and publications, Prang's art world also included both men and women. He employed women in his factory. He bought paintings from dozens of women artists, including Laura C. Hills, who later showed her work at the St. Botolph Club, and Ellen Bowditch Thayer Fisher, who studied at the Normal Art School and exhibited at the World's Columbian Exposition. She was also the sister of the painter Abbott Thayer.[127] Once the works of these women were reproduced as "Prang's American Chromos," their names appeared alongside the names of well-known male painters like Albert Bierstadt, Eastman Johnson, and Adolphe-William Bouguereau.[128] Prang also hired women artists like Elizabeth Bullock Humphrey to illustrate his books. He was so taken by Humphrey, in fact, that he published a "collection of her most popular designs, with a biographical sketch," in 1890.[129] Prang published lavish instructional materials by women like "Miss Grace Carter, of the South Kensington Art-School," who was also a member of Baltimore's Decorative Art Society (fig. 46).[130] And, many of Prang's prizes went to women; after Rosina Emmet's victory in 1880, the top prize in 1882 went to her friend Dora Wheeler. For Emmet, Prang's $1000 represented fully five times what she hoped to earn from a single sale at the SAA the following year.[131] Even for a woman with as extensive a network of art-world connections as Wheeler, Prang's $2000 prize could easily be the most lucrative sale of a career.[132]

Embracing the Media

Perhaps the greatest link between Prang and Koehler was their shared sense of the importance to the art world of the media—meaning, in this case, both printmaking *and* publishing. Both men shared a deep admiration for the capacity of the graphic arts to produce works of outstanding beauty and value. For Prang, as for Koehler, the graphic arts held the key to "true artistic expression."[133] At the same time, both men also saw that the mass media could play a central role in their art-world projects. In 1868, Prang thanked the press for its lavish praise of his images, and announced, "We shall be happy, at any time, to exhibit to editors or other journalists and writers for the press the entire process of chromolithography, whenever, in visiting Boston, they shall do us the honor of a call at our establishment."[134]

Within the wider publishing revolution, technological developments in image publishing also presented tremendous possibilities to Prang, Koehler, and their generation. As is well known, photography made visual information more precise and easier to obtain. But many other processes of image reproduction also emerged in the nineteenth century—including photo-chemical engraving, electrotyping, stereotyping and photo-electrotyping, as well as chromolithography—that also played key roles in making visual information circulate more widely and cheaply than ever before. This was important, because before the mid-1890s, when the halftone process facilitated the cheap mass printing of photographic images, even photographs could not themselves be mass-produced.[135] Before this time, the photographs the public saw in the press, such as the images by Napoleon Sarony and the Pach Brothers in *Harper's Weekly*, were—like the reproductions of paintings—actually images after photographs in another medium.[136]

There is no doubting Koehler's enthusiasm for the technology of image reproduction. As well as exhibitions on Dürer and Rembrandt, he also organized shows that focused specifically on the application of

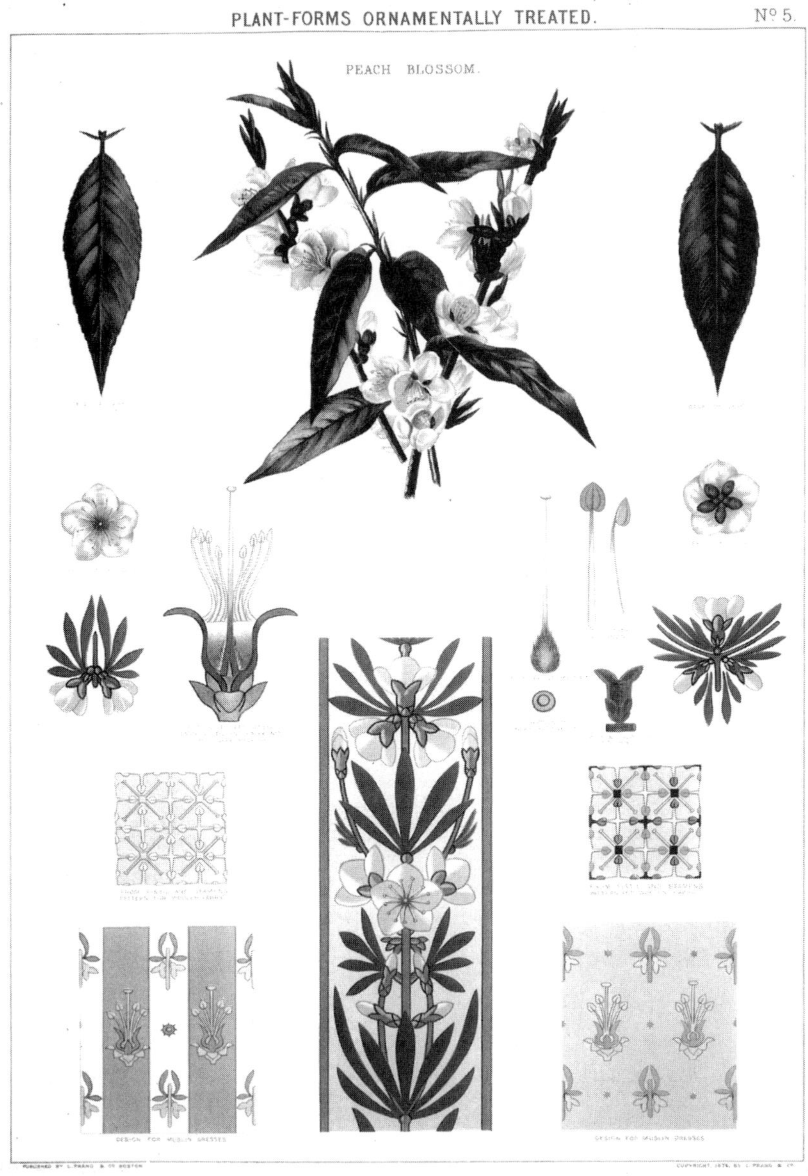

46. Grace Carter, *Peach Blossom*, 1874. Published in Grace Carter, *Plant-Forms Ornamentally Treated. Exhibiting a Number of Plants in Their Natural Colors, with an Analysis of Their Parts, and Their Application to Conventionalized Ornament* (Boston: L. Prang & Co., 1876). Boston Public Library

the graphic arts to the reproduction of images, including the 1892 *Exhibition Illustrating the Technical Methods of the Reproductive Arts from the XV Century to the Present Time: With Special Reference to the Photo-Mechanical Processes*.[137] In addition to his exhibitions, Koehler lectured publicly on the subject of "color printing," corresponded with Lathrop on this issue and on his translation, for Prang, of Von Bezold's *Theory of Color in Its Relation to Art and Art-Industry*, and wrote articles on "the photo-mechanical processes."[138] As a publisher, Koehler experimented with printing methods ranging from engraving to chromolithography to photomechanical reproduction, working to see which process produced the best results at least cost.[139]

Koehler was not alone in his zeal, as can be seen by the emergence of a journal, the *American Art Printer*, devoted specifically to this subject. Like the *Art Amateur* before it (and the *Keramic Studio* afterward), the *American Art Printer* published an "Art Supplement." Unlike the supplements in those journals, though, the *American Art Printer* frequently failed to note the names of the artists whose original works it reproduced, declaring instead that "this picture is printed from an electrotype made from a pen drawing, and reduced one-half in size" or was a "specimen of photo-zinc etching, by W. H. Bartholomew, 22 College Place, New York."[140] Copies were also widespread in other parts of the art world. As Alan Wallach has shown, plaster casts were in frequent use in the postwar museum, where they were prized for their educative and illustrative value; a glance at Koehler's *Art Directory* shows that many public art collections also proudly displayed copies of paintings in a variety of media, and even mechanical reproductions of coins and other objects, alongside original artworks.[141]

It is not hard to understand this enthusiasm. After all, these technologies met a basic desire for visual information, about both artworks and the world at large, that was not always so easily accommodated. Even well-placed New Yorkers like Alexander Wilson Drake encountered difficulty obtaining visual information, particularly when they were trying to find out what contemporary art looked like. In 1883, Drake wrote twice to Wood in pursuit of a list of French sculptors compiled by SAA president Augustus Saint-Gaudens, which he was sure would be "of great use to both of us especially if we get the photos."[142] This dependence was mutual. From Portland, Wood often demanded information and images from Drake and other eastern contacts. Drake readily complied, sending Wood exhibition catalogues and illustrated books, and filling his request to have a set of plaster casts made and shipped to Oregon by "De Comp, the plaster cast man."[143]

On one level, then, the acceptance—and even admiration—of copies can be explained by the need for visual information in the absence of originals. Viewers looked to original paintings and photographs, but more often to reproductions after them, for their capacity to convey visual information about Yellowstone or Niagara, about plants and birds, or about the day's latest technological marvels. If a lithograph after a painting could convey the same information as the original, then it was just as good as the original. This seems to have been the view of "Col. Higginson," who described the "delicate gradations of color" in Prang's reproduction of Ellen Robbins's nature studies as "perfection."[144] As a corollary, Higginson urged Prang to "continue these American subjects, for they educate the public taste far more than imported studies of foreign objects, whose correctness the popular eye cannot test."[145]

Americans did not accept copies just because they provided visual information, however. Koehler's enthusiasm for "reproductive etching" shows that this interest was not merely pragmatic, but was underpinned by a deep admiration for its practitioners, whose work was "sometimes spoken of as less valuable" than that of "original or painter-etchers." As Koehler saw it, "it would be folly to underrate the standing of the reproductive etcher," whose talent—akin, in Koehler's view, to translation—"is quite as rarely found in an approach to perfection as that of the creative artist." "The great reproductive etchers," he concluded, "will live in the memory of man as long as the masters themselves are not forgotten."[146]

This admiration for reproductions reflected wider aesthetic values. Generally speaking, American aesthetics in the postwar years prioritized the instrumental, as much as the ontological, qualities of art objects. What mattered, in other words, was not an artwork's objecthood or "aura," in Walter Benjamin's oft-repeated term, but what it could *do*. Could it convey nature, human character, or an original artwork faithfully? Could it provide moral, political, or social lessons? Could it teach viewers about the principles of art? Could it promote further interest in art? To critics, editors, and publishers in the postwar period, it was as essential that art images and objects meet these tests as that they be original or rare. This can be seen in the widespread admiration for copies, as well as in the way that works were classified within exhibition catalogues. Present-day exhibitions, and their catalogues, generally classify artworks by maker and medium, at least in the first instance. In contrast, exhibitions in the postwar period, and even after the turn of the century, sometimes used very different classificatory schemes. Earl Shinn's *Art Treasures of America*, for example, prized patronage above all; the Union League arranged art exhibitions around the political and historical significance of the figures and images the works represented.[147]

Along the same lines, the very abundance and portability of copies appealed, on an aesthetic level, to critics and publishers. In addition to catalogues and casts, Drake also sent Wood "a set of French lithographs of some dogs" as a Christmas present in 1886.[148] Drake seems to have chosen this present precisely because he already owned a version of the same images; the subject was "a great favorite of mine, I having saved a little wood cut of these dogs for years now find them taken up and lithographed by this superb French lithographers [*sic*]."[149] But, in the eyes of critics, editors, and publishers, abundance did not just bring personal aesthetic pleasure. It also served larger art-world goals, such as the quick development of collections without a big financial investment. In this spirit, an 1876 critic censured Vassar College's collection for containing a large copy of Raphael's *Madonna di Foligno not* because it was a copy, but because "a respectable gallery of large autotypes covering almost the entire range of art history" could have been bought for its price.[150]

A similar view was articulated by Prang, who was keenly aware that many more people would see his works than any unique paintings. Prang was not distressed by this thought, however, and not just because high sales meant high profits. As Prang saw it, the two essential goals of art—quality and accessibility—depended on high-volume production, because color lithographs were more expensive to make than oil paintings. Unlike paintings, they required the additional labor of the many artisans who produced the prints, on top of the cost of buying "original" art. "The cost of an artistic chromo," Prang wrote in 1872, "runs up into thousands, while an oil-painting of the same size is valued only by hundreds of dollars. . . . It follows that a chromo can be successful commercially only when several thousand copies can be disposed of; and hence, that it lies with the public whether good chromos shall be sold cheaply or not. For the better the chromos the more copies must be sold, unless the price of each copy shall be raised to an exorbitant amount."[151] For many reasons, in Prang's art world the aesthetics of abundance outweighed the aesthetics of originality.

At the "Borders of Art"

There was one other crucial element to Prang's and Koehler's embrace of the media. Like many of their contemporaries, Prang and Koehler lived and worked at the borders between art, craft, and industry. Both men entered their careers at a time when the crafts, as well as the art world, were undergoing rapid change brought about by industrialization. In many ways, these changes were negative: de-skilling came later to printmakers than to shoemakers or weavers, but it came nonetheless. Before Prang hit upon chromolithography, he tried and failed at several other artisanal occupations, including wood engraving, which were becoming obsolete even as he learned them.[152] Indeed, Prang's own chromolithography itself helped to put an end to the careers of engravers, as artists and audiences got a taste for full-color, "perfect" reproductions of artworks.[153] And before the end of his lifetime, Prang would even see chromolithography passed by, with the emergence of the halftone, the Hoe quadruple press, and other innovations that enabled newspapers to print photographs and to print cheaply in color.[154]

Prang and Koehler were not the only figures in the art world to negotiate the shifting terrain of a society undergoing industrialization. Others were the sons or the grandsons of artisans whose crafts had declined: both Thomas Eakins's grandfather and Thomas and Peter Moran's father were weavers who suffered great harm at the hands of industrialization. Others witnessed firsthand the same changes seen by Prang. A large number of American artists born between the 1820s and the 1850s—including some photographers, like Napoleon Sarony—began their careers as apprentice lithographers or even, in the case of Frederick Arthur Bridgman and Walter Shirlaw, as banknote engravers. These included many of the other artists whose work would be reproduced by Prang and Koehler, including J. Foxcroft Cole, R. Swain Gifford, Winslow Homer, and the somewhat older Eastman Johnson.[155]

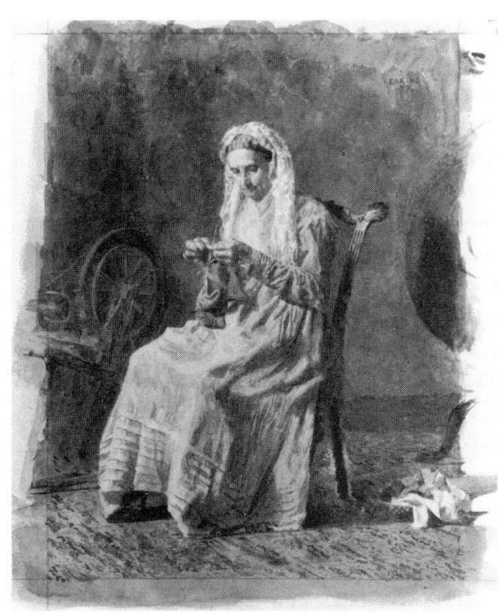

47. Thomas Eakins (1844–1916), *Seventy Years Ago*, 1877. Watercolor and gouache on cream wove paper, borderlines in pencil (watermark: J. Whatman), 15 11/16 × 10 13/16 in. (39.8 × 27.4 cm). Princeton University Art Museum, gift of Mrs. Frank Jewett Mather Jr.

Some artists negotiated the hard reality of social and economic change within their images. Some of the best-known nineteenth-century American paintings, such as George Inness's *The Lackawanna Valley* (1855; National Gallery of Art, Washington, D.C.), depict the changes wrought by industrialization. Other works, like Eakins's 1877 watercolors *Seventy Years Ago* (fig. 47) and *Fifty Years Ago (Young Girl Meditating)* (fig. 48), represented the subtle generational changes between a culture that made its own things and a culture that had lost the attributes of production. Like his photographic motion studies, which captured changes too rapid to be seen by the unaided eye, this diptych recorded a change whose gradualness made it nearly invisible—the disappearance of the spinning wheel from the American interior. Similarly, one of Dow's first ongoing efforts as an artist was to record the many old houses that were disappearing from Ipswich, and some of Prang's best-known early lithographs were his *Prang's Aids for Object Teaching: Trades & Occupations* (1874; American Antiquarian Society).[156] This series depicted the skilled work of figures such as *The Blacksmith*, *The Carpenter*, and *The Lithographer*. Particularly in the case of *The Shoemaker* (fig. 49), Prang offered viewers a clearly anachronistic image of the artisan as an independent producer. Contrary to Prang's lithograph, which depicted a shoemaker making complete pairs of shoes by hand for sale in his own showroom, shoemaking had been mechanizing in Massachusetts at least since the first decade of the nineteenth century, and by Prang's time was highly industrialized.

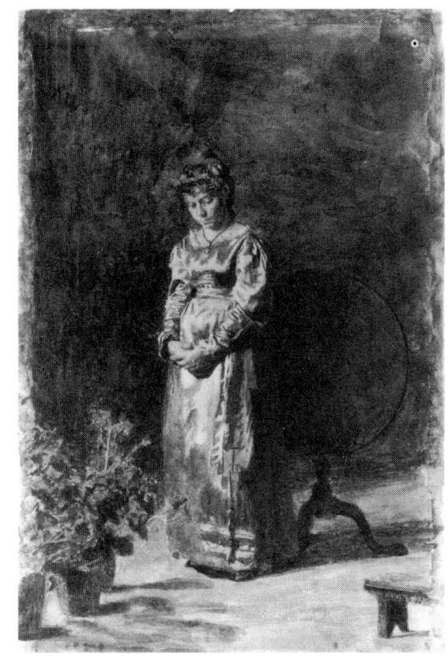

48. Thomas Eakins, *Fifty Years Ago (Young Girl Meditating)*, 1877. Watercolor and gouache on off-white wove paper, 9 9/16 × 6 1/8 in. (24.2 × 15.6 cm). The Metropolitan Museum of Art, Fletcher Fund, 1925 (25.97.2)

Artists did not just respond to industrialization by picturing its effects—or its noble victims. They also pursued a range of organizational

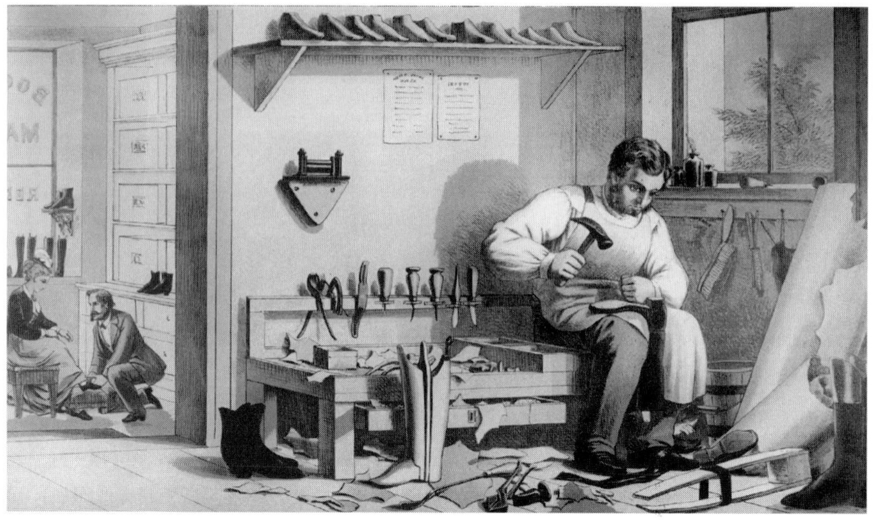

49. L. Prang & Co., *The Shoemaker*, 1874. From *Prang's Aids for Object Teaching: Trades and Occupations* (Boston: L. Prang & Co., 1874), pl. 2. American Antiquarian Society, Worcester, Massachusetts

strategies designed to make a place for artisans in the new economy. Some, like Dow, embraced a self-conscious return to craft traditions. Dow's interest in Japan, for example, was forged in this context: both Morse and Fenollosa saw Japan as a society that was rapidly and unfortunately forgetting its past. But in this "disappearing" culture, Japan also presented Dow with "authentic" tools and techniques of artistic practice that could be translated and taught to the next generation. Both Joseph Moore Bowles and Janet Payne Bowles also chose to respond to industrialization with a version of arts and crafts, reflected in *Modern Art*'s writings and in its William Morris–inflected presswork. In her painting and her metalwork, Janet Payne Bowles sought both motifs and technical models in Russian, Celtic, and other archaic traditions, many of which she found displayed in the Metropolitan Museum of Art's decorative collections. Perhaps not surprisingly, Payne Bowles, like Dow, became a teacher. Like Forsyth before her, she returned to Indianapolis in 1912, and spent the next three decades teaching metalwork and jewelry at Shortridge High School.[157]

Others chose a more entrepreneurial route. Like Prang, Milton Bradley industrialized and commercialized his operation, jumping from lithography to commercial amusements. This move made him wealthy beyond his imagination, and established his eponymous brand ("MB," in its worldwide incarnation) as one of the most recognizable symbols of the new consumer culture. As important, it allowed Bradley to do this without giving up the craft of printmaking. It is not accidental that his factory (fig. 50), proudly pictured in his catalogue, held up two signs: one, which advertised "Milton Bradley & Co. Publishers of Home Amusements," and another, which announced "Lithography · Engraving." Significantly, Bradley signed both this image and other images throughout the catalogue with "Milton Bradley & Co. Eng." Bradley's entrepreneurship also allowed him to promote his own vision of utopian educational reform, which, in turn, promoted both crafts and color as essential elements of primary education.

This was only one model of entrepreneurship. While Prang and Bradley created opportunities for themselves in the sphere of mass consumer culture, others glimpsed the potential the media presented for the marketing and sale of fine art. Like John White Alexander, many of the artists of the day combined careers as painters with careers as illustrators for books, magazines, and sheet music. Thomas Hovenden and Childe Hassam, for example, provided illustrations for the *Verses* of the popular poet Celia Thaxter; Elihu Vedder illustrated a very successful edition of *The Rubáiyát of Omar Khayyám* (1884); and Rosina Emmet designed the images for *Pretty Peggy and Other Ballads*, illustrated by chromolithography.[158] Along with Samuel Colman and other male artists, Emmet also contributed illustrations to Mrs. Burton Harrison's *Woman's Handiwork in Modern Homes*.[159] Even Whistler provided three drawings for Walter Thornbury's *Historical & Legendary Ballads & Songs*. Like Hovenden's contributions to Thomas Buchanan Read's *The Wagoner of the Alleghanies*, these drawings—*Lady Mabel*, *Dewfall*, and "Amid all the roar and the foam, I hear the hoarse shells of the Tritons"—were illustrations in the classic sense, depicting events and characters from the accompanying text rather than the artist's unique vision.[160]

Thomas Moran also pursued this strategy. Initially trained as an engraver, Moran worked simultaneously as a painter and an illustrator

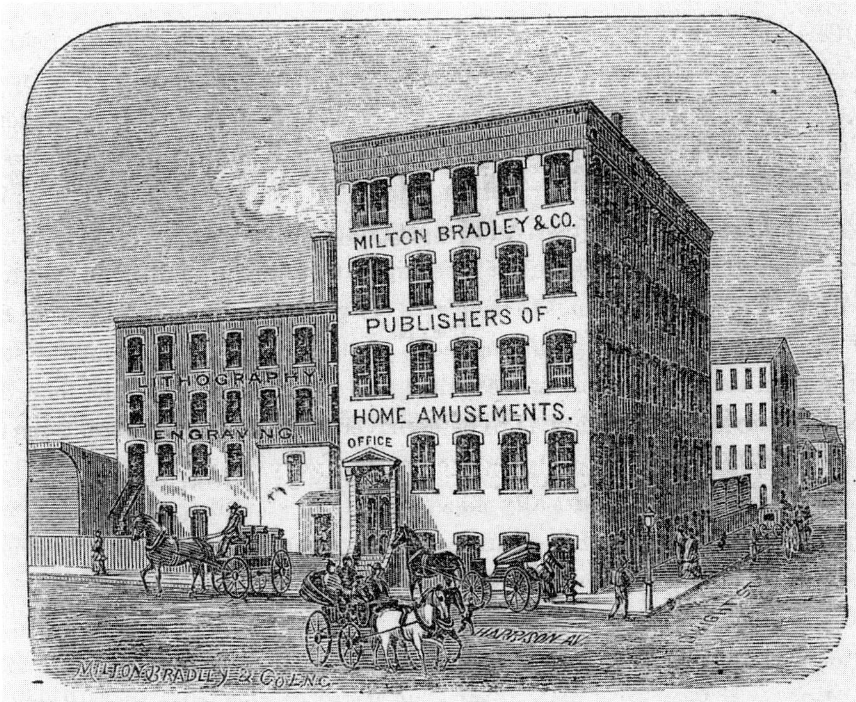

50. Milton Bradley & Co., *Milton Bradley & Co. Publishers of Home Amusements*, c. 1872. From *Work and Play Annual*, 1872. Widener Library of the Harvard College Library, Cambridge, Massachusetts

through much of his career. As Joni Louise Kinsey's *Thomas Moran and the Surveying of the American West* demonstrates, Moran was a clever entrepreneur who cannily persuaded *Scribner's*—for whom the artist had already made engravings after other artists' Western images—to press for his inclusion on geologist Ferdinand V. Hayden's survey of the Yellowstone in 1871.[161] This effectively provided Moran with markets for three kinds of images: his original drawings and paintings, many of which he sold to railroad man Jay Cooke; black-and-white images after them for *Scribner's* and for publications like the *American Art Review*; and the luxury portfolio of chromolithographs that Prang published as *The Yellowstone National Park and the Mountain Regions of Portions of Idaho, Nevada, Colorado & Utah* (see fig. 11).[162] Indeed, Moran financed his trip on credit advanced against these future works. As important, Moran's entrepreneurial foray to the West provided the artist with a new identity—"Yellowstone" Moran—and with monumental subject matter that would occupy his attention for much of his career. As Kinsey notes, Moran incorporated this nickname into the "brand" with which he subsequently signed his works, an "M" overlapping a "T" with wings to make the "T" look like a "Y" for "Yellowstone." The images in *The Yellowstone National Park* thus bore two trademarks: Moran's new signature, and "Prang's American Chromo." In Moran's case, as in Prang's, entrepreneurship enhanced and intertwined with creative passion.

At the same time that painters used the media as a source of sales and publicity to shore up their position in the fine arts market, it could also be argued that the general shift by artisans into the fine arts itself represented an entrepreneurial move—a kind of "up-skilling" that paralleled the emergence of couture (1858), whose practitioners also turned to "fine" modes of production as clothing manufacture became industrialized. It might be assumed that many printmakers who later became painters began their careers expressly with the purpose of "moving up" into the fine arts. Yet, the frequency with which this transition took place—and the fact that it happened at the exact moment that many print trades were declining, or at the very least, industrializing—suggests that there was more to it than coincidence. For while the new media offered many lucrative opportunities to printmakers, these opportunities were most definitely enhanced for those who were able to put one foot over the fine-art side of the border between art and printing.

It is in this context that Prang's and Koehler's desire to extend the reach of art, and their enthusiasm for the media, must be understood. These impulses were not driven by a love of art alone. In the end, their mutual embrace of the media was also driven by a sense of the need to chart a path for art's makers in an industrial age. If this can be seen in Prang's employment of artists, and in his own transition from craftsman to magnate, it can also be seen in Koehler's nonprofit entrepreneurship, which brought him from Prang's factory to the MFA. His many exhibitions and pronouncements on behalf of etching and the other graphic arts, as well as his prominent placement of "original" etchings in the *American Art Review* and the MFA, were designed to gain legitimacy for these media. Although this marketing of the graphic media took place within the context of nonprofit institutions, it was not essentially different from Prang's efforts to gain new niches for lithography. It also bears marked similarity to the efforts of Alfred Stieglitz and Edward Steichen—himself trained as a lithographer—to gain recognition for another print medium, photography, after the turn of the century.

Second, Koehler and Prang's support for institutional development in the art world, including art education, was also part of a larger movement to use art as a tool for social change. As historians have argued, initiatives like the Massachusetts Drawing Act emerged as much from the pressing social questions posed by industrialization and urbanization as from purely aesthetic concerns. The discipline of drawing appealed to reformers not only because it gave its possessors the means to find joy in their work in a time of rapid de-skilling, but because (like Bradley's games) it would keep the young out of the "traps of Satan." Particularly in schools that blended industrial and fine arts instruction, such as the Normal Art School and the McMicken School of Design, the push for art education was also designed to create new spheres of employment for artisans displaced by industrialization. This was not an unproblematic endeavor. As Jackson Lears points out, American arguments for art education at times glossed over real differences between ennobling labor and industrial drudgery; by looking for pragmatic and provisional remedies to industrial dislocation, moreover, reformers evaded making more sweeping changes in working conditions.[163]

Nonetheless, postwar cultural entrepreneurship cannot be dismissed as "therapy" for the bored middle classes, as "sacralization" on behalf of the elite, or as social control for the masses, not least because the educational reforms promoted by nonprofit entrepreneurs seem to have been supported by artisans themselves. The publisher of the *American Art Printer*, a trade journal printed in New York between 1887 and 1893, was unafraid to declare its allegiance to the cause of labor, even to the point of defending the anarchists accused in the Haymarket case. As the journal bluntly put it, "We believe in the organization of labor."[164] And yet, the journal also included many of the stock elements of middle-class art publications like the *Art Amateur*: lavishly printed art supplements, instruction "specimens" giving detailed explanation to would-be artisans (see fig. 37), and editorials proposing technical art education as a remedy for social dislocation.[165] The editors do not appear to have had difficulty resolving these two elements. They wrote: "We have faith that the toilers will get their education as they go . . . such an education that will lift them above and away from those lower levels where too many of them grope and grovel, and where the things of life are touched and swayed through the passions of the animal rather than through the reason of man."[166] We might surmise from this that the printer-editors of the journal were the victims of cultural hegemony. Or we might conclude that they understood the problems facing American artisans and workers, and they hoped that artistic virtuosity, like the organization of labor, would help them to reach a better future.

As for artists, both Koehler's and Prang's efforts did provide tangible help. Prang paid over $500,000 for art before 1892, much of it to living American artists. This figure does not include payments to the skilled art workers in his factory, many of whom were students at the Normal Art School.[167] These artists were not always pleased with Prang's prices, but some, like Homer, were satisfied enough with his patronage that they became lifelong colleagues and friends. More than forty years after Homer first began working for his "Dear Old Friend," the artist still turned to Prang's chromos as an aesthetically suitable alternative to reproduction by engraving, which by 1900 he vociferously rejected. Even at this advanced stage of his career, Homer still saw chromos as a means of circulating images without producing a glut of originals: "One a year," he wrote, "is enough to fill the market."[168] Others, too, benefited from Prang's patronage. First prize in his Christmas card contest, as I mentioned, was worth $1000 in 1880; this figure doubled to $2000 the next year. To put this in perspective, this was more than eight times what Frederick Dielman was asking for his entry at the SAA exhibition that year. Even for SAA vice-president J. Alden Weir, who could demand $1500 for a single canvas in 1881, this was still a good opportunity.[169] Koehler's efforts also provided artists with income and exposure. The painter and founder of the Ten, Cincinnati's John Twachtman–who attended both Cincinnati's Evening School for Mechanics and McMicken–exhibited at Koehler's 1881 exhibition at the MFA. His wife, Marthe (Mattie) Scudder Twachtman, exhibited at Koehler's *Women Etchers of America* and in the display he organized for the Ohio Valley Centennial; following this, the MFA bought several of her works. John Twachtman also sold Koehler at least eighteen of his etchings.[170] Not coincidentally, Twachtman was also an illustrator for *Scribner's*, which provided him with the income to buy a seventeen-acre estate in Greenwich, Connecticut.

I would suggest that the mutual embrace of the art world and the media by Prang and Koehler, and on the part of print dealers like Keppel, also had a more general impact on the mainstream art market in the longer term. Many of the artists who were involved with these entrepreneurs, including Homer, were the figures whose works would sell for the highest sums in the next decades. Although he would not live to see it, Homer's *Eight Bells* (1886; Phillips Academy, Addison Gallery of American Art, Andover, Massachusetts) would, by the 1930s, hold the record for a price paid for an American painting. Indeed, the emergence of modernism was not the only major change to sweep the American art world at the turn of the century. This period also saw a dramatic uptake in sales and increase in prices for the works of American artists. Even by 1919, the market in American art had become more profitable than anyone could have imagined a generation before. It was lucrative enough that Childe Hassam, who had once designed cards for Prang (fig. 51), could purchase a renovated East Hampton house full of fine furniture and write his friend Wood that he had "an assured income of about 12000 a year if things always pay." In turn, it was profitable enough that Wood could insist he "would not take less than twenty thousand net for [Albert Pinkham Ryder's] Jonah" (fig. 52), on top of the 10 percent commission and 10 percent tax that dealer Robert Macbeth had warned him would be taken out of the sale.[171] As for Macbeth—the son of Frederick Keppel's assistant, William Macbeth—the year 1919 also seems to have been a good one: Macbeth not only moved to better quarters at 450 Fifth Avenue, but also gave himself an impressive new letterhead.[172] Given that when Macbeth's father had started out in the 1890s, he was asking $225 for a pair of Ryder oils, given that just a year previously, before the Metropolitan Museum of Art commemorated Ryder's career with a retrospective exhibition, Wood had "value[d] the 'Jonah' at ten thousand," and given that in 1881, one of the years Ryder exhibited with the Society of American Artists, the entire

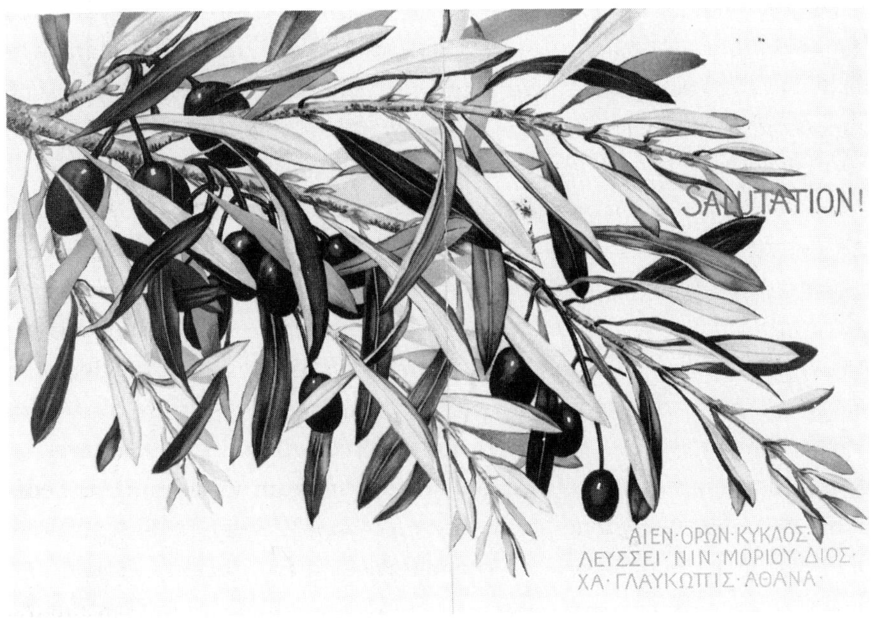

51. Unidentified artist after Childe Hassam (1859–1935), *Salutation!*, c. 1887. Chromolithograph. Published by L. Prang & Co., Boston. Special Collections, University of Virginia Library

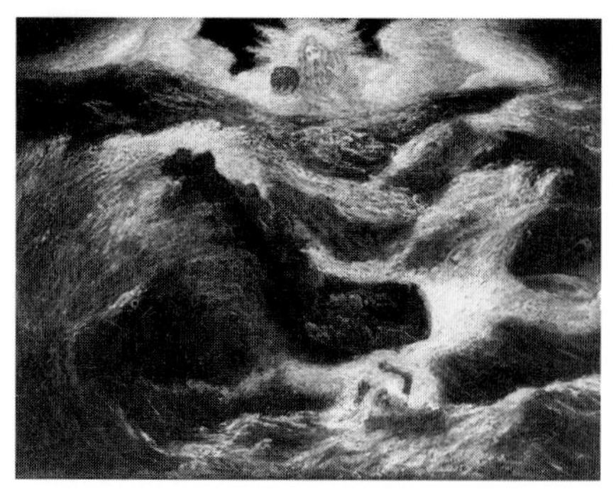

52. Albert Pinkham Ryder (1847–1917), *Jonah*, c. 1885–95. Oil on canvas mounted on fiberboard, 27¼ × 34⅜ in. (69.2 × 87.3 cm). Smithsonian American Art Museum, Washington, D.C., gift of John Gellatly

exhibition grossed only $2000, Macbeth had every reason to celebrate his success.[173] As for Wood, who bought the painting for $500 from Ryder and who did sell it to collector John Gellatly for $20,000, the growth of his investment in American art can only have been astonishing.[174] Although it would take another generation before American art would reach the center of the world stage, it is not too much to imagine that that rise was intimately connected to American art's ascendance at home at the turn of the century. And, it is not too much to imagine that this ascendance was helped, at least in part, by the development in the 1870s and 1880s of an organizational field for art.

Art and media also intersected at one additional frontier: the border between artist and amateur. While this can be seen from the *American Art Review*'s "American Art Chronicle," it is worth saying a few words about another branch of the art media that flourished in the postwar period: publications that provided direct instruction in the creation of ceramics, needlework, furniture, drawings, paintings, and other kinds of art.[175] This was not a new genre. At least 145 manuals of drawing instruction were published between the 1840s and 1860s, the most famous of which was John Gadsby Chapman's *American Drawing-Book* (1847). As Diana Korzenik shows, these books circulated widely both before and after the Civil War, finding their way beyond prosperous urban markets to the homes of relatively impoverished rural Americans like the Cross family of Manchester, New Hampshire, whose children became etchers, in part as a result of their influence.[176]

As in other spheres of art publishing, however, the range of publications devoted to art education and advice grew in content and scope after the Civil War. Books like W. N. Bartholomew's *Handbook No. 2 to Bartholomew's "National System of Industrial Drawing"* (1882), published by the editor of the *American Art Printer*, and J. C. Beard's *Painting on China: What to Paint and How to Paint It* (1882), expanded instruction to new areas. The emergence of periodicals devoted to art making expanded the range of this literature even further. These included *The Workshop*, *The Art Interchange*, *The Art Worker*, and *The Art Amateur*, subtitled *A Monthly Journal Devoted to the Cultivation of Art in the Household*, later shortened to *Devoted to Art in the Household*, and, finally, *For the Collector, the Artist & the Art Worker*. In the 1890s, these journals were joined by *Keramic Studio* and by *Brush and Pencil*, which advertised itself as an alternative to traditional schooling: "Counting the Cost deters many ambitious, talented students from completing their education under the instruction of the best teachers. Why Pay Full Tuition? By special arrangement with several leading institutions, Brush and Pencil is Prepared to give full courses in Drawing, Painting, Illustration,

Composition, Modeling and Designing . . . Pupils provided for in Day or Night Classes at all times, at Greatly Reduced Rates."[177]

Considered in terms of longevity, the *Art Amateur* was the most successful American art journal of the late nineteenth century. Published in New York, the journal survived from 1879 to 1903, no small feat in the volatile and competitive world of American publishing. But the *Art Amateur* was notable for more than longevity. It was also significant for its ability to blend seemingly disparate elements of the American art world into a broad, yet coherent vision in which the "cultivation of art in the household" meant not only the development of taste for the purposes of decoration or consumption, but "cultivation" in the sense of growing or making.

The *Art Amateur* approached "the cultivation of art in the household" from a wide perspective. In some respects, it was not that different from other art journals: like its competitors, it frequently published profiles of artists and accounts of new or historical art movements like "Tendencies in French Sculpture"; commentaries on exhibitions like "The St. Louis Exhibition: First Exhibition in America of Works by the Painters of 'The Secession,' of Germany"; and features promoting new developments in art education in the public schools.[178] Alongside these items, the *Art Amateur* also published engravings after paintings that readers could detach and display, similar to the giveaways and supplements of the *Art Union*, the *American Art Review*, and *Modern Art*.[179]

More importantly, the *Art Amateur* also published hundreds of articles and images designed to facilitate readers' *own* desires to create art. By publishing these features side by side, the *Art Amateur* suggested that the artistic efforts of amateurs were meaningfully linked to the labor and works of professional artists, and that the domestic sphere—like the studio or the museum—was a significant space within the art world. One of the journal's regular features was the "*Art Amateur* Working Designs," which offered oversized, foldout plates of designs. A plate published in 1896 (fig. 53), for example, included a "series of ancient embroideries copied by M. L. Macomber for *The Art Amateur*, from the Boston Museum of Fine Arts collection."[180] On one level, this image functioned like other art reproductions circulated by the journal: it gave readers a glimpse into the collections of one of the nation's best-known museums, without requiring them to visit the museum personally. By presenting these images as "Working Designs" that readers were expected to incorporate into their own work, however, the *Art Amateur* also invited readers to see art reproductions—and the museum collections from which they derived—as tools in the cultivation of their own artistic labor. For the *Art Amateur*, "art" inhered in both the images that readers removed from its pages and hung on their walls, and in the process of taking those images and setting to work.

Right:
53. "*The Art Amateur* Working Designs, Numbers 1693–1696." Published in *The Art Amateur* 35, no. 4 (Sept. 1896). Fine Arts Department, Boston Public Library

Opposite:
54. A. Leveille, *Portrait of M. Antoine Proust, by Auguste Rodin*. Published in *The Art Amateur* 35, no. 4 (Sept. 1896). Fine Arts Department, Boston Public Library

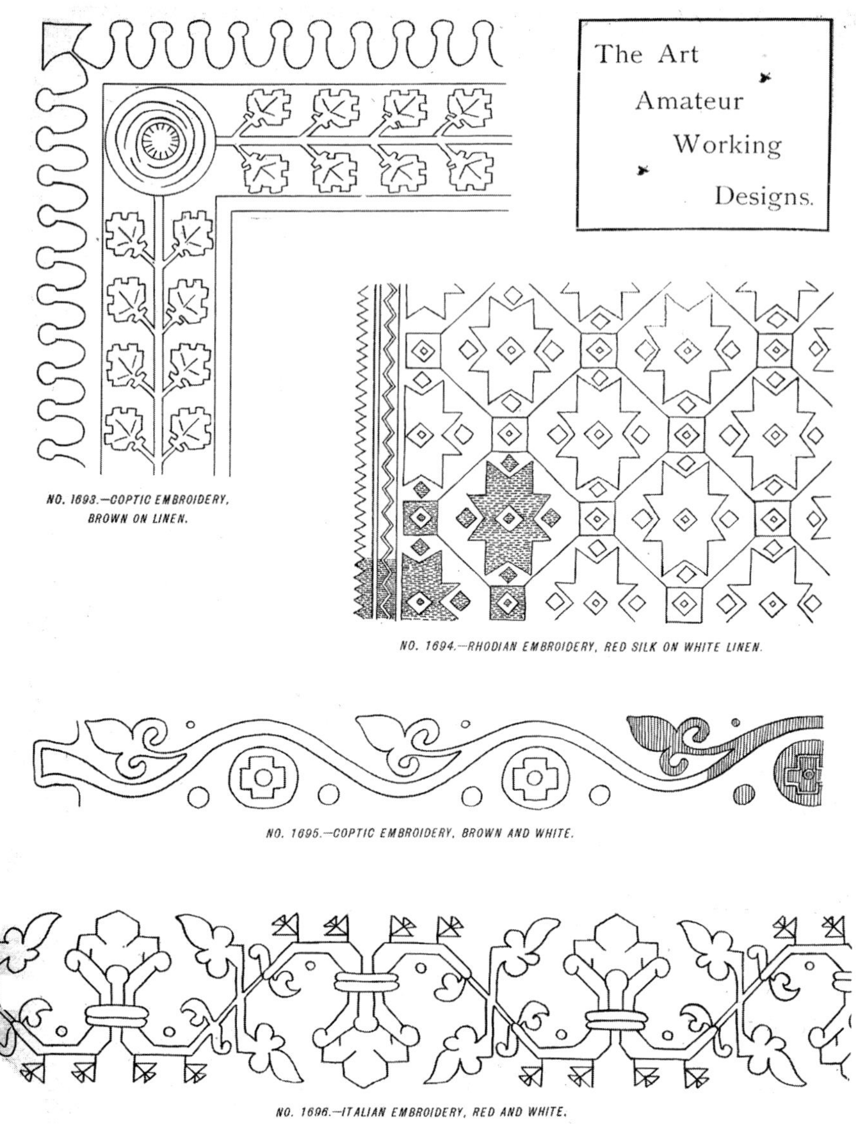

Beyond its "Working Designs," the *Art Amateur* also provided lists of art instruction books that could be purchased through its offices, and extensive advice and instruction of its own, ranging from "Practical Hints for Beginners" on how to clean brushes and prepare canvases, to tuition in needlework, jewelry, ceramics, and even taxidermy.[181] It also offered a recipe for making plaster casts, so that students could sell copies of their work to recoup the expenses of hiring models, studios, and teachers.[182] Significantly, this recipe appeared alongside an etching after Auguste Rodin's *Portrait of M. Antoine Proust* (fig. 54), which depicted the former French Deputy Commissioner of Fine Arts, and illustrated Roger Riordan's article admiring Rodin's unusual ability to combine "very great skill" with "that single-minded attention to the model which occasionally

ST. PAUL'S CATHEDRAL AND ITS MOSAICS.

WREN'S MASTERPIECE AND HOW ITS INTERIOR DECORATION IS NOW PROGRESSING AFTER THE LAPSE OF NEARLY TWO CENTURIES.

THIS great work of Sir Christopher Wren is not only the most imposing modern edifice in London, but in all England. Among the great domical structures of Europe, it ranks next to St. Peter's of Rome. The old Gothic cathedral of the same name was destroyed by the great fire of London in 1666. Wren begun the present building in 1675, and lived to see it completed in 1710. It is in the Italian style, and perhaps would not be considered very extraordinary but for the superb dome, surmounted by a stone lantern, reaching a height of 360 feet from the pavement, and the beautiful peristyle surrounding the drum upon which the dome is placed. St. Paul retains its original proportions of an English Gothic church, measuring 480 feet in length, with transepts 250 feet long, with the grand rotunda 108 feet in diameter at the crossing. It was long a matter of regret that the meagreness of detail in the decoration imparted rather a bare appearance to the whole interior; but this is now gradually being overcome, first by the magnificent reredos placed in position eight or ten years ago and now by means of an elaborate application of mosaics. It is in the dome where this is most needed, and where, in part, it has just been completed, to the intense admiration of all London. A representative of The Daily News reports an interview he has had with Mr. Henry Powell, one of the firm which manufactured the material used in the St. Paul's mosaics, and supplied the skilled workmen to put it in its proper place. As the subject is one of far more than local interest—the increasing demand for this mode of decoration, indeed, is already perceptible in this country—we reproduce the interview almost without abridgment:

"How much space do these mosaics cover, Mr. Powell?"

"The roof of the choir and the walls. Generally what you can see looking east from the dome—in fact, all the spaces left by Wren for decoration. There's no doubt you know that he left the spaces for color decoration of some sort, the three saucer domes, for example."

"What is a saucer dome?"

"A saucer dome is merely a very shallow dome. A saucer upside down expresses it exactly. There are three of them in the roof of the choir, and each of them measures 27 feet across."

"There is nothing corresponding to them externally—they merely carry on the idea of the dome?"

"Yes," replied Mr. Powell. "It is a sham ceiling, but then the whole of St. Paul's is one big sham, for that part. But I don't want to run down Wren, for I am a great admirer of Wren."

"And now as to the mosaics?"

"They are entirely of glass, in small pieces, little blocks of glass set in cement."

At my request Mr. Powell got me a slab of pinkish cement, four inches by three, with thirty-six of these cubes or tesseræ of opaque glass set in it, as it is in St. Paul's. We made a rough calculation, and arrived at 314,928 cubes of colored glass as the number contained in each of the saucer domes.

"What's the exact size of these cubes?"

"Well, you've got them there. About half an inch by three quarters; but they vary very much."

"And now as to the placing all this tonnage of glass where it produces these effects of richness?"

"Well, the saucer domes were left by Wren coated with stucco, being brick domes underneath. We've cut away the stucco, covered the bricks with cement, and inserted in the cement these opaque glass tesseræ or cubes."

"And where precisely does Mr. Richmond come in?"

"Mr. Richmond drew the plan of the pictures, and the workmen worked from that and to his colors. He drew his cartoons in colored chalks, full size."

"That must have entailed an enormous amount of work on him?"

"Enormous!" replied Mr. Powell, emphasizing each syllable so as to give its full value to the adjective. "He had to build a studio specially for it."

"In the pastels did Mr. Richmond only lump the color, or did he show exactly where each little cube should go?"

"He only drew the main lines of the figures."

"I have seen it stated somewhere that the workmen were in their way artists?"

"Well, they had to select their colors, of course, and they had to put them in the right places. They are men who draw with those colored cubes or tesseræ, instead of drawing with a paint-brush. Here you see them at work in this photograph. Hanging on one side will be Mr. Richmond's cartoon. There at their feet lies the box of cubes ranged in separate partitions."

"Just like a case of composing type?"

"Yes. They take a tracing of the cartoon, and then paste the tracing on the pink cement. With a brad-awl or other sharp instrument they prick out the outlines with holes made through the tracing in the pink cement."

"That seems mechanical work enough?"

"Yes, but they have to choose the right shades of the color in blues, greens, or what not."

Here Mr. Powell handed me a tray containing a big assortment of opaque glass in all shades of green.

"Then," he went on, "not only had they to display judgment in the matter of color, but they had to consider the effects of light in the placing of each tessera."

"How many men were at work?"

"Twenty-two."

"And how much glass did they use?"

"I can't say, I'm sure—but tons of it. You know, I think we have the beginning of a new industry."

"How will it develop? For churches mainly, I suppose?"

"There's no reason," returned Mr. Powell, "why it shouldn't be adopted for the external decoration of buildings. There's nothing so well adapted to our atmosphere; and then the material is everlasting. Nothing can touch it. You have a range of colors which is practically unlimited. You can get endless colors. . . . In combination with terra cotta it would produce the most magnificent effect that could be imagined. The aspect of London might be changed altogether. London would be a blaze of color instead of a murky, dirty place."

"And the mosaic won't foul or change color?"

"There's only one acid in existence that can touch it, and that isn't present in the atmosphere."

"But the cement?"

"That's been the crux, of course; but this pinkish cement we use won't go black. This cement, we believe, will be everlasting in its color and durability. We've made very careful experiments, and there's absolutely no lead in it. Mr. Richmond exposed some of it in the open air of his garden all through the hard winter of 1894-95, and it wasn't affected at all. Besides, we've tested it chemically, and we believe it to be absolutely imperishable."

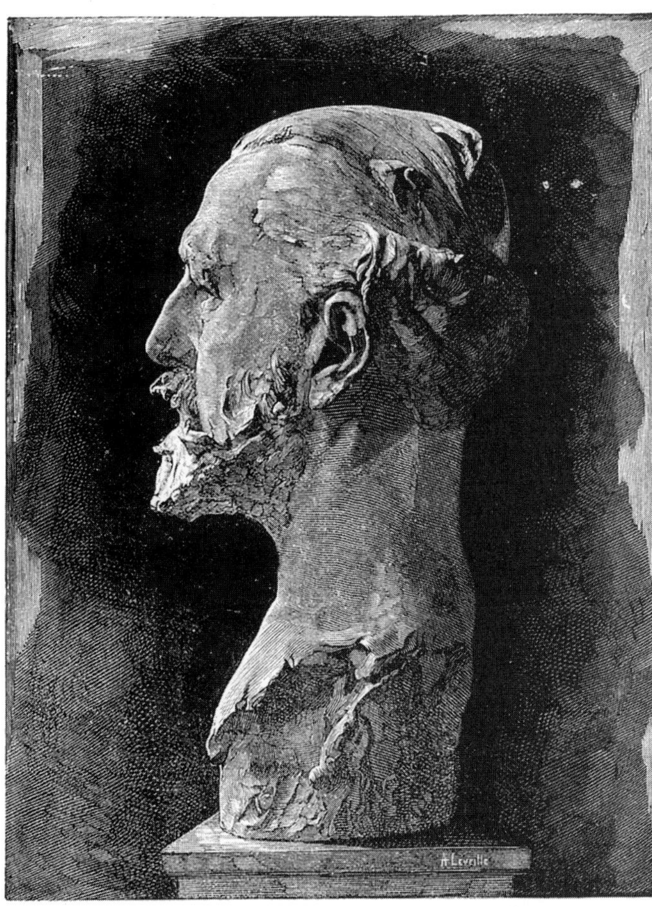

PORTRAIT OF M. ANTOINE PROUST. BY AUGUSTE RODIN.

SEE "TENDENCIES OF FRENCH SCULPTURE."

PLASTER CASTS FOR STUDENTS.

THE cost of good casts is sometimes very considerable, especially if they have to be transported any distance. Reduced copies are usually worthless. Full-sized busts from celebrated statues cost in New York anywhere from three dollars for Giuliano de' Medici to fifteen for Niobe. The bust of the Hermes of Praxiteles costs ten dollars; that of the Venus of Melos, three. "Masks"—that is, the faces of well-known statues—are very much cheaper, averaging from 50 cents to $1.50. The full-sized Venus of Melos costs fifty dollars; so does Donatello's David and Gondrou's anatomical figure. Smaller anatomical figures may be had for four or five dollars. Arms, hands and feet cost from fifty cents to three dollars each; reliefs after Della Robbia and Donatello, from one to twelve dollars each. Whenever possible, then, students should club together to buy models and hire a place in which to work, even if they cannot engage a teacher. But the student working alone may occasionally have a chance to recoup his expense, at least in part, by making casts for sale. If he wishes to preserve his own work, he should learn to cast it in plaster in any case. Plaster of Paris should be very white and free from lumps and grit. It should be kept dry until wanted for use. When mixed with water it will thicken quicker if a little salt be added, and may be kept fluid longer by the addition of a little isinglass in solution, or glue, which converts it into stucco. A cast may be rendered hard by applications of alum water, or it may be coated with wax dissolved in turpentine, and then be lightly baked in an oven to give it a tone approaching that of ivory. A way of ivorizing a cast that is adopted by many artists is to put it into a vessel of petroleum until it absorbs all the oil it will hold.

astonishes us in the work of wholly untrained persons."[183] Like the juxtaposition of Whistler and "Wood Carving for Women," this visual pairing of Rodin's art and advice for beginners offered Rodin not just as a figure of admiration, but aspiration.

The real chance that any of the *Art Amateur*'s readers would become internationally recognized artists was slim. However, the journal insisted that recognition and public success were attainable goals, even for amateurs—and even for women. Its series lionizing "Noted American China Painters" proved that this was possible. After all, "the first woman in America to become a potter," Susan Frackelton, had first "ground her clay in a small coffee-mill and rolled it with a pastry roller." From these domestic beginnings, the journal noted, Frackelton had "advanced so much that she now is at the head of a large manufactory," and had produced work that "won a medal at the World's Fair [and] was bought by Mr. John T. Morris, of Philadelphia, for the Pennsylvania Museum."[184] As both Frackelton and McLaughlin's prizes show, female art entrepreneurs *were* able to combine commercial success with the admiration and respect of museums, exhibition juries, and other "mainstream" art organizations and personnel. Similarly, McLaughlin showed her etchings at Koehler's *Women Etchers* exhibition at the Museum of Fine Arts.[185] Maria Longworth Storer's Rookwood Pottery won prizes at the 1889 Paris Exposition. Janet Payne Bowles earned commissions from J. P. Morgan and John White Alexander. And Alsop-Robineau's work was sufficiently well respected that, upon her death, a retrospective was held at the Metropolitan Museum of Art in her honor.[186] In part, this was because the developers of commercial enterprises, like Storer, were themselves linked to the creators of nonprofit art organizations. An ad for Rookwood that appeared in McLaughlin's *China Painting* advertised not only the company's prizes, but also the fact that Storer was the daughter of Joseph Longwood, founder of Cincinnati's art school and main patron of its museum.[187]

The *Art Amateur*'s advertisers certainly envisioned an active and ambitious readership for the magazine, which would demand equipment like "The New and Improved Wilke Kiln," "recommended highly by the best Amateur and Professional Artists in every City in the United States and Europe."[188] Advertisements specifically appealed to female readers as potential exhibitors and prize-winners; on the same page as the Wilke Kiln advertisement (fig. 55), a promotion for "Marsching's Roman Gold" china paint featured a fictional conversation "At the Exhibition!" between "Mrs. A," who "used Marsching's Famous Roman Gold, and took first prize," and "Mrs. B.," who "used one of those cheaper golds, and spoiled my vase." Not coincidentally, both Frackelton's *Tried by Fire* and Alsop-Robineau's *Keramic Studio* advertised Marsching products as well.[189] *Keramic Studio* also advertised "The Revelation China Kiln," manufactured in Detroit and endorsed by "well-known artists" such as "Mrs. Helen M. Clark, Chicago," and "Miss Helen D. Phillips, San Francisco" (fig. 56), and "Fitch Kilns," made by the firm of artist and inventor of "The Amateur's Portable Kiln," "Mrs. N. M. Fitch," which McLaughlin's *China Painting* praised. In both the real art world and the field of art envisioned by the late-nineteenth-century media, women flourished as artists and entrepreneurs.[190]

Like the wider efforts to create an organizational field for art, efforts to join the household labor of art amateurs to the work of recognized art

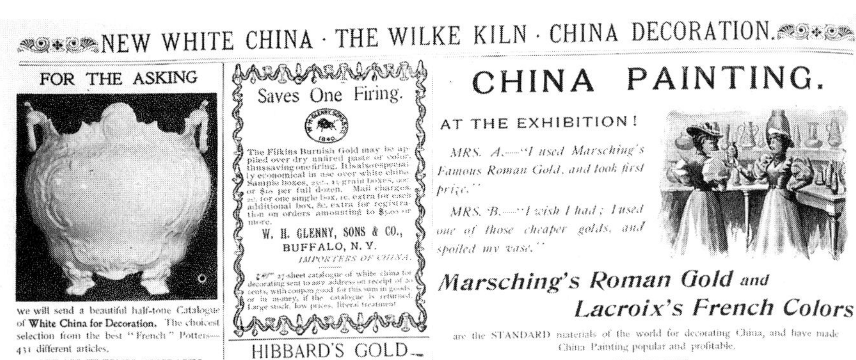

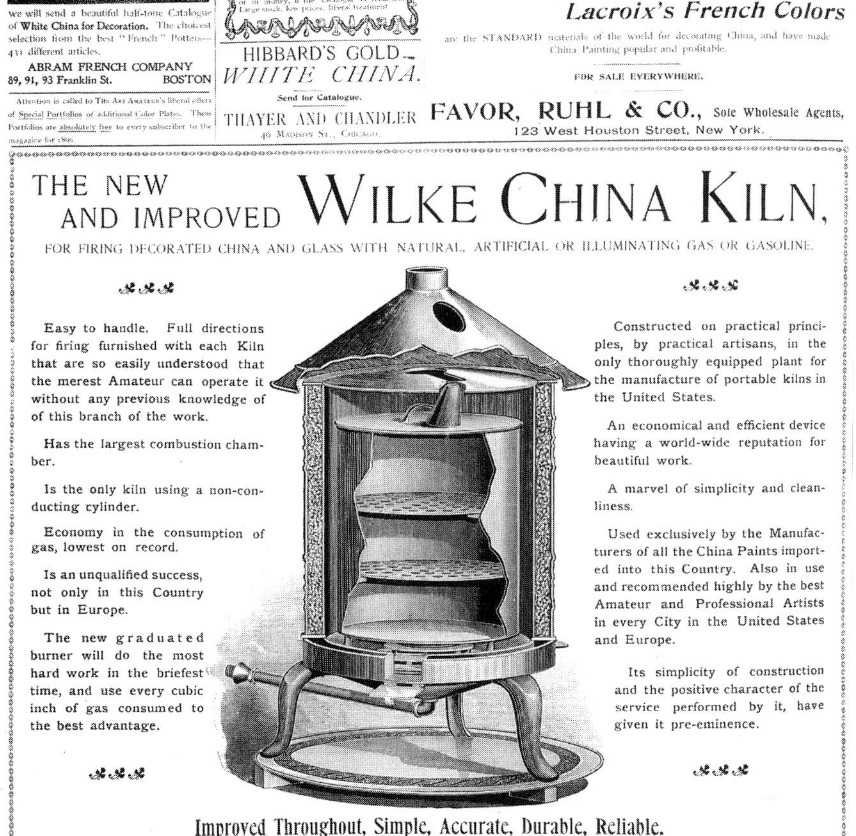

55. Advertisements for "New White China," "The Wilke Kiln," "China Decoration." Published in *The Art Amateur* 35, no. 4 (Sept. 1896). Fine Arts Department, Boston Public Library

The Lyman Press, Syracuse, N. Y.

professionals were highly significant. First, they had major implications for gender relations within the art world. As Kathleen McCarthy has shown, organizations such as Wheeler's NYSDA provided an entrepreneurial space that was difficult to obtain elsewhere in the art world.[191] While McCarthy argues that women's success in the decorative arts was attributable to their separation and marginalization from the mainstream art world, I would propose that it was precisely the blurring of art-world boundaries, facilitated by artist-entrepreneurs and by the media, that made this success possible. While the "field of art" in the present day is defined by indices like the Smithsonian's Inventories of American Painting & Sculpture, and replicated in a scholarly literature that persistently separates and diminishes the decorative, the industrial, and even the graphic arts, this was not always the case.[192] This can be seen not only in the pages of the *Art Amateur* and the *American Art Review*, but in the financial success of institutions like the NYSDA—Koehler's figures indicate that the Society's exhibitions were among the most lucrative in the art world in the 1880s. It can also be seen in the careers of women artists like Wheeler, Frackelton, McLaughlin, Payne Bowles, and Alsop-Robineau, who, alongside male artists like Louis Comfort Tiffany and John La Farge, made the decorative arts among the most appealing and successful branches of American art between the Civil War and the Armory Show.[193]

If an exploration into the worlds made by male entrepreneurs like Koehler, Prang, and Bradley can offer new insight into the aesthetic and social terrain of the postwar art world, so, too, can our unfolding awareness of women entrepreneurs like Wheeler. This new understanding is exemplified in the work of scholars like Mary Blanchard and the curators of the 2001–2002 exhibition of Wheeler's art at the Metropolitan Museum of Art, Amelia Peck and Carol Irish.[194] For too long, historians who examined this period, including McCarthy and Lears, employed distinctions between "amateur" and "real" artwork, and between the "fine" arts and other media, that did not accurately reflect the texture of the late-nineteenth-century art world. It is undoubtedly the case that these historians were motivated by the desire to rectify inequalities of the past. Nonetheless, it is necessary to note that many of these distinctions themselves emerged, at least in part, as a result of the efforts of professionalizing, proto-modernist critics who did not have such egalitarian goals in mind. Instead of replicating the "borders of art," we should ask ourselves what more we can learn from an art world that was very different from our own.

Opposite:
56. Advertisement for "The Revelation China Kiln." Published in *Keramic Studio: A Monthly Magazine for the Designer, Potter, Decorator, Firer* 1, no. 5 (Sept. 1899). Fine Arts Library, Harvard College Library, Cambridge, Massachusetts

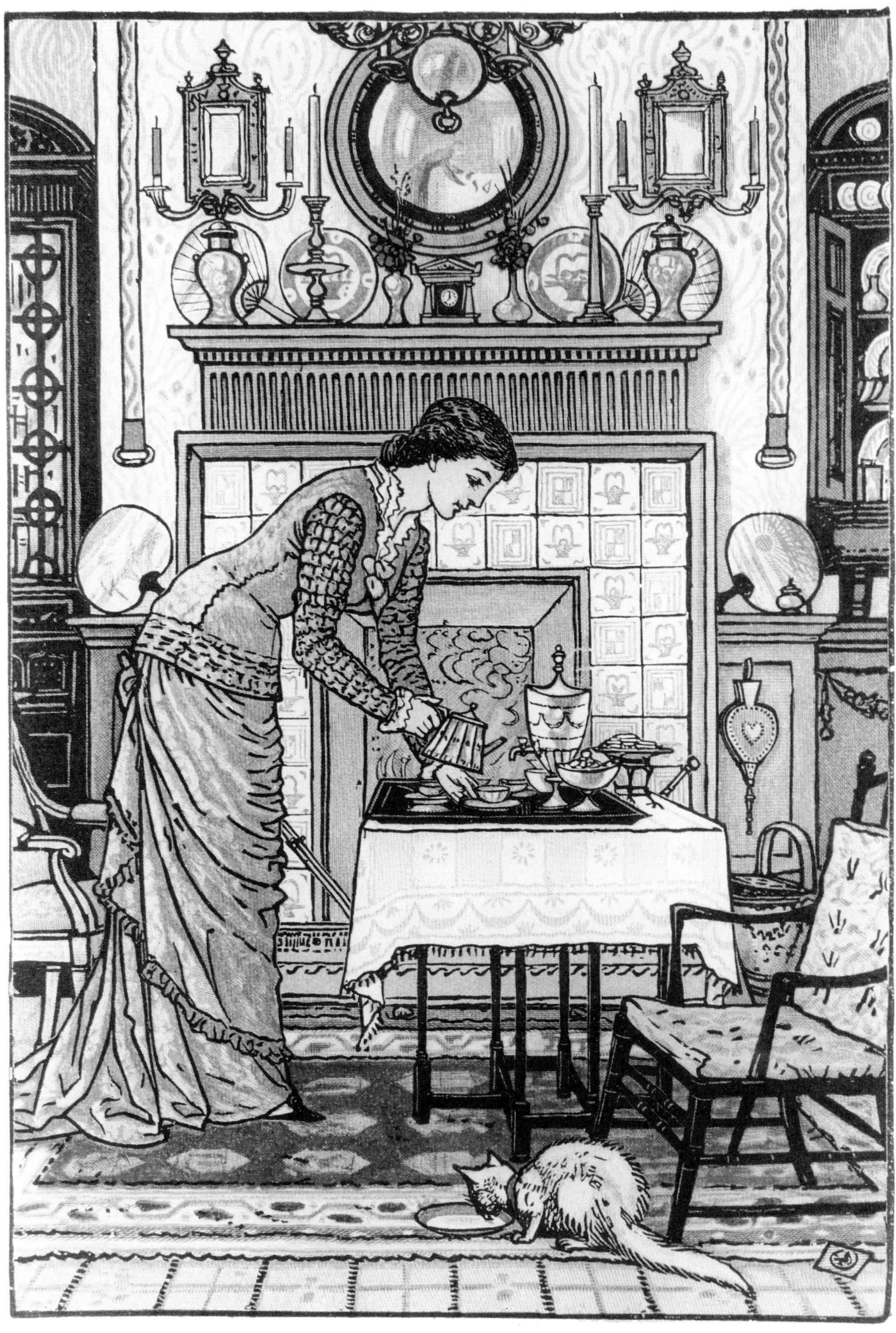

Chapter 3 Professionalism and a New Aesthetic Order

The number of men who are entering the field of art in these days, with the hope of achieving an easy conquest, is become so great that it is an absolute necessity to challenge every new comer with rigorous sharpness.
—Clarence Cook, 1866

How to chart a future path for artisans was only one of many questions posed by industrialization. For the middle classes, it also brought about a profound crisis of authority, sparked by massive economic growth and high levels of migration. One response to this challenge was professionalization. Professionalization, and the specialization it entailed, did not just solve the practical question of how to deal with production and administration on a vast new scale. More important, the division of intellectual labor along professional lines also offered an authoritative challenge to what historian Thomas Bender has described as "the competing . . . demands of a heterogeneous public," raising professional expertise as the legitimate and orderly successor to older sources of authority.[1]

In the United States, professionalization took two main forms. The first, which has been described at length by historians, consisted both in

57. Henry Marsh after Walter Crane (1845–1915), *My Lady's Chamber.* Frontispiece to Clarence Cook, *The House Beautiful* (New York: Scribner, Armstrong & Co., 1878). American Antiquarian Society, Worcester, Massachusetts

the organization of practitioners into independent corporate bodies with recognizable institutional structures and boundaries, and in the rationalization and assimilation of professional work.[2] Within fields that achieved the greatest degree of professionalization, the development of professional schools, the establishment of legal standards of qualification, and the institutionalization of systems of peer review all emerged as methods to control the "production of producers" and the content of professional knowledge within individual fields.[3] While organizational methods helped nineteenth-century professionals to maintain norms among practitioners, they also served to exclude outsiders. Complicated institutional gatekeeping systems (enforced, in some cases, by the state) prevented nonprofessionals from practicing, and erected real boundaries between lay people and experts.[4]

Yet, the professions did not rely solely on organizational routes to consolidation. Professionals also used less tangible means of self-definition, such as the development of professional languages, to foster their authority as experts. As historian JoAnne Brown has shown, early-twentieth-century American psychologists used metaphorical comparisons between themselves and physicians both to distance themselves from competitors and to gain authority and credibility for their enterprise. Indeed, these kinds of strategies were central to the professionalizing project; as Brown puts it, language "is uniquely suited to resolving the contradiction between popularity and monopoly that lies at the heart of the project of professionalization, because it advertises without disclosing, and sells without delivering, the special knowledge that is the professional's commodity."[5]

In the highly unstable atmosphere of the postwar period, struggles for interpretative and organizational control spilled from politics into the relatively peaceful cultural sphere, rendering debates about art and culture into questions of power, legitimacy, and authority. Within this context, art publishing participated in both linguistic and organizational forms of professionalization. Even though it was never subjected to licensing, compulsory training, or other requirements that characterize less porous professions, as a branch of journalism it was affected by the organizational transformation of work in the late nineteenth century. By the 1880s, American magazines were turning away from a policy of editorial restraint, characterized by the publication of unsolicited articles, to the strategy of what literary scholar Christopher Wilson has called "anticipatory production."[6] Magazines such as *Ladies Home Journal* and *McClure's* substituted commissioned work and the productions of internal writing staffs for occasional writings by outsiders, consolidating the production of opinion among closely linked, regularly employed editors and writers. American newspapers underwent a related metamorphosis, as individual writers fulfilled increasingly specialized tasks and journalism began to enjoy increased prestige and authority as an occupation.[7]

Art criticism was no exception to this trend. As in journalism as a whole, art critics and art criticism became more permanent and more deeply rooted in the last decades of the nineteenth century, as occasional art writings by amateurs began to give way to the work of staff writers and solicited outsiders, and as art writing emerged as a distinct subfield within journalism as a whole. In general, the relationship between art writer and periodical began to firm up during this period, with writers fulfilling a variety of more permanent roles than their amateur predecessors. Many publications began to depend entirely on staff writers for their criticism. In a parallel development, a growing cohort of critics emerged in the last third of the century, born in the 1850s and 1860s, who would devote all or a significant portion of their working lives to criticism. These included James Gibbons Huneker, Charles Caffin, Elizabeth Luther Cary, Clarence Cook, Mariana Griswold Van Rensselaer, and Sadakichi Hartmann.[8]

The structural change in art writing from irregular contribution to "anticipatory production" facilitated professionalism in two ways. First, the permanent institutional location of a regular column became in itself a marker of status and expertise. The critic's position as a paid and permanent writer also helped to transform criticism itself, in that it gave the critic not only increased authority but also an extended opportunity to develop particular lines of interpretation in print. Over the course of a few decades, the result was that the expert interpretation of professionals began to replace the ebb and flow of institution-building criticism, as critics strove increasingly to convey opinion rather than to produce new opinion-makers. In this way, art criticism served to confirm the professional status of its practitioners, as well as to redefine readers as nonprofessional clients of artists and critics alike.

Although this trend most certainly did not influence all art critics and editors to pursue a professionalizing agenda at this time, a growing sense of professional identity accompanied the reorganization of art criticism along occupational lines, witnessed by demands for tighter administration of the rules and rewards of the field. While art critics never formally organized into one overarching professional association, they adapted preexisting bodies such as the American Academy of Arts and Letters to perform the role of gatekeeper and back-patter for the field. As critic John Van Dyke wrote in describing election to membership in this organization: "One does not care much about the opinion of the man in the street. What the general public thinks of one's rank is not taken seriously by the lawyer, physician, artist, or writer. The lawyer seeks recognition from the bar association, his own professional associates, the physician looks to his medical society, the artist to his brother artists, the writer to his brother writers. Each regards his professional brethren as the best judges of his work, and when they say he is a good lawyer, doctor, artist, or writer it means something. It is an authoritative utterance and constitutes the best compliment he can receive. So I was honored, complimented, and pleased by my election to the Academy, that election having been brought about by the votes of fellow writers."[9] Although art critics did not establish the rigid professional boundaries that came to characterize law or medicine, they nonetheless promoted organizational solutions to the question of how to keep control over reputation and prestige within the boundaries of the profession, and jealously guarded those borders from competitors.

Professional Boundaries

While the trend toward professionalization affected a number of Gilded Age critics, it can be seen most clearly in the work of two writers, Mariana Griswold Van Rensselaer and Clarence Chatham Cook. Cook was one of the first Americans to make a living from art criticism, serving as a regular contributor and art editor of the *New-York Daily Tribune* and publishing both books and articles in *Scribner's Monthly* and the *Atlantic Monthly*.[10] Similarly, Van Rensselaer established a long-term relationship with the *American Architect and Building News*, a journal with a largely specialized and professionally distinct audience, as well as contributing to the *Century* and other journals. Unlike Cook, Van Rensselaer was not driven by economic necessity to earn her keep from criticism, but considered herself a professional nonetheless—indeed, she made a point of insisting on regular and prompt payment for her writing despite great personal wealth.[11]

These writers each had a highly developed sense of their work as a professional calling, separate and distinct from the activities of the public, artists, or other would-be participants in the art world. This did not mean that Cook and Van Rensselaer did not participate in the institutions developed by their peers. Indeed, Van Rensselaer contributed to the *American Art Review* and wrote the introduction to the catalogue of Koehler's *Women Etchers* exhibition when the show moved to New York's Union League Club in 1888.[12] Nonetheless, she presented the art world in a very different light than either Koehler or his counterparts at the *Art Amateur*. Unlike Koehler, who jointly promoted connoisseurship, broad-based art education, and institutional development, or the *Art Amateur*, which encouraged amateur readers to make themselves into artists, Van Rensselaer's goals for art publishing were more limited. Generally speaking, she focused on how professional critics could guide and foster the public's imperfect habits of perception and consumption. Coupled with an emphasis on the formal qualities of artworks, this consumerist vision of the public bolstered Van Rensselaer's drive for a separate and specialized professional criticism, and distinguished her from institution-building competitors in the field.

Cook's career also marked a departure in American art criticism. A Harvard graduate, Cook was perhaps the first American to make a living as an art critic for an American newspaper. In addition to his writings for the press, Cook also published numerous volumes of his own, including the highly successful *House Beautiful*, and was a founding member of both the Society for the Advancement of Truth in Art (1863) and the Society of American Artists.[13] The content of Cook's criticism is as relevant as his placement in the art world, for Cook consistently used it to promote professionalization as a model for criticism and the art world as a whole. This commitment to professionalization affected not only the content but the character of Cook's writings; as Barbara Stephanic notes, Cook was one of the first American critics to "write with the goal of providing the reader a thoughtful engagement with the work," or, in somewhat more neutral terms, to see the interpretation and judgment of individual artworks as the primary aim of criticism.[14]

The careers of Van Rensselaer and Cook are of consequence to this study not only because of their commitment to a new form of professionalization in art criticism, but also because they have emerged as two of the most studied critics of their era. Although hundreds of Americans wrote art criticism of one sort or another in the late nineteenth century, very few of them have received any attention from scholars, let alone been the subject of an individual monograph. In contrast, Cook and Van Rensselaer have each been the subject of doctoral theses and scholarly articles, many of which draw attention to "professionalism" as the two critics' chief merit. If it is true that the subjects we study divulge as much about the dispositions of our own time as they do about their importance in their own lifetimes, then it is telling that so much attention has been paid to these two critics and not to others who left equally lengthy paper trails. Indeed, no one is lining up to study Sylvester Rosa Koehler, George Parsons Lathrop, S. G. W. Benjamin, or many of the other writers whose contributions jam nineteenth-century periodical and book collections. There must be some reason for this divergence, which can be explained neither by a lack of sources nor by a lack of contemporary importance on the part of those who have been neglected.[15] Rather, I think it is that we can see ourselves only in Van Rensselaer, Cook, and the few later critics from the very end of the nineteenth century who have received similar attention (Caffin, Hartmann, Huneker), many of whom have escaped historical obscurity because of their ties to the Stieglitz circle. After all, they are like us in ways that many of their contemporaries were not. They wrote criticism that looks like our criticism: criticism that privileges, judges, and ranks artworks; criticism that ignores, excludes, or masks institution building;

criticism that values artistic objects over artistic labor; and criticism, in the case of the later critics, if not in that of Cook and Van Rensselaer, that overtly appreciates and admires modernism.

So, then, what was their program for professionalization? To begin, both critics placed a high premium on the erection of secure borders for the art world. Expressing a profound ambivalence about art-world expansion, Cook argued that Americans would do themselves more good by narrowing rather than widening public access to the hallowed shores of art. Unlike Koehler, who listed every artist and art teacher in an honor roll of American artistic expansion, who met the emergence of each new institution as one would greet a birth, and whose *American Art Review* and *United States Art Directory* contained obituaries of every artist whose death depleted the ranks of American art (even those as obscure as Firmin Bouvy of San Francisco, whose "favorite subjects were monks"), Cook feared that the art world would only be diluted by greater numbers.[16]

As his call to "challenge every new comer with rigorous sharpness" suggests, Cook believed the borders of the art world required stricter policing.[17] And who better to provide this service than critics? Although he grumbled that "the duty of passing judgment is a thankless office," Cook counseled that frank judgment by professional critics, although painful, would keep the unqualified from muddying the waters of culture. At the very least, he suggested, professional critics would do a better job than either the politic-ridden hanging committees and public officials who determined which artworks went before the public, or than the public itself, whose taste, he thought, was dubious in the extreme. Cook's "only fear at present is [that] our artists should become too prosperous, should find it too easy to sell their pictures, and test experiments upon the pockets of the public, which seems to bite at nothing so greedily as picture sales."[18]

Cook also proposed tighter standards for artists. He pleaded with Boston artists to form a "compact," suggesting that they work together "to procure models for the figure and to work systematically from the life" and to set firm criteria for works submitted for exhibition. The professional advantages of such an association, he argued, were clear, for once formed "we shall soon know the status of art in this locality. On all accounts it would be better to know this; for, in discovering deficiencies, we should also be made aware of strength sometimes unsuspected under the present lackadaisical mode of procedure."[19] As Cook saw it, American art was faulty, and only intense professional cooperation and the harsh discipline of uniform professional standards could remedy the situation.[20]

Cook's desire to curtail and control the making of art is also reflected in his writings on the decorative arts. Cook was fascinated by this subject, contributing a series of articles to *Scribner's* that was published as *The House Beautiful* in 1878. In contrast to contemporaries like Susan

Frackelton, whose writings about art included pictures of tools (fig. 58) and instructions on how to use them, Cook did not suggest that readers should strive to be artists. As the frontispiece to the book suggested, *The House Beautiful* was not a place for making art, but consuming and displaying it (see fig. 57). Within the text, Cook addressed the reader as a consumer, who required critical advice when choosing living accommodations and furnishings. This was necessary, he implied, because less honest tastemakers were always looking for ways to dupe their customers with inauthentic but flashy design. He contended that marbleized slate mantelpieces, for example, "by which invention Nature was taught what ugly things in the way of marble she might have made if she had been born

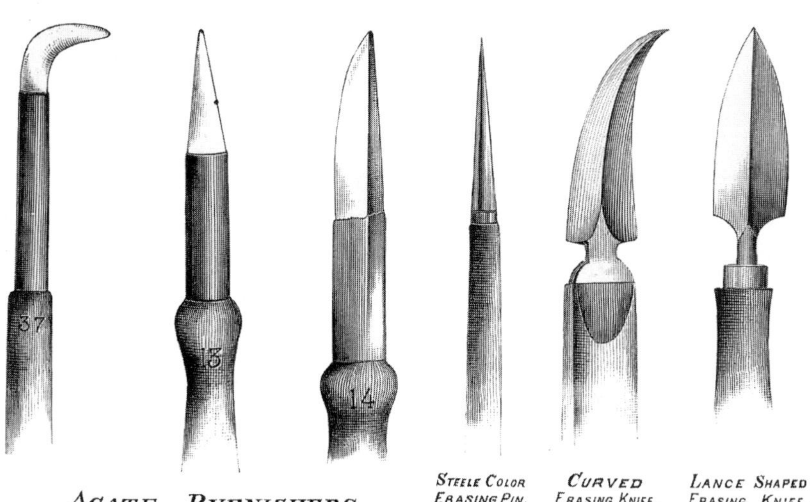

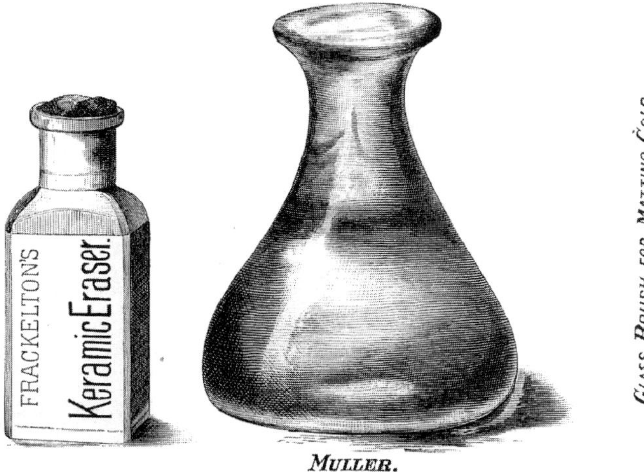

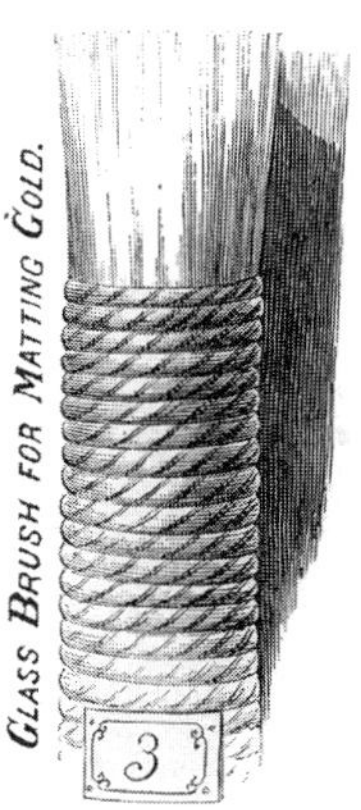

58. Susan Stuart Goodrich Frackelton (1851–1932), illustration from *Tried by Fire: A Work on China Painting* (New York: D. Appleton & Co., 1886). Fine Arts Department, Boston Public Library

a Yankee," were "supposed to make the rash gazer, while he wipes his eye, forget to remark the cracked and blistered plaster, the gaping wood-work, and the wind that whistles through the door and window-frames for want of thought."[21]

Cook's second volume on home decoration, *"What Shall We Do with Our Walls?"* (1880), also emphasized the reader's role as a consumer.[22] Rephrasing the question as "Whom shall we call upon to color our walls for us?" Cook never considered that readers might wish to decorate their interiors with frescoes or wallpapers of their own design.[23] Instead, he offered them a selection of tasteful suggestions for wallpaper to buy, manufactured by the publishers of his book, Warren, Fuller & Co., of New York. Cook further argued that readers could best contribute to the development of American art as a whole (as opposed to just the improvement of their own homes) by becoming *consumers* of art. "We wish these fellow-citizens of ours would see the truth, for it is a truth," he argued, "that the way to encourage the healthy, normal growth of any form of art, the true and only way to teach it, is to set it at some actual work intended to be paid for, and to be worth paying for."[24] Cook even explicitly suggested that fulfilling this role as consumers was *more* essential than supporting the development of art schools, which he suggested did little to promote true art. As he put it, "There never was talk heard of the necessity for schools-of-design in any country where art really flourished."[25]

Cook did not limit his negative comments to publicly funded art education; he also criticized public art patronage, at least as it was currently administered. Campaigning against the influence of "outsiders" within the art world, Cook argued that government patronage was tainted by the influence of judges who were chosen for their cultural, political, or social standing, rather than their professional expertise: "people of literary reputation, whose opinions on art are as valuable as their opinions on the whale-fishery." The consequence of this "indifference" and "ignorance of the members of Congress on the subject," Cook suggested, had been disastrous patronage decisions. He also suggested that outside influence had contributed to mistakes in patronage within New York, and joined the American Institute of Architects in agitating for greater control by architects over the commissioning of public buildings in New York.

If Cook found the use of "external" standards to have had a negative influence on public art, he was also critical of their impact on art education. Cook found the application of moral norms particularly galling, especially when it interfered with professional concerns such as the determination of art-school curricula. Cook's arguments against "prudery" can certainly be seen as a genuine sign of his progressivism. Nonetheless, they were also part of his program for professionalization. When he railed against a powerful cadre of older artists who had "carried prudery and what are called 'American' ideas to such a point that a lively fight is all the time waging on the subject of nude models, and the female students are subjected by these inquisitors to the most irksome rules," his complaint was not only that this had hampered student development, but that it had resulted in artists publicly siding with the general populace against their own professional brethren.[26] Unlike Koehler, who also championed the move to art study "from life," but who neutrally represented the transition away from study "from the antique" as a choice to be made by school personnel, Cook represented this change as a culture war between enlightened artists and Puritanical outsiders.[27] Seething against "the great bulk of the well-to-do people of New York," the "general public," and those artists who defected to the "public" position, Cook promoted professional solidarity and independence above art-world adherence to standard behavioral norms, even at or perhaps because of the risk of alienating audiences.[28] In Cook's view, art-world debates could be broken down into disputes between progressive "us" and prudish "them," and victory would be obtained only by adherence to professional standards.

As his own work on behalf of Warren, Fuller & Co. suggests, Cook was not afraid to offer his critical services to commercial clients. And, even as early as the mid-1860s, Cook hinted that art and profit could be joined, advising readers to consider the purchase of original artworks as a financial, as well as a cultural, investment.[29] Nonetheless, he criticized the market as another inappropriate "external" standard to the judgment of art, which interfered with the purer standards of professional independence. Presenting himself as a promoter of only principled aesthetic judgments, Cook speculated bitterly in 1866 upon his own favorable review of Henry Farrer's much abused contribution to the previous year's Academy exhibition. But, why, Cook asked, had he given his approval? "Because Mr. Farrer was the critic's friend? Because Mr. Farrer had paid him with pictures and sketches? Because he kept an Art-Gallery and had Mr. Farrer's pictures for sale? Was it for one or all these reasons? Or, was it because we believed it then, and believe it now, that we said it then, and repeat it now?"[30] Art critics must, Cook suggested, detach themselves from the trade in pictures.[31]

Similarly, Cook condemned the creep of the market into artistic conduct, worrying that the public's easy and sensationalistic taste provided a wrongheaded standard for artistic production.[32] Indeed, although he supported artists' organizations as a necessary step toward professionalization, he also disparaged associations that seemed to place financial interest ahead of the pursuit of aesthetic quality. He sneered that the Philadelphia Sketch Club's exhibition of 1866 "appears, then, to be a new speculation in picture-selling, and it seems to be in the hands of practical men, who will prosper in the undertaking if any one can," even though it contained "barely a dozen [works] of merit enough to deserve mention."[33] Along the same lines, Cook disparagingly described portraits as "mere merchandise—so much flattered vanity, and so many tubes of color at so many dollars."[34] Similarly, he argued against artists' militant support of the tariff on foreign art. As he saw it, artists who wished to block the entry of foreign art "have taken a mercantile view of their profession, and have used all their influence in a blind hostility to foreign art, merely as such, to subject art and artists in America to the bigotry of protection, to bring into the field of culture the jealousies and rivalries of trade."[35] By rejecting profit as a standard inappropriate to any of the art-world professions, Cook pursued a strategy that distinguished him from publishers like Prang, and that called into question the entrepreneurship of many of the artists of his day. It would, however, provide a link between professionals and the modernists, who considered the corrosion of the marketplace to be one of the crucial dangers facing modern culture.

Van Rensselaer also presented a forceful argument for professionalization in the art world, seen, for example, in her writings on architecture. Like Van Dyke, Van Rensselaer called on the public to recognize the authority of trained professionals, supporting her argument with bold comparisons between architecture and more established professions. "It may sound startling," she wrote, "but, believe me, none could be more true and wise" than the architect's recommendation that "the public must first learn to trust us as it does lawyers or doctors, before architecture can develop into a great art."[36] When she surveyed the built environment, Van Rensselaer seems to have seen a lot of ugliness, brought about by Americans' failure to depend upon professionals for their architecture. She wrote: "It is false to say that there are structures which need not be 'architectural' at all; that men may build at times, yet put all thoughts of art aside. Everything that ever was built is a good work of architecture or a bad one. . . . When we insist that our neighbors shall daily look upon barrenness or deformity, when we fill what before was placid, empty space with crying shapes of ugliness, we are bad citizens, brutal neighbors."[37] Embedded within this critique of amateur architecture was the idea that "good citizenship" within the art world was defined by good habits of consumption: if the public would stop building ugly buildings and start hiring professional architects, America would be more beautiful.

Even within the professional field of architecture, Van Rensselaer called for a further degree of specialization. She suggested that architects who meddled in areas outside their immediate specialty caused as much damage as amateurs. When "an architect who had devoted years to the study of" certain medieval buildings slated for restoration in Germany was replaced by "the government architect of the district,—a man who . . . had until this time been chiefly occupied with railway buildings," she argued, the result was "a monster neither old nor new, a lie . . . against which every tourist, every art-student, every German ought to be strenuously warned."[38] Only rigorous adherence to specialization and the absolute exclusion of outsiders, Van Rensselaer argued, could keep architectural works free from abuse and keep viewers safe from the depredations of ugliness.

This emphasis on professional modes of organization was frequently accompanied by a harsh attitude toward competitors in the art world and in publishing who had different definitions of the field of art. Cook did occasionally promote ventures like the Metropolitan's acquisition of the Cesnola Collection—an act that he would bitterly regret—but he generally seems to have harbored a deep bitterness against the publishing establishment. In 1886, for example, he railed in a personal letter that "I see that the late James T. Fields has written an article for the April 'Century.' Now that the dead men are having their turn, it may be hoped the living will soon begin to emerge. However, it is an old story that a dead man with a name (or half a one!) is better than a living man with no name at all (to speak of!)."[39]

In public, Cook cast his challenge to his competitors in the field of art in less conspiratorial terms. In particular, he challenged the media's ability to contribute meaningfully to art education. He disparaged much of the literature praised by other critics, questioning whether the "untrustworthy" tomes of Lübke, Woltmann, Ruskin, and Passavant, and the discussions of their ideas in the magazines, could properly educate Americans.[40] Cook also spoke harshly of the nation's art schools. He ridiculed "the foolish face of praise with which their performances are contemplated by the artists and the public," demanding to know how American art schools could "ever equal such a school as that of the Beaux Arts until they have . . . its corps of professors and teachers, in the co-operation of the best artists of the country, and the criticism of a body of men trained peculiarly for its work?"[41] Art education in the United States, Cook suggested, would flounder until the schools hired authorities in anatomy, criticism, and other subjects to replace ill-suited lecturers whose rhetorical skill outstripped their art expertise (not to mention the women who increasingly filled the ranks of the art-educational profession).[42] Both before and after the emergence of initiatives like the Massachusetts Drawing Act and the Normal Art School, Cook called for a radical reorganization of the art world along specialized, professional lines.

Van Rensselaer also assailed the cultural authority of professional criticism's competitors, by promoting and defending the cognitive superiority of professional critics. She regularly discounted the views of the public, denying at times that it even had an interest in art. The public's mode of viewing, she charged, was "flippant"; a true interest in art belonged only to "specialists more or less professional—artists, critics, and connoisseurs whose whole life is devoted to its service."[43] Her characterization of art-world amateurs, even those who participated in significant institutions, was hardly kinder than her assessment of the public at large. In describing the work of amateurs, Van Rensselaer suggested that they could not be trusted to further the interests of art without professional assistance. Unlike those who praised the Society of Decorative Art, she sniped at the "Ladies" of the Society both for their lack of knowledge in arranging their 1878 exhibition and for their inflated claims as to the show's educational merit. "It is doubly necessary," she wrote, "for enthusiastic and self-sacrificing amateurs . . . to go about their work not only with zeal, devotion, and liberality, but with prudence and wise severity, *and with the assistance of the best professional experience and the widest professional culture*."[44] Although as Koehler pointed out, the NYSDA provided a major source of funds and training for women designers, and, although Wheeler was herself a successful artist, Van Rensselaer represented the group as unprofessional and perhaps even harmful.

Van Rensselaer also appealed to the special quality of professional *critical* perception, in part by appealing to the complexity of art and the art world. This is visible in her commentary on the third exhibition of the Society of American Artists, in 1880. In this review, Van Rensselaer emphasized the Society's newness, arguing that this novelty made it difficult to provide a firm and precise description of the movement as a whole. She wrote: "As for the newer school, it is, of course, in its infancy, a school potential, or, as some may think, of future certainty, but still in process of development."[45] Readers' likely unfamiliarity with the group did not spur Van Rensselaer to provide a more elaborate explanation of its background or history, however. Despite her own admission that the movement had failed to take final shape, she wrote that "he who went to this third exhibition of the Society of American Artists and . . . did not know what names were absolutely new, what men were showing maiden efforts and trying 'prentice hands, who did not see the great advance others had made since their first appearance a year or two ago, who did not appreciate how they are all striking in the very teeth of our traditions, striving to win the public ear without sounding a single note such as it loves and listens for,—may indeed have got much pleasure from the pictures, but can have gained little knowledge as to the recent progress or the future prospects of our art."[46] As Van Rensselaer characterized it, the show would make sense only to those who already knew about it, not only because of the absolute newness of the movement, but also because the public itself presented an obstacle to progress. This twin conceptualization of the art world as a site in which time has begun to speed beyond the comprehension of normal understanding, and as a site of resistance to public norms, would become a commonplace in modernist and avant-garde thinking.[47] It also provided a useful wedge between professional critics and other judges of art.

This approach differed from S. G. W. Benjamin's review of the same show in the *American Art Review*. Benjamin, too, supported the SAA's efforts to reform the Academy. "It is tacitly understood," he wrote, "that an Academician, by right of the position he holds, is entitled to the first place. What is the result? As no man can be expected always to paint good pictures, bad ones are often awarded prominent positions, while better works are skyed almost out of sight."[48] He never suggested, however, that the new movement was particularly hard to comprehend. To facilitate this understanding, he devoted part of his review to breaking down the exhibition into comprehensible parts. He described the group's history and purpose as an Academy splinter group, and offered a lengthy explanation as to the significance of the SAA's change in hanging practices. He also gave readers information on the group's membership, including both participants in the exhibition and members who were not exhibiting in the current show but who might be known to readers, like Cincinnati's Frank Duveneck and "Miss [Mary] Cassatt." He also discussed "representative" works.[49] And, most importantly, Benjamin refused to represent the SAA's challenge to the Academy as a critique of the public. "If a work is of sufficient value to be admitted, do it full justice, and then leave the decision as to its qualities to the general public. This is the novel policy which has been adopted by the hanging committee in the case under consideration."[50]

Van Rensselaer did not argue that readers were unable to learn to appreciate art. She urged them to develop "a trained understanding of artistic technics, an acutely sensitive eye, a craving for beauty in its noblest forms, and an appreciation of it in its slightest and most evanescent,—these are the glories and delights of the true amateur, and these may be drawn from the study of materials open to any dweller in cities."[51] But, if they did not go about this task properly, she warned, dire results would follow. Without the training offered by professional criticism, viewers would never fully comprehend the pictures that dazzled and pleased them: "The untrained eye," she wrote, "will never see the audacious wrestling of Rubens with his mighty masses of seemingly intractable color, never perceive the subtle yet daring way in which Rembrandt's brush uses brown and yellow to give us sunlight and color and the blackness of darkness and the vividness of actual existence. It will never suspect the scientific planning of Veronese's composition, so casual in appearance, the scientific grace of his most careless draperies. . . . In a portrait by Velasquez, on the other hand, we have the most visible sober, realistic, yet noble and elevated way of working. The result is as magnificent in another way as Raphael's, as marvelous and inspiring to the trained eye, as utterly unappreciable by the untrained."[52] Untrained eyes might look, but they could not truly see.

Even more serious were Van Rensselaer's warnings against amateurs who aimed to *make* art on their own. Unlike the *Art Amateur*, which represented the border between amateurs and professionals, and between consumers and makers, as porous and unstable, Van Rensselaer defined amateurship solely in terms of art appreciation and connoisseurship. Calling this kind of amateurship a "beautiful and useful craft," she characterized amateur artists as "bungler[s] . . . half-taught enthusiast[s, and] idle trifler[s]."[53] This came at a high price. At a time when patterns for home art creation were still on the rise in art magazines and books, and in which many women were making the leap from kitchen to exhibition, Van Rensselaer charged such efforts with harming not only art education, but art itself. She wrote: "There might be a truer study of art carried on in every home than the attendance at drawing classes, the dabbling in water-colors, the so-called decoration of pottery to which we are accustomed. Results that are now so often but unmixed harm to the aesthetic sense of the student, unmingled distress to the eye of every educated observer, would be exchanged for very positive blessings. [By abandoning them] the world would be saved a vast quantity of untrained and false, and therefore contaminating, art. We should be spared the grotesque trophies of many sorts we know so well. And perhaps before a great while it would be impossible to find ladies capable of thinking themselves innocently, yea, even worthily, employed in sticking colored pictures on ginger-jars and drain-pipe,—capable of calling the burlesque effect 'decorative art.'"[54]

This definition excluded much of what was most vital about the "field of art" in the postwar decades. While contemporaries worked to join "amateur" and "professional," "fine" and "decorative," and "center" and "periphery," Van Rensselaer argued that the only appropriate relationship of the public to art was the consumption of artworks that had already met the approval of professional critics, made by artists who could claim membership in a "profession" that discriminated severely against women, and available for viewing and consumption only in metropolitan centers. Amateur artistic labor, and the institutions that supported it, were seen by Van Rensselaer to inflict harm upon American art and perpetuate delusions among those who clung to it. In the professionalizing art world of Mariana Van Rensselaer and Clarence Cook, those who thought otherwise were not artists, but fools.

"No Similar Lines in Nature"

In his 1939 essay "Avant-Garde and Kitsch," Clement Greenberg offered American readers a powerfully resonant vision of art's place in modern culture. He argued that historical self-awareness, sparked by the political and social turmoil of mid-nineteenth-century Europe, had given birth to an entirely new kind of artistic movement: the avant-garde. Preoccupied with the rise of European fascism and the hegemony of an insipid, propagandistic social realism in the Soviet Union, Greenberg presented the avant-garde as the only force that had been able "to keep culture *moving* in the midst of ideological confusion and violence."[55] Yet, although Greenberg presented historical conditions as the avant-garde's ultimate cause, he argued that the new movement had countered the decadence of the modern era by turning away from historical and social concerns and by abandoning representational content entirely in search of purely aesthetic truths. "Retiring from public altogether," Greenberg wrote, "the avant-garde poet or artist sought to maintain the high level of his art both by narrowing and raising it to the expression of an absolute."[56] Shifting rapidly from description to imperative, he apotheosized this turn away from history: "Content is to be dissolved so completely into form," he urged, "that the work of art or literature cannot be reduced in whole or in part to anything not itself."[57]

In the middle of the twentieth century, Greenberg provided a definition, a history, and a blueprint for modernism that would dominate American art for decades to come. First, by associating the modernist avant-garde with the struggle against "ideological confusion," as Serge Guilbaut has shown, Greenberg cranked the critical engine that propelled American painting and American modernism into the center of the international spotlight for the first time in its history.[58] More than that, however, Greenberg also formalized the place of a particular kind of art object within the modernist framework, positing the artwork that was "valid solely on its own terms, in the way nature itself is valid, in the way a landscape is valid, something given, increate [*sic*], independent of meanings, similars, or originals" as the only true challenger to both cultural decadence and ideological violence.[59]

As a definition of the modernist work of art, Greenberg's view is certainly compelling. With some notable exceptions, the defining attribute of the modernist artwork has been its claim to irreducibility, and the modernist imperative has been to produce works whose meaning does not derive from their adequacy as facsimiles of the nonfictive world but from their adherence to the same standards as "real" things. As William Carlos Williams demanded, "Now works of art . . . must be real, not 'realism,' but reality itself."[60] As a historical explanation of the emergence of this kind of work, however, Greenberg's account merely muddied the waters first stirred by early modernists. An echo of early vanguardist descriptions of their project as a revolutionary assault on the past, Greenberg's emphasis on the vague political roots of the modernist object merely perpetuated the legend of modernism as a revolutionary break from history.

If the emergence of modernism—defined, in shorthand, as the confluence of abstraction and irreducibility—cannot be attributed purely to a reaction against ideology, then, how can it be explained? One possibility lies within the other half of Greenberg's theory: that modernism was a response to internal imperatives (the "search for absolutes") within the history of painting itself. Until recently, this was the most commonly held view, and it is still one that deserves attention. Particularly if one allows for a broadly contextual view of the history of art—one which includes not only painting, but also printmaking and the decorative arts—then it is obvious that modernism in the United States did emerge as a response to formal and technical issues that emerged over the course of the nineteenth century. In granting the continued relevance of this kind of explanation, however, it is crucial to recognize the impact not only of the canon of French, German, or even Japanese painting or prints, but even less likely sources. Who can say, for example, that the highly popular art of psalligraphy or silhouette cutting did not have an impact on future artists? Like Japanese prints and decorative arts, and like arts and crafts printing, this widely popular pastime taught Americans to see nature in flat, conventionalized, semiabstract forms (fig. 59). As can be seen from an instructional manual published by Prang—it included a pair of scissors, as well as instructions and sample designs—this activity also taught readers to *render* nature in this way. While the question of psalligraphy's influence is beyond the scope of this book, it is suggestive of how the multimedia origins of modernist aesthetics might be pursued.

There is an additional possibility. It is that modernist aesthetics issued not only from painting, sculpture, or even the decorative and graphic arts, but also from a *critical* environment that was itself being transformed by the pressures of modernization. In other words, it is possible to suggest that modernist aesthetics, on some level, preceded modern art. The postwar art world was marked not only by changes within art, but also by a developing struggle between two competing models of criticism and art-world practice: a model that emphasized institutional development, that prized interchangeable multiples as well as authentic originals, and that sought to grant a significant measure of art-world sovereignty to the public and other nonprofessionals; and a professionalizing model that sought to promote the authority of experts as the key to artistic development. Aesthetics proved to be a powerful weapon in this struggle. For as critics worked to bolster their authority by direct claims to expertise, they also made a second, supporting set of ontological claims about art itself that replaced artistic labor and easily circulated, reproducible images with irreducible originals as the only "true" art.

It is in this regard, rather than as legitimators of already existing modernist artworks, that American art writers—even, perhaps, before American artists—first embraced arguments for abstraction and for a turn, in

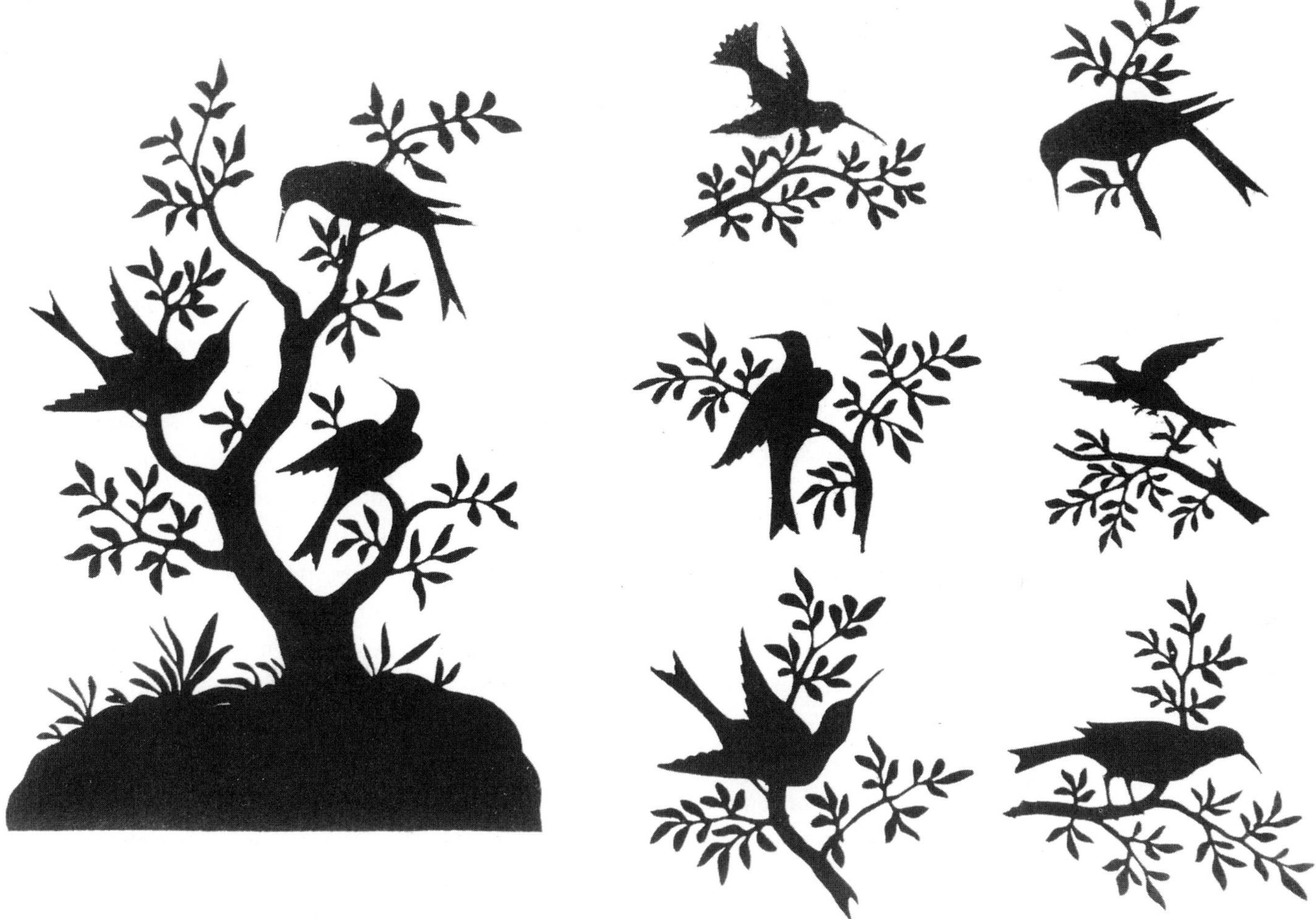

59. Design from George Schmidt, *Method of Teaching the Art of Psalligraphy by Self-Instruction* (Boston: L. Prang & Co., [1868]). American Antiquarian Society, Worcester, Massachusetts

Greenberg's phrase, "away from [the] subject matter of common experience."[61] Rewriting contemporaries' fondness for reproductions, literal transcriptions, restorations, and other insufficiently authentic productions as a taste for (at best) junk and (at worst) fraud, postwar critics established the authentic art object as the paragon of artistic worth. At the same time that critics' focus on difficult and esoteric objects helped to make the case for modernism, it also helped critics to legitimate their own existence as interpreters. Using art objects as their quarry, professionalizing critics did not just question whether the public could be made a full partner in America's cultural enterprise, but contested even the desirability of developing and maintaining shared cultural and artistic beliefs. Arguing that artistic standards were by their nature separate and distinct from commonsense norms of belief and practice, professional critics opened the door to a brand of modernism that valued iconoclasm among its chief virtues. Thus drawing sharp distinctions between professional and amateur, critics reified the division between the producers and consumers of art, promoting both a new degree of consumerism within high culture and an understanding of artists as isolated producers. As conceived, articulated, and enacted by Gilded Age critics, professionalism became not only a parent to modernism but a bulwark to cultural hierarchy in early-twentieth-century America.

Cook and Van Rensselaer both used straightforward appeals to authority to promote professional criticism and a professionalized art world, implicitly and explicitly rejecting models promoted by Prang, the *Art Amateur*, and even Koehler, for whom Van Rensselaer wrote in the 1880s. The heart of their argument, however, was aesthetic. It turned on two points: first, making the evaluation of artworks, rather than the support of institutions, the primary focus of criticism; and second, developing narrower standards with which to make such evaluations. A central part of their aesthetics was a challenge to the legitimacy of reproductions, imitations, and restorations, and the corollary definition of "art" as unique, irreducible, and authentic art objects. By promoting an aesthetic that valued authenticity and authentic objects, and that denigrated copies, professionalizing critics not only demonstrated their critical prowess, but also questioned the legitimacy of one of the most familiar and most accessible points of entry into the American art world.

The turn to aesthetic solutions for professional problems had unforeseen consequences for art itself. While bolstering critics' status as professional arbiters of public judgment, the aesthetic of the authentic, irreducible object proved to have lasting power in its own right. Initially promoted as a tool to foster the authority of professional critics to judge art, the aesthetics of authenticity eventually transformed American understanding of art so thoroughly and so completely that it is difficult to imagine what the art world looked like before its emergence. Professionalizing criticism promoted a proto-modernist aesthetics of authenticity on two levels. By undermining the legitimacy of common, everyday experience as a guide to artistic judgment, critics delegitimized representation as an aesthetic goal. By devaluing easily accessible but inauthentic works, moreover, they solidified the hegemony of difficult and esoteric objects. In this way, Cook and Van Rensselaer supplanted fidelity to the visible world with adherence to internal constraints within art itself as the primary standard for artistic production and judgment, and thus paved the way for the emergence of modernism in the United States.

As we have seen, copies were widely embraced by art publishers across the spectrum, including Prang, Koehler, and Drake. But Cook and Van Rensselaer questioned their legitimacy with increasing vehemence. They challenged the aesthetic merit of copies on two levels. First, they assailed reproductions of artworks, arguing that artistic value resided in original artworks and could not be lifted and transferred onto reproductions. Second, they began to question representation itself, arguing that artworks derived their value not by the faithful imitation of external reality, but by adhering to internal principles and processes within art itself. For both critics, these two arguments nourished and complemented each other, intertwining in a pointed attack on the goals and practices of the contemporary institution-building art world.[62]

Cook was initially suspicious of the value of casts and other reproductions as pedagogical tools. As a founding participant in the Ruskin-influenced Society for the Advancement of Truth in Art in the 1860s, and as editor of the *New Path*, Cook advocated study from nature as an antidote to training based on the "blind copying of other men's copies," a position which echoed that of many artists. Cook's concerns soon began to extend beyond pedagogy. Even in the mid-1860s, Cook commanded the public to "stop buying line engravings, copper-plates, etchings. . . . More pleasure, and of a more enduring kind, more love of Nature, more understanding of the real uses of Art, will flow to you out of one . . . drawing . . . than from all the Raphael Morghens, or Stranges, or Marc Antonios, that were ever sold to deluded buyers."[63] True artistic value, Cook argued, emanated from original, unique artworks. Those who thought otherwise were not beneficiaries of an expanding national interest in art, but victims of a pernicious fraud.

Although he was critical of etchings and other engravings, Cook's greatest ire was reserved for chromolithographs, which in the vast majority of cases were reproductions of paintings. In his judgment, chromolithographs were an excrescence; their cheapness and popularity only compounded their repulsiveness. Cook repeatedly attacked Prang, for instance, for "the pretension he makes to other ends in his business than the one legitimate end of selling to the best advantage. He is a trader, and a clever one, but he is nothing more, and his pretending to be something more, a connoisseur, a philanthropist, a teacher of the people, is displeasing to us, because it is merely a trick in trade."[64]

If Cook cast his argument against chromolithography as an attack on Prang's character, he also assailed the character of chromolithographs. Chromolithographs, he argued, could never educate the population because they were not themselves legitimate artworks.[65] Cook did not wish wholly to prevent the reproduction of images, as long as reproductions did not go by the name of "Art."[66] Rather, chromolithography's deception resided in its claim to be something, or at least to be like something, other than itself.[67] "Every art," he wrote,

> has its own independent field of work, and . . . nothing is gained by trying to imitate in one process the legitimate results of another. . . . Mr. Prang prides himself on having published imitations of oil paintings that will deceive even good judges. He uses a paper that is made to look

> precisely like canvas, and copies the strokes of the artist's brush. . . . Chromo-lithography is not Art at all, and we repeat it. It is a mere mechanic process, and one with a very useful, but a very narrow legitimate field. Its business is simply to reproduce, not to imitate—meaning by "imitation," "deception." It is the proper business of no art or process to deceive—any more than it is the business of a tongue to lie.[68]

Like Walter Benjamin, who would argue a half-century later that mechanical reproduction had transformed conventional definitions of art, "detach[ing] the reproduced object from the domain of tradition" and shattering the "aura" that had surrounded original artworks, Cook recognized that reproductive technologies had the capacity to alter completely the rules by which art was experienced and evaluated.[69] Where Benjamin would see the potential for liberation, however, Cook saw the makings of disaster. His response to mechanical reproduction, thus, was to contend that the "business" of art was not the imitation of things (in this case, artworks) but adherence to rules and constraints determined by the artistic process in which a producer worked. This definition ruled out not only slavish copies of the natural world, but also works that got away from the true formal principles of their own medium ("imitat[ing] in one process the legitimate results of another"). By making and disseminating copies under the name of art, Cook argued, Prang blurred Americans' critical sense, encouraging them to evaluate artworks on the basis of their faithfulness to external originals, rather than on their adherence to a particularized formal practice. Or, in more blunt terms, Prang taught Americans "to admire what is false."[70]

The hostility of certain late-nineteenth-century observers to the technology of mechanical reproduction is well documented. Perhaps most famously, E. L. Godkin wrote:

> A society of ignoramuses who know they are ignoramuses, might lead a tolerably happy and useful existence, but a society of ignoramuses each of whom thinks he is a Solon, would be an approach to Bedlam let loose, and something analogous to this may really be seen to-day in some parts of this country. A large body of persons has arisen, under the influence of the common-schools, magazines, newspapers, and the rapid acquisition of wealth, who are not only engaged in enjoying themselves after their fashion, but who firmly believe that they have reached, in the matter of social, mental, and moral culture, all that is attainable or desirable by anybody, and who therefore tackle all the problems of the day—men's, women's, and children's rights and duties, marriage, education, suffrage, life, death, and immortality—with supreme indiffer-

ence to what anybody else thinks or has ever thought. . . . The result is a kind of mental and moral chaos.[71]

Godkin's attack on chromolithography is usually explained as the product of growing class antagonism in the cultural sphere, and his comments are taken to represent the conservative cultural views of the declining Brahmin elite. To some extent, this is true. Godkin's views, and his career, were inextricably linked to those of his friend, Harvard professor and *Nation* cofounder Charles Eliot Norton. Nonetheless, this explanation is not entirely satisfactory.[72] For one thing, Godkin's antipathy toward chromos did not reflect the views of most elite consumers, at least when he first expressed it in the 1870s. Until Godkin, Cook, and others began to undermine it, the taste for chromos—like the taste for prints generally—was pervasive among the elite. Fighting the "chromo-civilization" meant fighting not only middle- and working-class consumers of chromos, but also Prang's many elite defenders like Charles Sumner, Thomas Wentworth Higginson, and Harriet Beecher Stowe.

Second, Godkin himself was not, by birth, a representative of either the Brahmin or the industrial elite; like Prang, Koehler, Keppel, and Macbeth, Godkin was an immigrant, in his case from County Wicklow, Ireland. As his biographer notes, the journalist went out of his way to disguise this fact, representing himself as "English" despite the fact that his family had been in Ireland for centuries—and despite the fact that his father, James Godkin, was a well-known campaigner for religious toleration and land reform in Ireland. Instead of representing the Brahmin or industrial elites, Godkin represented the interests of an emergent intelligentsia that he himself, and others like him, were helping to create—and that, like other professional and managerial elites, emerged directly from the wider crisis of authority ushered in by industrialization.

In other words, Godkin and Cook—a Harvard graduate who saw himself as "a man with no name at all (to speak of!)"—were cultural entrepreneurs, whose efforts to shape public opinion intertwined with the desire to create a *new* cadre of middle-class, reformist cultural critics. In some cases, this meant taking for themselves the causes of older liberal elites, such as racial equality and anti-imperialism. In others, it meant exposing the tastes of those elites as fraudulent, in order to create and control new hierarchies. Attacks on the chromo-civilization were a part of this campaign. So, too, was Cook's critique of engraving, whose target was not just a favorite of the middle class, but elite viewers like Sumner, who spent his convalescence after his infamous attack in the Senate exploring the Gray Collection. The engravers Raphael Morghen and Robert Strange, for example, whom Cook singled out for censure, were much admired by the senator, not least because of their abilities as copyists. Sumner was so inspired by engraving, in fact, that he wrote a treatise entitled *The Best Portraits in Engraving*, edited by Longfellow and published by Frederick Keppel.[73] In it, Sumner wrote that Strange "has a style of his own, which, soft and especially charming in the tints of flesh, [makes] him a natural translator of Titian," and that "a work of [Raphael], or any of the great masters, is better in an engraving of Longhi or Morghen than in any ordinary copy, and would probably cost more in the market. A good engraving is an undoubted work of art, but this cannot be said of many pictures, which, like Peter Pindar's razors, seem made only to sell."[74]

Cook and Godkin's campaigns against imitation and circulation thus did not represent a straightforward conservatism, or the interests of existing elites who supported art-world development. Rather, the attack on reproductions represented a plea for something slightly different: the domination by experts—"a jury of connoisseurs," as the *Nation* put it—over nonprofessionals, and the replacement of the cultural values of the nation as a whole, *including* the wealthy, the genteel, and the "cultured," by professional standards of judgment.[75] Indeed, Cook and Godkin seem deliberately to have challenged cultural forms and figures—like engraving and chromolithography—that were popular not just among the working and middle classes but among elite viewers like Sumner. One of the purposes of this challenge, I would suggest, was precisely to destabilize cross-class allegiances on matters of art.

This helps to explain why Cook did not just reject copies after what he saw as worthless, polluting originals—"strawberries-in-the-cabbage-leaves, upset cherries, Easter mornings, cats-with-work-baskets, chickens-forever, Magdalenas, and the rest"—but also reproductions of works, like those of Leonardo da Vinci, that he could not criticize on these grounds.[76] He blasted Leonardo's "hold on people who know nothing about art, and care nothing for it except as it is mixed up with their beliefs. They are drawn to him with a double sense, as a man far ahead of his time in his scientific tendencies, and a useful inventor, and for having painted a picture that can be accepted by people with a reasonable religion, hung up in their parlors, and given out in cheap reproductions as a prize to subscribers in their newspapers."[77] Cook's objection, then, was not to Leonardo's work, or even to the public's taste in itself. Rather, Cook condemned the standards and processes of judgment that produced that taste—to the fact that Americans used common sense rather than professional standards for judging artworks, and consequently valued the artist's qualities over the qualities of his works. For Cook, the problem with copies, like "paintings which draw the beholder by some interest more tangible to the common sense," was that they encouraged viewers to use inappropriate standards for judging art—profit, personal experience, social "reputation." Copies, in other words, allowed audiences to embrace the exact opposite of what Cook believed was necessary to create a flourishing American art based on works "which are purely pictorial": professional standards, based on aesthetic and art-world norms, devised and enforced by expert, critical professionals.

Cook's concern about imitation did not merely extend to reproductions; it turned into a deeper anxiety about representation itself. Although his critique of casts and other reproductions initially had been made in the name of a more sincere form of representation, nature alone would not hold Cook's interest forever. By the end of the 1860s, he had begun to turn away from a model of artistic authenticity based on natural appearances, expressing increasing skepticism toward artists whose methods relied on "too much hard, scientific work" and who had "shown no power to get beneath the surface of things." Five years later, Cook moved firmly toward an aesthetic that valued the intrinsic qualities of artworks over their referential and imitative aspects, disparaging "the purely materialistic school of art, by which we mean the school that believes in emphasizing all the externalities, bestowing more love and labor on a bit of tapestry or wall-paper . . . and troubles itself very little about an idea, or an imagination, or a feeling, in comparison with mere mechanical execution."[78] By this time, Cook had begun to question the legitimacy of representation itself in its most obvious forms.

One sign of this was Cook's ongoing effort to distinguish between artworks and "records." He greatly admired Mathew Brady's Civil War photographs, even calling them "art." Yet, Cook described these images as memory devices, rather than art objects, avoiding his usual attention to formal qualities and praising them solely on the basis of their historical value. They were, he wrote, "a condensed historical library; such a one as, for completeness, thoroughness, and accuracy, was never before made, [which] will give Mr. Brady a proud place among the men who have done their country honor by the part they played in her trial." A similar logic governed Cook's discussions of portraits of Lincoln. He breathed a sigh of relief that many photographs existed to combat the painted record of Lincoln's face. He wrote: "We take a good deal of comfort in the reflection that the counterfeit presentment of so good and wise a man as Abraham Lincoln is not to be at the mercy of any one or any half dozen of our professed portrait painters. That blunt truth-teller, the Sun, has recorded his face and figure so often and so well that the man's bodily presence is placed forever beyond the chances of fatal misrepresentation."[79]

This distinction did not derive solely from photography, moreover, as Cook argued that works in other media could fail as art and still retain their value as records.[80] Thus, he applauded F. B. Carpenter's

Emancipation Proclamation before the Cabinet (date and location unknown) even though "as a work of art—a piece of painting, Mr. Carpenter's picture was far from being a masterly work. But, as we have said, this was a secondary consideration in this case. What was essential was that we should have the facts."[81] Similarly, he refused to give a wholly positive assessment of Thomas Moran's *Chasm of the Colorado* (1873–74; Smithsonian American Art Museum, Washington, D.C.). He did admire certain aspects of the painting. Moran "has done us all a scientific service, and we admit that the work on this score was well worth doing," Cook wrote. "But no artist we have is better aware than Mr. Moran that, to do this alone, is not to make a picture, it is to make a map; and he meant to make not a map, but a picture." While "having the facts" was enough for maps or historical records, it did not make a painting or a photograph a true work of art.[82]

To be sure, Cook never completely broke with representation. Like so many of his counterparts both before and after the modernist divide, Cook continued to find redemption in the landscape, even while questioning its mere replication in the name of art. But Cook counseled artists to search for the formal truths underlying surface appearances, even when this meant stripping away visible details in order to paint form coherently.[83] Describing minute renderings of the surfaces of things as "tricks which have prevailed to set our uncritical public agape with admiring wonder, and keep the facile pens of certain critics busy with ridiculous praise," Cook celebrated works whose adherence to internal rules made them less immediately comprehensible to most viewers.[84] Thus, a "remarkable" winter scene painted by John La Farge, "glanced at casually, among other pictures . . . would not attract a moment's attention from the average amateur. Yet, as we let our eyes fall into it, the impression becomes increasingly stronger that there is invention in it, somewhere. That is, we are not altogether sure that Mr. La Farge saw just this, and no more, no less, out of his window, and then sat down to match the different parts, with carefully mixed colors; on the contrary, we get a feeling that he has developed this little reverie of faint tones as a tender fantasy, improvising, as he went on, turns and inflections of hue, as they became necessary to the general harmony."[85]

Here, Cook's argument foreshadowed Dow's claim, almost twenty years later, that he had not *represented* nature but used it to create "a purely imaginative treatment as brilliant and unreal as stained glass."[86] It is perhaps not an accident that Cook produced this argument when writing about John La Farge, who was as well known for his works in glass as on canvas. Yet, Cook's argument differed from Dow's, in that its emergent argument against representation was joined to a disparagement of "the average amateur," who in Cook's assessment would be unable to comprehend the image's irreducibility.

Van Rensselaer's critique of imitation was even more far-reaching than Cook's; it too was based on the idea that each artistic medium possessed unique qualities that distinguished it from the others. This can be seen in her discussions of etching. As she explained, a key "claim of etched work—one which is less easy to explain in words, however, and which cannot be fully understood from the wood-cut reproductions here put before the reader—lies in the fact that the lines obtained by it differ vastly in kind from those obtained by any other engraver's process. . . . Moreover, an etched line, of whatever degree of strength or delicacy, has a peculiar quality of its own."[87] Thus, she argued, etchings should not be evaluated by their faithfulness as representations or reproductions. Instead, "we shall prize most highly those prints in which [etching's] characteristic qualities are most perfectly exhibited, its limitations most loyally respected—since . . . an art is at its best when most thoroughly *itself*."[88] Indeed, Van Rensselaer argued, the search for etching's "characteristic qualities" necessarily led artists to deviate from representation: "Many facts in every theme must be omitted." The alternative to this process of selection was "too much useless elaboration, too little abstraction and condensation."[89] Put another way, "the etcher who can say a great deal with a few lines, who can suggest much while explaining, elaborating very little, is by this fact a greater etcher than the one who, to say as much, to suggest as much, needs many lines and full explanations."[90]

Like Cook's assertion that "every art has its own independent field of work, and . . . nothing is gained by trying to imitate in one process the legitimate results from another," Van Rensselaer's argument that art was "at its best" when it respected the rules of its own media foreshadowed one of Greenberg's main claims about "non-representational or 'abstract'" art: that it "must stem from obedience to some worthy constraint" and must "eliminat[e] from the effects of each art any and every effect that might conceivably be borrowed from . . . the medium of any other art." While her theory was never as fully articulated as either Greenberg's or Dow's, it did come close to presenting etching as an abstract art: or, in her words, the "translation into expressive linear language of something which has shown no similar lines in nature."[91]

Like Cook's critique of imitation, Van Rensselaer's analysis combined a plea for formalist authenticity with an appeal to her own critical authority. The appeal of etching was not "easy to explain in words." Even worse, it could not "be fully understood from the wood-cut reproductions here put before the reader." Like Cook's attacks on reproductions—and like her own comments on the dangers of "untrained" seeing—such arguments pointed to an unwillingness to release interpretative secrets to the public, a jealousy that could be supported by the adoption of particular aesthetic positions. The misappreciation of art was not the only bad result

Van Rensselaer feared. She also argued that the public's misconceived embrace of imitation had negatively affected the making of art, by leading artists to twist and warp their productions in an imitative and false direction. The public's admiration for imitation had forced many artists to adopt the "aims and methods . . . of the reproductive workman," a situation that debased the medium and drove it from its true purpose. "As a consequence—a natural and necessary consequence, and one with which we have not the smallest right to reproach our artists—many men who could etch and who have etched in the most purely etcher-like way are now beginning to etch in what I may call a pictorial way. We need not reproach them, I say; we have but ourselves to thank."[92] Van Rensselaer's use of "we" in this exhortation was most likely euphemistic.

I do not mean to suggest that these critics disparaged the public entirely or claimed that ordinary Americans had no role in the art world. Professions do not spread their authority merely by diminishing outsiders, but by appealing to them; it would not have served the interests of criticism to argue that the public could never make advances in taste and cultivation. At the same time, if critics granted too much autonomy to nonprofessional viewers, they risked losing their own authority as critics. The challenge for critics, then, was to provide a model of public participation in the art world that was both appealing and limiting at the same time. For Van Rensselaer, abstraction provided a neat solution to this dilemma. Because it severed any direct relationship between everyday visual experience and the world within the picture frame, Van Rensselaer's promotion of abstraction as a guiding aesthetic principle easily provided limits upon public comprehension. Abstraction, quite simply, was difficult stuff. She wrote: "One of the chief temptations which assail an artist in our day is the temptation to make a show of boldness and rapidity . . . if the real things are not at his command—to work in a rough and careless or pretentious way, which, with untrained eyes, may pass for the freedom and vigor and breadth of a master hand. And as etching is an art where freedom is especially prized, and where from the strictly interpretative nature of the method, the public may find it difficult to distinguish between an almost arbitrary yet truthful and brilliant interpretation of nature . . . and a 'free' but meaningless scribble on the copper,—it [is] to be feared that our young etchers might fall into sins of a careless or pretentious sort."

While freedom from the constraints of everyday vision had the potential to liberate and transform American art, it presented difficulty and danger, as well. For willing consumers, abstraction could provide untold aesthetic riches. For the unwary, it could also offer disappointment at the hands of artistic cheats. What made the situation even more dire was that viewers could be played for fools without even realizing it, because in the new and strange world of abstraction the differences between truth and meaninglessness were nearly impossible to detect. Luckily, Van Rensselaer was willing to step into the breach, reassuring her readers that artists had not yet made the fateful turn to trickery and that "trained eyes"—critics like herself—would keep artists honest. In so doing, she reasserted her capacity, as a professional critic, to make confident assertions of truth and falsehood when the public could not, again offering the public worry-free consumption and guaranteed taste as alternatives to active participation as judges and makers of the nation's art.

Irreducible Objects

As Cook and Van Rensselaer's acerbic descriptions of Prang and the NYSDA suggest, one of the reasons professionalism came into conflict with institution-building models of art-world practice is that professional critics explicitly adopted an adversarial approach. This is especially true of Cook, who became embroiled in yet another art-world controversy in 1882. This time, his opponent was the director of the Metropolitan Museum of Art, Luigi Palma di Cesnola. Cesnola had been under scrutiny since 1880, when numismatics expert and dealer Gaston Feuardent charged that Cesnola had improperly altered some of the works in the Cesnola Collection of Cypriote antiquities, which the director had "discovered" and sold to the museum himself. The museum responded by appointing a committee of inquiry, which exonerated Cesnola in 1881, hoping the controversy would die quickly. It did not. The next year, Feuardent filed a libel suit that resulted in a highly public trial. It was at this time that Cook entered the fray, after a period of hesitation that can be attributed to the fact that Cook's employer, the *Tribune*, had taken a virulently anti-Feuardent position. Cook's main contribution to the small but growing anti-Cesnola camp was a brief, but highly inflammatory, pamphlet published by Feuardent, entitled *Transformations and Migrations of Certain Statues in the Cesnola Collection*.[93]

Cesnola was an entrepreneur whose position as an art-world leader came only after a series of other careers, each of which he used to promote his next venture.[94] Italian by birth, he was expelled from military service in his native country for unmentioned indiscretions. Cesnola then migrated to New York in 1858, where he endured hardship and poverty and eked out a living teaching Italian to New York ladies. Making good use of the coming Civil War, he gave up this job to set up a cavalry school, and entered the Union army as leader of the Fourth New York Regiment. Inventing the title "General" for himself, after the war Cesnola was able to talk himself into the position of consul at Larnaca, in Cyprus, where he remade himself into an archaeological adventurer. His archaeological activities included the "discovery" of two major hoards, first at Golgos in

1870, and the second at Curium in 1875. Cesnola was hardly a model of archaeological scruple. He treated even legitimate sites very roughly and was not above inventing discoveries when it suited him. As it turned out, he wholly fabricated the Curium treasure, amassing the hoard from other digs and from traders.

While Cesnola's activities were dubious, they turned out to be quite lucrative. He used both the objects he acquired and his reputation as a discoverer to secure a profitable livelihood. Capitalizing on a developing public interest in archaeology, he cultivated the press, which was quick to cast him as an Italian-American Schliemann. He also courted well-connected figures in the art world like the Metropolitan trustees John Taylor Johnston and William Prime, and the writer Bayard Taylor.[95] As a result, Cesnola was able not only to sell both of his hoards to the Metropolitan—at a price of $140,000 in all—but to convince them to employ him to unpack and arrange them, as well.[96] In 1879, he was hired to become the director of the Metropolitan, at a salary of $5000 per year.[97] Cesnola went on to be one of the museum's longest-serving heads, keeping his position until his death in 1904.

The trustees could not have known that Cesnola's appointment, and the accession of his collection, would result in such unpleasant attention. Indeed, one of the critics who had most actively called upon the Metropolitan to acquire the collection was Clarence Cook, who hailed John Taylor Johnston's eventual decision to do so as an international art coup. "If there should be any educated person in any field who is ignorant of the nature of the Collection, or who hesitates to take our word as to its value," Cook wrote in 1874, "we would refer him to the journals of the learned societies the world over, to the communications of the most learned and scholarly men in England, France, Germany, Italy and America, who, without a dissenting voice, have declared that so great a treasure as this has not been unearthed in modern times."[98] In response, Cesnola cited Cook's initial commentary on his collection as his personal favorite.[99]

Cook's bitterness at his own complicity in Cesnola's publicity efforts may have contributed to the critic's animosity. Nonetheless, Cook tried to present his objections as professional, rather than personal. As in his earlier criticism, he distinguished between his own adherence to a model of art-world practice based on "disinterest," rather than on profit, reputation, or other external standards. Indeed, he was very critical of the museum for failing to censure Cesnola, and for allowing the director to continue in his position. Cook represented this as evidence of the museum's insularity and clubbishness: the committee, as he pointed out, was composed of three men chosen by the museum and two selected by those three, including two trustees, the president of Columbia University (who had been present at the museum's inception) and a relative of Cesnola publicist and confidant Hiram Hitchcock.[100] Cook's critique was intended, then, not only to expose fraudulent artworks, but also to set an example of proper art-world behavior. To be fair, Cook's charge of clubbishness was not wholly misplaced. Although the trustees genuinely seem to have been unmoved by Feuardent's criticism of Cesnola, they cannot have been pleased at the negative publicity generated by the case. A desire to shield the museum from embarrassment certainly must have played a role in their decision to appoint a committee with such close ties to the institution. Moreover, Cook paid a heavy price for his stance, eventually losing his job over it.[101]

In making his case against Cesnola, the first objection Cook voiced was to the director's "cruel and ignorant treatment" of the works during the excavation, which was the cause of their generally poor state. More than this, however, Cook was absolutely horrified by Cesnola's response to their destruction, which seemingly was to create new figures haphazardly out of the assorted rubble.[102] To Cook, this decision was unforgivable, in that it resulted in the production of monstrous amalgams like "Statue No. 39" (fig. 60) and No. 157, a statuette with a mirror that seemed to have been recently added.[103] According to Cook, this prevented observers from obtaining a true understanding of the art of ancient Cyprus; as gallingly, it had led to the waste of experts' time: "Knowing as he does now the fraudulent character of the whole collection of Cypriote antiquities," Cook mused, "how must Mr. Feuardent regret the time he has spent, in common with many others, in trying to classify these statues and statuettes." Like chromos, these fraudulent artworks filled Cook with rage. Joining the debate over whether No. 157 was, as Feuardent claimed, a statue of Hope, or, following Cesnola, that it represented Venus, Cook had another response. "Fraud," he concluded, "is the only name for this sorry figure, and all the other sculptures in the collection are her brothers and sisters."[104]

In the main, Cook used two sorts of evidence to prove the impropriety of Cesnola's behavior. First (and somewhat ironically), he used mechanical reproductions that had been made during the objects' wanderings in Cyprus, Europe, and New York to show that the statues had changed dramatically over time. Second, he used the direct accounts of knowledgeable witnesses, including himself, to demonstrate not only that the objects had been materially altered, but also to show that this had been done knowingly and at Cesnola's behest. One particularly damning narrative came from fellow art writer Earl Shinn, who, Cook wrote, "was walking about the Museum with Mr. di Cesnola, when his penetrating eye observed that one of the statues had . . . one finger-joint too many. This superfluity . . . was pointed out to Mr. di Cesnola by Mr. Shinn, and the

Migrations and Transformations of a Statue in the Metropolitan Museum

"*My answer is: In the entire collection I have not made a single restoration object in stone. . . .*"—CESNOLA before the Committee, Jan

1

STATUE No. 39.

As described by Mr. Hiram Hitchcock in *Harper's Magazine* for July, 1872. The head alone, with its "benignant face," to use the words of Mr. Hitchcock, is figured in the *Magazine*.

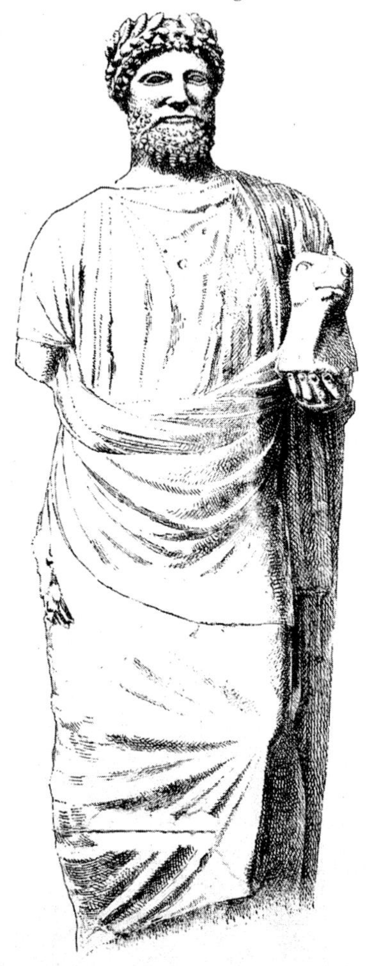

The body of this statue is made up of unrelated fragments: as a partial test, let the reader endeavor to connect the broken right arm with the portion of a hand attached to the thigh. This cannot be done without bending the arm. But the arm is not bent, it hangs down straight. Mr. Hitchcock tells us that Cesnola, in writing to him about the discovery, says he found the statue at Salamis. In the description nothing is said about the *feet*.

2

STATUE No. 39.

As represented in Doell's *Sammlung Cesnola* published in 1873. This is an exact copy of Doell's lithograph which, he says, he made "with great care" from Cesnola's own photograph of the statue.

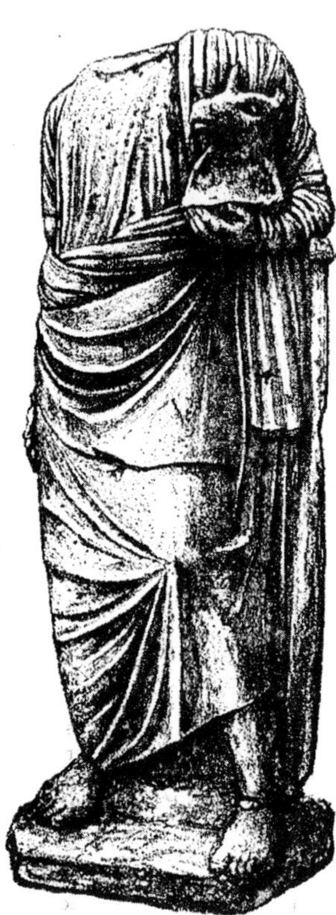

Remark the feet, legs, and base, and the absence of the head. When Hitchcock describes the statue from the photograph sent him by Cesnola, he places most emphasis on the head with its "benignant face." When Doell sees the statue, the head is no longer attached to the body, nor does he know that they were ever supposed to belong to one another. Doell places the body of this statue in the "good Greek" group. The head he calls "archaic." In the text, he says the statue was found at Golgoï, but in the preface, having probably read in Mr. Hitchcock's article in *Harper's Magazine*, that it was found at Salamis, he cautiously says that the responsibility for the information regarding the localities quoted in this book, rests solely with General di Cesnola.

3

STATUE No. 39.

As exhibited in the Museum in Fourteenth Street, from a photograph taken by Pach in 1874-1878.

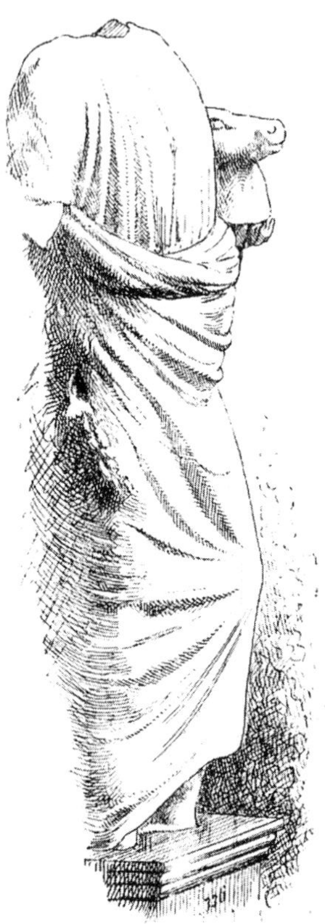

Remark the absence of the head, feet and base In the *Guide to the Cesnola Collection*, publishec by the Trustees of the Museum in 1876, this statue without head, feet, or base—though, as we have just seen, it once had them all—is numbered 33 and is classed as belonging to the Græco-Roma period—no longer, as in Doell, to the "good Greek period—and the head, numbered 217 is classed a "archaic." No mention is now made of Salamis the statue is classified among the Golgoï find.

head of the restoring room was immediately called up to set things straight. Then and there the offending joint was removed, the stump was shaped into a finger tip, and the superfluous joint was left on the floor of the case, where I have several times seen it."[105]

For Cook, this was too much to take. And it *is* an astonishing story. It is

ew York, numbered 39 in the Catalogue.

bject or part of any
81.

4

STATUE No. 39.

In this illustration the feet, legs, and base are seen as represented in Cesnola's *Cyprus* published in 1878.

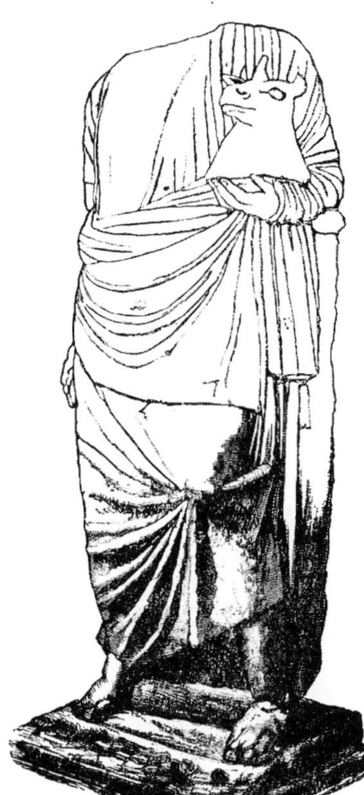

Remark the absence of the head, and the difference between the feet, legs and base of this illustration, and the same parts as shown in No. 2 from Doell. Compare also with No. 3 showing the same statue in Fourteenth Street. Cesnola in his book says the statue came from Golgoï. Says nothing about Salamis, and describes the head separately with its "benignant face," as coming from Golgoï.

5

STATUE No. 39.

Here we have the statue as it now stands in the Museum in Central Park. The illustration is from Mr. G. C. Cox's photograph on sale at the Museum.

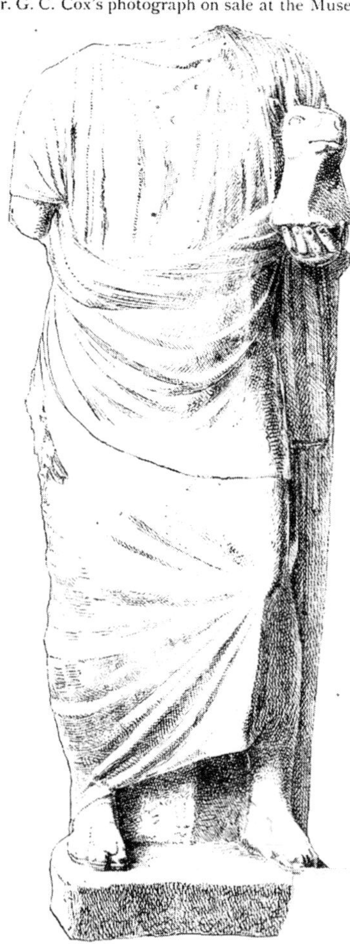

Remark the absence of the head anc
of entirely new feet, legs, and base
statue referred to by Mr. G. C. Cox i
testimony before the "Committee." ....
he himself saw the new feet made by stone-cutter, who came to the Museum for the purpose. He pointed out in Doell's illustration where the new pieces had been set in, and he told the Committee that if they would look at the photograph made by himself, and would go with him to the Museum, they could see the restoration for themselves. Mr. Cox's offer was not accepted. In the Museum Catalogue the statue is said to have been found at Golgoï.

60. "Migrations and Transformations of a Statue in the Metropolitan Museum of New York, numbered 39 in the Catalogue," 1881. From Clarence Cook, *Transformations and Migrations of Certain Statues in the Cesnola Collection* (New York: Gaston L. Feuardent, [1881?])

almost unbelievable that the director of the Metropolitan Museum of Art, not liking the number of finger joints on one of his statues, could simply have ordered it lopped off and reshaped. In the art world we currently inhabit, I think it is fair to say that this would not happen, and if it did, the perpetrator would most certainly face severe professional and legal consequences. Yet, what is perhaps even more astounding is that neither Cesnola nor the majority of his contemporaries seem to have seen this issue the way we do, at least not at first. As Cook himself argued, throughout the ordeal Cesnola could not be made to see why his actions had been objectionable; during the trial, he waved away fine distinctions between "restoration" and "repair." Indeed, as late as the 1890s, Cesnola was found directing his assistants to repaint the hooves in Rosa Bonheur's *Horse Fair* (1887; The Metropolitan Museum of Art, New York).[106]

The trustees' similar lack of conviction in the inviolability of art objects can be seen in another measure they enacted to disprove the charges against Cesnola. In the spring of 1882, they issued a curious invitation. Promising to treat the public's decision as the final word, they called upon "members of the museum, the general public, 'and especially editors of public journals, sculptors, workers in stone, and all persons interested in the truthfulness of archaeological objects . . . to make most careful examination'" of a group of the disputed sculptures. Over a period of five weeks, they expressly invited people to bring wire brushes, hammers, acid, and other tools that would prove that the statues were not fakes. Indeed, Cesnola wrote that it would be worth losing the statues entirely to the public's chisels if that would confirm their veracity and clear his reputation.[107]

This episode is significant in that it problematizes the idea of the museum as a temple to sacred objects, dominated by ideologically driven cultural entrepreneurs. The behavior of Cesnola and the trustees suggests, in fact, that Barnum's model continued to exert some influence even into the 1880s—even in an institution as "highbrow" as the Metropolitan Museum of Art. What was Cesnola's invitation, after all, but a summons to test whether the mermaid was a fake?[108] And what was Cesnola, but a chancer? He may have persistently reminded people of his lost Italian nobility, and he may have run the Metropolitan autocratically—it was under Cesnola's reign, infamously, that a plumber was turned away from the museum for appearing in overalls. And yet, it would be a mistake to see Cesnola's motives as purely, or even mainly, ideological, or to see Cesnola as any more representative of the class that controlled the museum than the Harvard-educated Cook. Cesnola's aims were venal and self-serving, but that is exactly my point: from beginning to end, Cesnola's involvement in the museum movement was motivated not by class control, but by personal gain. In this respect, his rise from the status of disgraced soldier and impoverished immigrant to a power broker who commanded the loyalty of New York's cultural elite shows his success at conning that elite as much as the hegemony of that elite over the art world.

It is also tempting to read this conflict in terms of Cook's wider arguments about authenticity. It is not possible to map the Cesnola controversy exactly onto the emerging divide between professionals and amateurs in the art press—curiously, the *Art Amateur* was among Feuardent's most consistent supporters. Nonetheless, I would argue that the controversy represents a definable point in the transition away from the aesthetics of the nineteenth century—instrumentalist, pleased with abundance, and not overly concerned with authenticity—to a modernist aesthetics that prized authenticity and irreducibility above all. This standard, which was still at the margins of American practice in the 1880s, would come to dominate the twentieth-century art world, not only proscribing actions like Cesnola's but making them unthinkable, and in the case of contemporary artworks if not antiquities, illegal.[109]

The ascent of a professionally driven, object-centered standard has had its benefits. Cook's opposition to Cesnola's Frankenstein methods may have been part of a larger agenda, but his revulsion was understandable. At the same time, the gradual erosion of institution-building standards also entailed palpable losses. The trustees' decision to play out their battle with Cesnola's detractors in the circuslike atmosphere of the public challenge may seem like a Barnumesque ploy, but it was consistent with a belief in public, rather than expert, judgment. In contrast, just as Cook's critique made it unthinkable that a museum director would violate the integrity of objects, it also guaranteed that amateurs like Cesnola or his constituencies—"members of the museum, the general public, 'and especially editors of public journals, sculptors, workers in stone, and all persons interested in the truthfulness of archaeological objects'"—would not get their hands on art again. The evolving standard of authenticity, in combination with professional models of organizing the art world, served without a doubt to undermine amateur participation in the art world as viewers and as makers.

For the moment, the emerging tensions exposed by the Cesnola controversy did not provoke a critical conflagration, and Cook's vision of an art world organized around professionalism and authenticity did not prevail. After the turn of the century, however, the brewing dispute over aesthetics, the art world, and the public's role in it would come to a head, as Americans confronted the large-scale display of modern art for the first time at the Armory Show of 1913. Although by 1913 the voices of a new generation were heard, the terms of the debate over the Armory Show and the positions of its combatants shared profound affinities to critical divisions produced in the decades following the Civil War. By successfully employing many of the aesthetic arguments and critical tools developed by critics like Cook and Van Rensselaer, a new generation of modernist critics completed a significant step in the twentieth century toward the ultimate hegemony of modernism and the ultimate end of the participatory ideal.

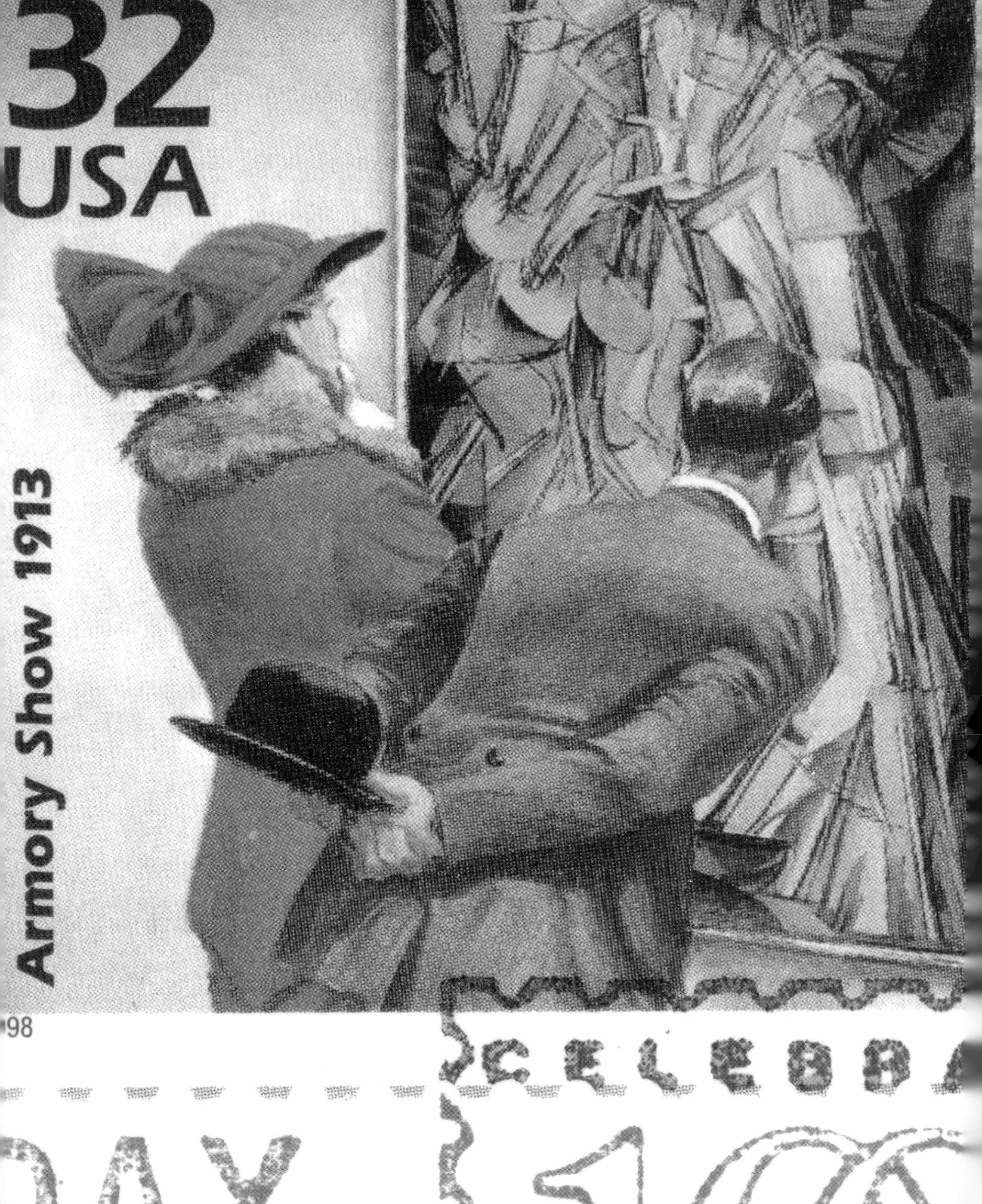
32
USA
Armory Show 1913
98
CELEB
DAY

Chapter 4

The Armory Show in Critical Perspective

It is of little importance what I or Mr. Advanced Progressive may *love* or *hate*. The important, very *important* point is, does the expression of our love or hate do harm? Does it retard the general knowledge and appreciation of art? Does it hinder development?
—Edwin H. Blashfield, 1914

Without a doubt, the most famous moment in the emergence of modernism in the United States was the 1913 International Exhibition of Modern Art, better known as the Armory Show. There is no question that the exhibition was a significant event. Arranged under the auspices of the American Association of Painters and Sculptors, it was the first large-scale exhibition of modernist art in the United States. It was arranged and masterminded by Arthur B. Davies, Walt Kuhn, and Walter Pach, who negotiated the display of approximately 1300 works, more than a third of them European, in order to show Americans what was new and exciting in the world of art. The show was a success in terms of sales and attendance: nearly $45,000 worth of art—including works by the likes of Picasso, Matisse, and Gauguin—changed hands, and approximately 275,000 people came to see it during its two months in New York, Chicago, and Boston, many of whom were drawn by the thrill of controversy.[1]

61. *Armory Show 1913* (postal stamp), 1998. Private collection

If the minutiae of the Armory Show are familiar, so is its legend. Over the past three-quarters of a century, it has assumed talismanic proportions in America's collective historical memory, not only of the early days of modern art, but of twentieth-century culture generally. In academic literature as well as in the more familiar textbooks read by secondary and college students, the Armory Show has come to stand as the singular moment at which the "new" vanquished the "old" in American culture with a single and stunning revolutionary blow,[2] a habit well-set by the 1952 publication of Meyer Schapiro's seminal essay within a volume entitled *America in Crisis*—a volume that tellingly ranked the Armory Show alongside "John Brown's Private War" and the Dust Bowl as one of "Fourteen Crucial Episodes in American History."[3] Most recently, in 1998 the United States Postal Service issued a commemorative stamp (fig. 61) of the occasion in its "Celebrate the Century" series, which not only graced the nation's letters but traveled the land by train alongside images like "immigrants arrive," "W. E. B. Du Bois, Social Activist," and "First World Series."

Although much recent scholarship on early-twentieth-century American art has emphasized the Armory Show's location in a series of art-world activities that, at least after the turn of the century, prepared the way for the emergence and acceptance of modern art in the United States—Alfred Stieglitz's exhibits at "291," American artists' pilgrimages to the Paris salon of Gertrude and Leo Stein and other hotbeds of European modernism, the collecting forays of John Quinn[4]—historians continue to veil the Armory Show in the language of crisis, and particularly in the language of political crisis. Often explicitly associating the "radicalism" of the new art with concurrent upheavals in manners, morals, and politics, historians have been all too willing to attribute modernism's emergence to political transformations, and particularly to the rise of socialism, feminism, free love, and other radical movements, without interrogating the explicit relationship between modernist aesthetics and nonconformist "modern" culture.[5] Mistaking superficial or nongenerative connections between the two as evidence that "modern" politics and modernist aesthetics shared the same parentage (and that, because these social and political changes were radical, so too was the art), scholars have forgotten that aesthetic politics are generated as much by internal transformations within the art world itself, and by sociopolitical changes that, on the surface, seem to have very little to do with the "spirit" of particular artworks, as by those political transformations that seem to have an obvious representational similarity to contemporary cultural productions. As I have already begun to argue in the preceding chapter, American visual modernism owed its parentage as much to the legacy of professionalization, which in some respects had as wide an impact on turn-of-the-century America as radical politics, and which struck the art world as surely as it did medicine, the law, and other fields of endeavor.

It is true that many American artists embraced modernism's break from nineteenth-century aesthetic traditions because they believed that aesthetic revolution would bring about democratic social change.[6] Nevertheless, it is important to remember that not all participants in the American art world were persuaded by this connection between aesthetic and political liberation, and that not all defenders of modernism were motivated by revolutionary fervor. The seemingly violent clash over modern art waged in the wake of the Armory Show, thus, must not be read solely or uncritically as an episode in the wider struggle by workers, women, and others for liberation in the first decades of the twentieth century. It must also be read as a chapter in a much less democratic struggle by an emerging art-world elite to limit and police access to artistic knowledge and the art world, which itself was part of the broader rise of professional and bureaucratic control in the half-century following the Civil War.

As historians, many of us are a little nostalgic for the Armory Show and the world that produced it. Upon looking back, the year 1913 seems like a time when radical political change was still possible, a time, moreover, when artistic experimentation still had meaning. We are not alone in this belief. An almost century-long vanguardist tradition of self-description, motivated by political as much as aesthetic desire, pleads modernism's case to us, promising personal and political liberation as the certain reward for those who abandon themselves to the modernist impulse. Like our modernist forebears, we believe that the world that produced the Armory Show was a world in which art and politics not only spoke to each other, but also joined together to break the shackles of convention and conformity—whether these shackles were the stifling bonds of Victorian manners or, in a later generation, the crushing censorship of totalitarian uniformity.[7]

This longing for a lost past of cooperation between artistic and political radicalism permeates even recent analyses of the Armory Show. This is summed up in Martin Green's *New York 1913*, a work that pairs the Armory Show and the Paterson Strike Pageant. Green writes: "The spirit of 1913 was an aspiration to transcend what most people accepted as ordinary and so inevitable. It was the ordinariness of capitalism and liberalism and class hierarchy, in the case of the IWW strike; and in the case of the Armory Show, it was old forms of art, appreciation, and beauty. But the radicals in both cases said no to certain 'facts of life.' One might even suggest that what they said no to was ultimately the same in both cases—in one important sense, it was ultimately the nineteenth-century bourgeois state."[8]

In coupling modernist revolt with a broad array of social and political transformations, historians' accounts of the Armory Show duplicate and magnify not only the chronology of crisis inherent in accounts of modernism's ascendance, but their characterizations of the two eras at odds in the show—the bourgeois "Victorian" and the radical "modern."[9] Like those broader accounts, they depict two separate and unmixable universes, constructed along inherently conflicting principles. Expressed most frequently by shorthand—"convention" versus "revolution," "White City" versus "skyscraper," "moral indignation" versus "experimentation" or "freedom," "tradition" versus "new spirit"—these two descriptive nexuses have become so embedded in historical accounts of the emergence of twentieth-century culture that they forbid alternative modes of explanation.

It is indisputable that the Armory Show did, in fact, mark a major transition in American culture. But in our haste to distance ourselves from those who would have stood in the way of revolution, we have failed to understand what could have motivated such an outcry. Believing as we do that the Armory Show was a radical, crisis-like event, we look for further evidence of radicalism to explain it—the personal relationships that clearly did exist between certain promoters of modern art and political radicals,[10] or the growth of "radical" artist organizations, critical of the authority of the National Academy of Design and other, older institutions—that easily confirms what we already believe. And when we do encounter the voices of those who questioned the show, we are inclined either to discount them entirely or to use their vehemence as evidence, again, that the struggle to promote modernism must have been radical indeed.

This is nowhere so evident as in historians' accounts of the supposedly uniform and monolithic denunciation of the exhibition by art critics,[11] who variously have been described as "genteel," "conservative," and "provincial,"[12] and whose motivation has been attributed generally to a selfish desire to defend the interests of a dying elite.[13] With the exception of a few critical "seers," historians have argued,[14] a conservative army of critics condemned the show unilaterally as not only an insult to the aesthetic norms of academic "classicism,"[15] but as an affront to moral decency, thereby poisoning public sentiment against modern art for decades to come.[16] Historians have thus allowed the highly publicized views of a few critics—most frequently, painter and writer Kenyon Cox—to stand for critical opinion as a whole and have argued that art critics, like the small-minded throngs who mobbed and mocked the exhibition in New York and who attempted to burn Matisse in effigy in Chicago,[17] failed to comprehend either the most significant artistic transformation of the era or the social and political transformations it accompanied.

Like all legends, this "story of the Armory Show" is partially grounded in truth. Cox and others like him did construct Post-Impressionism as the final, awful consequence of a half century of aesthetic decadence, a decadence that to him symbolized, fed from, and in turn nourished a more wide-reaching social and moral decline.[18] Writers such as Leila Mechlen, editor of the American Federation of Art's journal *Art and Progress*, joined Cox in deliberately linking modern art to dangerous trends in politics and manners, comparing "the 'Post-impressionists,' or the 'Modernists' or 'Expressionists,' whatever they may choose to call themselves" to "profligate[s]," "bomb thrower[s]," "defamer[s] and lunatic[s]," and demanded that a parallel system of discipline be devised to curtail artistic subversives, just as the law controlled political radicals.[19] By their hysterical response, critics such as Cox and Mechlen created in the public mind an association between artistic iconoclasm and political and social radicalism that has remained to this day, even though that association itself has come to be seen in an entirely different light.

This conceptualization of the critical response to the Armory Show as a monolithic screed against the new is misleading. In many ways, critical evaluations of the Armory Show, and the causes for critical opposition to it, were more complicated than historians have acknowledged. With the notable exception of Cox and Mechlen, very few writers condemned the show categorically. Most responses were mixed, demonstrating critics' profound appreciation of the changes taking place not only within the American scene at large or in art itself, but also within the American art world. Critics' primary preoccupation in evaluating the show, in fact, was not the fate of American politics and morality or the future of painting and sculpture in a purely aesthetic sense, but the future of the art world. While critics of the show's Post-Impressionist contingent did fear that unbridled change had caused European artists to slip into aesthetic decadence, the main cause of their concern was not the display of dangerous works *per se*, but the impact the new art—and the critical apparatus that was emerging to support it—would have on the art world, the public, and the very role of art in the American republic. Despite their distaste for many of the works displayed in the show, many of its most famous detractors argued that ultra-progressive European art, while unlovable in itself, had and would continue to have an indisputably positive effect on American artistic production, and expressed a far greater resistance to the "propaganda," secrecy, and exclusive expertise of modern art's "champions," who explained Post-Impressionist artworks in unfamiliar, unintelligible terms. "Conservative" critics' fears of the show, thus, were grounded not in mere conservatism or opposition to change, but in a deep suspicion of the interpretative machinery that accompanied the new art, which seemed to shake the very foundations of the American art world.

In order to understand this fear, which permeated critical responses to the Armory Show, it is important to reconsider the art-world context in which most early-twentieth-century critics wrote, rather than to link them to a vaguely defined Victorian past. In the decades following the Civil War, as I have argued, critics and publishers worked alongside the promoters of museums and art education to develop a comprehensive, national organizational field for art. This did not come to a sharp halt after the turn of the century, but continued in the careers of many critics who pursued institution-building, as well as evaluative, aims. With its demand for specialized, difficult modes of explanation—a demand that the show's most vocal supporters eagerly met—the Armory Show, and modernism in general, presented to these critics a dangerous turn toward a new, more exclusive art world in which experts, rather than the public, held the keys to the kingdom of American art. Thus, if to our eyes the exhibition was a watershed in the kind of artworks that would be seen and made in the United States, to contemporaries it also represented a pivotal change in the art world. It is in this context that responses to the Armory Show must be considered.

Like their opponents, critical supporters of the Armory Show owed a great deal to the art-world context in which they looked and wrote. Although their commentary often masked the importance of art-world concerns, unabashedly modernist supporters of the show also developed their understandings of art in response to the changing conditions of artistic production, as much as in response to the visual presence of works themselves. And, like modernism's institution-building detractors, supporters of the show drew upon critical practices developed in the previous generation. As we have seen, a powerful counter-current within postwar publishing was the emergence of a professionalized style of criticism. These critics, as I have argued, developed a professional language centrally concerned with issues of representation, authenticity, and abstraction, and used it to devalue both the commonsense knowledge that nourished most Americans' judgments about art and the amateurs who claimed, through their institutions, to augment public knowledge.

The generation of critics who supported modernism after the turn of the century followed in the footsteps of these critics, putting a heightened emphasis on the aesthetic qualities of artworks at the expense of art-world concerns, and using their claims to expertise to defend and promote a gatekeeping, as well as an aesthetic, agenda. The controversy over the Armory Show, which represented a head-on clash between the inheritors of the amateur, institution-building critics of the Gilded Age and their professionalizing rivals, was as much a struggle for power within the developing American art world as it was a debate about the merits or morality of artworks. Although institution-building critics outnumbered their modernist counterparts, in the end it has been the views of modernists that have persisted, along with their vision of artistic production and the public's diminished role in it inherited from the professionalizing critics of the late nineteenth century. The Armory Show did not produce this conflict, and it did not settle it; it merely provided the spark.

Skeptics

The first element that must be considered in re-evaluating the Armory Show's significance is the fact that most critics hardly opposed the Armory Show as a whole. Frank Jewett Mather, for example, whose critical imperative and reason for supposedly denouncing the show was recently described as "keeping art pure and society safe,"[20] greeted the show with enthusiasm and praise in two reviews in the *Nation*.[21] Although Mather described the attention garnered by the most recent European works as "the *succès de scandale* of the Post-Impressionists and Cubists," he defended the work of Van Gogh, Cézanne, and Gauguin. Perhaps as an attempt to prevent more narrowly based critiques of their work, Mather suggested that the selection chosen to represent these artists in the show was "far from superlative" and was quick to mention admirable traits he had witnessed elsewhere in their work, such as Gauguin's "classic serenity and monumental effect" and Cézanne's "immediate and primal sense of mass."[22]

Mather was not alone in his praise for the Armory Show. Many critics believed that the show contained fine examples of both European and American art, providing important evidence of American art's improvement over the preceding half century[23] and pointing the way beyond "stereotyped and fossilized standards" and "simpering, self-satisfied conventionality."[24] Many of those who were skeptical of the show saw a silver lining in it, arguing that even displeasing works served a useful purpose by providing a needed contrast to more worthwhile productions.[25] E. H. Blashfield, who defined the "'advanced' artist" as "the *intransigeant* [*sic*], the uncompromising man who enounces [*sic*] dangerous precepts" and who joined the show's angriest critics in denouncing the declining spiral away from "correct proportion, correct form, and correct values," still refused wholly to condemn either the show or the new movement. "I believe that the new movement is potential [*sic*] for great good," he wrote, "in its concentration upon color and light, its development, through experiment, of effects produced by broken color and the novel manipulation of material."[26] Even Royal Cortissoz—who generally and vociferously condemned the new art—praised Van Gogh's enthusiasm for painting and "solving technical problems." The painter was "passionately in love with color," Cortissoz suggested, and in "groping toward an effective use of it in the expression of truth, he gives you occasionally in his thick impasto a gleam of sensuously beautiful tone."[27]

Although critics like these praised the show for bringing specific *stylistic* innovations to light, many more critics praised it for its breadth and scope, arguing that the Association's organizational activities as an exhibiting body outweighed its predilection for controversial works. Thus, although Mather's review contained assessments of certain individual artists and works represented in the show, his primary evaluative criteria were organizational: he celebrated the "miracle of good taste and good management" that had allowed the organizers to set up a highly effective exhibition space, and softened his critique of the selection of foreign art by writing that "it is the fullest America has yet seen" and that "a consistent principle has been followed."[28] Indeed, Mather lauded the show's organizers for refusing to allow it to remain a mere "gorgeous family affair" of self-congratulatory American display. Far from condemning the exhibition as a threat to public safety, Mather held up the Armory Show as a model to be emulated by the National Academy of Design, which he feared represented only "a respectably obscure parochialism."[29]

To a reviewer in the *Outlook*, the eventual verdict on Post-Impressionism was not only inscrutable, but also irrelevant to considerations of the show's merit. For, while the public, critics, and artists locked horns over that judgment, "the Association's effort has already accomplished two welcome results for which we should be duly appreciative. It has shown conclusively that a large, interestingly selected lot of pictures attracts many observers, and, second, that when those pictures are selected to demonstrate certain theories they provoke instant, vivacious, and helpful discussion. That the present exhibition will be useful in popularizing painting no one can doubt, even if it does not popularize the latest tendencies in painting."[30] To the *Outlook*'s critic, the mere fact of organizing large-scale exhibitions that presented works in a coherent historical arrangement served the public interest not because it converted audiences to a particular line of development within painting, but because it converted them to painting itself. According to this critic's logic, the production and presentation of new and controversial styles served not as the harbinger of art's ultimate decline, but as the wellspring for public interest, manifested in hearty and enthusiastic debates among artists, critics, and the public alike.

Critical willingness to embrace the Armory Show as an organizational contribution to the enlargement of the American art world can also be seen in a review of the show in *Current Opinion*. While punchy editorials in the journal proclaimed "Bedlam in Art" and "Art Madness Recaptured,"[31] a longer review put the show in broader perspective, praising it for its scale and its breadth in representing "all the modern 'schools,' from Ingres to the Cubists and Futurists."[32] The scale of the exhibition alone, however, did less to convince the reviewer of its importance than its similarity to "another historic moment, over thirty years ago." At that moment, "the Paris art dealer, Durand Ruel, brought to America and hung in the galleries of the staid old National Academy of Design a collection of landscapes by the French Impressionist, Claude Monet," thereby integrating American viewers and buyers into the international contemporary art market for the first time in the nation's history.[33] The critic argued that, like the current show, Durand-Ruel's exhibition had produced its fair share of naysayers at first, but warned off Armory Show skeptics by reminding them that Monet's canvases now brought "large prices." "In the spirit of the old adage that history repeats itself," the critic mused, "is it utterly extravagant to prophesy that some of the works of Cézanne, Gauguin, Van Gogh, Matisse, and Picasso may become historic?"[34]

The critic's choice of Durand-Ruel's Impressionist exhibit as the basis for making the Armory Show (and artistic change in general) comprehensible to readers is significant. To the critic, the development of institutions for the display of art played as great a role in the direction and shape of artistic change as any internal qualities of works themselves. Thus, the critic praised the show not for the works contained therein—his breathless praise for the show's success hardly mentioned them, in fact—but for its similarity to an epic moment in the history of art-world institution building in the United States. Despite a crack at the "staid" Academy, the critic avoided a more inflammatory comparison between the show and the Salon des Refusés, emphasizing not the "revolutionary" character of the Association but its hierarchical and institutional qualities, and pointing out that "the selections were made by Arthur B. Davies and Walt Kuhn, President and Secretary of the Association." By accentuating the contrast between initial critical responses to Impressionism and its ultimate market value, moreover, the writer suggested that the critic's role was not to evaluate new styles as they emerged, but to promote institutions of display that would allow the market, acting as the agent of the public, to make final assessments of good and bad. While ephemeral critical evaluations might be seen as ridiculous a generation later, the reviewer suggested, critical support for exhibitions and the organizations that enabled them to take place was certain to retain its value.[35]

Another writer who made sense of the Armory Show by placing it in the context of the history of American art organizations was John White Alexander, by then president of the National Academy of Design. Although Alexander accused individual works within the show of "having offered us a few wholly indefensible sensations," he refused to condemn either the show's organizers or the spirit that had driven them to mount the exhibition.[36] Although Alexander doubted that "men who collected and selected this interesting exhibition" would appreciate the comparison, he equated the American Association of Painters and Sculptors with the Society of American Artists. "The creation of this society did for its day very much the same service that the Independent Exhibition has done for ours," he wrote, "and the freshness of the note it struck was quite as much an innovation and a breaking-away from accepted convention."[37] Reminding readers that the SAA had been absorbed by the Academy after "having done its work of regeneration," Alexander mused that the time would come when even Duchamp's controversial *Nude Descending a Staircase* (1912; Philadelphia Museum of Art)—the image at which the viewers in the postal stamp gaze so intently—would seem commonplace.[38] Alexander's motivation for praising the show to the degree he did, thus, had less to do with his opinions of particular works than with his understanding of the nature of the American art world. In Alexander's view, the show demanded critical recognition not just because it offered a glimpse into the stylistic future of American art (although it did do that), but because it provided powerful evidence of the art world's continued organizational innovation, a factor which critics since the Gilded Age had seen as crucial to the advancement of art in America. "Reactions against the academy's sober and restrained methods are not only inevitable," he wrote, "but necessary and very much to the interest of both the academy and those who, for want of a milder term, we must call rebels."[39]

Alexander's focus on the organizational aspects of the show, rather than on concentrated formal analysis of the objects displayed therein, was not accidental. In large part, the criticism practiced by many "conservative" writers who responded to the Armory Show was geared more toward building American interest in art through the general promotion of art-world institutions than toward legislating taste or interpretation for readers, and as such represented a continuation of the critical project pursued by *Modern Art* and the *American Art Review*. Like their predecessors, many critics who responded skeptically to the Armory Show conceived of criticism not as a pulpit for the espousal of particular evaluative viewpoints, but as the art world's institution-building institution.[40] As such, essays like Alexander's encouragement to the exhibition's organizers belonged to a critical context heavy with articles promoting art-world development and examples of journals' own attempts to serve as institutions for the promotion and dissemination of art,[41] as well as pleas for government support of American art and arts institutions.[42]

The art writing that surrounded the Armory Show owed a debt to the institution-building criticism of the nineteenth century in another respect: critics' attachment to a referential style of reporting that directed readers to further sources of commentary through the use of direct quotes from competing writers, which echoed postwar critics' eager and frequent recommendation that readers consult the views of competing authors and journals. While critics sometimes used these writings as a source of legitimacy for their own interpretations—or as fodder for ridicule—they often simply threw them upon the page without commentary.[43] By including these outside views and by identifying the institutional affiliation of their promoters, critics suggested to readers that art criticism was a communitarian venture, which crossed not only the boundaries of individual opinion, but also the divisions between institutional and commercial entities.

As a result, many critics who assessed the show vocally adhered to the dictum that "the public will make up its own mind" and bluntly refused to cast their comments in terms of evaluation. Writers such as the reviewer in the *Times*, for example, insisted that the ease of providing a record of his or her personal response to the Armory Show should not be allowed to tempt the critic to stray from the "less simple," though more essential, critical task. "For the critic," the reviewer wrote, "there is no such thing as taking sides. . . . He can heartily and with all his emotional being detest the eccentricities of a Matisse, and he can find his soul moved to something approaching ecstasy by the serene and noble rhythms of Puvis de Chavannes, but so can any one of us. His more dispassionate, although less simple, task is to try to discover what addition each of the innovators in the various schools has made to the sum of artistic achievement, what change each one has made in the prevailing taste of his time, and what step he has taken to broaden our perceptions."[44] What set critics aside, the reviewer suggested, was not their evaluative acuity, but their willingness to forswear passion in the name of duty—the duty to act as mediums for the expression of public opinion, which could only be ascertained by sifting through the mass of heated and contrary opinion. Side taking on "such a polyhedron as modern art" produced little benefit to readers, "any one of" them as capable of evaluation as the critic.

The sense that criticism used as a vehicle for the expression of opinion could produce undesirable fragmentation within the art world also pervaded E. H. Blashfield's contribution to the *Century*'s roundtable on "This Transitional Age in Art," in which the critic expressed some irritation at having been asked to express his *opinion* on contemporary art.[45] "Talk is so easily accomplished," he charged, adding that any criticism that unconditionally condemned particular styles "is hurtful, and above all is bewildering to the public."[46] Explaining that he had only agreed to write the article because he believed that many others shared his views, he insisted nonetheless that "it is of little importance what I or Mr. Advanced Progressive may *love* or *hate*. The important, very *important* point is, does the expression of our love or hate do harm? Does it retard the general knowledge and appreciation of art? Does it hinder development?"[47] The unbridled critical pursuit of a particular evaluative agenda, Blashfield suggested, could have terrible consequences for the art world, fracturing the structure that criticism was meant to create and undermining the very future of art.[48]

Antagonists

Despite the proliferation of positive critical assessments of the Armory Show's art-world impact, it would be foolish to suggest that the Armory Show engendered a critical love-fest. Writers did disagree sharply over the show's merits, and in condemning it, some demonstrated the willingness to abandon moderation that historians have long associated with the show's critical respondents. While many of those who believed that the right to evaluative judgment ultimately resided with the public declined to promote their own personal assessments of the show as law, some offered thinly veiled screeds against modernism under the guise of "letting the public have its say." Cox, for one, offered the following advice: "Do not allow yourselves to be blinded by the sophistries of the foolish dupes or the self-interested exploiters of all this charlatanry . . . you are not infallible, but your instincts are right in the main, and you are, after all, the final judges."[49]

Cox's intemperate condemnations of the Armory Show have rightly gained him the reputation of a man who feared and hated change. Despite their cartoonish vehemence, however, the contours of Cox's tirade bear some affinity to the objections of more thoughtful observers, and point the way to a more complete explanation of the sources of critical fear surrounding the Armory Show. Although the extreme tone of Cox's rant and the somewhat disingenuous manner in which he urged readers to be their own judges (as opposed to simply following his lead) disguise this affinity, Cox's nervousness about modernism had roots similar to those of many of his less vociferous contemporaries, whose fears were driven as much by the way in which modernism was being interpreted as by the simple fact that new and different works were being produced. Indeed, rather than this aesthetic agenda, it was this nervousness about the art-world implications of modernism—what its ascendance would mean for audiences, critics, and institutions—that linked Cox to more moderate writers who criticized the show. For, as his own work as an artist shows, Cox was committed to a kind of classicism that would have hardly moved some of his critical compatriots, some of whom were much more sympathetic than he was to the aesthetic changes represented by modernism. What united writers who criticized the show was not a unified aesthetic agenda, but a common attitude toward the art world, and in particular toward the role of critics and the public within that art world.

Many writers who voiced objections to the new art and to the Armory Show did so not on aesthetic grounds or on aesthetic grounds alone, but on the basis of the critical shroud that they believed had come to envelop modern art. Describing the proliferation of heated evaluative and interpretative commentary as "cant" and "propaganda," many critics disapproved of fellow writers' handling of modern art as a misappropriation of their position as critics. The adoption of an overtly partisan and evaluative criticism that relied on obscure language and reasoning, many writers argued, represented a dangerous turn for criticism to take, and threatened both to undermine the crucial relationship between critics and the public and to divide the art world dangerously. It was this threat to the delicate balance between educative, institution-building criticism, an active, judgment-forming public, and an aesthetic that valued common knowledge over specialized art-world expertise, rather than any challenge to public decency or even to specific stylistic norms that most worried critics of the Armory Show and that provoked their most heated condemnations of the new art.

In his lengthy attempt to expose "The Post-Impressionist Illusion," Royal Cortissoz frequently abandoned his discussion of the art displayed at the Armory Show in order to turn a wrathful eye toward the commentary that surrounded it. Like his many peers who condemned "the flood of recrimination" spilled by fellow critics, Cortissoz tellingly insisted that his own remarks on Post-Impressionism "sought merely to clear the ground of the cant which often encumbers it," a move he felt was necessary if readers were even to begin a meaningful examination of the new art. The unrestrained venting of partisan opinions on the show, he suggested, had so distorted it as to render it unintelligible to the public—had transformed it, even, into an entirely new entity. He thus promised to "look at Post-Impressionism for what it is, regardless alike of its acolytes and its equally furious opponents."

Despite his promise, however, Cortissoz spent little time *looking* at all, devoting most of his attention to the ways in which the new art had been interpreted. Before examining the work of a single artist, Cortissoz first attempted to discern the underlying principles of Post-Impressionism as a movement—as expressed in writing, not in paint—as the best way to "find out what the Post-Impressionists are driving at."[50] But Cortissoz found it difficult to locate a clear interpretative scheme he could relay to his readers, a situation which led him to conclude that Post-Impressionism's proponents had deliberately thwarted public comprehension of the new art as a way not only to guarantee the ascendance of the work itself, but to solidify their own position as its interpreters.[51] Deriding most critical decodings of the new art as a "sea of ecstatic but muddled exposition," and complaining that "there [wa]s a touch of mumbo-jumbo"[52] in even relatively helpful explanations like that given by English critic Roger Fry, Cortissoz suggested that critics had deliberately made the "Post-Impressionist hypothesis" seem much more complicated than it really was, in order "to further the propaganda" surrounding modernism.[53]

Cortissoz's objections to Post-Impressionism's critical scaffolding only gathered strength as his analysis progressed, and deeply colored his assessment of the movement itself. He complained that "invertebrate and confusing" thinking on the part of Post-Impressionist artists had "led them to produce work not only incompetent, but grotesque," and threw in the charge of insolence for good measure.[54] While this pronouncement is in itself relatively uninteresting, Cortissoz supported it with a fascinating choice of evidence. Turning not to the analysis of this "work" but again to its interpretation by critics, he wrote

> if these seem hard words, let me recall an incident of the Post-Impressionist exhibition in London two years ago. Mr. Roger Fry, writing in defense of the project, cited various persons who were in sympathy with it, and named among them Mr. John S. Sargent. In the course of a letter to the London "Nation" that distinguished painter said, "Mr. Fry may have been told—and have believed—that the sight of those paintings had made me a convert to his faith in them. The fact is that *I am absolutely skeptical as to their having any claim whatever to being works of art*, with the exception of some of the pictures by Gauguin that strike me as admirable in color, and in color only." [The italics are mine.][55]

In the end, Cortissoz's hostility to Post-Impressionism as a movement turned out to be as deeply rooted in his irritation at the conduct of its critical supporters as in any particular objections to the art itself. While he found Fry's misappropriation of Sargent's authority particularly disagreeable, he clearly believed that the rise of a modernist "gospel" had produced a wider crisis of interpretation, led by "Post-Impressionist impresarios and fuglemen [who] insolently proffer us a farrago of super-subtle rhetoric."[56]

As Cortissoz's outcry suggests, one of the elements critics found most disturbing about interpretations of the Armory Show and Post-Impressionist art generally was their tendency to use obscure language, which blocked the access of even educated readers familiar with the history of art. For their own part, many of the show's less friendly critics adopted a plain linguistic style (aside from the colorful terms of abuse) with which to record their impressions of the show, eschewing complicated or specific art terminology along with elaborate discussions of individual objects. Of course, the style adopted by these writers was itself limited by the boundaries of the middle-class press—critics only occasionally pretended to speak to those outside the boundaries of their educated readership—but within these boundaries, it did not work deliberately to exclude readers on the basis of their lack of professional, insider knowledge of the art world, an exclusion which many saw the new modernist criticism as performing. Like writers who condemned partisanship, some critics with doubts about the new art worked to distance themselves from their critical peers who concentrated on the minute analysis of individual objects. Alexander, for example, self-consciously distinguished his commentary from the "existing mass of purposeless and superfluous criticism,"[57] insisting that his purpose was "merely to review briefly the different phases through which our art has passed under his personal observation, mentioning names and individual work as rarely as is consistent with making himself fairly intelligible to his readers."[58] In championing the generality of his own criticism, Alexander elucidated many fellow writers' eagerness for an educative, plain style of criticism that provided comprehensive and intelligible overviews of subjects of interest to American readers. More significantly, Alexander deliberately eschewed the analysis of individual objects, arguing that it served the interests neither of intelligibility nor of the progress of American art.

Critics sometimes coupled this plain style of speaking with a self-consciously amateur persona, offering their own transparency as a form of protection to the public against cabalistic and self-interested criticism. Theodore Roosevelt adopted this strategy in his "layman's" comments on the exhibition, referring to modernism's supporters as "the champions of these extremists" and describing Cubist paintings as Barnumesque hoaxes. Derisively writing that "there are thousands of people who will pay small sums to look at a faked mermaid; and now and then one of this kind with enough money will buy a Cubist picture," Roosevelt hinted that his outsider's analysis might warn away at least a few willing dupes.[59] This was necessary, Roosevelt implied, because many critics preferred to promote shamelessly obscure interpretations of modernist artworks, such as those of Wilhelm Lehmbruck's *Kneeling Woman* (1911; Albright-Knox Art Gallery, Buffalo, New York). While his fellow critic Willard Huntington Wright would write "Doesn't she make you jealous?" on a post card of the image he sent home to his wife in Los Angeles (fig. 62), Roosevelt complained that the sculpture barely resembled a woman at all. More pointedly, he questioned the sincerity of critical admirers who described it as "'full of lyric grace,' as 'tremendously sincere,' and 'of a jewel-like preciousness.'" Suggesting that these words might just as easily represent "a conventional jargon" as the sincere views of critics, Roosevelt complained that the use of these phrases might in itself lead to an interpretative fracture between what critics saw and what they said. "In any event," he concluded, "one might well speak of the 'lyric grace' of

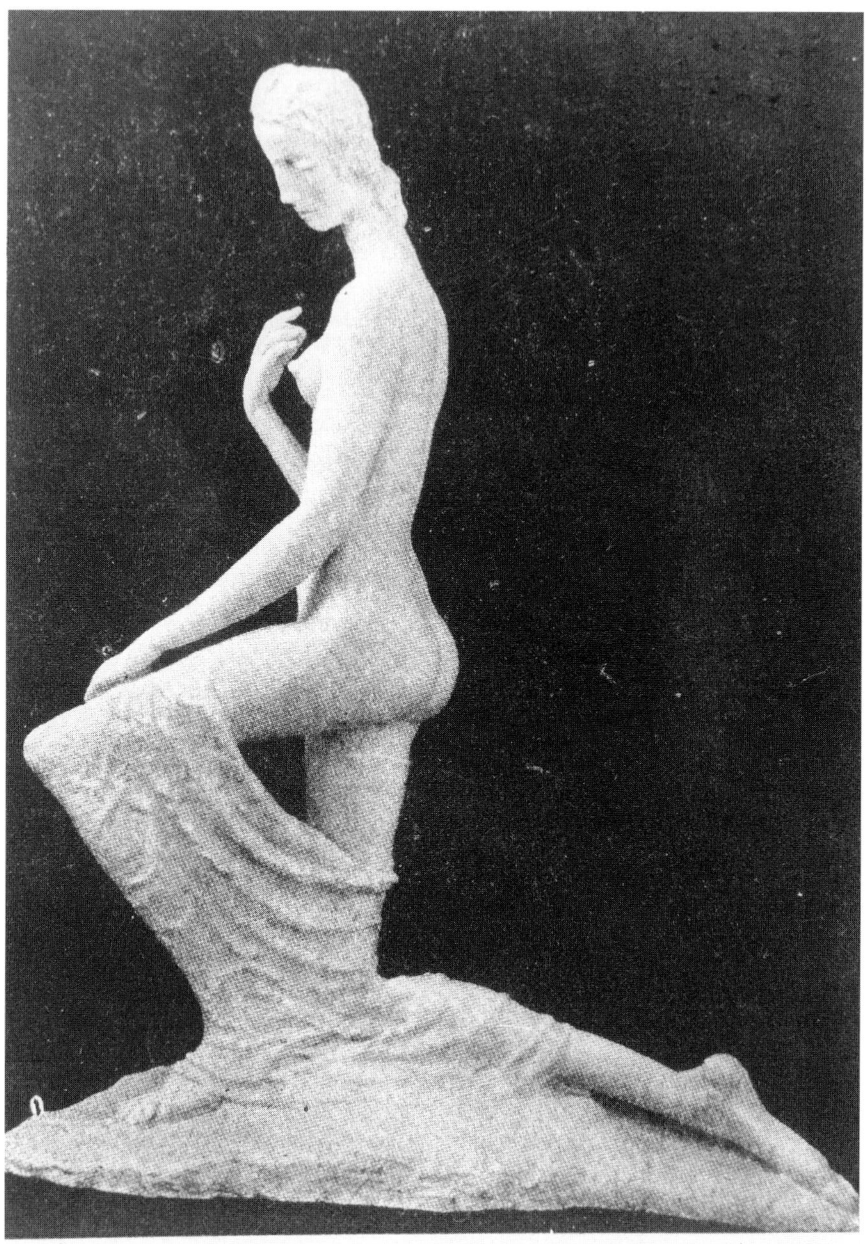

62. Armory Show postcard after Wilhelm Lehmbruck (1881–1919), *The Kneeling One* (*Kneeling Woman*), sent by Willard Huntington Wright to Katherine Boynton Wright, 22 March 1913. S. S. Van Dine Collection, Clifton Waller Barrett Library of American Literature, Special Collections, University of Virginia Library

a praying mantis, which adopts much the same attitude."[60] In this way, Roosevelt insisted that common experience, and not "inscrutable" critical whimsy, must guide the interpretative project.

But critics' frustration with modernism stemmed not only from its critical supporters, but also from the artists themselves. Perhaps the most intense locus for critical suspicion of the interpretative and discursive practices surrounding modernism was the adoption of seemingly referential titles to describe works and movements that did not live up to the promise of straightforward explanation. One writer in the *Outlook* mockingly referred to the creator of an especially enigmatic Cubist work as "zees coob" ("this cubist"), and contrasted the wholesome American skepticism of a policeman who exclaimed, "Aw, gwan wid yer . . . what er yer kiddin' us?" to the Frenchified defenses of those who claimed to explain it.[61] Indeed, critics objected to linguistic obscurity on the part not only of fellow writers, but also of artists, whom critics acknowledged as playing an important role in the interpretation of art.[62] Among the many "Layman's Views" expressed by Roosevelt was his casual denunciation of self-consciously named movements: "There is no reason why people should not call themselves Cubists, or Octagonists, or Parallelopipedonists, or Knights of the Isosceles Triangle, or Brothers of the Cosine, if they so desire; as expressing anything serious and permanent, one term is as fatuous as another."[63] Ignoring the fact that the identification of each fragmentary movement according to the method it promoted owed as much to the antagonism of European critics as to self-conscious naming on the part of participants, many critics shared Roosevelt's exasperation at what they saw as a foolish, indulgent, and ultimately unhelpful practice.[64]

Critics' objections to the naming of movements stemmed from a wider suspicion of the deep interpretative chasm that separated the pictures they saw from the titles and descriptions they read and heard. To many critics bred on an overwhelmingly representational style of artworks, and in a culture of the copy that admired pictures for their ability to convey visual information, as much as for their originality, the new works seemed random and perverse. The frustration critics faced at this situation can be seen in the comments of the reviewer in the *Outlook*, who complained that one painting "was only a jumble of cube-like forms. One is told that this and its neighbors represent 'A Dance' or 'A Procession;' that they depict 'Paris' or 'Seville.' One may have visited Paris and Seville and be fairly familiar with processions and dances, but one looks and looks and makes nothing at all out of 'zees coob.'"[65]

Here, as elsewhere, the critic's objections to the purely visual aspects of the work—that "it was only a jumble of cube-like forms"—played only a part in his or her resistance to it.[66] Instead, the critic seethed at being "told" its meaning by interpreters claiming special insight. Titles that referred to potentially familiar events and places provoked special hostility, moreover, not only because they brought home the growing disparity between the visible world and the visual content of modernist painting, but also because they suggested that the experience of nonexpert viewers was in itself somehow different from that of modernists. By assigning seemingly comprehensible titles to inscrutable images, modernism's interpreters appeared to call into question not only the quality of amateur judgments that were based on everyday experience, but also the quality of that experience itself.

The painting that most often produced this sense of interpretative dissonance and loss of control—and that, not coincidentally, aroused the most frequent and vehement outcries from critics—was Marcel Duchamp's *Nude Descending a Staircase* (see fig. 61). Observers of the Armory Show have focused a great deal of attention on the conflict this painting provoked, commonly describing all those who expressed reservations about the painting as the "'explosion-in-a-shingle-factory' school of commentators."[67] Most assessments of this "school" assume that the inability to recognize the merits of the work's formal qualities produced the now-infamous outpouring of critical hostility surrounding the piece.[68]

Although many writers focused an undeniably prejudiced eye on the piece, their biases against it turned not on mere incomprehension at its stylistic innovations, but on their unwillingness to accept the disjunction they perceived between work and title. Theodore Roosevelt famously compared the painting to "a really good Navajo rug" he had in his bathroom (a contest in which the rug readily won), and complained that "if, for some inscrutable reason, it suited somebody to call this rug a picture of, say, 'A well-dressed man going up a ladder,' the name would fit the facts just about as well as in the case of the Cubist picture of the 'Naked man going down stairs.' From the standpoint of terminology, each name would have whatever merit inheres in a rather cheap straining after effect."[69] Although Roosevelt insisted that the Navajo rug was superior to the modernist painting on aesthetic grounds, this was not his central preoccupation in condemning the work. What concerned Roosevelt most was neither the relative "artistic merit" of the two works nor the absolute requirement that works be representational, but that works whose titles demanded to be seen representationally carried through on that invitation and actually "fit the facts."[70] This issue also went to the heart of his concern with modernist criticism.

Critics did not reject Duchamp's *Nude*, then, simply because it looked like "an explosion in a shingle factory," but because it wasn't *called* "explosion in a shingle factory." For Adeline Adams, the problem with "the new school of emotion-painters who forswear representation, but label their pictures" was not their lack of obvious realism or referentiality *per se*, but the interpretative discomfort produced by their labels.[71] Recounting her own response to the painting, Adams wrote that

> that curious splinter-salad—made an unusually direct appeal to me, for the reason that it came upon me when I did not know it was there—in fact, when I was seeking something else; and, therefore, I would like to

> state what the appeal was. With my paleolithic bias toward representation fortified by an acquired taste for decoration, I found myself looking at I knew not what. My "emotional response" was rapid, for me. My mind asked, *method-madness*? *lost architect*? No! A drift of veneers piled up in the shop of a maker of musical instruments. That idea swiftly brought me the memory of a beautiful old man I once knew, a violin-maker, now dead; and with his image, as always, came crowding only elemental things, such as simplicity, home, pastoral country. It made me wish to find a human being in the canvas.[72]

Adams's fanciful interplay was quickly cut short. While the opening of interpretative space produced by the work's lack of clear representational content had at first liberated Adams to make her own meanings of the work—within, as she admitted, the confines of her own prejudices, experience, and canonical expectations—her freedom turned to "amusement-anger" upon seeing the work's title. This anger was twofold. In part, it derived from Adams's self-conscious feelings of exclusion; of the words that came to her mind upon seeing the title, two were "*épater*" and "*bourgeois*," both referring to Baudelaire's description of the bohemian project, and in clear conflict with Adams's understanding of her own place within both the art world and the larger culture. Yet the title's interpretative power provoked the greater portion of Adams's ire because it censored exactly the free play of meaning that had allowed her to enjoy the work in the first place. Although Adams tried to recapture this freedom within the narrower boundaries of interaction with the titled work, the result left her unfulfilled and anxious with self-doubt. "What was there to do but laugh at myself, entrapped sentimentalist assuming another person's burden of proof?" she asked, more convinced than ever of her relative lack of authority as a viewer in the face of modernism's tightening interpretative grip.[73]

Champions

The Armory Show's defenders also owed their critical practices to the legacy of nineteenth-century criticism. Unlike their skeptical peers, however, the Armory Show's strongest defenders relied on an aesthetic and an approach to criticism that emphasized the fracture between everyday experience and interpretation and valorized the integrity and irreducibility of art objects. While critical defenders of modernism celebrated what Armory Show impresario Walter Pach called "the fecund principle of making [a] picture a reflection not of the outer world, but of the domain of the mind,"[74] they also shared their professional forebears' ambivalent relationship to the public, using the evolving modernist aesthetic—and the esoteric critical language that attended it—to consolidate their own position as special and expert interpreters of the new art.

The dividing line between institution builders and professionals did not, it must be admitted, map exactly upon the division between defenders and detractors of modernism. Pach, for instance, clearly embraced large-scale organization as the most effective means of jump-starting modernism in the United States. Pach was not only one of the primary forces behind the Armory Show; he used similar strategies throughout his career, writing early pieces on Cézanne and Monet for the journal press, helping both Walter Arensberg and John Quinn to build their collections, and working to enable museums like the Metropolitan Museum of Art and the Louvre to acquire particular artworks. This is not surprising, as Pach himself was the son of Gotthelf Pach of Pach Brothers, the primary photographers for the Metropolitan Museum of Art (see fig. 60) and regular contributors to *Harper's Weekly*. As a result, Pach not only had the chance to study with Robert Henri and, as a man of twenty, to travel abroad to paint with William Merritt Chase, but also was exposed regularly and at an early age to the workings of the art world and in particular to the processes of circulation that made art available to the public.[75] Within this context, it is quite possible that Pach also encountered Louis Prang. For, although I do not know for sure whether the thirteen-year-old Pach saw Prang's 1896 exhibition at the Grolier Club, Pach did later own two lithographs that were displayed in the show: François Rudé's *Neapolitan Fishermen* and Antoine Louis Barye's *Study of a Tiger*, which he loaned to the Cincinnati Art Museum in 1948.[76] That the Club was run by Metropolitan trustee Robert Hoe, whom Pach's father undoubtedly knew, and that its shows were free, suggest that this was at least a possibility.

Despite the impact of organizational methods on figures like Pach, however, it must be noted that his sympathy for the public was tempered by a tendency to make distinctions between modernists and outsiders, experts and "laymen" or "amateurs."[77] In his defense of modernism in the *Century*, Pach divided art's audience into two camps, contrasting "those who oppose all change in the forms of art" to those who "break still further with the superstition that a picture must look 'just like nature.'"[78] Although he relished the public's newfound willingness to give the new art a try, this enthusiasm belied an undercurrent of suspicion toward nonexpert viewers. Remarking on the hostility Cézanne's work initially had met, for instance, Pach expressed near disbelief that "the esthetic and expressive phases of the work of art" had come to be appreciated by "even the laymen."

In any case, Pach was somewhat atypical; much of show's support came from critics whose writings bore a strong rhetorical similarity to those of the professional critics of the Gilded Age, and most of its strong disapproval from critics in the institution-building tradition. It is not difficult to see why many institution-building critics feared that the interpretation of art had come under the spell of a propagandistic cabal of modernist insiders with little interest in making art available to a broad audience. D. W. MacColl's lengthy defense of the exhibition in the *Forum*, for instance, contained this "explanation" of abstract art, which surely did little to stem the unease of critics who feared that the creation of an organizational field for art was no longer criticism's primary aim:

> An abstraction, I find in my dictionary, is "the name of a quality apart from the thing," and a quality is "that which makes a thing what it is." From which I infer that an abstraction is "the name of 'that which makes a thing what it is' *apart* from what it is,"—it is the name of that which makes a thing what it is Not what it is. It is a name: it is Not the thing. How really well established and settled in practice this is. And when we want to personify—quite a different matter—one of these names of things which will make, as we think, a thing what it is not what it is, when we really feel that we dare to call one of them from the vasty deep in which they abound, it is quite true: we must arouse ourselves from our timidities of mental habit; we must make a movement of our lips—a pass of our hands or feet. Men see that there has been a quickening. The name has become the thing. It has become what it is. IT is IT, and everyone else is a believer or an unbeliever.[79]

If MacColl's highly opaque, almost parodic language did not alienate observers used to plain and pedagogical accounts of aesthetic principles, his absolute partition of viewers and makers into believers and unbelievers—the aroused and the merely timid—was certain to be resented by critics who believed that the public could play a meaningful role in making judgments about art.

Modernist critics deliberately shunned this public-oriented position, offering their own vision of how aesthetic opinions were formed. In some cases, modernists developed a rhetoric that imitated their European counterparts' contempt for the bourgeoisie. Yet, American critics who adopted this language did not necessarily do so for the sake of promoting European art, and were not necessarily any less nationalistic than their institution-building peers. Like his predecessors who had appropriated the authority of European art while distancing themselves from it, Willard Huntington Wright evoked European critiques of the bourgeoisie while simultaneously promoting the American Synchromists as the true progenitors of abstraction. "While lacking a sense of rhythm," he wrote, "[Matisse] has a tremendous feeling of form in the static sense and a genius for color opposition which, while rare and delicate, is to the bourgeois shocking and savage. (All harmony to the untutored mind must be dark gray and black with but slight tone contrast.)"[80]

While Wright distinguished between modernist and bourgeois taste without explaining how those tastes were formed, other critics were more explicit. In a companion piece called "The Painting of Tomorrow" whose title clearly referred to Blashfield's "The Painting of To-Day," Ernest Blumenschein outlined his own conversion to modernist aesthetics, an account that reads more like an initiation into a secret society than the assimilation of common norms.[81] Describing his own furtive attempts to discern the meaning of various "passwords" overheard during his first untutored immersion in the salons of the "sandaled anarchists" and "disciples" of modernism,[82] Blumenschein suggested not only that aesthetic obscurity was an acceptable habit for Americans to adopt but that the job of getting to the meaning of new art and new aesthetics fell squarely on the unconverted outsider, rather than on critics and others who explained it, and that this conversion necessarily preceded any meaningful art-world participation. Under the pressure of a common aesthetic, Blumenschein complained, he "had always vaguely felt the bit in my mouth," and argued that in his own experience as an artist "the necessity of making my details thoroughly intelligible to the public often blocked my path when I was nearly at the goal."[83] Thus the modernist's main challenge as Blumenschein represented it was having the "courage to be different from our fellow-sheep" in the face of "derision," "contempt," and, in the case of artists, "a diminished income."[84]

It would be unfair to suggest that pro-modernist supporters of the Armory Show chose their language purely for its obscurity or that mere obscurity was the only purpose it served. If Armory Show skeptics had inherited their amateur predecessors' belief in the knowability of art, and their compelling interest in a style of criticism that stressed the pedagogical and the transparent, modernism's most vocal proponents tended to marginalize common experience as a guide to the interpretation of art, suggesting that aesthetic experience could be neither understood nor explained in conventional terms. According to MacColl, "the appeal which [modernist artworks] make is so direct and so personal that it removes life to another court by referring it not to any past experience of life, but exactly to a sense, a recognition of new life, new art. They give us something that was not in our life, that was not in the art of painting before, and it appeals to us with all the power and the charm of a quickened consciousness of the value and meaning of life itself."[85] Similarly, Willard Huntington Wright suggested that modern art's sources differed significantly from those of previous forms, describing Synchromism as a style in which "painting becomes almost entirely subjective and wholly creative," and in which works need only contain "that requisite leaven of the 'real.'"[86]

While modern art's liberation from common experience held out the promise of "quickened consciousness" and new creativity for critics like MacColl and Wright, it also presented them with a problem, in that it was extremely difficult to develop a plain way of speaking about an art that was hard for even its admirers to understand. A sense of the peculiar unknowability of modern (and particularly abstract) art affected modernist critics' decisions about how to express their judgments about art as much as it affected judgments themselves. In response to this, many promodernist writers chose a new and self-referential critical language that allowed them to focus on art objects as art objects, a decision that freed critics from making comparisons between objects and the external world. While jargon could be used to suit the professional needs of criticism, the turn to obscure language also marked critics' real struggle to express what they believed was incommunicable and, to a certain degree, unknowable.

Modernist critics' narrowing focus on art's aesthetic qualities also allowed them to abandon institution builders' concern with the art-world sources of artistic change, providing them with an explanatory framework that gave them greater power as experts and that helped them to distinguish themselves both from the past and from the public. Wright's analysis, thus, was not merely concerned with the relative significance of the subjective and the observed in modern painting, but contained a larger argument about the meaning of such narrowly aesthetic issues in the broader scheme of things. Of Impressionism, for example, he wrote: "Color juxtaposition is the main issue. Color had always been used merely for dramatic reinforcement or for decorative effects. These new men opened the eyes of all serious-minded artists to an entirely new conception in the making of a painting. The struggle to carry on this idea has been the history of painting for the last thirty years."[87] Abandoning all mention of institutional developments within the art world, Wright named a particular aesthetic innovation (and a relatively narrow innovation, at that) as the most significant accomplishment of the past generation. Indeed, Wright crowded the entire history of painting during the period into this development, thus displacing all nonaesthetic developments and all art-world participants who did not contribute directly to it from that history. By accentuating "most people's" simplistic attachment to easily grasped technical innovations "of secondary consideration," moreover, Wright further marginalized nonexperts from meaningful participation in the production and judgment of art—even while he privately relished the crude humor of the show's detractors (fig. 63).

Christian Brinton, who described artistic change in terms of aesthetic, rather than organizational developments, also promoted this decontextualized vision of artistic production. Although Brinton insisted that

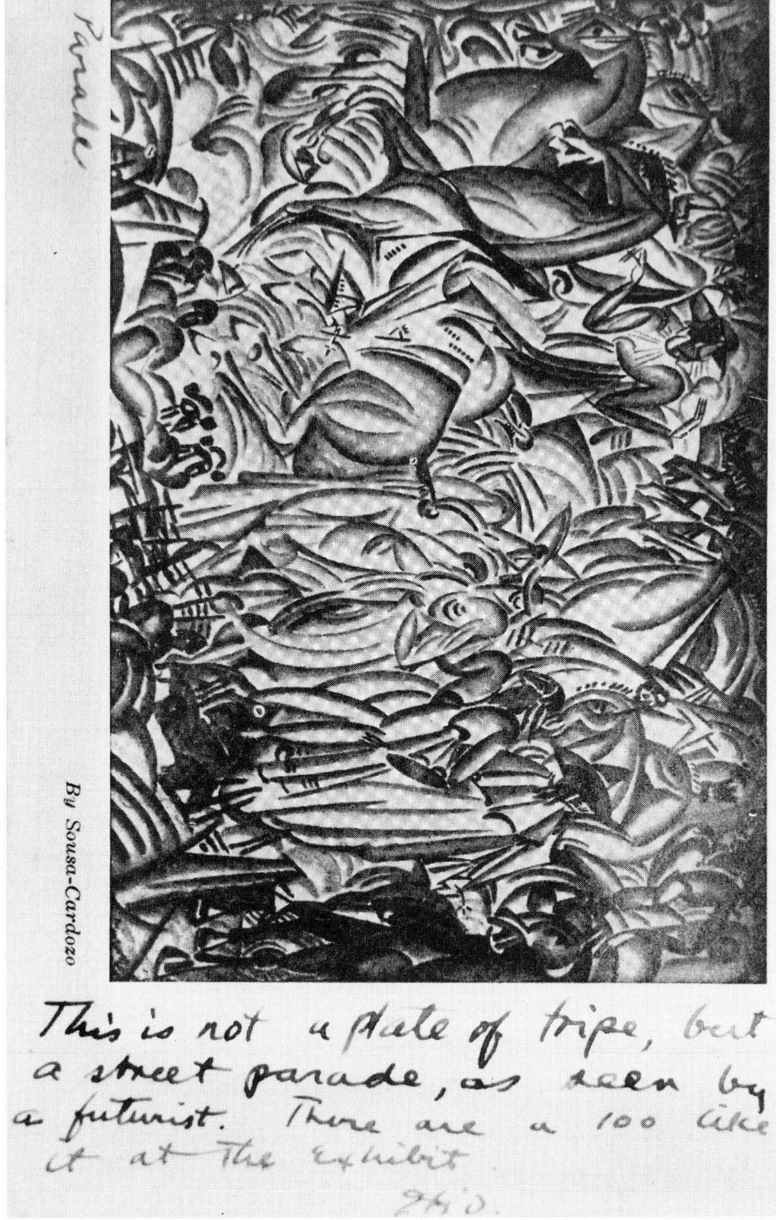

63. "This is Not a Plate of Tripe." Armory Show postcard after Amedeo de Sousa-Cardozo, *Parade*, sent by Willard Huntington Wright to Katherine Boynton Wright, 20 March 1913. S. S. Van Dine Collection, Clifton Waller Barrett Library of American Literature, Special Collections, University of Virginia Library

"Evolution, Not Revolution" powered artistic change, he depicted America's artistic "awakening" as a series of cataclysms enacted upon an empty landscape. He wrote: "We are indeed a fortunate people. Separated from Europe by that shining stretch of sea which has always so clearly conditioned our development—social, intellectual, and esthetic—we get only the results of Continental cultural endeavor. We take no part in the preliminary struggles that lead up to these achievements. They come to our shores as finished products, appearing suddenly before us in all their salutary freshness and variety. The awakening of the American public to the appreciation of things artistic has, in brief, been accomplished by a series of shocks from the outside rather than through intensive effort, observation, or participation."[88] To Brinton, as to Wright, then, the art-world development that had consumed the attention of a generation of critics and that still motivated so many writers to applaud the Armory Show for its institution-building qualities was meaningless.

While the desire to elaborate a nonreferential and object-based aesthetic may have driven pro-modernist accounts of the Armory Show and the new art in general, it is impossible to separate the purely aesthetic motivations that allowed certain critics to accept modernism from the broader trend toward an expert-driven, exclusive criticism begun in the Gilded Age. Like their professionalizing predecessors, America's first critical supporters of modernism adopted a criticism that placed the interpretation and evaluation of discrete art objects ahead of the promotion of wider art-world goals, and that disparaged those art objects whose referential character allowed their meanings to be unlocked through appeals to common experience alone. And, like their predecessors, modernist critics also expressed this emphasis on distinct and nonreferential art objects in an exclusive, esoteric discourse that served to further diminish public participation in the emerging modernist art world. It was to this potent combination of interpretative territorialism and obscure, clubbish language, as much as to the look or moral content of modernist artworks, that institution-building critics who responded to the Armory Show most violently reacted.

Like their nineteenth-century forebears, institution-building critics in the period of the Armory Show deliberately and purposefully shunned the exclusive use of purely evaluative criticism. Their resistance to a style of criticism that we take for granted as the style proper to professional critics should not be taken, as some scholars have suggested, as a sign of criticism's impoverishment before the second decade of the twentieth century, but rather as evidence that object-centered criticism is itself historically bounded, and that it serves the needs of certain interpretative communities better than others. The "story of the Armory Show" that has not been told is the story of this criticism's continued ascendance after 1913, the subsequent passing of a style of criticism that valued the expansion of the art world over the exclusive promotion of particular aesthetic norms, and the consequences of this loss for the American art world.

Camera Work

THE MAGAZINE WITHOUT AN "IF"—FEARLESS—INDEPENDENT—WITHOUT FAVOR □ □ □

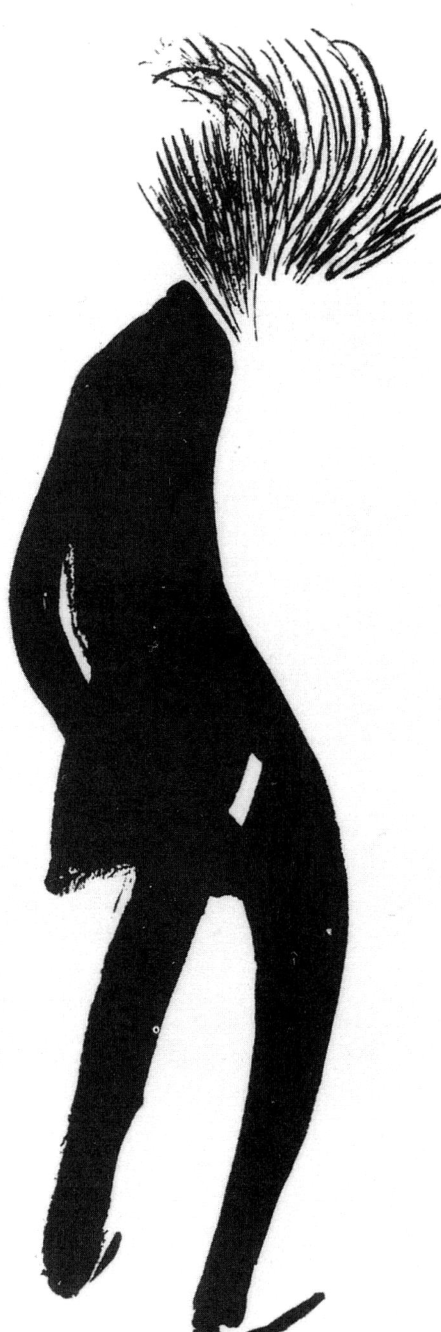

BY MARIUS DE ZAYAS

Chapter 5 *Camera Work*: Organizing the Avant-Garde

The Secessionists care little for popular approval, insisting upon works, not faith, and believing that their share having been done in producing the work, the public must now do the rest. A few friends, and these of understanding mind, a few true appreciators, this is all they expect and all they desire.
—Sadakichi Hartmann, 1904

At the beginning of the twenty-first century, it is clear who ultimately won the battle between professionals and institution builders for the control of American art. What counts for canons, after all, is how history treats art: what gets entrenched, what gets lost, and what remains but without remembered origins. In the case of American art, what we willingly preserve from the twentieth century tends to be modernism; from Alfred Stieglitz (fig. 64) to Jackson Pollock, from Frank Lloyd Wright to Georgia O'Keeffe, modernism is what put America on the map, and modernism is what we keep. The march toward preservation or oblivion affects art worlds as well as artists, practices as well as works. In a key respect, then, the approach taken by the art media after the Civil War represents an avenue not taken in the twentieth century. Perhaps because efforts to develop an arts infrastructure were so successful, by the mid-twentieth century, art publishing had lost its previous emphasis on

64. Marius de Zayas (1880–1961?), *Alfred Stieglitz ("Camera Work," the Magazine without an "If")*. Published in *Camera Work* 30 (April 1910). Yale Collection of American Literature, Beinecke Rare Book and Manuscript Library, New Haven, Connecticut

Stieglitz. If the 1913 Armory Show marked modernism's official American coming-out party, Stieglitz's intimate exhibitions of works by Rodin, Matisse, and Picasso between 1905 and 1912 served as the new art's formal letter of introduction to a small and powerful viewership.[2] Not merely an importer but an artist in his own right, Stieglitz has also been credited widely with transforming photography into one of the primary languages for modernist experimentation in the United States, a transformation which paralleled Frank Lloyd Wright's drive in architecture toward a vernacular American modernism.[3] Although scholars disagree on the degree to which Stieglitz himself initiated American photography's turn away from the academic, pictorialist style of the turn of the century toward the hard-edged, geometric productions of the following decades, few have denied Stieglitz and the photographic school he engendered a central place in the pantheon of American visual modernism.[4]

Yet, Stieglitz's talent as an artist and connoisseur of the new only partially explains his success within the art world, both occluding his relationship to his predecessors and prohibiting a more nuanced understanding of photographic modernism's emergence and rise to preeminence in the United States.[5] Stieglitz's proficiency as an art-world organizer, as much as the freshness of his vision, transformed the face of photographic production in America, and provided a model for artists working in other media, as well.[6] As both a preserver of the heavily organizational approach to artistic production championed by his nineteenth-century predecessors and an innovator on those forms, Stieglitz gave new shape to American understandings of artistic creation.[7] Like the Gilded Age entrepreneurs who had sought to promote the development of art in America through the establishment of museums, schools, and publishing, Stieglitz made a place for photography among the fine arts both by developing institutions devoted to its advancement and by constantly negotiating for its acceptance among the already established structures of the art world.[8]

Stieglitz reimagined the nature and function of art publishing in significant ways. If he utilized time-tested institutional means to build a place for artistic photography in a literal sense, he used publishing to achieve a more specific but more metaphorical construction, building his circle into an avant-garde, presumably independent of art-world ties, and constructing their works as the inevitable, natural next step in the development of artistic photography. By billing the promotion of a particular set of producers and works as a crusade for the promotion of artistic photography *per se*, Stieglitz closed off alternative definitions of artistic photography and represented his associates as the only and self-evident future of art.[9] Through this refashioning of criticism and publishing, and through the construction of a vertically integrated organizational structure that mirrored contemporary moves toward consolidation in business and industry, Stieglitz secured a lasting place in the American cultural imagination not only for modernist photography, but for the avant-garde itself.[10]

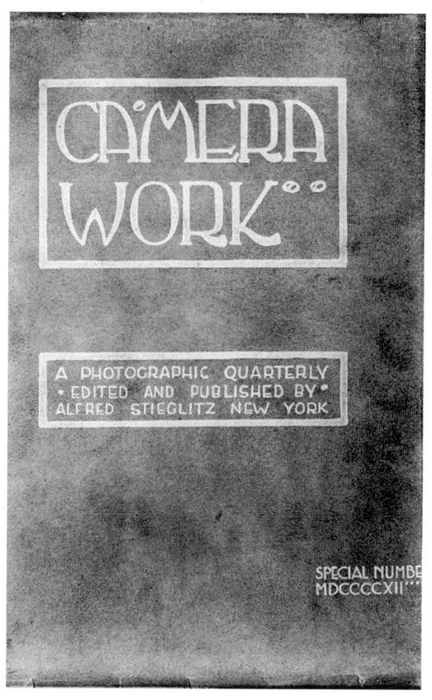

65. Cover of *Camera Work*, special number, 1912. Yale Collection of American Literature, Beinecke Rare Book and Manuscript Library, New Haven, Connecticut

Stieglitz's art-world empire consisted of three central organizations: the Photo-Secession, founded in 1902, *Camera Work* (fig. 65), a journal which ran from 1903 to 1917, and the Little Galleries at 291 Fifth Avenue, which operated between 1905 and 1917.[11] The Photo-Secession was not the first of Stieglitz's efforts in this direction: since before the turn of the century, he had been involved in the creation and restructuring of photographic associations, attending to the 1896 merger that had created the Camera Club, New York, out of the New York Camera Club and the Society of Amateur Photographers.[12] The Photo-Secession was self-consciously modeled after the various European splinter groups from which it took its name, joining photographers and sympathizers in an association devoted to the acceptance of photography as a valid artistic medium. Not only a convenient gatekeeping device, whereby membership readily distinguished insiders from outsiders, the association also helped to shape the boundaries of a united front for entry into competitions, exhibitions, and the like, undergirding aesthetic sympathy with the bond of formal association. Membership within the Photo-Secession, like membership within the Society of American Artists, the Ten, and the range of other formal and informal associations that artists formed throughout the nineteenth century, provided artists with sheltered opportunities for exhibition within the fold, as well as offering solidarity and common cause to those with grievances against the hanging committees that determined the composition of most large, public exhibitions.

The second key institution in Stieglitz's realm was the Little Galleries of the Photo-Secession ("291"), which hosted a range of exhibitions, comprising works by the photographers of the Photo-Secession, American painters including Marsden Hartley and Georgia O'Keeffe, and, as I mentioned, European artists such as Rodin, Cézanne, and Picasso. As the public face of the Photo-Secession, 291 also served as the starting point from which Stieglitz could develop and control a context of display amenable to Secessionist needs. Like the Society of American Artists' annual exhibition, it provided a seemingly "independent" space in which members' works could be displayed without outside "interference." In its commitment to the display of both photography and works in more established artistic media, 291 also bolstered claims that photography was a "fine" art.[13]

The journal *Camera Work* served as the linchpin of Stieglitz's enterprise. As in the case of the Photo-Secession itself, this effort was preceded by another journal, *Camera Notes*, which Stieglitz ran on behalf of the

Camera Club. In taking charge of *Camera Notes*, Stieglitz argued that the regular publication of criticism, examples of good photographic work, and information about the Club and "what is going on in the photographic world at large" would inspire creative advances among its readership.[14] *Camera Work* continued in this vein, but it also pursued another goal: the creation and definition of a vanguardist "field of art." Like their predecessors, *Camera Work*'s editors knew that the print media had the potential to reach more viewers than exhibitions alone. Hence, the journal often contained work that had been shown previously at 291, and entire catalogues of its exhibitions. In 1908, for example, the journal reprinted the catalogue from an exhibition of Rodin drawings, "for the benefit of the readers of *Camera Work* who did not have the pleasure of seeing the exhibition."[15]

If the images in *Camera Work* helped to define the vanguardist "field of art," so, too, did its commentary, which was often devoted to describing the Photo-Secession and explaining its relationship to other art-world organizations. Soon after publication began, *Camera Work*'s editors devoted a small supplement to answering the "many . . . enquiries as to the nature and aims of the Photo-Secession and requirements of eligibility to membership."[16] In response, this supplement explained that the Photo-Secession was comprised of a Council, Fellows, and Associates, and that its membership included photographers, as well as collectors, writers, and other supporters. In addition to explaining the Photo-Secession's structure, however, this supplement also allowed the editors to distinguish between its membership and outsiders. Suggesting that many applicants for membership had been refused, the editors wrote: "It must not be supposed that these qualifications will be assumed as a matter of course, as it has been found necessary to deny the application of many whose lukewarm interest in the cause with which we are so thoroughly identified gave no promise of aiding the Secession."[17] In so doing, the editors walked a fine line. For while they insisted that "'Camera Work' owes allegiance to no organization or clique," it was nonetheless "the mouthpiece of the Photo-Secession." What Stieglitz would have to do was to convince readers that "that fact will not be allowed to hamper its independence in the slightest degree."[18]

One of the difficulties Stieglitz faced was that many artists' associations that had claimed to be independent from the establishment had seemed to slide into conformity and decadence with the passage of time. The Ten, after all, had splintered off from the SAA, which within decades of its founding was seen by many artists as virtually identical to the Academy itself. If Stieglitz were to represent the Photo-Secession as truly independent from the establishment, it would have to be different from other vanguardist associations. In the main, the strategy pursued within *Cam-*

era Work was to suggest that the Photo-Secession was not, at heart, an organization in the conventional sense, but the embodiment of a visionary or spiritual purpose. Sometimes, arguments in favor of this interpretation emphasized Stieglitz's own formidable personal power. As Charles Caffin argued, "The Photo-Secession, in fact, is all that one particular strong personality stands for, syndicated."[19] At the very least, this attribution of the Secession imperative to a single, unified will, masked the complicated negotiations within the photographic community that had determined the group's membership.[20]

Nonetheless, it still suggested that one dominant personality (Stieglitz's) might have forced the rest to submit. Stieglitz's own analysis of the Secession's character thus further underplayed its organizational aspects, both avoiding the use of organizational metaphors (syndication) and replacing them with a spiritual metaphor. Characterizing the group's formation in terms of a vague seeking after honesty, Stieglitz described the Photo-Secession as the "Spirit of the Lamp; the old and discolored, the too frequently despised, the too often discarded lamp of honesty; honesty of aim, honesty of self-expression, honesty of revolt against the autocracy of convention. The Photo-Secession is not the keeper of this Lamp, but lights it when it may."[21] Other writers boldly denied that the Photo-Secession was an organization at all. In 1909, Paul Haviland exclaimed that "we are dealing, not with a society, not with an organization, as much as with a movement. The Secession is not so much a school or a following as an attitude towards life; and its motto seems to be:—'Give every man who claims to have a message for the world a chance of being heard.'"[22]

Camera Work's metaphorical description of the Secession as a movement, rather than a formal association, served a number of key purposes in the creation of an avant-garde. It rhetorically united a disparate group of artists, who in practice did not always agree on what "honesty of self-expression" actually meant. It allowed participants in the "movement" to forget the more earthly components of the artistic life—political intrigue, the constant struggle for fame and success—in favor of a seemingly purer notion of artistic production. This was accentuated by Stieglitz's decision to specifically identify Photo-Secession with European movements that overtly criticized the market, a decision that allowed Stieglitz to mask the Photo-Secession's indebtedness to corporate sponsors such as Kodak.[23] And, more generally, it allowed Stieglitz to naturalize his own aggressive role in the group's formation, as well as the group's similarities to both previous and contemporary associations within the art world.

It is crucial to note that this drive to define the Secession as a movement was not a drive toward professionalism *per se*. Although *Camera Work*'s purpose was, on the most obvious level, to challenge and redefine existing boundaries within the artistic guild in order to make room for photographers, it would be a mistake to interpret the Photo-Secession as simply a fledgling professional association. *Camera Work* brimmed with demands that photographers be treated as artists. Nonetheless, its writers bristled at the suggestion that artists in other fields could evaluate photography on the basis of their professional experience alone. As a distinct and quickly developing medium, they argued, photography resisted easy assessment even by experienced art-world professionals.[24] Cutting short suggestions that photographic juries be made up of painters and sculptors, *Camera Work* regular Charles Caffin[25] wrote that "prints that might have passed for notable a short time ago have been superseded in character and quality by later productions; and even among the photographers themselves it is only those who have kept themselves in touch with the important exhibitions that are in a position to judge of the kind of work which should be accepted as representative of the latest phase of the movement. Without such expert assistance a jury of painters and sculptors would hardly prove satisfactory in the judging of photographs, for so few of them have taken enough interest to acquaint themselves with the subject. Except as an assistance to their own work, they do not treat it seriously, and their attitude toward a print is generally one of surprise that it should be as good as or no worse than it is."[26]

Caffin's language here is reminiscent of Cook's and Van Rensselaer's appeals to "speeding time." Yet, he challenged the idea that professionalism within photography was enough to solve this problem. When the well-credentialed professional photographer Julius C. Strauss "presumed to act as spokesman for the photographic pictorialists," Stieglitz quickly undercut his authority. Freely acknowledging Strauss's status as "a well-known professional portrait-photographer," Stieglitz denied that membership in the photographic profession qualified him to speak for the group. "No doubt," the editor wrote, "Mr. Strauss was actuated by what he conceived to be the best interests of photography, and for taking the initiative is entitled to much credit; but his connection with the modern pictorial movement has hardly been such as to have given him the knowledge and experience necessary to impress the authorities with the history and consequent rights of photography as a fine art."[27] In part, *Camera Work*'s hostility to professionalism as an organizational model might have stemmed from the Secession's desire to be defined differently from other American artists' associations, as these associations were often organized around common professional aspirations, rather than shared artistic styles or methods.

If *Camera Work* questioned Strauss's right to interpret pictorialism, it also undermined his authority on another level. For while Stieglitz primarily excluded Strauss from commenting on the "modern pictorial movement," his comment implicitly challenged Strauss's competence to speak on *any* aspect of "fine art" photography. By blurring the distinction between the "modern pictorial movement" and "photography as a fine art," Stieglitz claimed both fields for the Secession. Moreover, he expanded the vanguard's claim beyond the production to the interpretation of artistic works, staking exclusive right to photography's history, as well as its future. By drawing boundaries between Secessionists and professionals in this way, Stieglitz laid the basis for Secession unity through self-interpretation and helped to exclude alternative visions of the possibilities for artistic photography.

Creating Contexts

In 1906, the Photo-Secession achieved a milestone in its struggle to gain acceptance for photography as an independent artistic medium: an invitation to mount an exhibition at the Pennsylvania Academy of the Fine Arts. The Academy had, after all, "helped to initiate the Salon movement in Philadelphia," only to close "its doors on the photographers and their claims" a few years later.[28] A sign of the Photo-Secession's coming-of-age, this invitation inspired *Camera Work* insider Joseph T. Keiley to pen a brief history of the group, in which he trumpeted Secessionist triumphs and set the stage for its future accomplishments.[29] Keiley did more than merely document the Secession's arrival, however; under the guise of recounting the group's past affairs, he used his critical history actively to shape and mold its identity. Burying the organizational content of Secessionist activity under a barrage of claims about the group's independence, Keiley transformed a moment of patent institution building into evidence not only that the group had stood apart from the surrounding art world, but also that its autonomy had guaranteed its success.

Keiley's announcement heralded the fact that a hallowed arts institution had agreed to support and shelter the Secession. Nonetheless, Keiley maintained that the invitation proved the Photo-Secession's remove from art-world intrigue. The Photo-Secession, he wrote, "had kept apart from all entanglements with other organizations. Effort was repeatedly made to affiliate it with other organizations, or to draw it into controversy. Experience had taught it the lesson of the safeness of standing alone. Into controversy or politics it always declined to enter. On the other hand, it opposed no recognition, and sought to secure it for its own exhibitions."[30] By presenting independence as the cause of present and indisputable events (the Photo-Secession's current success, exemplified by the Pennsylvania exhibition), Keiley lent it the force of historical fact. In this way, he surpassed the celebratory and promotional rhetoric endemic to Gilded Age criticism, positing a new relationship between critics and the events at hand. Most nineteenth-century writers had rendered their observations about the art world rather transparently, perhaps noting the place of particular events within the larger trajectory of American progress in the arts. Keiley's history had a more definite end point. Keenly aware of the invitation's potential to confirm a larger set of claims about the Photo-Secession and pictorialism generally, Keiley transformed it from a simple marker of success into evidence for the group's independence from art-world affiliations, and for its single-minded adherence to an aesthetic, rather than a political, goal.[31]

This event—and its representation in *Camera Work*—is important because it points to one of the central strategies employed by Stieglitz in the establishment of an American avant-garde: the creation of contexts of display that would serve the aesthetic and institutional needs of his allies, while effacing or denying the acts of organization that underpinned them. In furthering this dual aim, Stieglitz and his associates employed a wide variety of rhetorical strategies in describing the Secession, its exhibitions, and its links to the rest of the art world. This included the editors' consistent appeal to a central dichotomy by which they judged all opportunities for exhibition. *Camera Work* divided exhibition situations into two clearly marked categories: those in which the Photo-Secession was free to display its works, unencumbered by outside interference, and those in which the taint of external meddling prohibited viewers from experiencing pictorialist works in the correct manner. Insisting that the Secession itself have full control over the judgment and selection of its members' productions, *Camera Work* announced in 1903 that "it is the policy of the Photo-Secession to exhibit only upon invitation, and this necessarily implies that its exhibit must be hung as a unit and in its entirety, without submission to any jury."[32] Such proclamations emphasized the unity and impenetrability of the Photo-Secession, while warning trespassers to respect its boundaries.[33]

If the Secession worried that juries' invasive, individualized appraisal of its members' works would compromise its independence, it also fretted that outside organizers lacked the capacity to show photography to its best advantage. S. L. Willard expressed this fear in the journal's second issue, writing of the Third Salon at Chicago that "remarks on juries and on hanging may seem less pertinent than a criticism of the prints; but a poor setting will mar a good play; cheap typography and binding a good book; inexperienced performers an artistic musical composition. Pictorial photography may well claim a place among fine arts, but dignity and sanity are needed in its every relation if it is to attract the approval and recognition of people of taste and cultivation."[34] By relinquishing its works to the inexpert hands of outsiders, Willard suggested, the Secession would never be able to convince the world of photography's true merit.

Stieglitz's appeal to "independence" as the standard for Secession entry into exhibitions served several purposes. It allowed him to explain the Secession's uneasiness concerning competing institutions, and enabled him to distance the group from the many friendly associations it had made. Moreover, it allowed Stieglitz to perform this distancing while continuing to portray the approval of these outside groups as evidence of the Secession's merit. In describing Secessionist participation in exhibitions outside the Little Galleries, the editors oscillated between self-congratulation for having been recognized by galleries, critics, and other art-world players, and carefully placed barbs about the inadequacy of non-Secessionists to make aesthetic decisions. In assessing one of "the two most important exhibitions of pictorial photographs held in recent years in this country . . . at the Corcoran Art Galleries in Washington and at the Carnegie Art Galleries in Pittsburg [*sic*] in February," *Camera Work* announced that "at Pittsburg the interest is equally great, the exhibition being still open at this writing. In order to insure the complete carrying out of our ideas, the Director of the Photo-Secession, accompanied by Messrs. Steichen, Keiley, and Coburn, traveled both to Washington and Pittsburg to superintend the hanging of the prints, a matter of great importance which is generally underestimated, as well as formally to open the halls to the public. The local press showed much interest, devoting a large amount of space with the usual inadequate newspaper illustrations to the Secession and all its works."[35] Disguised by their mildness of tone, and inserted within the larger, congratulatory framework of tributes to Photo-Secession success, these criticisms nonetheless hit their mark, proving the distance between Secessionists and their peers.

Camera Work also used the dichotomy between independence and interference to explain and naturalize the founding of 291. A frequent argument voiced within the journal was that 291, unlike other exhibition venues, was a "neutral" and "independent" space in which "quality" alone determined content. This distinguished it from "academic and art-organization exhibitions," Keiley argued, which "with few exceptions, have degenerated into being conservators of aesthetic snobbery or of the commercialization of art."[36] Indeed, the editors even expressed gratitude that the number of such exhibitions was declining: "We are devotedly thankful that there are fewer photographic 'Art Exhibitions' now than there were several years ago. What has been lost in quantity, however, has been gained in quality. (We wish the same could be said of the 'real' art exhibitions.)"[37] In the presumably neutral space of the Little Galleries, the editors suggested, works spoke loudly, clearly, and forcefully for themselves, necessarily winning an audience of thrilled supporters. In this way, *Camera Work* transformed an organizational issue—how to promote and disseminate artworks—into a purely aesthetic matter, independent of its institutional context.

In reality, Stieglitz and his associates paid close attention to the details of display, creating contexts that enhanced the reception of Secessionist productions and distinguished Photo-Secession exhibitions from those of its competitors.[38] Besides arguing for photography's inclusion among the fine arts through a concurrent display of drawings, paintings, and photographs,[39] Stieglitz surrounded Secessionist productions with the trappings of artistic display. This gained him the scorn of critic Charles Fitzgerald, who sneered that "the exhibition at present open at No. 291 Fifth Avenue is simply reeking with 'art' down to the very catalogue with its eccentric lettering, its pretty little gold seal, and its ragged edges. There is surely nothing wanting in the way of refinements; if there is a question, it is whether all these excrescences are traceable to a foundation as solid as the photographers would have us believe. They suggest, not the struggles of exploration, but the easy satisfaction of established convention, not to say the refinement of decay."[40]

More important than the catalogue were Stieglitz's efforts within the gallery itself. From at least the late 1850s onward, American artists had realized that the way their art was displayed—not just the art itself—was an important factor in the making of sales and reputations. Frederic Church and Albert Bierstadt staged elaborate events at the Tenth Street Studio Building to exhibit monumental works like Bierstadt's *The Rocky Mountains, Lander's Peak* (1863; The Metropolitan Museum of Art, New York), complete with elaborate drapery, dramatic lighting, and promotional catalogues written by the artists' friends. Even at the extravagant admission price of twenty-five cents, Church's similarly spectacular month-long display of *Heart of the Andes* (1859; The Metropolitan Museum of Art, New York) in 1859 drew over ten thousand visitors—some of whom had to be turned away as the exhibition shut its doors.[41] The savvy use of these kinds of exhibitions helped to make Church and Bierstadt among the highest-paid artists of the day, each commanding as much as ten or even twenty thousand dollars for a single canvas in the 1860s. As we have seen, this entrepreneurial approach to the display of art continued in the 1880s, most notably in the hands of Chase and Whistler. Whistler arranged a series of exhibitions—including two in New York in the 1880s—that showcased his own work within a context entirely of his own invention. Leaving no details to chance, Whistler not only directed the placement of pictures—hung in single or double file across the line of sight—but selected frames, materials and color for the walls, and the design and content of exhibition catalogues. In one case, the artist even instructed guests to wear black and white, so as not to disturb his carefully devised color scheme.[42]

As important to later exhibitors was the move by associations of artists, beginning with the SAA, to devise hanging practices that would suit their membership's needs. As we have seen, one of the significant sources of SAA hostility to the Academy in the 1870s was the older institution's method of selecting and displaying works. Like founding member Clarence Cook, who increased his own critical authority by narrowing the boundaries of art, the vanguardist SAA worked to improve the fortunes of its members by distinguishing them from "mainstream" competitors. As Trudie Grace observes, however, this hostility derived from the Academy's *expansiveness*, as much as from its exclusivity. In its exhibitions, the SAA was persistently more exclusive than the Academy; according to Grace's estimate, the SAA showed around twenty-five percent of the pictures it received, while the Academy's acceptance rate was closer to "sixty percent during many years."[43] The SAA's shows were also considerably smaller than Academy annuals, and minimized the number of rows of pictures hung in any given space; it even experimented with single-row hanging. That this was a successful strategy is borne out by Koehler's "Statistical Table of Exhibitions" for 1882, which shows that in the two previous years of Society exhibitions, the value of works sold doubled while the number of works displayed increased only by a third.[44]

Stieglitz appropriated this strategy to distinguish the Secessionist vanguard from its competitors. Within 291, works were hung sparsely within a minimally decorated, neutrally colored space (fig. 66) that was at odds with the still comparatively crowded Academy-style installations (see fig. 28). This served not only to distinguish the Photo-Secession from the Academy and other "mainstream" organizations, but from fellow critics of the Academy like Robert Henri, who also organized "independent" exhibitions throughout the period but who, to Secessionist tastes, was too unselective. As an article by James Gibbons Huneker, reprinted in *Camera Work*, exclaimed: "No, messieurs et mesdemoiselles, les Independents [*sic*], you'll never beat the Academy at its own stupid game by substituting quantity for quality! Two wrongs don't make a right. Oppose quality to quantity. Slash off the heads of two-thirds of your applicants and try to kill the demon of vain display."[45]

The "opposition of quality to quantity" provided the Photo-Secession with a means of distinguishing itself from its competitors. Moreover, the radical visual and material simplification of 291's installations also paralleled the wider argument, within *Camera Work*, that the Photo-Secession was a spiritual and aesthetic "movement," rather than an organization. As Caffin argued: "I have never seen an exhibition presented with so discreet a taste. . . . The secret of its discretion . . . consisted in *adopting the photographic print itself as the unit of the scheme of arrangement*. This sounds obvious enough, but observe the result of conforming to it logically."[46] In other words, 291's interiors were not made by the hand of

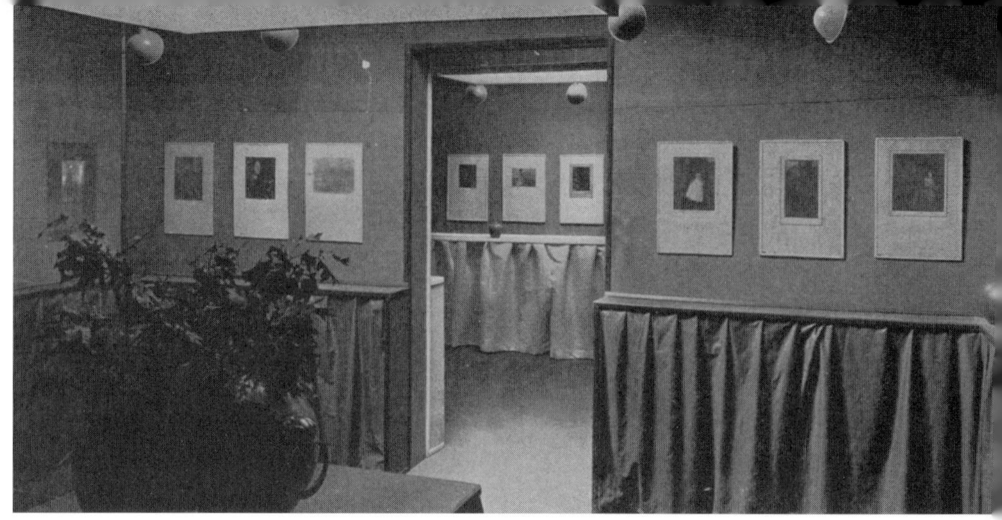

66. The opening exhibition at 291, Nov. 1905–Jan. 1906. Published in *Camera Work* 14 (April 1906). Yale Collection of American Literature, Beinecke Rare Book and Manuscript Library, New Haven, Connecticut

Stieglitz, but followed "logically" from the works themselves. While Benjamin had made similar remarks regarding the SAA's exhibitions as early as the 1870s, Caffin's tone suggested to readers that this method, like other Secession innovations, represented a radical break with the art world of the past.

This rhetorical strategy could also be used to describe Secession exhibitions outside 291, such as the show at the Pennsylvania Academy of the Fine Arts or the Secession-juried photographic exhibition of 1910 at Buffalo. As Caffin described it, "One received a suggestion that the exhibition represented not an incident, but for the time being the purpose of the building's existence," once again blurring the distinction between Secession jurying and "adopting the photographic print itself as the unit of the scheme of arrangement."[47] In contrast, Stieglitz refused to participate in the St. Louis World's Fair because it did not offer such an amenable context in which to embed the Secession's work. Unlike the Pennsylvania and Buffalo exhibitions, participation at St. Louis would have demanded the dispersal of the group's oeuvre among the productions of nonmembers. As photographs, the Secessionists' works would have been banished from the Fine Arts section at St. Louis and hung with the productions of professional portrait photographers, rather than with paintings or etchings. Unlike Koehler, who combined a campaign for etching with a respect for the "Interstate Industrial Exhibition" and the "National Manufacturing and Mining Exhibition," Stieglitz boycotted the St. Louis exhibition. He also described the decision of some pictorialists to participate as "a pity."[48] Cast in this way, what was really an exercise in the optimization of context within the confines of the conventional network of artistic display came off as a battle between independents and insiders.

Like nineteenth-century entrepreneurs, who realized that magazines could be used to circulate the "original" works of graphic artists to a wide and potentially lucrative audience, Stieglitz recognized the potential of

Camera Work to display the Photo-Secession and its works.[49] This may have been Stieglitz's wisest adaptation of nineteenth-century organizational strategy. A single image from *Camera Work* can now sell for two to three times what an entire year of the *American Art Review*, with plates intact, will fetch on the market. In public collections, even the rarest post-war art magazines, and the images inside them, are usually found only on the library shelves of those universities that happened to collect them when they came out, often as not sitting in remote storage areas waiting for the end times. In contrast, *Camera Work* is almost exclusively to be found, when accessible to the public at all, in the paper vaults of America's museums alongside the Picassos and the Rembrandts. The canon, as it turns out, is climate-controlled.

In *Camera Work*, as in 291, Stieglitz and his associates created carefully constructed venues for the display and reception of the Photo-Secession's work, and for the organization itself. And, in both cases, they did this while effacing this effort at contextualization in favor of interpretations that portrayed the three institutions as "honest," "independent," and derived solely "from the works themselves,"—rather than insincere, entangled, or deriving from less "logical" sources. One of the ways in which Stieglitz fashioned a positive context for the reception of the Photo-Secession was by appealing to Europe, which can be seen in the group's name, as well as in 291's displays of "progressive" European art. It also can be seen in *Camera Work*'s inclusion of a wide range of articles that recounted the group's success at European exhibitions, and that noted the praise it had garnered from international museums, galleries, camera clubs, and "His Majesty the King of Italy," who had given the Secession a "special award."[50] Lest readers think the Photo-Secession was too entangled with the establishment, it also made frequent mention of "progressive" European institutions like Britain's Linked Ring and the Salon des Refusés.[51] At the same time, however, the journal took pains to emphasize that it had foresworn opportunities to sing its own praises: "In recent numbers we spoke of printing some reviews of the Photo-Secession Invitation Collections which had been sent to various European capitals. We had hoped to publish in this number extracts from these articles, but upon mature consideration have deemed it best to omit them. The Photo-Secession and its workers have so often been accused of over-weaning arrogance and conceit that the eulogistic tone of all these critiques would seem, if reprinted by us, to lend some truth to these charges, and therefore, to save our modesty, we feel constrained to forego publishing these reviews."[52]

Innovative editorial strategies also encouraged *Camera Work*'s audiences to read the Photo-Secession as an independent movement, driven by aesthetic imperative rather than expediency. As mentioned, the editors specifically stated that "'Camera Work' owe[d] allegiance to no organization or clique."[53] This impression was enhanced by a number of less obvious strategies, such as Stieglitz's avoidance of a fixed staff, or at least the appearance of one, in favor of a constantly evolving cast of critics and sharp limitations on the amount of space devoted to views designated as official, editorial opinion. The journal bolstered this impression of editorial restraint by frequently reprinting large blocks of text taken from competing publications. And finally, they implied that even the pieces penned by their own associates had arrived upon *Camera Work*'s pages by a mysterious process of revelation, rather than intentionally. This led to some strange results, such as when the editors "wish[ed] to reiterate for the *n*th time that the articles published in the magazine do not necessarily reflect [ou]r own views. As a matter of fact, few of them do. It has been our policy—and it will continue to be our policy—to print such articles as we deem timely, interesting, or provocative of ideas."[54] By creating contexts that erased the hand of the editor and the gilded frame of the Salon, Stieglitz and his associates represented modernist photographs and modernist opinion as revealed truths, rather than as things that belonged to a corrupt and intrigue-laden "mainstream" art world.

In truth, *Camera Work* did supply readers with a wide array of views on artistic and photographic issues, not all of them friendly and some of them quite hostile to the modernist project. Indeed, Stieglitz seemed to revel in the words of his enemies, which appeared with regularity within the journal's pages. *Camera Work*'s critical "regulars," moreover, did not cheer unceasingly for the Secessionist cause; the usually sympathetic Charles Caffin, for example, brandished his own critical independence on a number of occasions, exposing the egotism and folly of artists who belittled the public but then expected it to interpret their scorn as genius.[55] Yet, although roomy enough for multiple voices, *Camera Work* was hardly a haven for dissent. At the same time that they printed rancorous views from insiders and outsiders alike, the editors took steps to ensure that readers could distinguish challenges from the "party line." They did this through another editorial tactic: the employment of metadiscursive strategies, such as contextualization, which guided readers through the maze of critical opinion.[56] While allowing Stieglitz to marginalize the views of the Secession's critics, this strategy also provided a powerful mechanism by which to mask the bonds between Stieglitz and his allies.

This can be seen in the journal's treatment of Caffin's errant columns, such as one polemical piece on artists that the editors crudely named "As Others See Us." Caffin's essays were accompanied by corrective spin on other occasions, as well.[57] Caffin's "Is Herzog Also Among the Prophets?" of 1907, for example, provoked a lengthy commentary in which the editors struggled to avoid giving the appearance of interference.[58] At great length they wrote:

> We are glad to print the article which appears in this number from the pen of Mr. Caffin, the art critic, giving his impressions of these studies. We have no intention of commenting in any way upon Mr. Caffin's views, but feel that it may be interesting, in passing, to supplement an incomplete statement made by him of Mr. Herzog's method of achieving some of his results. Mr. Caffin alludes to Mr. Herzog's composite groups, but omits to mention his actual method of producing, let us say, The Banks of Lethe, assuming that he posed the group of figures as rendered in that composition and then photographed it. As a matter of fact Mr. Herzog proceeded approximately as follows: having made innumerable single- or occasionally double-figure studies on 4 × 5 plates, and having made bromide enlargements from each of these negatives, and having from these enlargements cut out the figures, paper-doll fashion, he then proceeded, on a large panel, and with these figures and a paper of pins, to group and re-group, arrange and re-arrange—in short, carry on experiments in his "hunt for the line!" When finally the composition satisfied his eye, he pasted down the pinned figures and with brush and pigment filled the gaps and pulled together the sections of his composition. Lastly, he photographed this result in various sizes, thus producing a number of "original" negatives. From one of these the accompanying photogravure was made without any tool work or retouching whatever.[59]

This lengthy commentary accomplished two tasks. First, it corrected Caffin's critical oversights, putting a more modernist spin on Herzog's photographs by demonstrating that his methodology had consisted neither in the narrative posing of figures nor in the alteration of negatives, but in compositional "experiments" with the raw materials of the medium. Second, it reversed the normal priority of text over gloss, and thereby quietly reasserted editorial control, by elevating the anonymous "supplement in passing" on Caffin's original interpretation to a central place in the text.

The employment of these strategies can also be seen in the journal's publication of "outside" reviews of Photo-Secession activities, which gave the immediate impression of vanguardist nonchalance in the face of criticism. If these outside views suggested that the group was willing to take on all challengers, however, the manner in which they were sewn into the text of the journal tells a very different story, in that the seams between text and gloss were always left showing. For one thing, outside opinions were often visually distinct, printed in smaller typeface than the surrounding sanctioned text. As well, these extracts did not always stand alone, but followed introductions that provided readers with the keys to deciphering the narratives that followed.

One notable example of this was *Camera Work*'s republication of reviews of the 1908 exhibit of Rodin drawings at 291, including some that were quite negative.[60] These responses were contextualized in such a way, however, that readers would have little trouble distinguishing between true and false opinion. For one thing, the editors also reprinted the text of the catalogue in full.[61] They also prefaced the extracts with the following exclamation: "It may be said to the credit of New York—provincial as it undoubtedly is in art matters generally—that in this instance a truer and more spontaneous appreciation could nowhere have been given to these remarkable drawings."[62] More subtly, the editors also carefully sequenced the "outside" views in descending order of sympathy to Secession opinion. The most antagonistic responses lamely brought up the rear, like W. B. McCormick's assertion that "these drawings should never been shown anywhere but in the sculptor's studio, for they are simply notes dashed off, studies of the human form—chiefly of nude females—that are too purely technical to have much general interest except that of a not very elevating kind. Stripped of all 'art atmosphere' they stand as drawings of nude women in attitudes that may interest the artist who drew them, but which are not for public exhibition."[63] Coming on the heels of J. N. Laurvik's assertion that the exhibition was "a challenge to the prurient purity of our puritanism" and J. E. Chamberlin's contention that the show was "of very great importance to artists and sculptors, though doubtless it will be pretty nearly incomprehensible to the general public," McCormick's warning against depictions of "nude females" of a "not very elevating kind" and his resistance to the "purely technical" were thereby discredited.[64] While the publication of "outside" opinions proved Stieglitz's vanguardist skill at the "gentle art of making enemies," the context created by *Camera Work* made them easy to dismiss.

Untrained Eyes

Camera Work also pursued another main goal: to recast the engagement of viewers and artworks. An important part of this process was a redefinition of the "public" for art, which the journal consistently represented as retrograde and antagonistic to the cause of advanced art. As the editors lamented in 1910: "Why is a man who fights for an ideal of humanity, no matter whether a poet, reformer, philosopher or artist, always hooted by the crowd, and pelted with mud, even by his friends! It cannot be otherwise. . . . The public has no time to reflect. It is only concerned with the effect. Its esthetic appreciation lives on memories or reminiscences. It admires only what it has seen before. It is always opposed to real originality. The road of novel ideas is too rough for them. Discrimination is not granted to the Philistines."[65] This, too, represented a significant change from views expressed by many critics in the 1870s, who had called upon "ignoramuses, babes and sucklings" to express their views about art, and had insisted that "the only safety is in a multitude of counsellors . . . our faith in the average perceptions, the average taste of the world at large is strong, and we think the critics are more like in the end to come round to the average opinion than the average opinion is to give up to the critics."[66] It followed, however, from an emerging tendency within *Modern Art* to publish vanguardist descriptions of artists like Theodore Child's description of Edgar Degas: "M. Degas is very little known to the public; he never exhibits in the annual salons, and very rarely in any other exhibitions. His aristocratic temperament and his strong respect for his art disincline him to expose to the general and unintelligent gaze works to appreciate which demand highly developed artistic education."[67]

While *Modern Art* employed such claims sparingly, *Camera Work* often cast art as a battle between vanguardists and Philistines. This can be seen in Sadakichi Hartmann's assertion that "the Secessionists care little for popular approval, insisting upon works, not faith, and believing that their share having been done in producing the work, the public must now do the rest. A few friends, and these of understanding mind, a few true appreciators, this is all they expect and all they desire."[68] Similarly, Hartmann disparaged the idea that education could teach the public to appreciate "an art as virile and fascinating, individually local and bitter as that of" Toulouse-Lautrec, whom he described as a "Montmartre bohemian." This was, in Hartmann's view, because "art appreciation can not be taught. It may be fostered, gradually developed in some naturally responsive and neglected individual, but even then it will lack freedom and spontaneity. Appreciation is an individual growth, like art itself, and it necessitates inborn talent from the start. . . . For that reason art is by the few and for the few. The more individual a work of art is, the more precious and free it is apt to be; and at the same time, as a natural consequence, the more difficult to understand."[69] Art appreciation could not be taught, in other words; it belonged only to the aristocracy of taste.

If Hartmann cast ordinary viewers as dense, he also described them as lazy. Unlike Milton Bradley and many others who promoted engaged public participation in art, music, and other disciplines, Hartmann suggested that music was more popular than art precisely because it provided passive enjoyment. Hartmann wrote: "People understand a Tschaikowsky symphony as little as an Impressionist exhibit, nevertheless ninety-nine out of a hundred will prefer to hear the concert, while one solitary individual will derive a similar pleasure and satisfaction from the paintings, for the simple reason that music is easier to enjoy. One pays a comparatively small admission, sits down and listens, and the music drifts without any personal effort into one's consciousness."[70]

This redefinition of the public set the Photo-Secession's progressivism, its inborn talent, and its commitment to art into sharp relief. As such, it helped to define the "field of art" as a battleground between a vanguardist elect and a hostile, feeble, and inferior public. This was not the only dimension of this argument, however. Crucially, the promotion of a vanguardist aristocracy of taste also contributed to a wider redefinition of seeing within *Camera Work*. This definition cast "proper" seeing as a moment of revelation, in which works alone won viewers without their consent, much less their consideration.[71] This was possible, however, only for viewers who were already prepared for it. Like *Camera Work*'s characterization of the Photo-Secession as a "movement" of seekers after "honesty of self-expression," and like its characterization of Photo-Secession exhibitions as "logical" arrangements of "the photographic print itself," *Camera Work* denied that this preparation could be provided by the institutions of the art world. Instead, critics like Hartmann proposed that inborn talent was the key to sight.

Interestingly, one of the clearest reformulations of seeing came from J. M. Bowles, who made an appearance in *Camera Work* in 1907 to describe his own conversion to the cause of photography. Like Caffin, who sometimes appeared as an "outsider" in the journal despite strong ties to it, Bowles prefaced his remarks by writing that he was "merely an interested and sympathetic outsider. At the outset I was neither for nor against photography; it made its way with me solely by the sheer force of good work. My mind was open—'a fair field and no favor' being my creed in matters pertaining to art—and I hope to be able to keep it so."[72] It is, of course, possible that Bowles did not have views on photography before 1907, although his interest in and engagement with a multiplicity of other artistic media make this somewhat unlikely. His claims to be an outsider are even more difficult to accept. After all, he had published and publicized the works of Secession intimates, allies, and teachers—including Hartmann himself—well before the Photo-Secession had even existed, which is undoubtedly why "Mr. Stieglitz has asked me to write 'at any length and on any subject.'"[73]

More important than Bowles's self-description as an "outsider" or his assertions of "fairness" was the relationship of this claim to his declaration that photography "made its way with me solely by the sheer force of good work." Bowles emphasized this connection by arguing that he had deliberately avoided educating himself on the subject, so that his opinion could be as neutral as possible: he was, he wrote, "uninfluenced by any reading or 'talk' on the subject. In fact, I have deliberately refrained from informing myself on many points which have arisen in my mind since I started to prepare these notes."[74] Given Bowles's own history, this is a surprising claim; after all, *Modern Art*'s "Tables of Art Reading" indicate that he had a formidable command of a wide range of art publications, and that he believed the dissemination of these materials to be valuable.

Bowles's own comments suggest, however, that by 1907 he really was "a fatalist as to the progress of the arts," and that he may well have believed, "with Whistler[,] that art happens, that it depends entirely upon the individual worker, and that we can do little to either accelerate or retard its progress."[75] This transformation had dangerous consequences. For when Bowles worked with Prang in the 1890s, he appears to have believed that the very provision of "reading [and] 'talk'," alongside support for a wide range of museums, schools, and associations, was one of the central purposes of art publishing, that this provision would help readers to understand and appreciate art, and that this understanding and appreciation would contribute to the overall development of American art. When he worked with Stieglitz after the turn of the century, in contrast, this vision seems to have given way to the idea that works alone were sufficient for those who were ready to receive them, and that nothing more could be done.

Bowles did not suggest that publishing no longer served a purpose in the art world. Although "the purpose of this paper is to record emotions produced on a rank outsider solely by the work," he also argued that his "very ignorance may have its value, perhaps even show which way the wind of public opinion blows, and blazon the way for a campaign of publicity upon points regarding which the genuinely interested should be informed."[76] Nonetheless, this idea of a "campaign of publicity" differed significantly from what he himself had attempted in *Modern Art*. For one thing, it defined "insiders" as a very small group indeed, for only a very few people could have as thorough a knowledge of the art world as someone with Bowles's experience. It also suggested that the goal of art publishing was not to provide a comprehensive overview of art and its institutions, to help make a broad public for art. Rather, it promoted the idea of publishing as "publicity," or the management only of those self-selecting audiences whose "genuine interest" was already known.

In this way, Bowles recast looking as a passive act, in which works alone held sway, and abandoned a notion of art publishing as an institution that could create a public for art by providing the contexts that made it comprehensible. Together with *Camera Work*'s general redefinition of the public as antagonistic and uncomprehending, and its attacks on the art world as a corrupt "establishment," this marked a devastating undoing of the field of art championed by many nineteenth-century critics. While promoting a new and highly successful artistic vanguard, *Camera Work* dismantled the machine that had made art go.

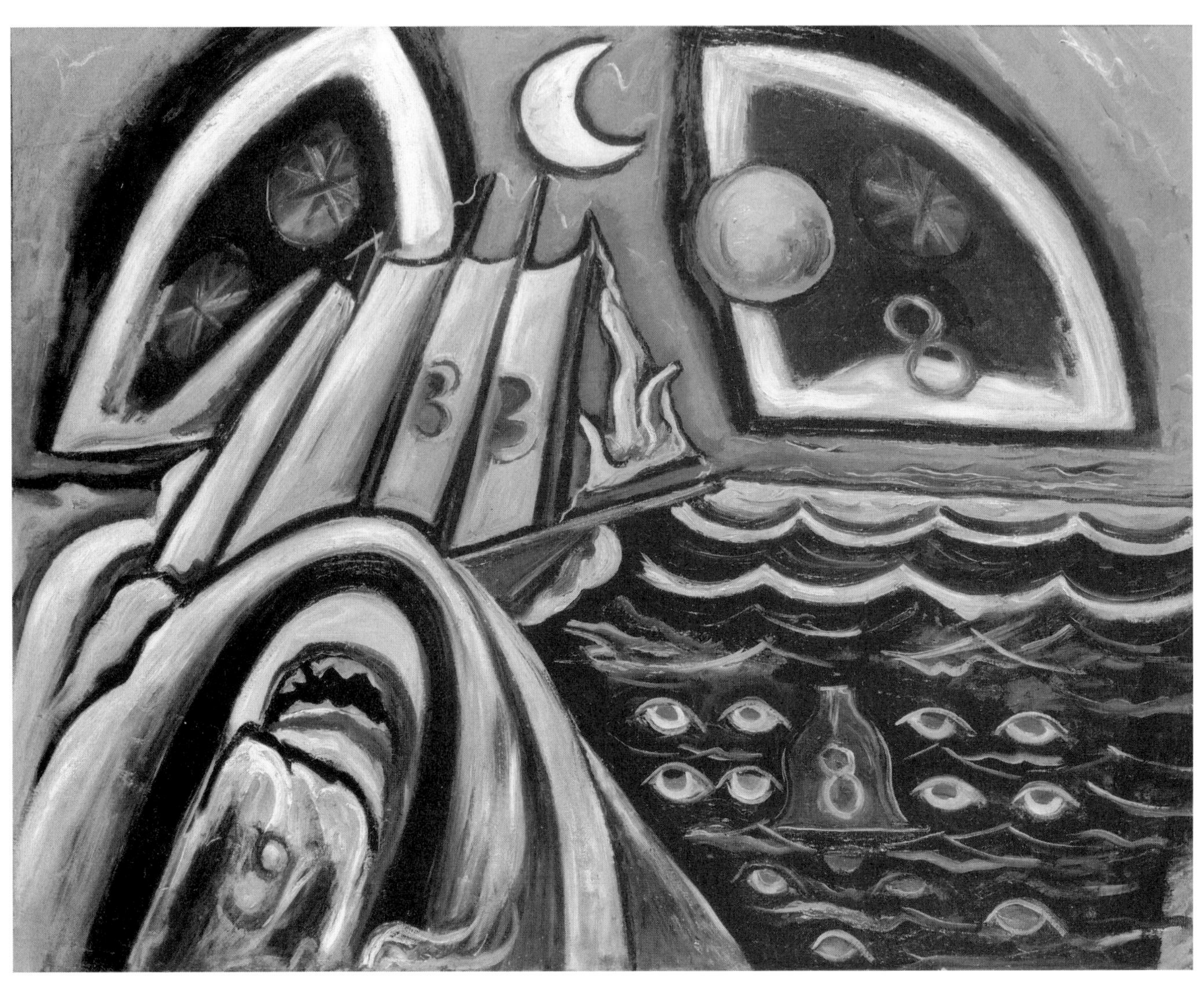

Chapter 6 Continuity and Rupture

The turn to bohemia was one manifestation of gathering revulsion against a society that seemed locked in a stranglehold of bourgeois resolve.
—Christine Stansell, 2000

67. Marsden Hartley (1877–1943), *Eight Bells Folly: Memorial to Hart Crane*, 1933. Oil on canvas, 21¾ × 13⅛ in. (55.2 × 33.3 cm). Frederick R. Weisman Art Museum at the University of Minnesota, Minneapolis, bequest of Hudson Walker from the Ione and Hudson Walker Collection

The mythology of revolution that surrounds American modernism portrays the Gilded Age as a hostile and separate historical reality from the innovative, iconoclastic culture that followed it, and explains, too simply, the transition between the culture of the late nineteenth and early twentieth centuries in terms of sudden, radical rupture. Although signs of this mythology are not hard to find, they are perhaps nowhere so common as in the many individual and collective biographies written about the first "modern" generation, which nearly universally emphasize the difficulties faced by early American modernists, their isolation from both an art world and a wider society that failed to understand their personal or artistic deviation from established norms, and their psychological and professional need to break away from stifling convention.[1] As part of this larger representation of modernism as a radical rupture with the past, much conventional modernist biography also tends to portray the modernists as social and political radicals, whose aesthetic and social radicalism were mutually constitutive and mutually necessary.[2] And finally, because the model of change that drives most interpretations of the emergence of modernism is underpinned by an unexplained mechanism of radical rupture, historians have tended to under-analyze the organizational techniques modernists employed to bring about cultural change. Emphasizing only modern-seeming historical changes like the rise of Bohemia, the importation of "radical" immigrant culture, and the emergence of apparently new forms of labor radicalism in the decades surrounding the turn of the twentieth century, historians have almost entirely failed to notice that modernists were also savvy managers of organizational and professional strategies that originated in the Gilded Age, and that the employment of these strategies enhanced modernism's emergence in the United States.

This conventional view of modernism has also strongly affected representations of those who failed to become bona fide modernists: those of the previous generation whose roots in the Gilded Age made them too old, or those whose representational aesthetics made them seem too tame to be "moderns." Thus, as a corollary to the collective biography of modernism as a radical rupture with the past, historians after modernism have argued that those who came before the true modernists—with a few isolated forefathers like William James and James McNeill Whistler—were conformists whose genteel taste meshed perfectly with their conventional social ideals, and who could never come to terms with the radicalism of the next generation.[3] As I have argued, this has led historians to portray the early-twentieth-century American art world as two unmixable universes inhabited, on the one hand, by "Gilded Age," "academic" conservatives like Kenyon Cox, Frank Jewett Mather and E. H. Blashfield, and on the other by "modern" radicals like Walter Pach and Edward Steichen. What this shorthand rendering of the turn-of-the-century art world obscures is that the boundary between them was permeable and unfixed, and that figures from both sides crossed it regularly throughout the period between the Civil War and the First World War. Cox worked with his contemporary, the modernist Rockwell Kent, in the National Society of Mural Painters; Mather was a key early influence on the Museum of Modern Art's Alfred H. Barr; and Blashfield was an early member of the American art world's first anti-Academy splinter group, the Society of American Artists, who collaborated with Augustus Saint-Gaudens and others both on projects (like the SAA) that challenged the Academy and on others, like the celebration of the centennial of George Washington's inauguration, that did not. On the other side, Pach spent his youth watching his father photograph the collection of the Metropolitan Museum of Art, and Edward Steichen learned his love of art by reading illustrated magazines in the public libraries of Gilded Age Wisconsin.

Although this book, unlike many other books on early American modernism, is not a work of collective biography, the power and persistence of the biographical method compels me to venture into this territory to offer some new thoughts on the matter. To my mind, the evidence against the view of modernism's emergence as a radical generational rupture is powerful and twofold. First, as the preceding chapters show, profound structural and discursive continuities within art criticism served as a platform for modernism that went beyond mere individual "inspiration." Beyond that, however, an examination of the biographies and the careers of many individual figures who lived through this transitional period, including those of artists, critics, and institution builders, shows quite clearly that the radical ruptures we should expect to have taken place did not necessarily happen even in the lives of single individuals, and that to varying degrees it was possible for many cultural and social "moderns" to live in both the "genteel" (or retrograde) world of the Gilded Age and the "radical" world of the early twentieth century at the same time. Within this framework, an examination of the more general, if less familiar, contexts in which modernists grew up—a rising art world marked by dramatic innovations both in institution building and in professionalization; a boom in commercial image publishing; and an expanding and changing era of art education—suggests that there was much more to modernism's emergence than a straightforward rejection of a wholly unusable past.

There is a disjunction between the way in which the late-nineteenth-century art world has been represented in conventional collective biographies and a subtler reality. A brief examination of a few figures shows that while many modernist artists did follow unusual paths, and while many of them did suffer indifference, there were often strong continuities between the late-nineteenth-century art world development and the activities of the modernists. In the case of modernist painter Marsden Hartley, for example, it can be argued that the Gilded Age art world not only failed to hinder his career, but also contributed directly to his establishment as an artist and to the very possibility of his becoming an artist in the first place. Second, an examination of the modernist brothers Willard Huntington Wright and Stanton Macdonald-Wright shows not only that aesthetic modernism could exist comfortably alongside deep social and political conservatism, but that the stuff of aesthetic modernism had strong roots in Gilded Age popular culture and media, art-educational practice, and art theory. Third, an examination of People's Art Guild founder John Weichsel—recently featured prominently in a book called *Anarchist Modernism*—shows that modernists were not only well aware of the organizational methods of the late nineteenth century, but that they cannily fused these methods, along with approaches developed by the Progressives, both to promote modernism and to bring about social change.[4] And finally, a perusal of the biography of collector, critic, and institution builder C. E. S. Wood shows that nineteenth-century institution builders were not necessarily cultural conservatives who gazed upon the social and cultural revolutions of the early twentieth century with horror and contempt. Rather, they could be enthusiastic supporters of social change who embraced radical causes with the zeal of moderns.

Marsden Hartley: Isolation in Context

One figure whose portrayal is typical of modernist biography is Marsden Hartley. Historians have emphasized the artist's genius, his lack of financial success, and above all his loneliness and isolation from both the art world and society at large. In the first full-length biography written about the artist in 1952, Elizabeth McCausland introduced Hartley with the following words: "Only at the end of his life, when he had long been driven by ill health and economic anxieties, did he come back to nature. He had scorned the lonely, desolate land of his birth. In it at last he found not only peace and human company but the fulfillment of his need to be himself. In the companionship of drowned fishermen, eroded shells, sea birds dead on the beach after the hurricane, he found that sense of persisting and meaningful life he had not found in art coteries and salons. Still a lonely man, he was less lonely because he learned to share the loneliness of the elements."[5]

With these words, McCausland provided an image of Hartley as a modern artist that would stick for half a century. In 1992, Townsend Ludington emphasized different aspects of the artist's identity to explain the artist's "loneliness, his peripatetic nature, his ideas, and the subjects of his paintings," including his homosexuality and the fact that he "was a native of Maine, brought up in the late nineteenth century and deeply aware of New England's, not to mention America's puritanical codes."[6] Nonetheless, the biographical image of Hartley that remained in 1992 was that of an isolated and misunderstood outsider, driven to the margins of existence by his inability to acclimatize to mainstream art and social norms.

It is obvious that Hartley did have trouble getting along with people, as Ludington's work shows. Even in his relations with allies like Alfred Stieglitz, who provided comradeship, gallery space, and financial assistance to the artist, Hartley could be bitter and self-aggrandizing.[7] Hartley's sexuality did make his assimilation into mainstream society difficult.[8] Indeed, as Jonathan Weinberg's more recent work establishes, the avant-garde could also be unforgiving toward homosexuality.[9] It is obvious that Hartley experienced a deeply ambivalent relationship with his upbringing in the industrial hinterland of Maine—as an impoverished immigrant mill hand's son who, after his mother's death, was sent away from his father to live with an older sister at the age of eight, the artist had anything but an easy childhood.[10] Hartley did, along with his fellow modernist Stanton Macdonald-Wright, suffer both real (if short-term) exclusion for his embrace of unpopular views like the admiration for Germany during the First World War, and a deeper sense of alienation at the fact that history had not seemed to recognize his genius as a progenitor of modern art.[11] And finally, Hartley did draw on his own personal anguish in the creation of works like *Eight Bells Folly: Memorial to Hart Crane* (fig. 67).

At the same time, however, Hartley's life cannot be read entirely as a story of a man whose career was determined by exclusion. For, as Ludington himself points out, Hartley first decided to become an artist after a visit to John Semon's studio in Cleveland, where Hartley had moved in 1893 to rejoin his father and stepmother.[12] Taking off Monday mornings from his job as an office boy in a marble quarry, Hartley began to study art first with Semon and then with Nina Waldeck of the Cleveland School of Art. After a period of study with Waldeck and in the summer school of Cullen Yates, Hartley's "work was good enough to attract the attention of one of the School of Art's trustees, Anne Walworth, who offered him a stipend of four hundred and fifty dollars a year for study."[13] It was this money, which supported Hartley from 1899 until 1904, that allowed him to move to New York, to study with William Merritt Chase, the "talented, if extremely conservative" Kenyon Cox at the Art Students League, and at the National Academy of Design; to join the summer art colony of Charles Fox and Curtis Perry in Maine; and to begin to forge the ties that would link him to the modernist art world of Alfred Stieglitz and Mabel Dodge.[14] When the money ran out, Hartley was assisted by Mrs. Ole Bull, widow of the Norwegian violinist and friend of the Brahmin elite, who after meeting Hartley at a utopian religious community in Maine let the artist use her home as a studio and as a gallery for an exhibition of his works in 1907. Hartley also received assistance from the critic and artist Philip Leslie Hale, who was a contributor to *Modern Art* and member of the St. Botolph Club, where both he and his sister, painter Ellen Day Hale, exhibited their work.[15] Hale took Hartley's works to Boston's Rowland Gallery, where they were seen by collector and fellow St. Botolph Club member Desmond FitzGerald, who paid Hartley $400 for one canvas in 1908.[16] The next year, Hartley met Stieglitz, who promptly gave the artist a one-man show at 291 and, as Ludington puts it, "saved him financially."[17]

During the crucial early years of his early career—from the transformative moment when he decided to become an artist, until the moment he made his début in modernist New York—Hartley was consistently supported and encouraged by individuals who were enmeshed in the institution-building art world of the Gilded Age. Who, after all, were his early teachers? Semon, whose studio, although "gloomy," was in Cleveland's City Hall; Yates, who had returned from Paris to teach in, of all places, Cleveland, and who (although Ludington does not mention it, implying that Hartley's works alone drew Walworth's attention) not only displayed his pupil's works at an exhibition but (in Hartley's words) "courteously called the attention of one of the trustees to my little labors";[18] and Waldeck, who taught at Cleveland's art school, founded in 1881 "to establish and maintain a School of Art, to afford facilities for the acquirement of a practical knowledge of the arts [and] to procure, for the use and benefit of members and others, such appliances and material as may be necessary to further this purpose; to create and maintain a Gallery of Art."[19]

Beyond teachers like Waldeck, who Hartley later wrote "was to mean everything for later development because she was a real artist through and through," Hartley's other benefactors also played an inestimable role in establishing him as an artist, and did so not just as individuals but as participants in a wider institution-building moment that was only beginning to come to a close.[20] Just as Walworth was a trustee of the Cleveland School of Art, Hale too was enmeshed in the institution-building art world of Boston. Hale, the son of Unitarian clergyman and reformer Edward Everett Hale, was an artist as well as a critic. He was also an art teacher, who spent a lengthy career in the school of the Museum of Fine Arts, Boston, and who actively supported the movement to bring art classes into the settlement houses.[21] Within these spheres, Hale's career bridged the gap between the accessible and the exclusive in the art world, and also between Gilded Age and Progressive approaches to building an organizational field for art. Seen in this context, it is not at all surprising that Hale, like both the MFA and the St. Botolph Club, would work to promote the career of a fellow New Englander—even a budding modernist like Hartley.

Regarded in this light, historians' overarching emphasis on Hartley's development of a unique modernist style in "virtual isolation"—a phrase that Ludington takes from Barbara Haskell—is misplaced.[22] For while it was undoubtedly true that Hartley felt deep personal loneliness, and while it is possible that some of Hartley's teachers, like Cox, had "scant effect" on the specific form that his art would take, Hartley was far from alone in the art world that institution builders had made. Nor was he alone within Stieglitz's *Camera Work* and 291, which were, at least in part, avant-garde adaptations of earlier organizational efforts. While the young Hartley's mind may, as Ludington argues, have "swirled with the crosscurrents between big city and small town, between family and independence, between orthodoxy in art and what he felt," it also lingered on "the face and distinction of Miss Waldeck," whom as late as the 1930s Hartley declared he would "never . . . forget."[23]

Like his friend Rockwell Kent, who exiled himself in Newfoundland, where "men seem to be confronting the universe, not merely themselves," and yet gratefully immersed himself in the catalogues, newspapers, and art-world contact offered by his correspondence with dealer Charles Daniel, Hartley combined psychological isolation with immersion in the art world.[24] Hartley's mind may have been lonely, but it was also full of both Hale's "treatise in yesterday's (Sunday's) Herald," and Hale's praise, which was enough of a triumph that Hartley wrote about it to his friend Horace Traubel.[25] In this joining of isolation and immersion, he also followed in the footsteps of Winslow Homer, whose rugged, masculine depictions of the Maine coast Hartley emulated and whose title, *Eight Bells*, Hartley borrowed for Crane's memorial. More than that, his pockets were full enough of Anne Walworth's and Desmond FitzGerald's money that during his crucial formative years of study and networking—the years that would decide his future—he could avoid both his father's fate as "a spinner at the mills" and his own "work in Auburn for three dollars a week in a shoe factory, where his task was to check the lots of shoes as they passed from one department to another."[26] Indeed, what is perhaps most important to remember when one reads about Hartley's poverty and isolation is that Walworth's "one hundred fifty for summer" provided him with as much income as a *year* of full-time work would have provided in either the shoe factory or in the marble quarry where he was working shortly before he met her. And this, of course, was on top of the three hundred dollars she gave him for winter study each year for five years running.[27]

Now, I do not wish to suggest that Hartley was wrong to take this patronage or to undermine the value of his art by pointing out its material and institutional, as well as psychological and personal, roots. For it was not in the least "ironic" that a modernist could have benefited materially from the efforts of nineteenth-century institution builders. Indeed, this was one of the constituent relationships that many organizers envisioned between artists and the art world, not only in their own time but in the future. When institution builders talked about providing meaningful careers that would keep the working class out of industrial drudgery, this is surely what they had in mind. When they talked about the role of critics, museums, and patrons in "creating" American art, this is what they were proposing. And, when they invited the sons of artisans and workers like Hartley and Munsell into the St. Botolph Club or the MFA—not as visitors, but as artists—this is what they meant. That Hartley was a modernist, rather than an academician or an industrial designer, should not mask this fact. The art world made by nineteenth-century institution builders made it possible for young Americans to become artists by creating the networks that would keep those artists from being alone. This is the historical and art-world context that hides in plain sight behind the myth of Hartley's "virtual isolation."

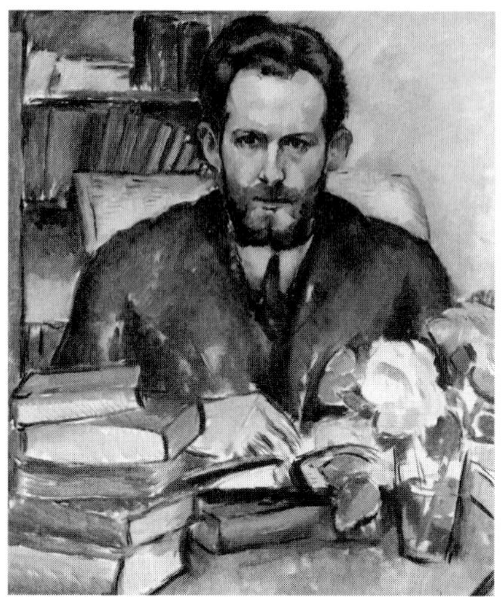

68. Stanton Macdonald-Wright (1890–1973), *Willard Huntington Wright (S. S. Van Dine)*, 1913–14. Oil on canvas, 36 × 30 in. (91.4 × 76.2 cm). National Portrait Gallery, Smithsonian Institution, Washington, D.C.; this acquisition was made possible by a generous contribution from the James Smithson Society

Willard Huntington Wright: Retrograde Radical

The myth of the artist as isolated outsider is but one element of the modernist legend. Just as frequently pushed by modernists, and just as commonly repeated by historians, is the idea that modernism, and the modernists, were social radicals who not only pushed the envelope of aesthetic innovation, but also were responsible for dramatic political and cultural transformations. Take, for example, Christine Stansell's nostalgically revolutionary description of the Armory Show: "Images of violent revolution and of the dawning of an age swirled around the show. John Sloan compared it to a charge of dynamite, a metaphor that resonated in 1913 with suspicions of the Wobblies and industrial sabotage."[28] This interpretation, which is far from unusual, pairs aesthetic and sociopolitical radicalism as mutually constituent and mutually necessary components of the emergence of American modernism.

Like other modernist myths, this account is only partially true. Some aesthetic modernists did promote radical social and political change. But other Americans embraced aesthetic modernism, in the clearest possible terms, without ever making the transition to social and cultural radicalism. Or, in some cases, modernists sampled a few items from the menu of nonconformity, without committing themselves meaningfully to political or social change. Perhaps the best example of an aesthetic modernist who failed to embrace radical political and social ideals is the critic Willard Huntington Wright (fig. 68). It is indisputable that Wright was an early and avid advocate of modernism. As the previous chapters illustrate, he championed the aesthetic innovations witnessed in the Armory Show, a position he elaborated in his numerous columns, in the books *Modern Painting: Its Tendency and Meaning* and *The Future of Painting*, and in his co-organization of the 1916 Forum Exhibition of Modern Painters, whose object was "to put before the American public . . . the very best examples of the more modern American art."[29] He was also the principal critical promoter of Synchromism, the modernist style developed by Morgan Russell and Wright's brother, painter Stanton Macdonald-Wright, with whom he had a close intellectual and personal relationship.

Wright may have been fighting an aesthetic revolution, but he was certainly not interested in radical social change. Indeed, despite provocative printed proclamations against marriage and other conventions, he was retrograde in nearly every possible respect when it came to social issues, and seems to have been motivated not by radicalism but by the same things that drove the capitalist, patriarchal, imperialist system that modernism is supposed to have shunned: money, fame, and power. Wright had a strong appetite for material success. As a young man in Los Angeles, he wrote gleefully to his wife, Katherine Boynton Wright, about the lavish dinners his father "blew" him, measuring and cataloguing "3-in. thick steaks, drinks . . . pudding (45 c. per plate) & other good things" in size, plenitude, and price. In the same year, the twenty-one-year-old Wright wrote to Katherine that he had "decided to stay over in Chicago a day to see a publisher. Turkish bathed, got manicured, suit pressed, shaved, etc. etc. When I got through it was 4:30."[30] Wright's desire for the good life was matched by a strong sense of his own social, racial, and gender superiority, and he described those he considered his inferiors with brutal scorn. Not only did he recount his interactions with his fellow train passengers in a ridiculing dialect, but he forbade Katherine to name their child Ramona because it "brings up in my mind Helen Hunt Jackson, dirty squat Mexican females & that *awful* western country" he was desperate to leave for New York.[31]

After moving to New York to edit the *Smart Set*, a move that brought him into contact with Alfred Stieglitz, Robert Henri, and John Weichsel, with whom he would organize the Forum Exhibition, and which certainly contributed to the development of his modernism, Wright did not lose these attitudes. Rather, at a time when we might expect him, in his private moments, to have been thinking about social revolution, Wright seems mostly to have been concerned that labor radicalism would interrupt mealtime. As he wrote to his wife, he "was at dinner the other night . . . & shortly after we had ordered, a brick came crashing through the window & struck not 4 ft from [his] chair. It was the strike signal, & immediately the waiters, cooks etc took off their aprons & walked out. No dinner there! The strike of the cooks & waiters in NY is pretty bad. You never know when you go into a restaurant whether or not you will be able to finish your meal."[32]

Indeed, even as Wright made a name for himself as a critic who self-consciously scorned the "old maid's antipathy for such words as dam [*sic*] & God & . . . mistress," Wright's major personal preoccupations were with the famous publishers and writers he met, the size of his salary, and his office perks. His excitement was palpable, for example, when he had the chance to make a speech at the Book Men's League banquet, "in which is represented I suppose every man of importance who has to do with the writing or publishing of books in N. Y.," and as he became known to figures such as H. L. Mencken, Bliss Carman, and "Perkins of Scribner's." Significantly, he seems to have gotten an equal charge out of his success at bohemian events like George Jean Nathan's 1913 costume party, where Wright "made a speech & was soused enough not to care . . . grabbed 3 wenches, bribed the orchestra to play ragtime, & began a most scandalous turkey trot," and at the same weekend's "annual banquet of the mag. Editors," where "men like Chas. Dana Gibson, Wm Dean Howells etc." gathered "at Delmonico's—$25 a plate." As Wright wrote, "I had a great time. On one side sat Frank Munsey & on the other Geo Bar McCutcheon!!! Wasn't that a scream?" For Willard Huntington Wright, the New York of 1913 was full of promise. He was on his way up in a world in which modernism could provide the ticket to success, fame, and fortune. Best of all, he could challenge the aesthetic standards of the past without giving up either his place in the social hierarchy or his place next to "Gutsen Borglum [*sic*], John W. Alexander, Edward Bok!" For this successful modernist, "the service here is fine—girls, niggers and office boys do everything for me."[33]

And how did women fit into Wright's modernist world? Stansell tells us that "certainly never before, and probably not since, did a group of self-proclaimed innovators tie their ambitions so tightly to women, and not just a token handful but whole troops of women, waving the flag of sexual equality."[34] It's a nice story, but unfortunately in this case, it is false. For although Wright, like his brother Stanton Macdonald-Wright, seems to have embraced a free enough attitude toward love, an attitude which led both men eventually to leave their first wives for more compelling matches, his desire for sexual freedom does not seem to have been motivated by feminism. On the contrary, Wright opposed women's suffrage and embraced the conventional, un-modern view that women's value rested on their prettiness, small waists, and delicate feet; as he exclaimed upon another train voyage, "And the people! My god! I never saw such a collection. . . . The women are out at the waist, flat-footed & pock-marked. There isn't a human being aboard."[35] More systematically, Wright wrote an entire book, as he explained to Katherine, on the premise that "not only do men of ideas not need feminine help, but it is a downright hindrance to their highest development." In this story, published as *The Man of Promise* in 1916, Wright's protagonist "marries an admirable unusual & sympathetic woman & later runs away with an advanced & modern one: but fundamentally they are little different, & he is finally defeated in his life's purpose."[36]

Wright's particular blend of clever amorality and patriarchal egomania proved to be a tragic mixture. As Willard became famous, Katherine's own career as a writer (and arguably her entire life) disintegrated as he abandoned her on the West Coast with their infant daughter Beverley and refused to support them except in the meanest possible fashion. Indeed, Wright's daughter recalled that he even went so far as to allow himself to be put on the cover of the *New Yorker* as "the most eligible bachelor in New York City" while Katherine lived a life of increasing desperation, working as a cook and boarding herself and Beverley out because they could not afford a home of their own.[37] While the ideology of free love certainly worked to the advantage of women like Mabel Dodge who had the power and position to wield it, for women without independent means—even those married to modernists—it could be deadly. As Willard and Stanton's mother, Annie van Vranken Wright, saw it, "both he & Stanton are convinced that those whom they consider their inferiors should in all cases be sacrificed if necessary to the superior being. . . . He & Stanton are of one mind & day by day & little by little, as I learn the heart-breaking tragedy of [Stanton's first wife] Ida's life & realize Stanton's attitude towards the whole situation the burden of woman is almost more than I can bear."[38]

It is imperative to emphasize at this point that it is not the "irony" of Willard Huntington Wright's life that I aim to convey, or its impropriety. I do not believe that authors or artists need conform to a particular political agenda to be historically important. Rather, what I wish to convey is that there was a great deal of variation within the individual careers, beliefs, and courses of development among the modernists. A shared aesthetic agenda simply did not translate into a sameness of attitude toward social or cultural issues. Although some modernists most certainly did embrace radical causes, the case of Willard Huntington Wright demonstrates that others emphatically did not. Beyond that, I wish to argue that our romantic attachment to the moderns' sociopolitical "radicalism" is misplaced, and that this nostalgia has prevented us from seeing the multiple contexts from which modernism emerged. If we can leave aside the assumption that modernists were radicals, and that all that came before modernism was its unworthy opposite, we may learn that modernism had deep and sometimes surprising roots, and that there is something to be gained by examining them. The time has come, then, to stop transferring our own romantic yearnings for political and social revolution upon the past, and to look beyond our own "revulsion against . . . bourgeois resolve" for answers as to why modernism emerged, and why it took the shape it did.

Stanton Macdonald-Wright: Shades of Prang

If Willard Huntington Wright inherited his retrograde social views from the Gilded Age, it is possible to argue that his modernism, and the modernism of his brother, Stanton Macdonald-Wright, also had roots in that period. Unfortunately, any definite arguments along these lines are difficult to prove, as his widow restricts Stanton Macdonald-Wright's papers, including nearly all of his early correspondence with Willard.

Color thus was everywhere in Gilded Age America, and very much on Americans' minds, as is evident from the wave of experimentation with color in industry, art, and science that accompanied the ascendance of color in the American media. As mentioned previously, figures as seemingly disparate as Prang, Koehler, and Lathrop were joined by a fascination with the new print technologies, including technologies for color printing. They disseminated their findings through charts (fig. 69), lectures, and books like Koehler's translation, for Prang, of Von Bezold's *The Theory of Color in Its Relation to Art and Art-Industry*, whose purpose was to expand the reach of Michel Eugène Chevreul's color system to a wider audience.[50] While it is difficult to gauge the impact of any single publication in this field, the presence of this volume in the library of the former State Normal School in Cedar Falls, Iowa, suggests that it did travel fairly widely.

Americans themselves were also experimenting with color. Indeed,

69. "Chart of the Prang Color Theory to Accompany Miss Ball's Paper." Published in *Modern Art* 1, no. 2 (spring 1893). Fine Arts Department, Boston Public Library

CHART OF THE PRANG COLOR THEORY

TO ACCOMPANY MISS BALL'S PAPER

LL R	LL RRO	LL RO	LL ORO	LL O	LL OYO	LL YO	LL YYO	LL Y	LL YYG	LL YG	LL GYG	LL G	LL GBG	LL BG	LL BBG	LL B	LL BBV	LL BV	LL VBV	LL V	LL VRV	LL RV	LL RRV
L R	L RRO	L RO	L ORO	L O	L OYO	L YO	L YYO	L Y	L YYG	L YG	L GYG	L G	L GBG	L BG	L BBG	L B	L BBV	L BV	L VBV	L V	L VRV	L RV	L RRV
R	RRO	RO	ORO	O	OYO	YO	YYO	Y	YYG	YG	GYG	G	GBG	BG	BBG	B	BBV	BV	VBV	V	VRV	RV	RRV
D R	D RRO	D RO	D ORO	D O	D OYO	D YO	D YYO	D Y	D YYG	D YG	D GYG	D G	D GBG	D BG	D BBG	D B	D BBV	D BV	D VBV	D V	D VRV	D RV	D RRV
DD R	DD RRO	DD RO	DD ORO	DD O	DD OYO	DD YO	DD YYO	DD Y	DD YYG	DD YG	DD GYG	DD G	DD GBG	DD BG	DD BBG	DD B	DD BBV	DD BV	DD VBV	DD V	DD VRV	DD RV	DD RRV

LL—lighter
L—light
N—normal
D—dark
DD—darker

R—red
RRO—red-red-orange
RO—red-orange
ORO—orange-red-orange
O—orange, etc.

Y—yellow
G—green
B—blue
V—violet, etc.

GRAYS

LL Gy	LL RGy	LL OGy	LL YGy	LL GGy	LL BGy	LL VGy
L Gy	L RGy	L OGy	L YGy	L GGy	L BGy	L VGy
Gy	RGy	OGy	YGy	GGy	BGy	VGy
D Gy	D RGy	D OGy	D YGy	D GGy	D BGy	D VGy
DD Gy	DD RGy	DD OGy	DD YGy	DD GGy	DD BGy	DD VGy

RGy—red-gray or russet
OGy—orange-gray or brown
YGy—yellow-gray or citrene
GGy—green-gray or olive
BGy—blue-gray or slate
VGy—violet-gray or heliotrope
Gy—neutral gray

color became a major area of scientific study in North America beginning in the 1870s, leading to the publication of influential works like Ogden Rood's *Modern Chromatics, with Applications to Art and Industry*, which the *American Art Review* hoped would, along with Von Bezold's book, make the language of color "part of the common stock of intellectual furniture with which the everyday work of life is to be performed."[51] The next decades also saw the publication of Mary McArthur Tuttle's *Color: Theoretically and Practically Considered*, and Munsell's *A Color Notation*.[52] Color also became a key area of research in the developing field of psychology, at institutions like Columbia University and the University of Toronto. Toronto, for example, executed an entire series of research projects on this subject, resulting in publications like William James Dobbie's *Experiments with School Children on Color Combinations* (1900). Interestingly, this research created another niche for Bradley to market his books and products; while *Elementary Color* appealed to the need for aesthetic training, it also proposed that color should be studied because it was important to "the psychological or psycho-physical study of the nature, duration and delicacy of color vision and color judgment."[53] Bradley seems to have received his wish; at least one Columbia University researcher used the "Milton-Bradley papers" to test for color blindness, and the university invested in his *Two-Axle Color Mixing Device*, patented in 1893.[54] An adaptation of a Victorian optical toy, the chromatrope, which was initially manufactured in London, this device facilitated psychological experimentation with color by giving experimenters the mechanical means to flash colors before subjects' eyes in rapid sequence.[55]

Perhaps an even truer testament to color theory's currency in Gilded Age America was its seepage beyond scientific and book publishing into the educational and periodical press. To find out about color theory, late-nineteenth- and early-twentieth-century Americans did not have to seek out anything quite so weighty as Von Bezold. Rather, in the late 1880s, all they had to do was to open a copy of the *American Art Printer* to find an exhaustive, multipart series on color that began in its first issue and spanned more than a year of the journal's run. The journal explained the need for such a series: "Good color-pressmen are scarce. They rank as leaders in their department, and, as a rule, deserve all the credit they get. Their acquirements have cost them years of time, which might have been seriously shortened had they had taste or gumption for the study of working principles that are easier to learn than they think. We do not allude here to such matters as consistency of inks, the use of varnishes and oils, the treatment of rollers, etc.: these are strictly manipulative features. We mean the theory of colors, the knowledge of their composition, and the accepted laws that control all combinations of them."[56] As was typical of the art press at this time, however, the journal backed up its theoretical discussions with practical, illustrated instructions, like "The Press Room—Working Red Ink," on how to print economically and well in color.[57]

If the emergence of a culture in color affected the teaching of industrial art in the magazines, it also had a profound influence on art education in the more traditional sense. When it was initially introduced into the schools, free primary art education focused almost wholly on one aspect of artistic training: drawing. This was mirrored in American art textbooks, which before the 1890s focused virtually exclusively on teaching students to see and convey form and mass through a language based on drawing. As Walter Smith argued in an 1880 teachers' manual published by Prang, the first requirement of "A proper course of instruction in Art Education" was "instruction and practice in drawing, as the language for expressing ideas in regard to forms," instruction that had to be backed up at all times by a thorough appreciation of the "disciplinary training of the mental powers which the study of form and the practice of drawing alone can give, as well as an appreciation of the value of such training and knowledge in scientific and aesthetic culture."[58]

By the 1880s and 1890s, however, this was beginning to change. While standard textbooks of the 1870s stressed the importance of learning the visual language of line and geometry, by the 1890s and 1900s these concerns would begin to be matched by a new fascination with color. This pivotal moment is captured in A. H. Munsell's *Color Notation*, which emphasized "balanced and measured color" in art education while still making use of the author's training in drawing under the Massachusetts Drawing Act. It can also be seen in Bradley's system of instruction. *Elementary Color* specifically appealed to the success of drawing in the schools, arguing that "the foundation of art in black and white is laid in form study."[59] But Bradley insisted that "color is the one thing in which we are deficient and in which we are making no advance[.] Is it not necessary that we adopt a new line of operations for our color instruction in the primary grades?"[60]

This dual emphasis on line and color is also reflected in Arthur Wesley Dow's *Composition*. In a classic modernist formulation, Dow immersed himself in Japanese drawing techniques (fig. 70), recuperating a declining tradition in order to "make it new." The pre-modernist twist on this was that Dow inscribed his meditation on line within a teaching manual, rather than in an artwork *per se*. In this way, he was able not just to remake his *own* art, but to teach his readers how to use tradition to remake *their* art, as well. As *Along Ipswich River* and "Painting with Wooden Blocks" show, however, Dow's modernism was equally concerned with how *color*, independent of line, could provide the material basis of abstract form, particularly in print media.[61]

In promoting their visions of color education, Munsell, Bradley, and

LINE DRAWING AND MATERIALS

Dip it into the ink, and holding it perpendicular to the paper, draw your line. It must be held in a perpendicular position in order to move freely in all directions as does the etcher's needle.

The line is not drawn with the fingers, but by a movement of the whole hand and arm in one sweep. This gives greater force. The hand may be steadied if necessary by resting the end of the little finger on the paper.

Determine the width of the line at the start, by pressing the brush-point firmly down till it spreads to the desired width. Slowness of drawing is most important, as an expressive or artistic line is not made by mere momentum of the hand, but by pure force of will controlling the hand. In slow drawing, the line can be watched and guided as it grows under the brush-point.

Slight waverings, when not resulting from weakness or nervousness, are not objectionable; in fact, may add to the individuality and expressiveness of the line.

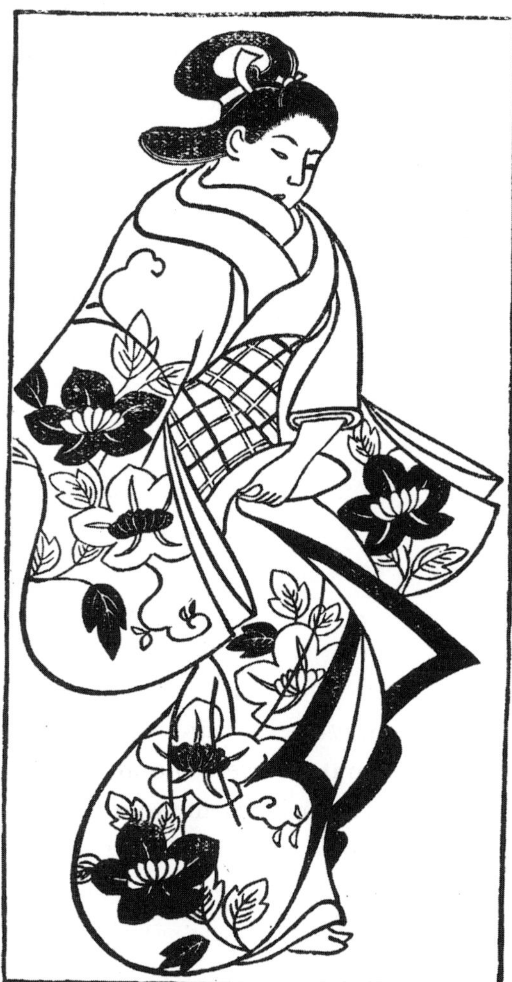

No 10 Okumura Masanobu (Japanese) 18th cent.

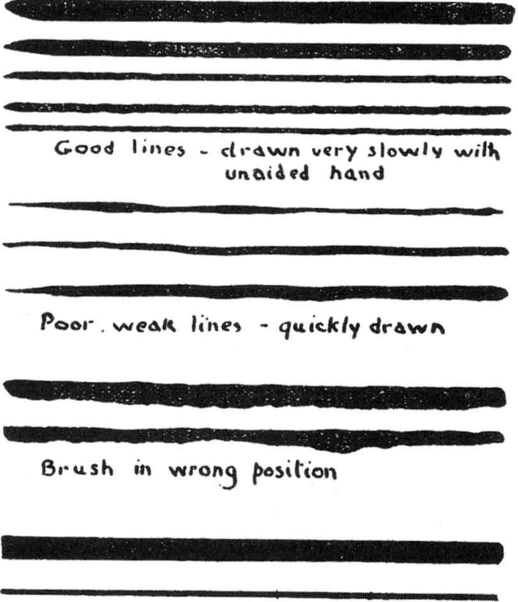

13

70. Arthur Wesley Dow, "Line Drawing and Materials." From *Composition* (Boston: J. M. Bowles, 1899). Fine Arts Library, Harvard College Library, Cambridge, Massachusetts

Dow had another competitor with whom to reckon: Prang, whose well-established art education "system" provided the business model for art-instructional publishing on a mass scale. By the 1890s, Prang himself was moving into color instruction, as Walter Smith's textbooks were joined—and eventually replaced—by books like Mary Dana Hicks's *Art Instruction in Primary Schools*.[62] Hicks, whom Prang would marry after his first wife's death, still advised teachers to emphasize striving and virtuosity with the brush. Yet, her emphasis was different from Smith's. "While free painting is carried on, it will be found beneficial to have some work done

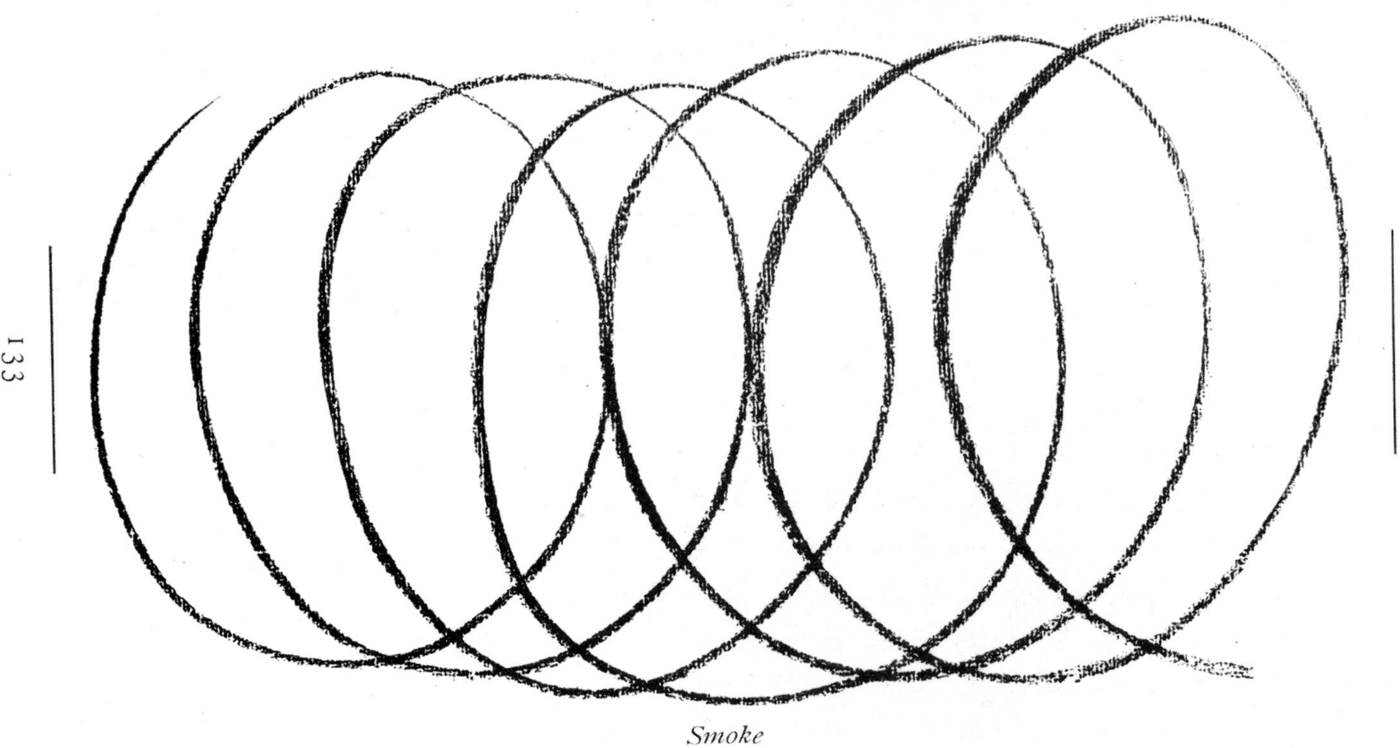

71. Leila Maude Wilhelm, *Series I. Curved Line Drawings (Smoke)*, 1905. From Jane L. Hoxie, *Hand Work for Kindergartens and Primary Schools* (Springfield, Mass.: Milton Bradley & Co., 1905). Widener Library of the Harvard College Library, Cambridge, Massachusetts

also with reference to even effects—technically known as flat washes—in given spaces to obtain increasing control over the brush. For this purpose decorative outlines are well fitted. The children enjoy this work, as it presents some difficulties to overcome, something to strive for; and as the outlines are already printed, they do not have to consider form at all, but can give their whole thought to color effects."[63] In classrooms that used her book, drawing (and form that was based on drawing and geometry) began to cede its dominance to a new concern with color.

What is essential to keep in mind about Hicks's prescriptions for the study of color without form is that they emerged from a context in which visual culture had dramatically changed. Not only had chromolithography brought color images into the homes of millions of Americans, but the process of chromolithography, like lithography before it, also subtly altered the materiality of depiction in the print media. Unlike engravings and woodcuts, lithography was neither an intaglio nor a relief process. Rather, it was a planographic chemical process; although the images depicted by lithographs and chromolithographs did often rely upon line and geometry, they were not inscribed upon the plate. Instead, as Prang put it, lithographs and chromos were materially based, like photographs, in

21. SMOKE.

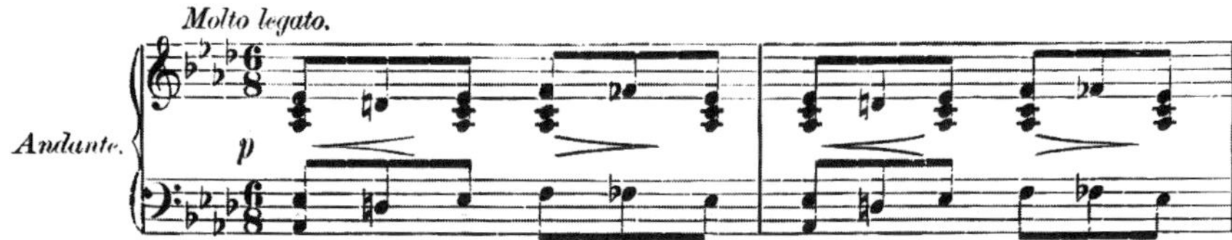

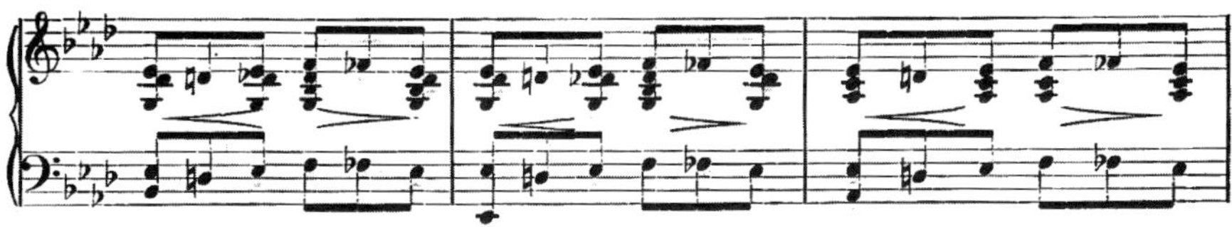

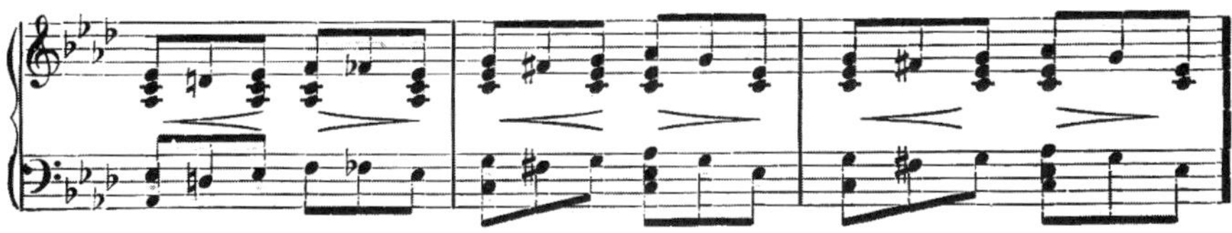

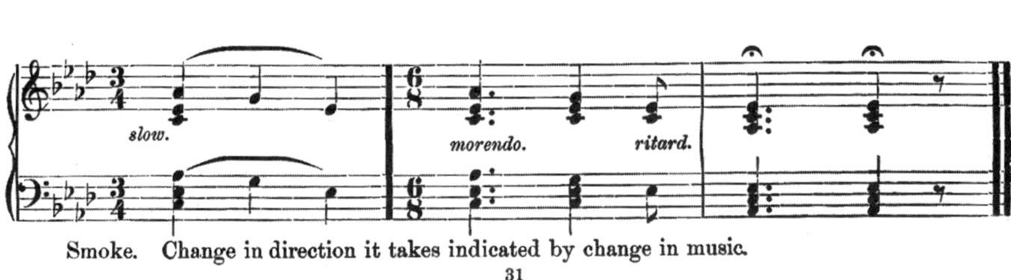

72. Katherine Montz, "Smoke," 1894. From *Instrumental Music* (Springfield, Mass.: Milton Bradley & Co., 1894). Widener Library of the Harvard College Library, Cambridge, Massachusetts

"flat even tints . . . gradated from the darkest shades to highest light."[64] Although this seems like a small point, and it might seem fanciful to make too much of it, it is possible to suggest that lithography's flatness—self-consciously recognized by Prang—might have provided another kernel for the fusion of flatness and color that would later come to play such an important role in modernist painting.

Periodicals like the *American Art Printer* and the new art education books, plus the widespread psychological research on color, provided an important context for modernist painters who emphasized color after the turn of the century. More specifically, I would suggest that these sources also provided a context for a more specific element of the work of Macdonald-Wright, which is crucially distinguished by the connection between sight and sound. Like color more generally, discussions of synaesthesia emerged in all of the spheres I have mentioned: art publishing, art education, and psychology. The *American Art Printer*, for example, specifically mentioned the experiments of British scientist Francis Galton, marveling at the fact that for some people "certain sounds always call up certain colors. In one case a whole language was developed for translating colors into sound and back again, and this favored individual could read words out of a wall paper pattern, or paint a pattern in order to represent a word."[65] Closer to home, this connection was also explored by American scientists, including Clark University President G. Stanley Hall and William O. Krohn of the University of Illinois, who founded one of the nation's first psychology laboratories.[66] Mary Hicks Prang also took up this theme, publishing an article entitled "Color Hearing" in the journal *Science* after her husband's death.[67]

Bradley and Munsell also explored the link between sound and sight, and integrated it into their educational systems. Like many modernists, proponents of the kindergarten movement worried about the psychological and developmental impact of modern, urban life. As Jane Hoxie wrote in one Bradley publication, *Hand Work for Kindergartens and Primary Schools* (1905), "in the early history of our country, before the growth of our large cities, many activities were possible to the child that are now almost wholly denied him. This is especially true of the child born and brought up in the city. Under former and more primitive conditions, the child's environment contributed directly to sturdiness of character and robustness of physique."[68] In order to replicate this wholesome "primitive" environment, both Hoxie and Katharine Montz, who published *Instrumental Music* for Bradley in 1894, advocated a synaesthetic program of study that intertwined "gesture and movement of the body" with creative activities. More specifically, Montz and Hoxie argued that exercises that allowed children to represent familiar things in diverse art forms—music, crafts, drawing—would encourage the holistic development of all of the senses, and counteract the evil effects of urban life. In other words, "Smoke" should be both pictured (fig. 71) *and* sung (fig. 72). In combination, kindergarten advocates hoped, such synaesthetic exercises would "requite the child of to-day for the loss of a life near to nature."[69]

While this particular example did not specifically link sound and *color*, Munsell's system—which also advocated a model of sense development that emphasized making, rather than just looking—explicitly made this connection. Color, Munsell argued, was just like music. Foreshadowing both Macdonald-Wright and Macdonald-Wright's mentor in color theory, Canadian painter Ernest Tudor-Hart, Munsell offered the following challenge: "And why should any one balk at the suggestion of measured color? Is not music measured? Are not the sensations of sound, of time, of weight, of space, and of temperature, all measured and taught to children by different scales? . . . The child who is to become a singer or composer begins the study with fixed intervals of related sound, and the freest flights of artistic freedom can succeed only through respect for these fundamental measures."[70] Whether for the generations of students who used Munsell's system in the primary school, in the art school, and in the teacher's college between 1905 and the Second World War, or for color entrepreneurs like H. G. Maratta, who in 1916 copyrighted his own pigment system based on the analogy between color and sound, this was the question to ask.[71]

These trends in art education, publishing, and psychology had serious implications for the ways Americans saw and made art. At the most basic level, they opened the door to a kind of painting that valued color among its primary properties. In Macdonald-Wright's case, this meant color that could be measured and represented systematically, color that made form, and color that, like music, could be made to perform according to its own rules and rhythms. Although it is not possible to document the full extent of Macdonald-Wright's debt to the nineteenth-century culture in color, it would be interesting to try.

John Weichsel: The People's Organizer

One welcome change within the collective biography of modernism is its increasing attention to the roles played by immigrants in the early-twentieth-century American art world (evident in both Stansell's *American Moderns* and Allan Antliff's *Anarchist Modernism*). Despite this positive development, it is striking how little the insertion of immigrants into the modernist biography has done to challenge the idea of modernism as a radical break with the past. Like scholarship on native-born artists, collective accounts of immigrant artists have tended to separate the experience of twentieth-century immigrant artists from that of their predecessors. In both Stansell's and Antliff's analyses, for example, immigration is specifically associated with artistic radicalism after the turn of the century. Similarly, even accounts of immigrant artists that are not strictly about modernism—Cynthia Jaffee McCabe's massive exhibition and book *The Golden Door: Artist-Immigrants of America, 1876–1976*, for example—cast the impact of immigration in strictly twentieth-century terms.[72] While that exhibition technically began in 1876, it did not feature a single artist who arrived in the United States before the 1890s; instead, it waited for the arrival of modernists Max Weber, Oscar Bluemner, and Abraham Walkowitz to begin the "century of artist-immigrants."[73] Moreover, when it comes to immigrant participation in other areas of the premodernist art world, such as dealing, collecting, publishing, and art education, even less interest has been shown by scholars. Like the literature on the emergence of modernism more generally, the accounts of immigrant modernism tend to focus exclusively on artists who worked to "radicalize" art and politics in obvious ways.

Like other modernists, immigrants themselves contributed to the shaping of the image of the immigrant-artist-as-radical. From the days of the early transatlantic modernists like Marcel Duchamp, whose entrepreneurial shocks to the art world were as much a part of his art as the objects themselves, through the Second World War, and even in more recent years in the works of visitors like Jean Baudrillard, modernist (and postmodernist) Europeans have represented themselves as cultural exiles in a land of barbarous plenty. Consider, for example, the account of post-Second World War America given by émigré poet and dramatist Carl Zuckmayer: "Artificial Christmas trees with electric candles in all imaginable colors, chiefly pink, orange, and silvery blue, stood in front of the houses. I had been invited to a party given in the Beverly Hills Hotel. A slide had been covered with artificial snow and men in bathing trunks, women in silk jersey, skied down it directly into the cocktail tent. Huge crimson poinsettias bloomed in all the gardens. The sight of all this nauseated me."[74] In both the historical literature and the accounts of many participants, the role of the European immigrant has been cast as that of a radical cultural critic who transplants vanguardist art and vanguardist institutions into a climate barely hospitable to art.

What these accounts neglect is the involvement of immigrants in the American art world from the earliest days of the colonies, and their persistent significance in shaping both American art and the art world well before the emergence of modernism. In the pre-modernist period, many of the most influential cultural entrepreneurs were immigrants, including Prang, Koehler, Keppel, and Macbeth. So, too, were a number of the best-known artists, including the Moran family and Thomas Hovenden of Dunmanway, Cork, Ireland, who painted the public's favorite artwork at the World's Columbian Exposition (*Breaking Home Ties* [1890; Philadelphia Museum of Art]). Like the "radical" newcomers after the turn of the century, these immigrants shaped the twentieth-century art world in meaningful ways. Macbeth's gallery was the site for Robert Henri's landmark 1908 exhibition; Hovenden was Henri's teacher. And, even those immigrants who imported "radical" new political and aesthetic ideas after the turn of the century *also* engaged with the existing context. When considering the impact of immigrants on American modernism, it is important to recognize both this ongoing engagement with the art world *and* the "radical" immigrant shaping of it.

One immigrant who both brought new ideas to the art world and built upon existing practices was John Weichsel. Weichsel was engaged in a number of pursuits in the art world, but he is best known as the founder of the People's Art Guild (1915), whose chief mandate was to encourage the development of art in the poor, immigrant areas of New York. This involved not only "bringing art in" to the neighborhoods, but also encouraging the careers of immigrant artists. Weichsel's career provides both corroboration for, and contrast to, the conventional view of immigration's role in modernism's emergence. In one respect, it shows that immigrants did take the lead in the introduction of new styles—within the People's Art Guild and in other exhibitions he organized, Weichsel displayed the works of modernists Stanton Macdonald-Wright, Morgan Russell, Charles Sheeler, Charles Demuth, and Marsden Hartley; immigrants Abraham Walkowitz, William and Marguerite Zorach, and Jules Pascin; and Ash-can and *Masses* realists George Bellows and John Sloan. He also showed the works of artists who worked in more traditional styles like Everett Shinn, who employed a decorative fusion of Impressionism and academic realism.[75] What Weichsel's career also shows, however, is the influence of nineteenth-century organizational strategies, which undergirded many of his projects. In the hands of an innovative organizer like Weichsel, both these older strategies and new organizational techniques being developed by Progressive reformers in the first decades of the twentieth century helped to encourage modernism.

John Weichsel was born in Poland in 1870, the son of Jewish merchants of modest means. Because he was discovered at an early age to have a great mathematical talent, Weichsel was sent to Berlin to study. After obtaining a degree in mechanical engineering, he went to the University of Zurich to pursue a doctorate in psychology. In the early 1890s, lacking the funds to complete his degree, he migrated to the United States, where he took up employment as a machinist's helper in Bound Brook, New Jersey. Finishing his psychology degree as a night student at New York University, Weichsel went on to head the Department of Mechanics and Drafting at New York's Hebrew Technical Institute from the turn of the century until shortly before his death in 1946.[76]

As far as can be established, Weichsel never aspired to be an artist. Yet, his education and his temperament contributed to a deep and abiding interest in culture that led him during his years in New York not only to establish the People's Art Guild, but to promote organizational efforts on behalf of Polish-Jewish artists, to co-organize (with Willard Huntington Wright, Alfred Stieglitz, and Robert Henri) the Forum Exhibition, and to take an interest in efforts like the Société Anonyme. Unlike Weichsel's People's Art Guild, whose exhibitions were free, this organization charged people money to look at modernist artworks and to listen while "Mrs. Charles Knoblauch told of her friendship with Miss [Gertrude] Stein while Marsden Hartley and Henry McBride read from her unpublished works!"[77]

Weichsel did not limit himself to original modernist artworks, however.

He also worked toward the establishment of a Jewish Museum, and promoted the circulation of cheap prints of street scenes—which he specifically hoped would be sold in working-class neighborhoods—and Jewish devotional handicrafts.[78] In his ceaseless pursuit of variety, Weichsel's interests mirrored those of many nineteenth-century organizers, whose aesthetics also blended the cheap with the priceless, the original with the reproduced, and the spiritual with the commercial.

If Weichsel's agenda was varied, it ran in certain definable directions. First, he placed an overarching faith on the importance of organization. As his notes on a proposed Jewish Museum indicate, Weichsel believed that museums were both the conservators and the progenitors of culture. Like postwar museum organizers, Weichsel proposed a curatorial role for the institution: to "rescue from obscurity and to prevent possible loss or destruction of the many objects of Jewish culture."[79] At the same time, however, he did not see the conservation of unique and irreplaceable artworks as the institution's only purpose. He also planned that it would "bring real art into the homes of the Jewish masses . . . through popular sales of works of art, and through the dissemination of meritorious reproductions of pictures, sculpture, brasses, etc. etc."[80] Along the same lines, Weichsel also planned "the establishment of a Jewish Art Publication Branch of the Jewish Museum" and "a library of Jewish culture (especially of literature and art)." And, finally, Weichsel proposed that a single museum in New York was not enough; rather, it would be beneficial "to establish a bureau for the extension of the work of the Jewish Museum over the United States."[81]

It is easy to see why Weichsel might have taken this approach to a religious project like the Jewish Museum, which was obviously suited to an organizational, instrumental, and proselytizing view of the art world. What is significant is that this view also underpinned Weichsel's involvement in secular projects, such as the People's Art Guild, which promoted modernist art that claimed to be its own end. For Weichsel, these projects seem not to have been radically different; for if Weichsel saw art as the means to further specific religious aims, the form of institution building he embraced was blind to aesthetic creed. Like Koehler's correspondence, Weichsel's papers are marked by the overarching desire to expand the art world outward. Although I have not scrutinized his many letters written in Polish and Yiddish, what remains in English are receipts and budgets for press releases, for shipping, for framing, for packing, and for posters; catalogues and invitations; letters from artists who participated in his initiatives; tracts and letters selling his project to whoever would listen, plus their responses; and plans for adjunct institutions like the "Library of the People's Art Guild."[82]

If the People's Art Guild built upon late-nineteenth-century practices, it also incorporated more recent organizational innovations, particularly Progressive theories of social life and social organization. Weichsel seems to have shared his contemporaries' conviction in the merits of community intervention, and their faith that such interventions would prevent or diminish future social problems. His innovation was to incorporate this idea into the organization of the art world, by mounting shows in settlement houses, in cafés and restaurants, and in public schools and libraries.[83] As a 1915 receipt for "carting 1 painting from Kroll" and "1 painting by M. Stern from Montross to University Settlement" shows, this entailed the actual removal of artworks from sites within the art world, like commercial galleries, to sites within immigrant and working-class communities.[84] Between 1915 and 1918, the People's Art Guild installed approximately fifty exhibitions at locations ranging from the Lower East Side's Jacob A. Riis House and Neighborhood Playhouse, to the Bronx YMHA, to the Federation Settlement in the immigrant neighborhood surrounding East 105th Street, to Brooklyn's socialist Williamsburg Culture Club, to Harlem's "Young Women's Association" of 110th Street.[85]

Weichsel's organizational portfolio contained another element shared by "reformist" Progressives and "radical" modernists alike: the sense that his generation was the first truly to recognize the problems of the day, and that their efforts represented something entirely new in the world of art. This made it difficult for Weichsel to see the continuities between his project and earlier efforts to bring art "to the people," such as the Drawing Act and the art education movement more generally. Indeed, although Weichsel's desire "to counteract the debasing influenc[e]s of present industrialism . . . by endowing the masses with a deeply seated habit of participation in the diverse phases of surrounding life, in a beautiful manner," was shared by Bradley, Lathrop, and many others, he cast his work as a corrective to "the usual passive veneration for art" and "art work of the traditional, priestly kind."[86] And, even though the nineteenth-century art press routinely valorized the labor of amateurs, the industrial and decorative arts, and images that by later standards would count as neither original nor authentic, Weichsel presented as revolutionary the idea that "it is not the art article but the selfexpressive [*sic*] artistic manifestation that is the ultimate end of art activity" and the proposal that "settlement houses . . . will not limit [their efforts] to plastic art."[87]

And finally, Weichsel was also in touch with Progressivism's psychological side, and thus was able to tap into another deep Progressive vein: the profound sense of ambivalence felt by many reformers toward their own privileged pasts. Like the Progressives themselves, who since Jane Addams had used guilt as a catalyst for activism, Weichsel skillfully manipulated this anxiety to gain even greater cooperation from reformers, a manipulation that may have been aided by his own status as an immigrant.[88] In a 1919 letter to Albert J. Kennedy of the National Federation of Settlements that was largely critical of settlement house directors, Weichsel complained that the "social realization" of "the artists and the public," as well as "the best intentions of progressive head workers in settlement houses" had been "frustrated by lack of backing on the part of their directors who usually belong to a social class only too amply favored by present art production." Arguing that to be successful the settlement houses could not "confine their art effort within class walls," Weichsel implied that the lofty social position of these heads had kept them from truly believing in the art-world capacities of the "wage-earning classes." As he put it, "one of the best known settlement heads at one time told me that his time is largely occupied 'by getting my neighbors out of jail.' It is too bad that this man's gifts can not be applied to work that would forestall the jailing of his neighbors. If his be a typical instance in neighborhood work, then it is high time to institute new neighborhood agencies for the enhancement of popular life to a degree that would make it jailproof."[89]

Although Weichsel's plea for greater art efforts in the settlements turned out to have been ill-timed—he could not have known that the Progressive movement would collapse under the pressure of postwar xenophobia and prosperity—its reception shows that Weichsel had fundamentally mastered the language of Progressivism. In his response to Weichsel, Kennedy wrote that Weichsel's letter was "one of the most compelling statements of the relation which should exist between the artist as producer and the consuming public that I have ever been privileged to read," and asked if he could circulate it to the settlements in the Federation.[90] And indeed, throughout the People's Art Guild years Weichsel seems to have enjoyed nothing but support from Progressives for his ventures.

While Weichsel's organizational approach represented a canny fusion of nineteenth-century institution building and Progressive community action, it also tapped another important source of organizational innovation at the turn of the century: immigration itself. Although neither Weichsel's public nor his artists were exclusively immigrants, immigrants represented a significant constituency for his projects. As Weichsel himself frequently argued, the People's Art Guild contributed to the cultural life of immigrant communities by bringing exhibitions to neighborhoods that were distant from the center of the art world, and by helping immigrant artists to make a living in their chosen field. Beyond his work in the Guild, Weichsel also provided concrete personal assistance to individual artists, helping those like Jules Pascin to straighten out the immigration problems that plagued many recent arrivals during and after the First World War.[91]

In return, Weichsel received the cooperation of immigrant artists, as well as the financial and organizational assistance of immigrant groups like the "Committee of Hostesses for the Exhibit of the Work of Polish Jewish Artists" and the Hebrew Sheltering and Immigrant Aid Society, whose work for a 1921 exhibition contributed to the raising of $6,943.83 in remittances to artists. He also received help from the immigrant press: the *Jewish Daily Forward* provided space and sponsorship for an exhibition in May 1917 that included over three hundred works by eighty-nine artists, many of them immigrants themselves.[92] Weichsel's papers also contain numerous receipts for advertisements in both mainstream media outlets and papers like *Novy Mir* (*The New World*), a Russian daily; *The Day: National Jewish Daily*; and *Russkoye Slovo*, "the only daily Russian newspaper in America."[93] Just as nineteenth-century entrepreneurs had used technological and organizational developments in the media to further the "field of art," so Weichsel used the thriving immigrant media of the prewar years to expand the art world yet again.

What is perhaps most significant about these efforts is not that they contributed to the ascent of modernism in the United States—which they certainly did—but that they did so without excluding other styles. In nearly all of Weichsel's shows, with the notable exception of the Forum Exhibition, the work of Wright, Hartley, and even Stieglitz sat side by side with work that was fairly conventional even for the day. Unlike Stieglitz's organizational efforts, which were designed to create a vanguardist empire in America for Stieglitz and his allies but which to those like Thomas Hart Benton who were pursuing another path could be "especially irritating;" and unlike the overtly professionalizing style of the Wrights, which although geared toward making them famous, valued aesthetic "creed" above all, Weichsel's brand of organization happily fused different kinds of art in the search for a broader aim: the expansion of the art world in the United States.[94] What Weichsel's career as an immigrant organizer in the world of art shows, then, is that modernism did not always arrive as a rupture, a bang, or a *succès de scandale*. Sometimes, for the price of "two boys carfare," it just showed up in people's neighborhoods.[95]

Finally, however, it must be said that although Weichsel's work reveals the continuities between modernists and their institution-building predecessors, it also provides a glimpse at the more sinister influence of professionalism. Although Weichsel's generosity, his emphasis on bringing art to the people, and his faith in organizational over aesthetic principles provide a model for democratic art-world practice, there was a competing element of professionalism in Weichsel's project. For while Weichsel worked to build a machinery that would bring about "social realization" in American urban communities, what he seems to have meant by this was that immigrant and working-class neighborhoods needed their own professional artists. Despite Weichsel's best intentions, his vision undermined itself: for if professional artists were to be the sole engines of "social realization," the public would necessarily be passive. What the art-world career of John Weichsel shows, then, is that immigrants did not just influence American modernism as radical catalysts. More than that, they were carriers of organizational methods from the Gilded Age that would contribute to modernism's emergence; they were negotiators of the transition to Progressive modes of organization in the art world; and they were instigators of the professionalism that would undermine the continued viability of both. As such, John Weichsel and his forgotten peers played a much more subtle but no less important role in the emergence of modernism than Duchamp, the café anarchists, and the other immigrant radicals who influenced American art and politics after the turn of the century.

Charles Erskine Scott Wood: Gilded Age Modern

If the careers of John Weichsel, Marsden Hartley, and the Wright brothers are instructive in reminding us of the institutional and cultural continuities that shaped the first modernist generation, the lives of older figures also challenge conventional wisdom about the nature of the transition from the "genteel" to the "modern." It is a common assumption within history and sociology, if not within the history of art, that Gilded Age culture was conservative and retrograde, dominated by two trends: first, the cancerous spread of capitalism, which was responsible not only for the economic domination of the populace but also for the aesthetic oppression of those subjected to the cracked cake-icing grandeur of the White City; and second, the organizational villainies of urban elites, who created a soul-killing and antidemocratic system of cultural hierarchy in their quest to find new spheres of hegemony after the Civil War. According to modernists themselves, and some of the most influential historical scholarship of the past generation, late-nineteenth-century culture has come to stand as a fortress whose banners read "social control—capitalism—gentility" and which was demolished by forms of cultural and political radicalism that produced fear and anguish in the hearts of the older generation.

But was this true? Were institution builders merely out to preserve the status of commercial or industrial elites, and did nineteenth-century capitalism make only for retrograde politics and a stifling and false Gilded Age culture? At the level of the individual, it is difficult to draw such easy conclusions. Take, for example, the case of Moncure D. Conway. Conway was one of the most consistent champions of museums in America, and was one of the first people to try to serialize the work of Matthew Arnold in the American press. As such, we might expect him to have been out to preserve the privileges of his class. In fact, it was not so simple. A southerner who made his name as an abolitionist, Conway embraced every radical cause he could find, from anti-slavery, to anti-imperialism, to feminism. Indeed, Conway lamented in 1882 that feminism in Britain was not moving quickly enough: he complained in a letter to Susan B. Anthony that "as women do not 'boycott' their opponents nor assassinate them in the high Irish and Nihilist style, the progress is slow."[96]

And what about Louis Prang? As the embodiment of the culture of consumption, surely he must have been a political conservative, surely he must have worked to hinder the emergence of "radical" aesthetic forms, and surely he must have represented the industrial elite to which his staggering wealth surely provided an entry. Again, this was not entirely the case; Prang never foreswore his past, continuing like Bradley to identify with the declining *artisanal* elite even as he joined the industrial bourgeoisie. While this may have made him a nostalgic figure, it did not cause him to reject progressive art or politics: as we have seen, Prang (fig. 73) was responsible for the first American exhibition of works by Redon and one of the earliest displays of works by Manet, and he was the publisher of *Modern Art*. Prang can also hardly be blamed for promoting a retrograde political agenda. Like the abolitionist and art critic Conway, he embraced feminism and anti-imperialism. A close friend of William Lloyd Garrison Jr. and California women's rights leader Caroline Severance, Prang condemned the American colonial foray into the Philippines as a "more than criminal action," advocated Henry George's Single Tax, and railed against "the monopoly of the natural resources by the use of which alone the life of man can be sustained."[97]

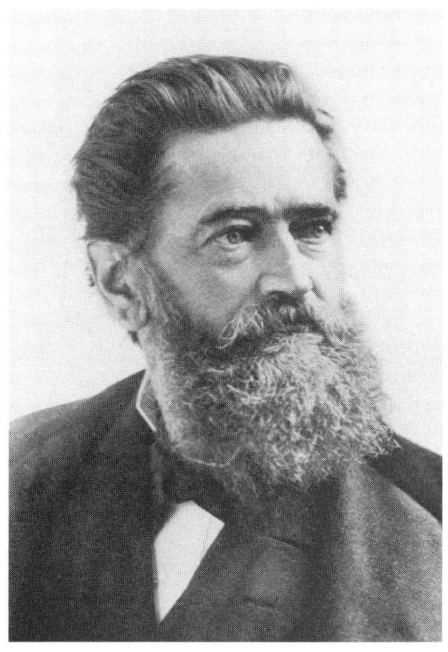

73. Louis Prang (1824–1909), 1880. Massachusetts Historical Society, Boston

And finally, it is worth considering the life of C. E. S. Wood.[98] Wood was, in many ways, a classic nineteenth-century institution builder. Himself an amateur painter who exhibited in New York, Philadelphia, Chicago, and San Francisco, Wood was a founding member of the Portland (Oregon) Art Association, and helped to establish the Portland Art Museum. He orchestrated the commissioning of Olin Warner's *Skidmore Fountain* (1888, Portland, Oregon), one of the most significant works of public sculpture in the nineteenth-century American West. He was an amateur painter, who broadened his friendships with artists like Warner and Albert Pinkham Ryder and dealers like Jimmie Inglis over wine, opera, and cigars. Along with Childe Hassam, he went with brush in hand to paint the wilderness of Oregon.[99] He was an avid collector whose taste combined a rather typical desire for bronzes and snuff boxes and a slightly more risky, but not exactly radical, admiration for his contemporary Americans—Ryder, Warner, Hassam, and even the pastels of a young Sadakichi Hartmann, whose work he introduced into local Western

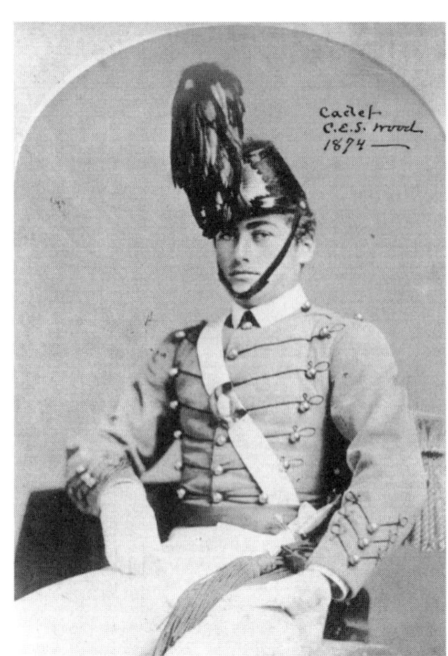

74. C. E. S. Wood (1852–1944) as a cadet, 1874. Papers of C. E. S. Wood, Box 296 (30), The Huntington Library, San Marino, California

markets.[100] He played a central role in the establishment of the *Pacific Monthly*, deliberately titled as a Western bookend to the famous Boston journal, to which he himself contributed writings on art and other topics.

And where did Wood learn his love of art? In part, he learned it from his mother, who like many well-positioned nineteenth-century women was an amateur watercolorist.[101] More significant to Wood's own development as a painter and an art-world figure, though, was his time at West Point between 1870 and 1874 (fig. 74), when as a cadet Wood came under the tutelage (and danced with the daughters) of Robert Weir, and in the early 1880s when he returned as Adjutant of the Academy.[102] By this time, the senior Weir had retired, but Wood forged a lifelong friendship with his son, the painter J. Alden Weir, who had been in Paris during most of Wood's training. These are striking facts. Today, it is hard to imagine young cadets or officers learning a lifetime love of art at any of America's military academies, or that an institution like West Point could both encourage art instruction and provide the venue in which two very distinct social universes—the New York art world and the military elite—would meet and mix. In the nineteenth century, however, drawing was a required element of the curricula of the nation's military academies—just as it was obligatory in its burgeoning schools of technology, a number of its universities, and many of its public schools. As a result, West Point seems to have been the perfect place for the son of the Navy's first surgeon general to have had his first face-to-face contact with the art world—and to begin a life that would lead him farther and farther from his father's "joyless tyranny," as Wood put it.[103]

Wood was also a classic representative of the late-nineteenth-century elite. His father's success gave him entry into the highest military and political circles, as is suggested by the fact that, upon Wood's appointment to West Point, President Ulysses S. Grant personally met him in the White House to discuss Wood's father's renowned service.[104] Following this, Wood continued to mix in these circles, marrying Washington socialite Nannie Moale Smith and enjoying friendships with people like Mrs. Douglas Robinson, the sister of Theodore Roosevelt. Indeed, Wood was probably best known and most successful in the nineteenth and early twentieth centuries not for his art-world activities, but for his primary careers—first, as the Army officer who "recorded" Chief Joseph's "fight no more forever" speech at the end of the U.S. military's campaign against the Nez Perce, and second, as a phenomenally successful Portland lawyer who helped the international banking firm Lazard Frères retain a land claim in a case argued by Wood before the Supreme Court. This victory changed Wood's life, netting him an immediate $50,000 plus sole commission on the dispersal of $6,000,000 worth of land in eastern Oregon.

Although Wood's activities were certainly unusual, their diversity was not atypical of the postwar generation of institution builders, who often were amateurs in the art world (but, in the case of Gilded Age arch-villains like Henry Frick and Charles Lang Freer, to whom Wood was introduced by Eugene Meyer Jr. of Lazard Frères, *were* intimately connected to processes like the usurpation of the Nez Perce and the rise of continental capitalism).[105] What is perhaps more surprising is that Wood also became a proponent of anarchism, an advocate of birth control and divorce, and a champion of the right to discuss them. Bitterly disillusioned by his early experiences in the army, Wood also became an anti-imperialist, campaigning strenuously against both the annexation of the Philippines and the First World War and renouncing the war against "the Indian" as a war to defend "the powerful capitalists and 'captains of industry.'"[106] He publicly defended Emma Goldman and gave legal counsel to the IWW.[107] He had radical friends, including John Reed. He contributed to and was praised by the *Masses* and the *New Masses*.[108] He also corresponded with Harriet Monroe, and published poems in *Poetry* and alongside Wallace Stevens in the *Measure*.[109] As Wood liked to claim, "Rebellion is in my blood and I esteem discontent and revolt as the noblest of all human attributes."[110] In short, although his own work was never aesthetically modernist, he did meet many of the criteria set by historians for inclusion among the "moderns."

Seeing these two halves—"two rooms," as the title of a recent anthology of Wood's writings puts it—of his life and career, it is tempting to cast Wood's life in terms of great ironies, as his biographer, Robert Hamburger, has done.[111] And there were certainly many aspects of Wood's life and career that are hard to reconcile. Although he assailed capitalism's grip on the masses, and although he occasionally enjoyed slumming (particularly when it consisted of listening to the underworld reminiscences of someone else, like his friend Jimmie Inglis, and could be framed by brandy and "Johannesberger Cabinet" wine), Wood was reluctant to give up the creature comforts of his own class. Thus in 1913 he "tried to take Mrs. Burke to a Bohemian restaurant Couldn't find one—all dirty and adjuncts to saloons—Finally had to end in great respectability at the Oregon Hotel—upstairs dining room."[112] Even more ironic is another episode recounted in Wood's diary for 1913. Here one comes across Wood in bed, writing a "'True Fairy Tale' for the Masses . . . intended to show their desperate condition [illeg.] against Capitalism." Fair enough. And yet, as the diary's next line tells us, the bed he was writing in was in the Hotel Astor, where he was working on the Lazard Frères case that would make him rich by keeping eastern Oregon in the hands of the banks. Indeed, the fortune Wood would make from this venture was so great, as Wood's son wrote, "that he was enabled to provide for my mother and us children and retire and go to California with Mrs. [Sara Bard] Field," the suffragist and poet. In other words, it was Wood's very engagement with capitalism—embodied by his morning in the Hotel Astor—that allowed him to promote his radical agenda, including his critique of capitalism and his personal embrace of "free love."

And yet, perhaps there is more to this episode than simple irony or contradiction. Perhaps it is not ironic that speculative capitalism is what made free love possible as an ideal and, in Wood's case, a reality. Despite the fact that modernism is predicated on the idea of challenging the bourgeoisie, of challenging the grotesque and unequal wealth of the Gilded Age, it was also and profoundly a product of that wealth. Wealth, or the pursuit of it, was one of the links that most consistently and firmly connected the first modernists—the wealth of the Steins, to meet and collect and talk of revolution; the wealth of Stieglitz, to do the same in New York instead of Paris; the wealth of Mabel Dodge to bring together aesthetic and political "radicals" in Greenwich Village and Taos; the wealth of Hartley's benefactors, who sent an immigrant mill hand's son to New York to become, of all things, an artist; and the wealth of Ida Wright, Stanton Macdonald-Wright's first wife, to fund not only his study in Paris, but a private studio.[113]

Indeed, Wood himself did not conceive of his own life ironically. This is not surprising, as people can be blind to their own inconsistencies. And yet Wood seems to have been motivated by more than a simple lack of self-awareness, as he also avoided another trope that contradictory figures often turn to in order to explain their own irreconcilable pasts: that of radical rupture. For although Wood did self-consciously flout convention and reject the "joyless tyranny" of his parents, he embraced many aspects of their characters, particularly their abolitionism, their "contempt for pedigree and ancestry," and their resistance to the prevailing culture of antebellum Baltimore.[114]

Beyond this, Wood also failed to reject his own institution-building past. Indeed, there is strong evidence to suggest that he actively believed that the organizational methods that worked for the art world would also work for radical politics. Thus, in addition to borrowing the strategies of his Eastern counterparts in his cultural endeavors in Portland, he also turned to methods such as the tireless use of the expanding periodical press as a forum for the promotion of particular ideals, a clearinghouse for the advertisement and promotion of corollary publications, and the establishment of networks of like-minded associates. Wood also realized the potential held by ephemeral publications, circulating pamphlets marked "Not copyrighted. Free use invited" and even Christmas cards with his favorite lessons on free speech, the dangers of imperialism, and the like.[115] Similarly, Wood's career as a political activist, like his career as a cultural organizer, is marked by two other institution-building hallmarks: continuous, vocal participation in the construction and refinement of organizations and institutions, and the frequent utilization of the club and lecture circuit.[116] This helps to explain why Wood, an "anarchist" who gave legal counsel to the IWW, also had a lifelong, if provocative, relationship with the Democratic Party, serving as a delegate at both the state and national levels, and played a central role in the ascendance of Progressive reforms like initiative and referendum and the direct election of senators.[117] Far from being the lugubrious Victorian quoter of Whitman that Christine Stansell makes him out to be, Wood was a savvy organizer whose Christian anarchism, like that of the abolitionists he so admired, was based on an understanding of the flow of information in an age of mass circulation, and an awareness of the need to develop and employ new organizational methods as time went by.[118] While the emergence of the modern may have entailed rupture, in Wood's case it also was driven by its continuities with the nineteenth-century past.

Far from arguing that Wood, or Hartley, or the Wrights, or Weichsel were ironic anomalies in a trajectory of radical rupture, I believe that they were each in some way typical of the first modernists. Just as broader (and generally unrecognized) institutional and organizational changes in the art world contributed to the emergence of modernism on a structural level, continuity also marked the lives lived by modernists. Even in a biographical context, which has so frequently been presented in terms of "before" and "after," it is important to recognize that modernism did not always emerge out of simple ruptures between outsiders and stifling convention, or out of clear and defining moments of individual conversion. If modernism derived from the bohemianism of Greenwich Village, with its radical politics and seemingly "free" social mores, then it also derived from the institution-building matrix of the Gilded Age art world, with its publishing networks, its schools and museums, its plentiful circulated images, and its eager patrons. In a key sense, the emergence of this world after the Civil War made people in the next generation want to become artists, made them realize they could become artists, and provided the structures that would enable them to be artists. More than that, it helped to make them modernists.

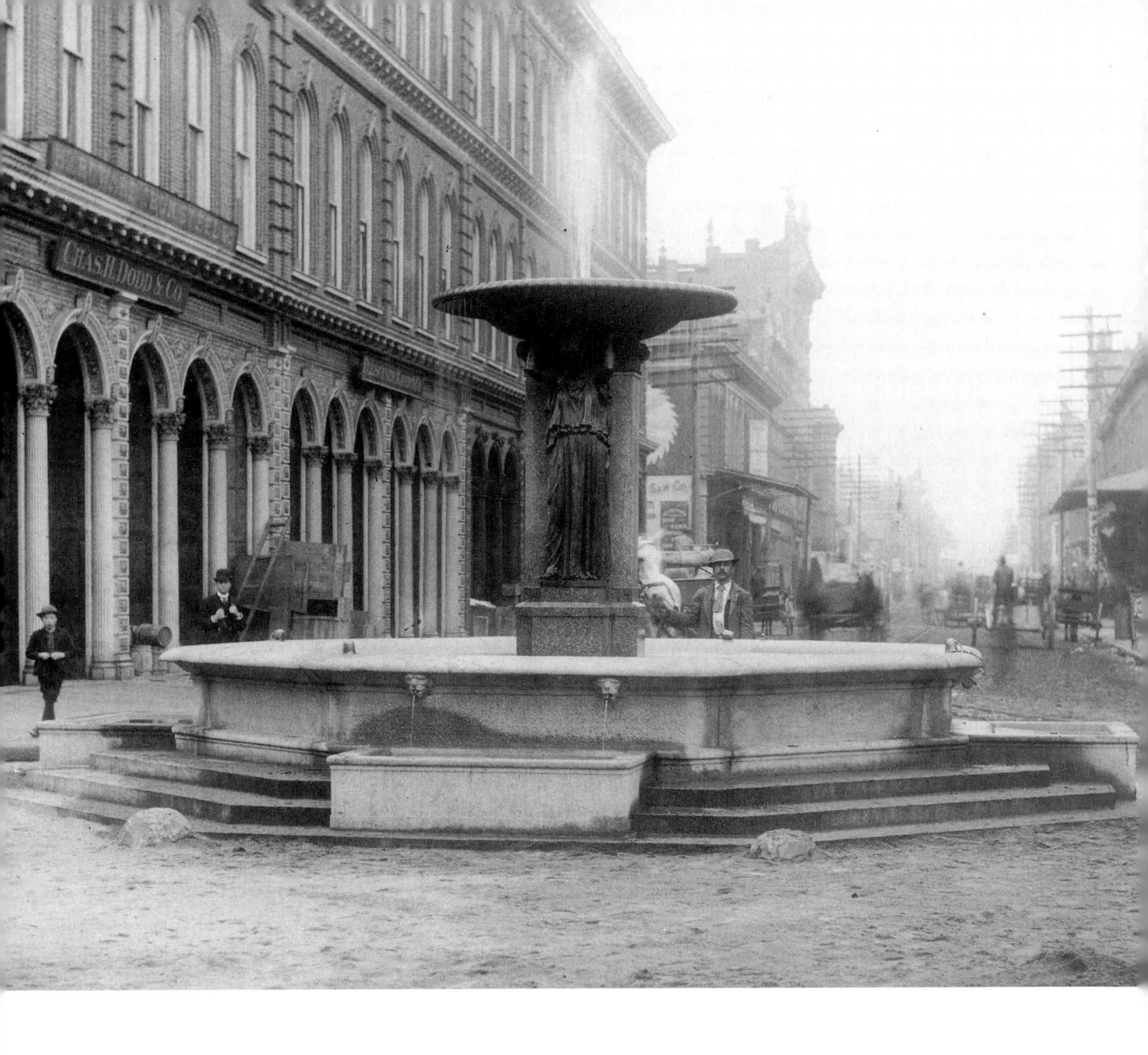
CHAS. H. DODD & CO.

Postscript

Pre-Modernism and Postmodernism: Reflections on the *Tilted Arc* Crisis

Rigorous procedural mechanisms were devised to ensure an invulnerable process for selecting artists of achievement and art of enduring qualities.
—Richard Serra, 1985

75. Olin Levi Warner (1844–1896), *Skidmore Fountain*, 1888, Portland, Oregon. Oregon Historical Society

Throughout this book, I have made two central arguments about American visual modernism. The first is that modernism should not be seen as a revolutionary upheaval, but as the product of complex, long-term changes. The second is that these changes, although gradual, did eventually produce an art, and an art world, that differed in key respects from the art and art world of the late nineteenth century. Over the course of the decades between the Civil War and the Armory Show, the exclusive idea of "art" as unique works, created and vetted by art-world professionals, traveled from the margins to the center of the art world. Together with artistic vanguardism, with its emphasis on the opposition to "outmoded," "mainstream" traditions, professionalism became the dominant mode of practice in the modernist art world.

In making these arguments, it has been my intention to shed new light on the beginnings of visual modernism in the United States, and the consequences of those beginnings for the history of American culture in the twentieth century. As the twenty-first century begins, however, the history of pre-modernism might also provide some insight into how we might approach the defining artistic change of our *own* time: the *end* of modernism. Like the emergence of modernism, its decline was also marked by conflict. The 1980s and early 1990s, in particular, witnessed the eruption of numerous art controversies in the United States. Many of these controversies centered on the issue of public funding for artworks (for example, the photographs of Robert Mapplethorpe) whose postmodern emphasis on the representation of marginalized racial, gender, and sexual identities outraged certain viewers. Others, most notably the controversy surrounding the commission, installation, and removal of Richard Serra's sculpture *Tilted Arc* (1981, New York City) by the federal government's General Services Administration, reflected the weakening hold of works in an abstract style. As Harriet Senie suggests in the most comprehensive treatment of the controversy to date, "Modernism was in decline, and various postmodern styles with implicit and explicit political content enjoyed greater acclaim at modernism's expense."[1]

Whether they involved early postmodern or late modern art, however, virtually all the controversies of this transitional period shared a common source: severe disagreement over the shape and direction of the art world, as much as over art itself.[2] As in the Cesnola case, the Armory Show, and other pre-modernist conflicts, professionalism once again provided one of the key sources of dissent in these postmodernist controversies, particularly in the case of *Tilted Arc*. As Casey Nelson Blake argues, the often acrimonious debate over whether or not to remove *Tilted Arc* turned largely on three antagonistic discourses: the largely conservative voices of government bureaucrats who objected to the work in the name of a privatized public sphere (and who called for its removal); the professionalized language of art-world insiders (who called for it to stay); and an intelligent but marginalized public (whose interests were not fully represented by either side).[3]

It is possible to gauge how deeply professionalization permeated the *Tilted Arc* crisis by looking briefly at some of the arguments made by art historians, artists, and critics against removing the work during the public hearing convened in March 1985. At this time, art historian Benjamin Büchloh declared:

> Only once in the history of the twentieth century was the domain of art and culture officially removed from the competence of its producers and the professional judgment of its academic and administrative supporters, and handed over to the spontaneous "practice of the collective prejudice." That was the moment when the Fascist demigods of the Nazi party encouraged populists to destroy the culture of which the

> bourgeois capitalism had deprived them all along. . . . At that time, the public collections acquired by progressive museum directors and art historians were first denounced as frauds and [as a] deceit of the public and subsequently [were] destroyed. Fortunately, some of them were at least sold, and they entered international collections such as that of the Museum of Modern Art in New York. The art that was removed at the time by the quacks and vigilantes on behalf of the so-called public included, among others, works by Picasso, Brancusi, Tatlin, and others. In many respects, these were the antecedents of the world of Richard Serra, whose work, as most art historians and critics throughout the world by now unanimously agree, places him in that line of complex definitions of sculpture that make him simply the most important sculptor of the post-World War period.[4]

The intensity of Büchloh's comments reflects the very real threat that the Reagan administration's cultural platform posed not just to specific public art programs, but to the very idea of public spending for art. Nonetheless, his comments also provide evidence of a starkly Manichean view of the art world that indicates a much deeper jealousy toward nonexpert involvement in art matters. Casting professionals as the defenders of "important" artists against fascist "quacks and vigilantes," Büchloh's testimony suggested that the art world had no real laypeople: only a "so-called public" so mesmerized by "bourgeois capitalism" that it could be made to do anything. In this vision, professionalism is represented not as a historical outgrowth of capitalism's ascendance, but as a heroic barrier between a courageous avant-garde and a cowardly, moblike public.

It would be unfair to single out Büchloh for holding this view. Indeed, the reason his comments are so important is that they reveal a pattern of (vanguardist, professionalizing) thinking that was pervasive in the testimony of those who argued on Serra's behalf. Many of the artists who testified described the public and its tastes in scornful tones, threatening that if *Tilted Arc* were removed then all art that is "*too* honest," that "challenges the homogenization of contemporary bureaucracy," and that above all is "important" would be replaced by "art of second-class or third-rate quality," perhaps "academic figures of justice, or old cannons or cannonballs."[5] Abigail Solomon-Godeau's testimony, which began with a professional self-identification ("critic and historian") moved quickly to the vanguardist suggestion that "the incomprehension and outrage that have historically accompanied the productions of modern artists" was normal.[6] And, although she argued that "the notion of 'the public' was . . . problematic" and "could be manipulated to mask other agendas," she nevertheless was able to define a "public" to which the government *should* listen: "experts and laymen . . . public servants . . . museum curators . . .

public sculpture foundations . . . artists . . . critics . . . doctors . . . lawyers."[7] In other words, professionals at work and professionals using their leisure time to defend the interests of other professionals.

While this classificatory scheme may seem casual, it recurred repeatedly throughout Serra's defense and the commentary that soon followed it. For example, the American Council for the Arts' primer *Public Art, Public Controversy: The Tilted Arc on Trial* organized its transcript of the public hearing into handy professional blocks, headed "Architects and Builders," "Art Critics," "Art Historians," "Painters" and the like.[8] This scheme was applied only to the testimony of those speakers who supported Serra and challenged the government's right to remove or relocate the sculpture. Those who thought it should be removed, although classified individually by name and occupation, were identified collectively by their opinions rather than their professions under the heading "The Case Against *Tilted Arc*," to which were devoted six out of ninety-four pages of "selected testimony."[9] Although the book's foreword claimed that "every effort ha[d] been made to preserve the character of the original spoken testimony," it failed to record a single objection to the sculpture by an art-world professional, despite the fact that a number of artists, including sculptor and public art advocate Virginia Maksymowicz, had called for its removal.[10] Indeed, although there were certainly many people within the art world who were genuinely dismayed at the obvious rift between "public" and "art," for many professionals it was more important to police the art world's borders—even against errant artists—than to see what might be done to repair this rupture.

This is set into relief by an earlier controversy over the relocation of public art: the campaign to move Olin Warner's *Skidmore Fountain* (fig. 75) in the 1930s. Like the campaign against *Tilted Arc*, this movement was met with outrage by some figures in Portland's art world. As C. E. S. Wood argued, the sculpture's removal from the center "of a city, where the stream of human life flows longest and thickest" and placement in a park, with "a widening of space, with trees for environment, would be simply ignorant vandalism." Seething at the thought, he wrote that "if the city fathers . . . wish to show their ignorance, I suggest that they put the Skidmore fountain on wheels . . . and move it from place to place, as the mood changes, with a card 'This is our one and only work of art, the world-celebrated Skidmore fountain. Bids will be accepted for its next location.'"[11] To Wood, as to Serra, the dislocation of this work from its site posed three distinct threats: aesthetic degradation due to removal; an unacceptable capitulation to the market; and, as he also pointed out, a transgression of legal obligations incurred at the sculpture's commission.

What is interesting about Wood's argument, however, was what lay behind this outrage: not just fear for the *artist's* reputation and the precedent that removal would set for future artists, but anger on behalf of the work's original *patrons*. Like Serra's defenders, Wood certainly held the artist in high esteem: at Warner's death, he had railed, "I cry out. Oh the pity of it. The pity of it . . . a thousand drunkards and fools left and the one supreme genius taken." And yet, when the campaign to move the *Skidmore Fountain* began, his concern for Warner was matched by an equally strong concern for the impact of the work's relocation on the donors and institution builders who had had the foresight to put in place a sculpture that benefited the young city both aesthetically and practically.[12] As he wrote in exasperation: "If they are actually so bourgeois and new-rich that they cannot bear to leave their one and only work of art where Steve Skidmore clearly willed it to be, where Henry Failing and those men who reverently carried out Skidmore's will from their own pockets, wished it to be, where the sculptor placed it and came across the continent to view the site, that all might be harmonious, then move it."[13] What Wood realized is that artists' legal rights are only one of the things that must be safeguarded to ensure a future for art; so, too, must be protected the enthusiasm and the love of art that makes audiences want it to exist.[14] What Wood saw was that this enthusiasm sometimes turns viewers into patrons, so that public art can be made even in the absence of government patronage. What Serra failed to see is that without this enthusiasm even a "blue-ribbon panel" cannot create meaningful public art.[15]

I have not introduced the *Tilted Arc* crisis here in order to take sides on the question of its removal. As Senie persuasively argues, there is more to be gained by analyzing the causes and the consequences of that event than by fanning the flames of controversy. Furthermore, the sculpture's opponents hardly provided a model that should be emulated. My purpose in introducing *Tilted Arc*, instead, is to illustrate how modernism and professionalism continued to be conjoined in the American art world as modernism declined; and to suggest the limits of an art world in which vanguardist "oppositionality" is expressed through a language that is itself a sustaining element of the very structures of power it purports to critique. Within and outside the art world, both at the turn of the twentieth century and in the present day, professionalism does not "challenge the homogenization of contemporary bureaucracy." Emerging as it did out of the crisis of authority created by industrialization, professionalism helped to create that bureaucracy, and reaffirms it today. It will never have the transformative power Serra's defenders ascribed to it.

Neither this postscript nor this book is meant to be entirely bleak. I have not described the decline of the pre-modernist art world merely to lament its passing, and I have not introduced *Tilted Arc* in order to say, "I told you so." My hope, rather, is that a fuller understanding of the art world before modernism might offer some ideas about what might be done to overcome the malaise left in its wake. And the pre-modernist art world does offer some encouraging suggestions for what might enable the growth of truly "public" art. These include the revitalization of the ideal of universal, free art education; the rehabilitation of amateurship and the reinstatement of artistic labor within the definition of art; and the renewed support for accessible public art institutions. In both its good and its bad aspects, pre-modernism has something to teach postmodernists.

Consider the question of art education. Senie rightly claims that current levels of art education are insufficient to inculcate a love or understanding of art among most people, and that this lack of understanding fueled public hostility to *Tilted Arc*. She argues that "if one's only exposure to art is making it in kindergarten or rare encounters with 'visiting artists,' then art remains a diversion (a hobby or entertainment) rather than an expression of serious content in visual form." As a remedy, she proposes that public art installations be preceded and accompanied by educational programming.[16] I would go a step further. Why not bring back universal free art education, at all levels of schooling? We would not think of teaching people to read without also teaching them to write; so how, then, can we think that people will be visually literate unless we also teach them to draw, to photograph, to sculpt, or to master today's new visual arts and media? "Kindergarten" art was not initially meant as a mere diversion: it was meant to teach all people, regardless of background, to see like artists and to see like lovers of art. There is no reason why we should sell ourselves short in the present day.

Related to the question of education is the question of artistic labor. As Julian Stallabrass argues, one of the consequences of the rise of conceptual art has been a declining engagement with artistic practice.[17] Although Stallabrass is primarily concerned with British art, his comments reflect Senie's fear that recent American art is only about the *representation* of identity politics, and fails meaningfully to concern itself with aesthetics or the materiality of art. One of the solutions to this "hollowness"—and one that does not require the making of stylistic or narrative prescriptions—is to look for ways to rehabilitate virtuosity as a prized aesthetic value; and, furthermore, to think about how ordinary people, rather than just professional artists, might pursue this goal. If, as Senie argues, *form* was the content within abstract art, then it certainly seems possible to envision an art in which *labor* is content.

And finally, there is the question of support for public art institutions. Of course, museums should not be used to further cultural hierarchy, racial exclusion, or other social evils.[18] But neither should art institutions be dismissed because their history is complicated. Like Frederick Paul Keppel, I believe that it is possible to imagine a world in which museums are as "vital to public education as libraries."[19] However, at a time in which the political omens foretell the dismantling of *all* public institutions—even those which, like libraries and schools, have been more sheltered than museums—it is getting more difficult all the time. Given the fragile future of public art institutions of any sort, it does not seem to be a good strategy for historians of culture to continue to expend so much effort on the project of unmasking them and deriding their potential supporters. Instead, we should be reimagining their place in a democratic twenty-first-century culture.

Unlike some critics of postmodernism, I do not believe that art should not have a social or a political content; and I do not think that the modernists who genuinely strove for change were wrong to do so. But the politics of art reside as much outside the frame as inside it, in the "mainstream" institutions of the art world as much as in the institutions of the avant-garde. Neither a modernism that is built upon the compromised "oppositionality" of "difficult" aesthetics, nor a postmodernism that is focused exclusively on the *representation* of disaffection with the status quo is enough. As important as are the look and shape of art, so too are the look and shape of the art world. Is it accessible? Is it democratic? Does it allow for the meaningful participation of all people, as creators and decision-makers, as well as as viewers? There is a distinction in politics between "citizenship," in which even marginalized people participate meaningfully in the development and operation of political institutions, and "governance," in which bureaucrats and professionals offer us a menu of services, but at the expense of our autonomy. In art, as in politics, we need to ask a fundamental question: are we going to be citizens, or are we going to be onlookers? Only time will tell.

Acknowledgments

Everyone who writes a book incurs debts. As this project has taken many years—and many moves–to complete, I have incurred a lot. I would like to thank, first of all, the teachers whose guidance and support at Johns Hopkins University made this project possible, especially Dorothy Ross, Ronald Walters, and JoAnne Brown. For sparking my interest in earlier years, I am grateful to Joseph Kett and Fred Green.

I also owe a deep debt of gratitude to the many art historians who generously shared their knowledge and time. As a guest in the discipline, I have been continually impressed with its hospitality. Thanks, then, to Alan Braddock, Sarah Burns, Erika Esau, Marian and Phil Kovinick, Michael Leja, David Peters-Corbett, Alan Wallach, the fellows and staff at the Smithsonian American Art Museum, and the anonymous reader for Princeton University Press. I am especially grateful to Katherine Manthorne, for her tremendous generosity and critical acuteness.

I would not have been able to write and illustrate this book without the financial assistance of the Arts and Humanities Research Board, the Huntington Library, the Massachusetts Historical Society, the Smithsonian Institution, and University College Cork. I am also grateful to the staff at the American Antiquarian Society, the Archives of American Art, the Baltimore Museum of Art, the Boston Public Library, the Huntington Library, the Johns Hopkins University Libraries, the Massachusetts Historical Society, the Smithsonian American Art Museum, and the other libraries and archives mentioned in the text for their patient and assiduous help with research. Thanks, too, to Marcus Wood for giving the book its title; to Princeton University Press for giving me something to put it on; and to Robert and Brownie Allen, in whose house it was such a pleasure to write it.

I am grateful to the many colleagues, friends, and allies who lived with me while I lived with this project, including Andy Bielenberg, Jonathan Brody, Vittorio Bufacchi, Mark Canuel, Mark Chu, Amie Cole, Linda Connolly, Elizabeth Ferry, Cathy Jurca, Mara Keire, Michelle Lesperance, Sandra Macpherson, Dan McGee, Stacey McGraw, Chris McKenna, Mervyn O'Driscoll, Rebecca Plant, Charlene Porsild, Susanne Pralle, Nancy Press, Raluca Radulescu, Mark Rigstad, Laura Riley, Silvia Ross, Jon Rottenberg, Leo Shin, Mike Szalay, Christopher Wild, David Wood; all the folks in Calgary; and new friends in Brighton and Dublin.

Finally, I owe this and so much more to Anthony, Ellen, Bart, T.J., and Cindy Mancini; Ali Bothwell; David, Sybil, and Peter Finlay; and, most of all, to Victor and Graham Finlay, for their patience and love.

Abbreviations

Periodicals and Newspapers

AABN *The American Architect and Building News*
AAP *The American Art Printer*
AAm *The Art Amateur*
AAR *The American Art Review*
AE *Art Education*
AM *Atlantic Monthly*
CO *Current Opinion*
CW *Camera Work*
HM *Harper's Monthly*
JSAH *Journal of the Society of Architectural Historians*
KS *Keramic Studio*
MA *Modern Art*
NAR *North American Review*
NYDT *New-York Daily Tribune*
PC *Prang's Chromo: A Journal of Popular Art*
SM *Scribner's Monthly*
USAD *The United States Art Directory and Year-Book*, compiled by Sylvester Rosa Koehler (New York, London, and Paris: Cassell, Petter, Galpin and Co., 1882)

Societies, Institutions, and Individuals

AAA Archives of American Art
AAA-EM Elizabeth McCausland Papers, Archives of American Art
AAA-JW John Weichsel Papers, Archives of American Art
AAA-SRK Sylvester Rosa Koehler Papers, Archives of American Art
AAA-WHL Winslow Homer Letters, Archives of American Art
AAS American Antiquarian Society, Worcester, Massachusetts
AAS-LP Louis Prang Papers, American Antiquarian Society
AWD Alexander Wilson Drake
CCC Clarence Chatham Cook
CESW Charles Erskine Scott Wood
HEH The Huntington Library, San Marino, California
HEH-CESW Charles Erskine Scott Wood Papers, The Huntington Library
HEH-KAEE Korzenik Art Education Ephemera Collection, The Huntington Library
KBW Katherine Boynton Wright
MFA Museum of Fine Arts, Boston
MGVR Mariana Griswold Van Rensselaer
MHS Massachusetts Historical Society, Boston
MNAS Massachusetts Normal Art School
NYSDA New York Society of Decorative Art
SAA Society of American Artists
SRK Sylvester Rosa Koehler
UVA-WHW S. S. Van Dine Collection, Clifton Waller Barrett Library of American Literature, Special Collections, University of Virginia Library
WHW Willard Huntington Wright (S. S. Van Dine)

Notes

Introduction
Interrogating Modernism

1. Mabel Dodge to Gertrude Stein, Jan. 24, 1913, quoted in John Rewald, *Cézanne and America* (Princeton, N.J.: Princeton University Press, 1989), 175; originally published in Donald Gallup, ed., *The Flowers of Friendship: Letters Written to Gertrude Stein* (New York: Alfred A. Knopf, 1953), 70–71.
2. See, for example, Christine Stansell, *American Moderns: Bohemian New York and the Creation of a New Century* (New York: Metropolitan Books, 2000); Ann Douglas, *Terrible Honesty: Mongrel Manhattan in the 1920s* (New York: Farrar, Straus, and Giroux, 1995); Arthur Frank Wertheim, *The New York Little Renaissance* (New York: New York University Press, 1976); Edward Abrahams, *The Lyrical Left: Randolph Bourne, Alfred Stieglitz, and the Origins of Cultural Radicalism in America* (Charlottesville: University of Virginia Press, 1986); Wanda Corn, *The Great American Thing: Modern Art and National Identity, 1915–1935* (Berkeley and Los Angeles: University of California Press, 1999); Martin Green, *New York 1913: The Armory Show and the Paterson Strike Pageant* (New York: Scribner's, 1988); Abraham Davidson, *Early American Modernist Painting, 1910–1935* (New York: Harper and Row, 1981); Daniel Joseph Singal, "Towards a Definition of American Modernism," *American Quarterly* 39, no. 1 (spring 1987): 7–26.
3. See, for example, J. G. A. Pocock, *The Machiavellian Moment: Florentine Political Thought and the Atlantic Republican Tradition* (Princeton, N.J.: Princeton University Press, 1975); Bernard Bailyn, *The Ideological Origins of the American Revolution* (Cambridge, Mass.: Harvard University Press, 1967); Michael Warner, *The Letters of the Republic: Publication and the Public Sphere in Eighteenth-Century America* (Cambridge, Mass.: Harvard University Press, 1990); Gordon S. Wood, *The Creation of the American Republic, 1776–1787* (New York: W. W. Norton, 1972).
4. Lawrence Levine, *Highbrow/Lowbrow: The Emergence of Cultural Hierarchy in America* (Cambridge, Mass.: Harvard University Press, 1988); Paul J. DiMaggio, "Cultural Entrepreneurship in Nineteenth-Century Boston: The Creation of an Organizational Base for High Culture in America," in *Rethinking Popular Culture: Contemporary Perspectives in Cultural Studies*, ed. Chandra Mukerji and Michael Schudson

Elementary Color (Springfield, Mass.: Milton Bradley & Co., 1895).
53. Henry Lefavor, "Introduction," in Bradley, *Elementary Color*, 3.
54. See Milton Bradley & Co., *Milton Bradley, A Successful Man: A Brief Sketch of His Career and the Growth of the Institution which He Founded* (Springfield, Mass.: Milton Bradley & Co., 1910), 30 and passim.
55. Ibid., 14; James J. Shea, *It's All in the Game* (New York: G. P. Putnam's Sons, 1960), 47–57.
56. *Milton Bradley, A Successful Man*, 43.
57. Ibid., 66–67.
58. Edgar Kaufmann Jr., "'*Form* Became *Feeling*,' a New View of Froebel and Wright," *JSAH* 40, no. 2 (May 1981): 130–37 and "Frank Lloyd Wright's Mementos of Childhood," *JSAH* 41, no. 3 (Oct. 1982): 232–37; Jeanne S. Rubin, "The Froebel-Wright Kindergarten Connection: A New Perspective," *JSAH* 48, no. 1 (Mar. 1989): 24–37.
59. Milton Bradley & Co., "Dear Sir, in introducing to your citizens our new scientific combination of the stereopticon" (c. 1860, AAS).
60. Shea, *It's All in the Game*, 47–57.
61. *Work and Play Annual of Home Amusements and Social Sports* (Springfield, Mass.: Milton Bradley & Co., 1872).
62. Ibid., inside cover, 3, 33, 42, 45–47.
63. See Henry Turner Bailey, "Milton Bradley" and Emile Poulsson, "Mr. Bradley as I Have Known Him," both in *Milton Bradley, A Successful Man*, 42–46 and 47–50.
64. Clapper, "Popularizing Art in Boston," 24–25.
65. Wilhelm von Bezold, *Theory of Color in Its Relation to Art and Art-Industry*, trans. S. R. Koehler (Boston: L. Prang & Co., 1876); *Illustrations of the History of Art. A Series of Above 2000 Woodcuts Selected, by permission, from the Works of Kugler, Lübke, Burckhardt, Overbeck, Dohme, C. von Lützow, Falke, Woltmann, Lacroix, etc. Chronologically Arranged, and Forming a Universal Atlas, to be Used in Connection with Any Work on the History of Art. Authorized American Edition, Published under the Supervision of S. R. Koehler* (Boston: L. Prang & Co., 1879); see also Joseph Langl, *Modern Art Education: Its Practical and Aesthetic Character Educationally Considered*, trans. S. R. Koehler (Boston: L. Prang & Co., 1875).
66. "Competitions," *AAR* 1, div. 2 (1880): 59, 60, 66, 135; Clapper, "Popularizing Art in Boston," 25.
67. See Mary Cassatt, *Mother and Child*; photogravure from a drypoint etching, *MA* 3, no. 1 (winter 1895): 2.
68. See, for example, the front matter of *MA* 2, no. 3 (summer 1894): n.p.
69. J. M. Bowles, ed., *Some Examples of the Work of American Designers* (Philadelphia: Dill & Collins, 1918).
70. Ibid., n.p.
71. Mary W. Blanchard, "Embroidery, Enterprise, and the Modernist Vision in Gilded Age America," *American Quarterly* 54, no. 4 (Dec. 2002): 664.
72. Kathleen Waters Sander, *The Business of Charity: The Woman's Exchange Movement, 1832–1900* (Urbana: University of Illinois Press, 1998), 49–59.
73. Mary W. Blanchard, "'It Is Surprising That There Are Any Happy Wives': *The Art Interchange*, 1878–1886," *Journal of Women's History* 8, no. 3 (1996): 40–41.
74. These included "*The Winged Moon*, designed by Dora Wheeler and executed in needle-woven tapestry by the Associated Artists, 1883" (Candace Wheeler, *The Development of Embroidery in America* [New York: Harper and Brothers, 1921], facing 123).
75. Blaugrund, "Tenth Street Studio Building," 2.

Chapter 2
Building an American Art World

1. On Lathrop, see *The Catholic Encyclopedia*, http://www.newadvent.org/cathen/16051b.htm, May 19, 2003.
2. George Parsons Lathrop, "The Study of Art in Boston," *HM* 58 (May 1879): 818.
3. Ibid.
4. Ibid., 819.
5. Ibid.
6. Carrie J. Rebora, "The American Academy of the Fine Arts, New York, 1802–1842" (Ph.D. diss., City University of New York, 1990); Nina de Angeli Walls, "Art and Industry in Philadelphia: Origins of the Philadelphia School of Design for Women, 1848–1876," *Pennsylvania Magazine of History and Biography* 117, no. 3 (1993): 177–99; Sarah Allaback, "'Better than Silver and Gold': Design Schools for Women in America, 1848–1860," *Journal of Women's History* 10, no. 1 (spring 1998): 88–107; April F. Masten, "The Work of Art: American Women Artists and Market Democracy, 1820–1880" (Ph.D. diss., Rutgers University, 1999).
7. William C[rary] Brownell, "The Art-Schools of New York," *SM* 16, no. 6 (Oct. 1878): 762, 774.
8. On the history of the museum in the United States, see Nathaniel Burt, *Palaces for the People: A Social History of the American Art Museum* (Boston: Little, Brown, 1977); Steven Conn, *Museums and American Intellectual Life, 1876–1926* (Chicago: University of Chicago Press, 1998); Paul J. DiMaggio, "Cultural Entrepreneurship in Nineteenth-Century Boston: The Creation of an Organizational Base for High Culture in America," in *Rethinking Popular Culture: Contemporary Perspectives in Cultural Studies*, ed. Chandra Mukerji and Michael Schudson (Berkeley and Los Angeles: University of California Press, 1991), 374–97; Neil Harris, "The Gilded Age Revisited: Boston and the Museum Movement," *American Quarterly* 14 (winter 1962): 545–66; Helen Lefkowitz Horowitz, *Culture and the City: Cultural Philanthropy in Chicago from the 1880s to 1917* (Lexington: University of Kentucky Press, 1976); Lawrence Levine, *Highbrow/Lowbrow: The Emergence of Cultural Hierarchy in America* (Cambridge, Mass.: Harvard University Press, 1988); Alan Wallach, *Exhibiting Contradiction: Essays on the Art Museum in the United States* (Amherst: University of Massachusetts Press, 1998). For the antebellum period, see Neil Harris, *The Artist in American Society: The Formative Years, 1790–1860* (Chicago: University of Chicago Press, 1966); Lillian B. Miller, *Patrons and Patriotism: The Encouragement of the Fine Arts in the United States, 1790–1860* (Chicago: University of Chicago Press, 1982).
9. SRK, *USAD*, 14–16. See also *The Act of Incorporation, By-Laws, Etc. of the Museum of Fine Arts* (Boston: Alfred Mudge, 1870); Charles C[allahan] Perkins, "American Art Museums," *NAR* (July 1870), reprinted Boston, 1870; Walter Muir Whitehill, *The Museum of Fine Arts, Boston: A Centennial History* (Cambridge, Mass.: Belknap Press, 1970).
10. *Catalogue of an Exhibition of Contemporary Art, Held under the Direction of the Boston Art Club, the Boston Society of Architects, and the Schools at the Museum, also of the Paintings Shown by the Museum* (Boston: Museum of Fine Arts, 1879); SRK, *USAD*, 14–16; SRK, "American Art Chronicle—Exhibitions and Sales," *AAR* 1, div. 2 (1880).
11. SRK, *USAD*, 29–30.
12. L[uigi] P[alma] di Cesnola, ed., *The Metropolitan Museum of Art* (New York: Harper & Brothers, 1882), 32; Winifred E. Howe, *A History of the Metropolitan Museum of Art* (New York: Metropolitan Museum of Art, 1913), 122; Conn, *Museums and American Intellectual Life*, chap. 6.
13. SRK, *USAD*, 42, 69.
14. Ibid., 60–61.
15. "The Museum of Fine Arts, Boston," *AABN* 8, no. 253 (30 Oct. 1880): 205–16. As the plan was reduced to fit the format of the *AABN*, these inscriptions are only visible by magnifying glass.

16. *Act of Incorporation of the Museum of Fine Arts*, 7.
17. On the SAA and its role in the art world, see Jennifer A. Martin Bienenstock, "The Formation and Early Years of the Society of American Artists: 1877–1884" (Ph.D. diss., City University of New York, 1983); Eliot Candee Clark, *History of the National Academy of Design, 1825–1953* (New York: Columbia University Press, 1954), 105–10; Barbara Stephanic, "Clarence Cook's Role as Art Critic, Advocate for Professionalism, Educator, and Arbiter of Taste in America" (Ph.D. diss., University of Maryland, 1997), 185–93.
18. G. W. Sheldon, *American Painters: With Eighty-Three Examples of their Work Engraved on Wood* (New York: D. Appleton and Co., 1879), 169–74.
19. Trudie A. Grace, "The National Academy of Design and the Society of American Artists: Rivals Viewed by Critics, 1878–1906," in *Rave Reviews: American Art and Its Critics, 1826–1925*, ed. David B. Dearinger (New York: National Academy of Design, 2000), 107.
20. SRK, *USAD*, 95, 102, 105, 109, 119, 123.
21. Ibid., 47, 74, 18.
22. St. Botolph Club Records, MHS MS N-237, Box 21, Folder 15.
23. SRK, *USAD*, 38.
24. Hale and Wheeler are listed alongside Winslow Homer, J. Alden Weir, and John Twachtman in *Catalogue of Spring Exhibition 1886 from Apr. 15 to May 1* (Boston: St. Botolph Club, 1886). For Bellows, Glackens, Henri, and Luks, see St. Botolph Club Records, MHS MS N-237, app. B, app. C.
25. H. Wayne Morgan, *New Muses: Art in American Culture, 1865–1920* (Norman: University of Oklahoma Press, 1978), 12; Oliver Larkin, *Art and Life in America* (New York: Holt, Rinehart, and Winston, 1960). It should be noted that collecting and dealing were not new, but expanded and altered ventures after the war; international dealers had had ventures in New York at least since the 1840s. Also see Samuel Putnam Avery, *The Diaries, 1871–1882, of Samuel P. Avery, Art Dealer* (New York: Arno Press, 1979) and "Some Notes on the History of the Fine Arts in New York City during the Past Fifty Years," in Benson J. Lossing, *The History of New York City* (New York: Perine Engraving and Publishing Co., 1884), 840–43.
26. "A Chat with a Dealer," *AAm* 3, no. 4 (Sept. 1880); Frederick Keppel, *The Golden Age of Engraving* (New York: Baker & Taylor, 1910).
27. *Catalogue of the Etched Work of Peter Moran* (New York: Frederick Keppel & Co., 1888); Peter Moran, *The Noonday Rest*, 1877, etching, published in *AAR* 1, div. 1 (1880): facing 149; Thomas Moran, *The Passaic Meadows*, etching, published in *AAR* 1, div. 1 (1880): facing 151; Peter Moran after Van Marcke, *Landscape and Cattle*, engraving in *AAR* 1, div. 1 (1880): facing 66; Annin after Thomas Moran, *Walls of the Grand Cañon*, engraving, in *AAR* 1, div. 1 (1880): facing 380.
28. "Diary of William Macbeth," 31 Mar. 1892, William Macbeth Papers, AAA; Macbeth Gallery, *Fiftieth Anniversary Exhibition 1892–1942* (New York: Macbeth Gallery, 1942).
29. *Exhibition of Paintings by Arthur B. Davies, William J. Glackens, Robert Henri, Ernest Lawson, George Luks, Maurice B. Prendergast, Everett Shinn, John Sloan: Feb. 3 to 15, 1908* (New York: Macbeth Gallery, 1908). See Bennard Perlman, *The Immortal Eight: American Painting from Eakins to the Armory Show, 1870–1913* (New York: Exposition Press, 1962); William Innes Homer, *Robert Henri and His Circle* (Ithaca, N.Y.: Cornell University Press, 1969).
30. Jane Gorjevsky, Curator, Carnegie Collections, to J. M. Mancini, 30 Apr. 2003.
31. Paul J. DiMaggio, "Constructing an Organizational Field as a Professional Project: U. S. Art Museums, 1920–1940," in *The New Institutionalism in Organizational Analysis*, ed. Walter W. Powell and Paul J. DiMaggio (Chicago: University of Chicago Press, 1991), 275.
32. Ibid., 272.
33. SRK, *USAD*, 42; Susan Stuart Frackelton, *Tried by Fire: A Work on China Painting* (New York: D. Appleton and Co., 1886).
34. M. Louise McLaughlin, *China Painting. A Practical Manual for the Use of Amateurs in the Decoration of Hard Porcelain* (Cincinnati: Robert Clarke & Co., 1890); on McLaughlin, see Eileen Boris, *Art and Labor: Ruskin, Morris, and the Craftsman Ideal in America* (Philadelphia: Temple University Press, 1986).
35. "Noted American China Painters XXI.–Miss Louise McLaughlin," *AAm* 35, no. 4 (Sept. 1896): 79.
36. SRK, *USAD*, 34, 36–37.
37. Ibid., 33–34.
38. Walter Smith, *School Document No. 7. Report on Drawing. Addressed to the School Committee of the City of Boston, Massachusetts* (Boston: Rockwell and Churchill, 1880), 11.
39. Section 1 of "An Act Relating to Free Instruction in Drawing" reads: "The first section of chapter thirty-eight of the General Statutes is hereby amended so as to include Drawing among the branches of learning which are by said section required to be taught in the public schools" (*Acts and Resolves Passed by the General Court of Massachusetts, in the Year 1870* [Boston, 1870], 183).
40. *Annual Report of the School Committee of the City of Boston: 1866* (Boston, 1867), 109, 333.
41. Ibid., 107.
42. Ibid., 109, 107.
43. Ibid., 107–8.
44. Lathrop, "The Study of Art in Boston," 819.
45. Smith, *School Document No. 7*, 22.
46. Ibid., 39.
47. *Rules of the School Committee and Regulations of the Public Schools, of the City of Boston* (Boston: City Printers, 1871), 42–44. For more information on wages for night-school drawing instructors, see Smith, *School Document No. 7*, 30.
48. On art education, see Diana Korzenik, *Drawn to Art: A Nineteenth-Century American Dream* (Hanover, N.H.: University Press of New England, 1985); Randolph Benton Miley, "A Critical Examination of Henry Turner Bailey's Method of Pedagogical Art Criticism in Context" (Ph.D. diss., Florida State University, 1994).
49. "Form of Application for Admission to the Massachusetts Normal Art School," in *Circular of the MNAS . . . Second Year, 1874–5* (Boston: Wright & Potter, 1874), n.p.; SRK, *USAD*, 18.
50. On the early curriculum and aims of the Massachusetts Normal Art School [MNAS], see *Prospectus of the* MNAS (Boston: Alfred Mudge & Son, 1874); *Report of Proceedings at the Meeting for the First Distribution of Certificates to Students of the* MNAS*, and Address by His Excellency Alexander H. Rice, Governor of the Commonwealth of Massachusetts, Jun. 23, 1876, in the School* (Boston: Alfred Mudge & Son, 1877); *Circular of the* MNAS*. . . . Third Year, 1875–6* (Boston: Wright & Potter, 1875); *Circular of the* MNAS*. . . . Fourth Year, 1876–7* (Boston: Albert J. Wright, 1876); *Circular of the* MNAS*. . . . Eighth Year, 1880–1* (Boston: Franklin Press, 1880); *Circular of the* MNAS*. . . . Ninth Year, 1881–2* (Boston: Franklin Press, 1881).
51. *Circular of the* MNAS*. . . . Fourteenth Year, 1886–7* (Boston: Wright & Potter, 1886), 12.
52. "The New Revolution," *AAP* 1, no. 1 (Jan.–Feb., 1887): 3; SRK, *USAD*, 18; *Circular of the* MNAS*. . . . Fourth Year, 1876–7*, 16.
53. *The Antefix Papers. Papers on Art Educational Subjects, Read at the Weekly Meetings of the Massachusetts Art Teachers' Association, By Members and Others Connected with the Massachusetts Normal Art School* (Boston: Printed for Private Circulation, 1875), in HEH-KAEE.
54. *Acts and Resolves*, 359.

55. MNAS, *Circular and Catalogue for the Thirty-Fifth Year, 1907–1908* (Boston: Wright & Potter, 1907), 25–63.
56. Ibid., 27, 31, 34.
57. Ibid., 25, 33, 34.
58. *AE* 4, no. 6 (May 1898): 191.
59. MNAS, *Circular and Catalogue . . . 1907–1908*, 27, 41.
60. Georgia W. Fraser, "John W. Alexander: His Paintings," *AE* 4, no. 6 (May 1898): 171–72; Fred H. Daniels, "Historic Ornament and Its Application to Design," *AE* 4, no. 6 (May 1898): 183–85; Clarence Moores Weed, "Bamboo Flower Holders," *AE* 4, no. 6 (May 1898): 169–70; E. W., "An Experiment with Applied Art in Newcomb College, New Orleans," *AE* 4, no. 6 (May 1898): 166–68; "In the Field," *AE* 4, no. 6 (May 1898): 191.
61. MNAS, *Circular and Catalogue . . . 1907–1908*, 31.
62. Walter Smith, *Second Annual Report on the Promotion of Industrial Art Education in the State of Massachusetts*, 23. This report is bound in *First Annual Report of The Board of Visitors of the* MNAS, *Together with the Second Annual Report on Industrial Art Education* (Boston, 1874), in MHS.
63. *Circular of the* MNAS. . . . *Eighth Year, 1880–1*, 1–4.
64. Duties and pay of the curator are proposed in the *First Annual Report of The Board of Visitors*, 8; Munsell is listed as curator in *Circular of the* MNAS. . . . *Ninth Year, 1881–2*, 2.
65. SRK, *USAD*, 18; *Circular of the* MNAS. . . . *Ninth Year, 1881–2*, 12.
66. SRK, *USAD*, 11.
67. *Circular of the* MNAS. . . . *Eighth Year, 1880–1*, 4, 12.
68. The exhibitions were held on 27 Jan.–8 Feb 1890; 29 Dec. 1890–17 Jan. 1891; and 24 Dec.–11 Jan. 1892. See St. Botolph Club Records, MHS MS N-237, app. B. An example of Munsell's paintings is *Seascape* (1890; Worcester Art Museum, Worcester, Mass.).
69. A. H. Munsell, *A Color Notation: A Measured Color System, Based on the Three Qualities, Hue, Value, and Chroma, with Illustrative Models, Charts, and a Course of Study Arranged for Teachers* (Boston: G. H. Ellis Co., 1905) and *Atlas of the Munsell Color System* (Malden, Mass.: Wadsworth, Howland & Co., 1915).
70. MNAS, *Circular and Catalogue . . . 1907–1908*, 25, 35.
71. Prang's system was influential. For example, Scottish manufacturer and writer on color theory David Paterson wrote to Prang: "This autumn I have found it very interesting to match some of the soft indescribable shades of the Autumn leaves with your Color Standard & thus record their tints with scientific accuracy. For example, the russet leaves of the Beech I find correspond to *Orange 3rd Shade*. The red of the wild cherry with 1 *RRO*. & all the many varieties of soft citrines in the chestnut leaf–range from Yellow, 1st shade to 1.YYO & 1 YO. With all their various *tints*" (David Paterson to Louis Prang, 5 Nov. 1905, AAS-LP, folder 1).
72. This included a booklet, *The Munsell Color System: Children's Studies in Measured Colors* (Boston: Wadsworth, Howland & Co., 1910), HEH-KAEE, Box 44, envelope 5, p. 1).
73. Typical prices included $2.50 for a teacher's color sphere, and ten cents for a box of seven crayons (ibid., inside back cover).
74. "Munsell Crayons No. 3 Box, 22 Colors," HEH-KAEE, Box 71, Set 4.
75. *Annual Report of the School Committee . . . 1866*, 109.
76. The first two journals were the organs of a successor to the *American Art Union* and the *Art Union of Philadelphia*, respectively. On criticism before the Civil War, see Stephanie Wasielewski Fay, "American Pictorial Rhetoric: Describing Works of Art in Fiction and Art Criticism, 1820–1875" (Ph.D. diss., University of California at Berkeley, 1982); Emily Julia Halligan, "Art Criticism in America before *The Crayon*: Perceptions of Landscape Painting, 1825–1855" (Ph.D. diss., University of Delaware, 2000); Janice Simon, "*The Crayon*, 1855–1861: The Voice of Nature in Criticism, Poetry, and the Fine Arts" (Ph.D. diss., University of Michigan, 1990); Dearinger, *Rave Reviews*.
77. See Theodore P. Greene, *America's Heroes: The Changing Models of Success in American Magazines* (New York: Oxford University Press, 1970); Frank Luther Mott, *A History of American Magazines* (Cambridge, Mass.: Harvard University Press, 1938). For art publishing in California, see Nancy Dustin Wall Moure's invaluable *Publications in Southern California Art*, 3 vols. in 1 (Los Angeles: Dustin Publications, 1984).
78. For a few examples of exhibitions other than the Academy annual, see "An Exhibition of Decorative Art," *SM* 10 (Aug. 1875): 518–19; "Ninth Exhibition of the Water-Color Society," *SM* 12 (Apr. 1876): 901–3; Philip Quilibet, "Drift-wood–Art and the Centenary," *Galaxy* 19 (May 1875): 696–99; Quilibet, "Art at the World's Fair," *Galaxy* 2 (Feb. 1876): 271–72; "Characteristics of the International Fair: Closing Days," *AM* 39 (Jan. 1877): 94–100; D. M. A., "Art at the Paris Exposition," *SM* 17 (Dec. 1878): 276–81. On the Ohio Valley Centennial, see SRK, *Catalogue of the Contributions of the Section of Graphic Arts to the Ohio Valley Centennial Exposition, Cincinnati, 1888* (Washington, D. C.: Smithsonian Institution Press, 1888); Helena E. Wright, "The Smithsonian in Cincinnati: Exhibiting Prints at the Ohio Valley Centennial Exposition, 1888," in Alice M. Cornell, ed., *Art as Image: Prints and Promotion in Cincinnati, Ohio* (Athens: Ohio University Press in association with the University of Cincinnati Digital Press, 2001), 131–65.
79. "Taine's Art Lectures," *SM* 2 (Oct. 1871): 666–67; James T. Bixby, "Taine's Philosophy," *NAR* 117 (Oct. 1873): 401–38; Sarah B. Wister, "Pater, Rio, and Burckhardt," *NAR* 121 (July 1877): 155–90; "Viollet-le-Duc's Discourses on Architecture," *HM* 52 (Mar. 1876): 616; "Ulrici's Treatises upon Art History," *NAR* 125 (July 1877): 175–77; "Couture's 'Conversation's on Art,'" *SM* 18 (Sept. 1879): 794; "Editor's Literary Record–Veron's Aesthetics," *HM* 58 (Apr. 1879): 787.
80. "Talks on Art," *SM* 10 (Oct. 1875): 787; "Popular Arts," *SM* 10 (May 1875): 110; "Some Heliotype Reproductions," *SM* 9 (Jan. 1875): 383–84; "Editor's Literary Record–Putnam's Sons' Art Books," *HM* 57 (Sept. 1878): 629.
81. "Examples for Stump-Drawing," *SM* 14 (Jun. 1877): 267; "Editor's Literary Record–Duffield's The Art of Flower-Painting," *HM* 58 (Jan. 1879): 311–12; "Books on Art," *SM* 8 (Aug. 1874): 503–4.
82. "Dredging in New York Harbor.–Drawn by J. W. [*sic*] Twachtman," *Harper's Weekly* 26, no. 1329 (10 Jun. 1882): 356; this image accompanies "Dredging in New York Harbor," 364–65.
83. "Plate CXIX.–Decorative Designs Designed from Plants, Contributed to *The Art Amateur* by John Williamson, of Louisville, Ky. (For explanation, see page 88)," *AAM* 5, no. 4 (Sept. 1881).
84. Charles Wyllys Elliott, *Pottery and Porcelain, from Early Times down To The Philadelphia Exhibition of 1876* (New York: D. Appleton and Co., 1878), 5; John Treadwell, *A Manual of Pottery and Porcelain for American Collectors* (New York: G. P. Putam & Sons, 1872), 22, 32–39 and passim.
85. "Red Cedar Lumbering at Cedar Keys, Florida.–from Sketches by S.G.W. Benjamin," *Harper's Weekly* 26, no. 1325 (13 May 1882): 300.
86. AWD to CESW, 8 Sept. 1883, WD Box 128 (14), HEH-CESW.
87. Charles C[allahan] Perkins, "American Museums," *NAR* 110 (July 1870): 1–29; James Jackson Jarves, "Museums of Art," *Galaxy* 10 (July 1870): 50–59; "The Art Museum," *SM* 3 (Apr. 1872): 756–57.
88. S. G. W. Benjamin, "Contemporary Art

in England," *HM* 54 (Jan. 1877): 161–79; John Arbuckle, "About Greece and Greek Museums," *SM* 14 (May 1877): 65–72; Sofia Bompiani, "The New Museum in Rome," *SM* 18 (May 1879): 1–13. There were many articles relating to South Kensington, in journals ranging from the *Art Amateur* to *Harper's Monthly*. They include Phebe D. Natt, "London Art-Schools," *Lippincott's* 25 (May 1880): 629–35; "Foreign Notes," *Studio*, n.s., 6, no. 13 (1891): 125–27; M. D. Conway, "Decorative Art and Architecture in England," *HM* 49 (Oct. 1874): 617–32. For other museums, see "A New Southern Art Museum," *Art Union* 1, no. 4 (1884): 91–93; "An Infant Museum," *Studio*, n.s., 1, no. 14 (1885): 163–65; Lathrop, "The Study of Art in Boston;" "A Word of Suggestion," *SM* 7 (Nov. 1873): 120–21; "Comment and Review," *American Art* 1, no. 10 (July 1887): 286–88; "Art Notes," *Art Review* 1, no. 3 (1887): 10–24.

89. "A New Southern Art Museum," *Art Union* 1, no. 4 (1884): 92.
90. M. G. Humphreys, "The Provincial Art Gallery," *AAm* 16, no. 4 (1887): 88–89; "Art Objects Viewed by Electric Light," *AAm* 23, no. 2 (1890): 33–35.
91. Carol Duncan, "Art Museums and the Ritual of Citizenship," in *Exhibiting Cultures: The Poetics and Politics of Museum Display*, ed. Ivan Karp and Steven D. Lavine (Washington, D.C.: Smithsonian Institution Press, 1991), 90. On the museum and the "sacralization" of art, see also DiMaggio, "Cultural Entrepreneurship"; Levine, *Highbrow/Lowbrow*.
92. J. R. G. Hassard, "An American Art Museum: The Designs Submitted by Wm. H. Beard," *SM* 2 (Aug. 1871): 409.
93. [Attr. to Thomas G. Appleton], *Boston Museum of the Fine Arts. A Companion to the Catalogue* (Boston, 1877), 8. MHS copy inscribed "Mrs. G. Dexter, May 15, '85." This link is also explicitly mentioned in Whitehill, *Museum of Fine Arts, Boston*.
94. Humphreys, "Provincial Art Gallery," 88. On the Boston fire, see Korzenik, *Drawn to Art*, 141–42.
95. The standard work on the "White City" is Alan Trachtenberg, *The Incorporation of America: Culture and Society in the Gilded Age* (New York: Hill and Wang, 1982); see also Kathryn Fanning, "American Temples: Presidential Memorials of the American Renaissance" (Ph.D. diss., University of Virginia, 1996).
96. "The Art World," *The Art Collector* 9, no. 3 (Dec. 1898): 35.
97. DiMaggio, "Constructing an Organizational Field," 267.
98. Ibid., 268. "High culture" is DiMaggio's phrase, taken from the subtitle of his account of the founding of the MFA, "The Creation of an Organizational Base for High Culture in America."
99. Ibid, 268.
100. AWD to CESW, 1 Feb. 1886, WD Box 128 (22), HEH-CESW.
101. This reference might be to a work by Edward Sylvester Morse, but I have not located the exact source.
102. SRK, *American Etchings: A Collection of Twenty Original Etchings, by Moran, Parris, Ferris, Smillie, and Others* (Boston: Estes and Lauriat, 1886); SRK, *American Art: Illustrated by Twenty-five Plates, Executed by the Best American Etchers and Wood Engravers, from Paintings Selected from Public and Private Collections* (New York: Cassell, [1886]).
103. SRK, *Museum of Fine Arts: Exhibition of American Etchings*, 2d ed. (Boston: Alfred Mudge & Son, 1881), 3–14.
104. T. Tokuno, *Japanese Wood-Cutting and Wood-Cut Printing*, ed. SRK (Washington, D.C.: Government Printing Office, 1894); Nancy E. Green and Jessie Poesch, *Arthur Wesley Dow and American Arts and Crafts* (New York: American Federation of Arts in Association with Harry N. Abrams, 1999), 62–63.
105. *Society of American Artists Fourth Annual Exhibition* (New York: Society of American Artists, 1881), 11–12; Pennsylvania Academy of the Fine Arts, *Catalogue of the Fifty-second Annual Exhibition, Apr. 4–May 29, 1881* (Philadelphia: Pennsylvania Academy of the Fine Arts, 1881), 18–19; S. P. Langley to SRK, 2 Apr. 1890, AAA-SRK, Reel D-187; W. W. Greenough to SRK, 10 Sept. 1887, AAA-SRK, Reel D-182; Charles Loring to SRK, 18 Apr. 1889, 21 Oct. 1880, AAA-SRK, Reel D-182; E. H. Greenleaf to SRK, 21 Apr. 1887, 15 July 1886, 17 July 1884, 20 Jan. 1881, AAA-SRK, Reel D-182.
106. S. G. W. Benjamin, "The Exhibitions. IV.–Society of American Artists. Third Exhibition," *AAR* 1, div. 1 (1880): 258–62.
107. "The Works of the American Etchers: Introduction and I.–R. Swain Gifford," *AAR* 1, div. 1 (1880): 3–6.
108. W. J. Linton, "The History of Wood-Engraving in America. Chapter 4," *AAR* 1, div. 2 (1880): 55–61; W. J. Linton, "The History of Wood-Engraving in America. Chapter 5," *AAR* 1, div. 2 (1880): 98–105; *AAR* 1, div. 1 (1880): 144–48; *AAR* 1, div. 1 (1880): 166; *AAR* 2, div. 1 (1881): 151–54; *AAR* 2, div. 1 (1881): 229–34.
109. *AAR* 1, div. 2 (1880): 87.
110. "American Art Chronicle," *AAR* 1, div. 2 (1880): 132.
111. Ibid., 133.
112. "American Art Chronicle," *AAR* 1, div. 2 (1880): 85.
113. "American Art Chronicle," *AAR* 1, div. 2 (1880): 137, 132; emphasis in original.
114. SRK to Dr. William W. Folwell, 21 June 1880, AAA-SRK, Reel D-187; James G. Ardrey to SRK, 6 June 1881 and 28 June 1881, AAA-SRK, Reel D-182.
115. *AAR* 1, div. 2 (1881): 269.
116. SRK, *USAD*.
117. DiMaggio, "Cultural Entreneurship," 381; SRK, *USAD*, 16.
118. *PC* 1, no. 4 (Christmas 1868): 5.
119. Edward S. Morse to Louis Prang, 27 Dec. 1887, MHS MS S-255.
120. *Catalogue of Publications by L. Prang & Co., 159 Washington St., Boston* (Boston: L. Prang & Co., 1867), 6–10; "Miss Robbins's Pictures," *PC* 1, no. 4 (Christmas 1868): 2.
121. Louis Prang, *Catalogue of an Exhibition Illustrative of a Centenary of Artistic Lithography, 1796–1896* (New York: Grolier Club, 1896); SRK, *A Chronological Catalogue of the Engravings, Dry-Points and Etchings of Albert Dürer, as Exhibited at the Grolier Club* (New York: Grolier Club, 1897).
122. R. G. Ingersoll to Louis Prang, 2 Jan. 1880, HEH HM 27044.
123. Henry I. Bowditch, "A Memorial of Lieut. Nathaniel Bowditch A.A.G., 1st Cavalry Brigade, 2nd Division, Army of the Potomac" (Nathaniel Bowditch Memorial Collection, 1851–1886, MHS).
124. Katharine Morrison McClinton, "L. Prang and Company," *Connoisseur*, Feb. 1976, 99; S. A. Schoff after Elihu Vedder, *The Sea Serpent*, in *AAR* 1, div. 2 (1881).
125. *Catalogue of Louis Prang's Collection of Oil and Water-Color Paintings including the Famous Prize Christmas Cards*, AAA Reel N300, 83; "Competitions," *AAR* 1, div. 2 (1880): 59, 60, 66, 135; *Society of American Artists Fourth Annual Exhibition*, 3, 9, 10; SRK, *USAD*, 103; SRK, *Museum of Fine Arts: Exhibition of American Etchings*, 4. Kruell was a frequent contributor to *Modern Art*.
126. *Collection of the Société Anonyme: Museum of Modern Art 1920* (New Haven, Conn.: Yale University Press, 1950), 78.
127. *Catalogue of Louis Prang's Collection*, AAA Reel N300, 82, 83, 92; Larry Freeman, *Louis Prang: Color Lithographer, Giant of a Man* (Watkins Glen, N.Y.: Century House, 1971), 169–80; Harry T. Peters, *America on Stone: The Other Printmakers to the American People, A Chronicle of American Lithography other than Currier & Ives* (Garden City, N.Y.: Doubleday, Doran and Company, 1931), 327–28; St. Botolph Club Records, MHS MS N-237, app. C. Ellen Bowditch is listed as a Normal Art School student

in *Circular of the MNAS. . . . Eighth Year, 1880–1*, 3.

128. "Prang's American Chromos," *PC* 1, no. 5 (Apr. 1869): 8.

129. Celia Thaxter, *The Yule-Log*, illustrated by L. B. Humphrey (Boston: L. Prang & Co, [1889]); Mary J. Jacques, *Child Life: A Souvenir of Elizabeth B. Humphrey* (Boston: L. Prang & Co., 1890).

130. Grace Carter, *Plant-Forms Ornamentally Treated: Exhibiting a Number of Plants in Their Natural Colors, with an Analysis of Their Parts, and Their Application to Conventionalized Ornament* (Boston: L. Prang & Co., 1876); SRK, *USAD*, 124.

131. The asking price for Emmet's *In the Fields* is listed in Bienenstock, "Formation," 332.

132. Freeman, *Louis Prang*, 169–80; Bienenstock, "Formation," 13–16.

133. Louis Prang, *Catalogue of . . . Artistic Lithography*, 10.

134. "A Word to Journalists," *PC* 1, no. 1 (Jan. 1868): 4.

135. David Clayton Phillips, "Art for Industry's Sake: Halftone Technology, Mass Photography, and the Social Transformation of American Print Culture, 1880–1920" (Ph.D. diss., Yale University, 1996).

136. See, for example, "The 'Namouna.' From a Photograph by Pach," *Harper's Weekly* 26, no. 1324 (6 May 1882): 276.

137. SRK, *Catalogue of A Selection of Prints: Arranged Chronologically to Illustrate the Various Processes of Engraving Invented from the 15th to the End of the 18th Century* (Boston: Alfred Mudge & Son, 1893); SRK, *Exhibition Illustrating the Technical Methods of the Reproductive Arts from the XV Century to the Present Time: With Special Reference to the Photo-Mechanical Processes* (Boston: Alfred Mudge & Son, 1892).

138. G. P. Lathrop to SRK, 9 Sept. 1880 and 15 Sept. 1880, AAA-SRK, Reel D-187; SRK, *The Photo-Mechanical Processes* (Boston: reprinted from *Technology Quarterly*, 1892).

139. Boston Art Club notice, 18 Jan. 1875, AAA-SRK, Reel D-182.

140. "Art Supplement to *The American Art Printer*," *AAP* 1, no. 3 (May–June 1887); "Art Supplement to *The American Art Printer*," *AAP* 1, no. 4 (July–Aug., 1887): n.p.; see also "Listening to the Fairies. (From painting, by the Ives Process.) Plate furnished by the Photo-Electrotype Engraving Co., 20 Cliff Street, New York City," *AAP* 1, no. 2 (Mar.–Apr. 1887): n.p.

141. Wallach, *Exhibiting Contradiction*; "The Art Collection of Vassar College," *SM* 11 (Feb. 1876): 593–94; "Perkins's Eastlake's Household Taste," *NAR* 116 (Jan. 1873): 206–8; Moncure D. Conway, "The South Kensington Museum, Second Paper," *HM* 51 (Oct. 1875): 649–66.

142. AWD to CESW, 16 May 1883, WD Box 128 (6), HEH-CESW; AWD to CESW, 26 June 1883, WD Box 128 (8), HEH-CESW.

143. AWD to CESW, 13 Mar. 1884, WD Box 128 (20), HEH-CESW; 26 Jan. 1886, WD Box 128 (21), HEH-CESW; statement of account in AWD to CESW, 1 Feb. 1886, WD Box 128 (22), HEH-CESW; AWD to CESW, 7 May 1886, WD Box 128 (23), HEH-CESW. Drake also encouraged Wood to have a coin he owned electrotyped (AWD to CESW, 18 Aug. 1882, WD Box 128 [2], HEH-CESW).

144. "Miss Robbins's Pictures," 2.

145. Ibid., 2.

146. SRK, *Museum of Fine Arts: Exhibition of American Etchings*, 10–11.

147. Edward Strahan [Earl Shinn], ed., *The Art Treasures of America: Being the Choicest Works of Art in the Public and Private Collections of North America*, 3 vols. (Philadelphia: G. Barrie, 1879–1882); *Catalogue of the Works of Art in the Union League of Philadelphia* (Philadelphia: J. B. Lippincott, 1908).

148. AWD to CESW, 6 Nov. 1886, WD Box 128 (25), HEH-CESW.

149. AWD to CESW, 2 Dec. 1886, WD Box 128 (27), HEH-CESW.

150. "The Art Collection of Vassar College," *SM* 11 (Feb. 1876): 594.

151. *Catalogue of Publications Issued by L. Prang & Co.* (Boston: Alfred Mudge and Son, 1872), 5, quoted in Clapper, "Popularizing Art in Boston," 71.

152. Ibid., 36–38.

153. See Korzenik, *Drawn to Art*.

154. Robert Hoe, *A Short History of the Printing Press and of the Improvements in Printing Machinery from the Time of Gutenberg up to the Present Day* (New York: R. Hoe, 1902); Phillips, "Art for Industry's Sake."

155. These are only a few examples. Short biographies of these artists can be found in Annette Blaugrund, ed., *Paris 1889: American Artists at the Universal Exposition* (Philadelphia and New York: Pennsylvania Academy of the Fine Arts and Harry N. Abrams, 1989), 122–23, 130–31; 154; 173–74; 176.

156. Frederick C. Moffatt, "The Education of the New England Artist: The Early Years of Arthur Wesley Dow," *Essex Institute Historical Collections* 112, no. 4 (1976): 275–89.

157. Barry Shifman, *The Arts and Crafts Metalwork of Janet Payne Bowles* (Indianapolis: Indianapolis Museum of Art in cooperation with Indiana University Press, 1993), 16.

158. See Thomas Hovenden, *The Wreck*, published in Celia Thaxter, *Verses: With Twenty-Five Full-Page Illustrations by Famous Artists* (Boston: D. Lothrop Company, [1891]), n.p.; *Pretty Peggy and Other Ballads, Illustrated by Rosina Emmet* (New York: Dodd, Mead & Company, 1880).

159. *Woman's Handiwork in Modern Homes, by Constance Cary Harrison; with Numerous Illustrations and Five Colored Plates from Designs by Samuel Colman, Rosina Emmet, George Gibson, and Others* (New York: Charles Scribner's Sons, 1881).

160. See Walter Thornbury, *Historical and Legendary Ballads and Songs* (Boston: W. F. Gill & Co., 1876), 129, 157, 175; T. Buchanan Read, *The Wagoner of the Alleghanies* (Philadelphia: J. B. Lippincott Company, 1885), frontispiece, 66.

161. Joni Louise Kinsey, *Thomas Moran and the Surveying of the American West* (Washington, D.C., and London: Smithsonian Institution Press), 1992.

162. "Moran's 'Mountain of the Holy Cross,'" *SM* 10 (June 1875): 252–53; Ferdinand V. Hayden and Thomas Moran, *The Yellowstone National Park* (Boston: L. Prang & Co., 1876).

163. T. J. Jackson Lears, *No Place of Grace: Antimodernism and the Transformation of American Culture, 1880–1920* (New York: Pantheon Books, 1981), 66–82.

164. "Hang the Anarchists?" *AAP* 1, no. 1 (Jan.–Feb. 1887): 7; "Who Should Hang?" *AAP* 1, no. 6 (Nov.–Dec. 1887): 2–3; "Can Afford Just Prices," *AAP* 1, no. 2 (Mar.–Apr. 1887): 2. The quote is from "Organization," *AAP* 1, no. 3 (May–June 1887): 2.

165. "Dissecting a Job," *AAP* 1, no. 2 (Mar.–Apr. 1887): 6–7; "Art Supplement to *The American Art Printer*," *AAP* 1, no. 4 (July–Aug. 1887): n.p.; "Technical Training," *AAP* 1, no. 1 (Jan.–Feb. 1887): 3.

166. "Organization," *AAP* 1, no. 3 (May–June 1887): 2.

167. Clapper, "Popularizing Art in Boston," 64; L. Prang & Co., "Weekly Letter" [#4], 1 Nov. 1888, AAS-LP, folder 1.

168. Peters, *America on Stone*, 327–28 and pl. 71; Winslow Homer to Florence Fuller, 9 Dec. 1900, AAA-WHL, Reel 3483; Winslow Homer (WH) to Louis Prang (LP), n.d. [marked "Nov. 28.65 around"], AAA-WHL, Reel D24; WH to LP, 30 Dec. 1893, AAA-WHL, Reel D24; WH to LP, 6 Nov. 1895, AAA-WHL, Reel D24; WH to LP, 22 Nov. 1895, AAA-WHL, Reel D24; WH to LP, 14 Mar. 1896, AAA-WHL, Reel D24; WH to LP, 22 Oct. 1905, AAA-WHL, Reel D24; Homer's quote on the market is from WH to LP, 18 Oct. 1905, AAA-WHL, Reel D24.

169. SAA *Fourth Annual Exhibition*, 8, 9.

170. [SRK], *Museum of Fine Arts. Print Department. Exhibition of the Work of Women Etchers of America, Nov. 1 to*

Dec. 31, 1887 (Boston: Museum of Fine Arts, 1887), 5; "Chronology of John Henry Twachtman with Emphasis on Etching," Mary Baskett Gallery, http://www.marybaskett.com/mbg_artists/twachtman_3ex.html, May 12, 2003. On the Ten, see William H. Gerdts et al., *Ten American Painters* (New York: Spanierman Gallery, 1990); Ulrich W. Hiesinger, *Impressionism in America: The Ten American Painters* (Munich: Prestel, 1991).

171. Childe Hassam to CESW, 21 Oct. 1919, WD Box 149 (12), HEH-CESW; CESW note, WD Box 166 (42), HEH-CESW.
172. Macbeth Gallery, *Fiftieth Anniversary Exhibition, 1892–1942*.
173. Robert William Macbeth to CESW, 29 Mar. 1919, WD Box 166 (42), HEH-CESW; Macbeth to CESW, 2 Feb. 1895, WD Box 166 (40), HEH-CESW; CESW to Metropolitan Museum of Art, 18 June 1918, WD Box 235 (3), HEH-CESW; SAA *Fourth Annual Exhibition*, 8; SRK, *USAD*, 136.
174. Katherine Field (Ehrgott) Caldwell, note on verso of photograph of drawing of John Gellatly by Abbott Thayer, 25 June 1975, WD Box 296 (9), HEH-CESW.
175. Charles Alfred Barry, *Primer of Design* (Boston: Lee and Shepard, 1878); John Leighton, *Suggestions in Design* (New York: D. Appleton and Co., 1881); L. B. Urbino and Henry Day, *Art Recreations: Being a Complete Guide to Pencil Drawing, Oil Painting... Moss Work... Papier Maché... Wax Work, Shell Work... Enamel Painting, etc., ... with Valuable Receipts for Preparing Materials* (Boston: S. W. Tilton, 1863).
176. Korzenik, *Drawn to Art*, 73 and passim.
177. "Counting the Cost," *Brush and Pencil* 8, no. 1 (1901): 4.
178. Isabel McDougall, "The Autumn Exhibition at the Chicago Art Institute," *AAm* 35, no. 5 (Oct. 1896): 109–10; L.M.R., "The St. Louis Exhibition," *AAm* 35, no. 5 (Oct. 1896): 110; Roger Riordan, "Tendencies in French Sculpture," *AAm* 35, no. 4 (Sept. 1896): 65–66; "How to Interest Children in Drawing: Surprising Results from the System Employed in the Chicago Public Schools," *AAm* 35, no. 5 (Oct. 1896): 112.
179. "Head of a Steer by James M. Hart from the Original Oil Painting," *AAm* 1 (1879): n.p. Hart's work was also reproduced by Prang in "Our Artists," *PC* 2, no. 9 (Christmas 1870): 6.
180. "The Art Amateur Working Designs," nos. 1693–96, *AAm* 35, no. 4 (Sept. 1896): supplement. See also "Working Designs on Supplements," *AAm* 1, no. 3 (Aug. 1879): supplement pl. III; "The Art Amateur Working Designs," *AAm* 35, no. 6 (Nov. 1896): supplement.
181. "Art Instruction Books," *AAm* 1, no. 4 (Sept. 1879): iii.
182. "Plaster Casts for Students," *AAm* 35, no. 4 (Sept. 1896): 67; "Practical Hints for Beginners," *AAm* 35, no. 5 (Oct. 1896): 94.
183. On Proust, who was a key organizer of the 1889 Paris Universal Exposition, see Annette Blaugrund, "Behind the Scenes: The Organization of American Paintings," in Blaugrund, *Paris 1889*, 13–39. Roger Riordan, "Tendencies in French Scuplture," *AAm* 35, no. 4 (Sept. 1896): 66.
184. "Noted American China Painters XXVI: Mrs. S. S. Frackleton," *AAm* 35, no. 5 (Oct. 1896): 123.
185. [SRK], *Women Etchers of America*, 5; Phyllis Peet, *American Women of the Etching Revival* (Atlanta: High Museum of Art, 1988), 147.
186. Joseph Breck, *A Memorial Exhibition of Porcelain and Stoneware by Adelaide Alsop Robineau, 1865–1929* (New York: The Metropolitan Museum of Art, 1929).
187. Advertisement for Rookwood Pottery, from M. Louise McLaughlin, *China Painting* (Cincinnati: Robert Clarke & Co., 1890).
188. Advertisements for "New White China," "The Wilke Kiln," and "China Decoration" in *AAm* 35, no. 4 (Sept. 1896): n.p.
189. Frackelton, *Tried by Fire*, n.p.; *KS* 1, no. 5 (Sept. 1899): inside back cover.
190. "The Revelation China Kiln," *KS* 1, no. 6 (Oct. 1899): 3; "Fitch Kilns," *KS* 1, no. 6 (Oct. 1899): vi; McLaughlin, *China Painting*, 11.
191. Kathleen D. McCarthy, *Women's Culture: American Philanthropy and Art, 1830–1930* (Chicago: University of Chicago Press, 1991), 37–56.
192. This can be accessed at http://www.siris.si.edu. An example of a work that detrimentally excludes media other than painting and sculpture—except for the works of Whistler—is Annette Blaugrund's otherwise excellent *Paris 1889*. While this book provides a wealth of information about the "fine arts" contributions to this event, and the expatriate careers of participants, its exclusion of artists in other media is troubling because many of these excluded figures won prizes and had important and complex links to the rest of the art world.
193. The only exhibitions to earn more in 1881 than the NYSDA did in 1880 were the National Academy's annual show ($42,838) and the Interstate Industrial Exhibition ($30,075) (SRK, *USAD*, 136).
194. Amelia Peck and Carol Irish, *Candace Wheeler: The Art and Enterprise of American Design, 1875–1900* (New Haven, Conn., and London: Yale University Press, 2001).

Chapter 3
Professionalism and a New Aesthetic Order

1. Thomas Bender, "The Erosion of Public Culture: Cities, Discourses, and Professional Disciplines," in Thomas Haskell, ed., *The Authority of Experts: Studies in History and Theory* (Bloomington: Indiana University Press, 1984), 98. See also George Frederickson, *The Inner Civil War: Northern Intellectuals and the Crisis of the Union* (New York: Harper and Row, 1965); Peter Dobkin Hall, *The Organization of American Culture, 1700–1900: Private Institutions, Elites, and the Origins of American Nationality* (New York: New York University Press, 1982); Thomas Haskell, *The Emergence of Professional Social Science: The American Social Science Association and the Nineteenth-Century Crisis of Authority* (Urbana: University of Illinois Press, 1977); Robert Wiebe, *The Search for Order, 1877–1920* (New York: Hill and Wang, 1967).
2. Jeffrey Lionel Berlant, *Profession and Monopoly: A Study of Medicine in the United States and Great Britain* (Berkeley and Los Angeles: University of California Press, 1975); Burton Bledstein, *The Culture of Professionalism* (New York: W. W. Norton, 1976); Peter Dobkin Hall, "The Social Foundations of Professional Credibility: Linking the Medical Profession to Higher Education in Connecticut and Massachusetts, 1700–1830," in Haskell, *Authority of Experts*, 107–41; Magali Sarfatti Larson, *The Rise of Professionalism* (Berkeley and Los Angeles: University of California Press, 1977).
3. On the "production of producers," see Larson, *Rise of Professionalism*.
4. Paul Starr, *The Social Transformation of American Medicine* (New York: Basic Books, 1982).
5. JoAnne Brown, *The Definition of a Profession: The Authority of Metaphor in the History of Intelligence Testing, 1890–1930* (Princeton, N.J.: Princeton University Press, 1992), 33. See also Andrew D. Abbot, *The System of Professions: An Essay on the Expert Division of Labor* (Chicago: University of Chicago Press, 1988).
6. Christopher P. Wilson, "The Rhetoric of Consumption: Mass-Market Magazines and the Demise of the Gentle Reader, 1880–1920," in *The Culture of Consumption: Critical Essays in American History, 1880–1980*, ed. Richard Wightman

Fox and T. J. Jackson Lears (New York: Pantheon Books, 1983), 39–64.

7. Correspondingly, journalists increasingly came from the ranks of the college-educated. See Michael Schudson, *Discovering the News: A Social History of American Newspapers* (New York: Basic Books, 1978).

8. Arlene Rita Olson, *Art Critics and the Avant-Garde: New York, 1900–1913* (Ann Arbor, Mich.: UMI, 1980); Jane Calhoun Weaver, ed., *Sadakichi Hartmann, Critical Modernist: Collected Art Writings* (Berkeley and Los Angeles: University of California Press, 1991); Sandra Lee Underwood, *Charles Caffin: A Voice for Modernism, 1897–1918* (Ann Arbor, Mich: UMI, 1983); Arnold T. Schwab, *James Gibbons Huneker: Critic of the Seven Arts* (Stanford, Calif.: Stanford University Press, 1963); Peter Plagens, "The Critics: Hartmann, Huneker, de Casseres," *Art in America* 61 (July–Aug. 1973): 66–71; Ann Uhry Abrams, "Catalyst for Change: American Art and Revolution, 1906–1915" (Ph.D. diss., Emory University, 1975).

9. *The Autobiography of John C. Van Dyke* (Salt Lake City: University of Utah Press, 1993), 180–81.

10. On Cook, see John Peter Simoni, "Art Critics and Criticism in Nineteenth-Century America" (Ph.D. diss., Ohio State University, 1952); Barbara Stephanic, "Clarence Cook's Role as Art Critic, Advocate for Professionalism, Educator, and Arbiter of Taste in America" (Ph.D. diss., University of Maryland, 1997); Joann W. Weiss, "Clarence Cook: His Critical Writings" (Ph.D. diss., Johns Hopkins University, 1976); "Clarence Cook," in *In Pursuit of Beauty: Americans and the Aesthetic Movement*, ed. Doreen Bolger Burke (New York: The Metropolitan Museum of Art and Rizzoli, 1986), 412–14.

11. On Van Rensselaer, see Lois Dinnerstein, "Opulence and Ocular Delight, Splendor and Squalor: Critical Writings in Art and Architecture by Mariana Griswold Van Rensselaer" (Ph.D. diss., City University of New York, 1979); Cynthia D. Kinnard, "The Life and Works of Mariana Griswold Van Rensselaer, American Art Critic" (Ph.D. diss., Johns Hopkins University, 1977) and "Mariana Griswold Van Rensselaer (1851–1934): America's First Professional Woman Art Critic," in *Women as Interpreters of the Visual Arts, 1820–1979*, ed. Claire Richter Sherman with Adele Holcomb (Westport, Conn.: Greenwood Press, 1981), 181–205.

12. MGVR, "Introduction," *Catalogue of the Work of the Women Etchers of America* (New York: Union League Club, 1888).

13. Clarence Cook, *The House Beautiful: Essays on Beds and Tables, Stools and Candlesticks* (New York: Scribner, Armstrong and Co., 1878).

14. Stephanic, "Clarence Cook's Role," 78.

15. In addition to Koehler's publications, there are thirteen rolls of microfilm in the Archives of American Art in the S. R. Koehler Papers (reels D30, D182–D191, 3533–3534). As far as I have been able to determine, this has resulted in exactly two publications on Koehler in the twentieth century: Phyllis Peet, *American Women of the Etching Revival* (Atlanta: High Museum of Art, 1988); Helena E. Wright, "The Smithsonian in Cincinnati: Exhibiting Prints at the Ohio Valley Centennial Exposition, 1888," in *Art as Image: Prints and Promotion in Cincinnati, Ohio*, ed. Alice M. Cornell (Athens: Ohio University Press in association with the University of Cincinnati Digital Press, 2001), 131–65.

16. SRK, *USAD*, 95–123, 129; SRK, "American Art Chronicle—Art Education," *AAR* 1, div. 2 (1880): 43–44.

17. [CCC], "Fine-Arts," *NYDT*, 20 Nov. 1866, 6.

18. [CCC], "Opening of the Thirty-ninth Exhibition of the Academy of Design," *NYDT*, 15 Apr. 1864, 5.

19. [CCC], "Art," *AM* 34 (July 1874): 122.

20. The lack of hard-headed professional judgment Cook perceived at an 1865 exhibition of the Artists' Fund Society, for example, led him to cry, "What hope is there for any genuine improvement in our Art when such work as this is not only bought by prominent men, but given the place of honor by the artists themselves?" ("The Artists' Fund Society," *NYDT*, 27 Dec. 1865, 5).

21. Cook, *House Beautiful*, 112–13.

22. Clarence Cook, *"What Shall We Do with Our Walls?"* (New York: Warren, Fuller & Co., 1880).

23. Ibid., 2.

24. Ibid., 32.

25. Ibid., 33.

26. [CCC], "Art," *AM* 35 (Feb. 1875): 250.

27. SRK, "American Art Chronicle—Art Education," *AAR* 1, div. 2 (1880): 133.

28. [CCC], "Art," *AM* 35 (Feb. 1875): 250.

29. [CCC], "Fine Arts," *NYDT*, 13 May 1865, 9. Cook was also not afraid to use monetary metaphors to describe art's value; he was fond of goading artists, for example, to "give us the worth of our money" at exhibitions ("Fine Arts," *NYDT*, 24 Oct. 1866, 6).

30. [CCC], "National Academy of Design: Fortieth Annual Exhibition (Fifth Article)," *NYDT*, 23 June 1865, 6.

31. See, for example, "Fine Arts: Mr. Rothermel's 'Republican Court in the Time of Lincoln,'" *NYDT*, 12 Mar. 1867, 2. Interestingly, Cook did not generally apply this critique to dealers, whom he praised in particular for bringing European art to the New World. Perhaps he saw dealers' self-interest, unlike that of artists, as a necessary and proper part of their professional activity ("The Reception at the Academy of Design," *NYDT*, 1 8 Jan. 1866, 5; "Fine Arts: The Fourth Exhibition of French and Flemish Pictures," *NYDT*, 22 Feb. 1866, 4).

32. [CCC], "Opening of the Thirty-ninth Exhibition of the Academy of Design," *NYDT*, 15 Apr. 1864, 5; CCC, "Table Talk," *Putnam's Magazine*, n.s., 3 (Apr. 1869): 511–15.

33. [CCC], "Opening of the Exhibition of the Philadelphia Sketch Club," *NYDT*, 19 Jan. 1866, 8.

34. [CCC], "National Academy of Design: Fortieth Annual Exhibition (First Article)," *NYDT*, 13 May 1865, 9.

35. [CCC], "Art," *AM* 34 (Oct. 1874): 508; see also "Art," *AM* 33 (June 1874): 753–57.

36. MGVR, "Client and Architect," *North American Review* 151 (Sept. 1890): 320.

37. Ibid.

38. MGVR, "The Restorations at Goslar," *AABN* 3 (6 Apr. 1878): 120–21.

39. CCC to "Dear Will," 22 Mar. 1886, HEH *HM* 29481.

40. [CCC], "Art," *AM* 34 (July 1874): 123.

41. [CCC], "Art," *AM* 34 (Oct. 1874): 506; see also "National Academy of Design: Fortieth Annual Exhibition (Fourth Article)," *NYDT*, 9 June 1865, 6.

42. Sea Urchin [CCC], "From Boston," *NYDT*, 25 Nov. 1865, 10; [CCC], "Art," *AM* 35 (Feb. 1875): 250.

43. MGVR, "Spring Exhibitions and Picture-Sales in New York—II," *AABN* 7 (8 May 1880): 202; MGVR, "Antique Sculpture in Berlin," *AABN* 7 (13 Mar. 1880): 106. Among the few "connoisseurs" MGVR included in this company was dealer Samuel Putnam Avery, whose efforts to bring art to American consumers she valued highly.

44. MGVR, "The 'Loan Exhibition' in Aid of the Society of Decorative Art," *AABN* 3 (26 Jan. 1878): 35.

45. MGVR, "Spring Exhibitions," 190.

46. Ibid.

47. This idea is most thoroughly examined in Stephen Kern, *Culture of Time and Space, 1880–1918* (Cambridge, Mass.: Harvard University Press, 1983); see also William Everdell, *The First Moderns: Profiles in the Origins of Twentieth-Century Thought* (Chicago: University of Chicago Press, 1997).

48. S. G. W. Benjamin, "The Exhibitions. IV.—Society of American Artists. Third Exhibition," *AAR* 1, div. 1 (1880): 259.

49. Ibid., 258.

50. Ibid., 259.

51. MGVR, "Artist and Amateur," *AAR* 1, div. 2 (1880): 383.

52. Ibid., 382.
53. Ibid., 383.
54. Ibid.
55. Clement Greenberg, "Avant-Garde and Kitsch," in John O'Brian, ed., *Clement Greenberg: The Collected Essays and Criticism*, vol. 1 (Chicago: University of Chicago Press, 1986), 8.
56. Ibid.
57. Ibid.
58. Serge Guilbaut, *How New York Stole the Idea of Modern Art: Abstract Expressionism, Freedom, and the Cold War*, trans. Arthur Goldhammer (Chicago: University of Chicago Press, 1983).
59. Greenberg, "Avant-Garde," 8. Scholars have, of course, doubted this characterization. Most notably, Rosalind Krauss has spelled out the disparities between avant-garde and modernist claims to originality and actual practice in *The Originality of the Avant-Garde and Other Modernist Myths* (Cambridge, Mass.: MIT Press, 1985), esp. 151–70; see also Gregory Currie, *An Ontology of Art* (Basingstoke, United Kingdom: Macmillan in association with the Scots Philosophical Club, 1989).
60. Williams is quoted in Miles Orvell, *The Real Thing: Imitation and Authenticity in American Culture* (Chapel Hill: University of North Carolina Press, 1989), 240.
61. Greenberg, "Avant-Garde," 8–9.
62. Cook argued that an attempt "to show the relations of art with theology," for example, "will be regarded by most readers as a blemish on the work" ([CCC], "Samson's Art Criticism," *NYDT*, 14 Feb. 1867, 6). There was one brief period during Cook's career when he did appeal for art's morally and socially uplifting character, though, during his brief stint at *Putnam's Magazine* in the 1860s and during his earliest years at the *NYDT*. It is interesting to note that Cook's responsibility at *Putnam's* was not to write about art per se (that job belonged to S. S. Conant), but to comment upon larger political, social, and cultural issues in the "Table Talk" column. Overall, Cook's art writings in the *NYDT* from the same period are less moralistic in tone, and are more likely to combine moral concerns with an attention to the characteristics of artworks as objects; in urging that a permanent New York home be found for James Jackson Jarves's collection of early Italian paintings, he argued both that the "pictures are the fruit of earnestness, of sincere religious feeling, of deep intuitions," and that they must be given "solid respect for the way in which they are painted," especially since American "pictures not yet thirty years old are faded, cracked and tarnished, while these, dating from the Thirteenth Century, are nearly as perfect to-day as when they were first painted" ("The Jarves Collection of Pictures by Early Italian Masters," *NYDT*, 27 Dec. 1864, 6). For examples of Cook's early reformist writings, see CCC, "Table Talk," *Putnam's Monthly*, n.s., 3 (Feb. 1869): 254–59; "Table Talk," *Putnam's Monthly*, n.s., 3 (Mar. 1869): 380–83; [CCC], "The Exhibition of Pictures at the Metropolitan Fair," *NYDT*, 9 Apr. 1864, 12.
63. [CCC], "National Academy of Design: The Thirty-ninth Exhibition, Fifth Article," *NYDT*, 14 May 1864, 3.
64. CCC, "Fine Arts—Chromo-Lithography," *NYDT*, 8 Aug. 1868, 2. It must be noted that Cook initially responded favorably to chromolithography, hoping that it would "educate the taste of the masses, by placing within their reach facsimiles of the finest works of the great masters in painting. This response, however, was short-lived ("Chromo-Lithography," *NYDT*, 25 May 1866, 2).
65. "The Fine Arts: The Jarves Collection of Early Italian Pictures," *NYDT*, 12 Feb. 1868, 2. Cook's architectural writings are marked by a similar sensibility; he condemned, for instance, the new Boston City Hall as "a slavish copy" of the Tuileries, and savaged Hunt's designs for the gates to Central Park, writing that "these Gates are copies, tame and spiritless, indeed, but still copies, in every part and detail, of modern French work—nothing springs out of the needs of the place, nor is dictated by conditions that exist and ought to be respected" ([CCC], "The Fine Arts," *NYDT*, 21 Oct. 1865, 9; "Mr. Hunt's Designs for the Gates of the Central Park," *NYDT*, 2 Aug. 1865, 8).
66. Cook urged, for example, that plaster casts be made and distributed of busts of Civil War heroes, not for their artistic value, "but as lofty home-examples of high intellectual and moral powers used in the service of Duty" ("Fine Arts," *NYDT*, 19 Aug. 1865, 6).
67. By the same token, Cook chastised publishers who altered photographic reproductions of paintings, writing of a book of photographs of works by Van Eyck that "we wish . . . the publishers had been willing to give the photographs to the public, without 'touching them up' with India ink. It seriously detracts from their value as record, without adding anything to their agreeableness as mere pictures which can atone for the unpleasantness of feeling that the master's work has been meddled with" ("The Fine Arts," *NYDT*, 30 Sept. 1864, 6).
68. [CCC], "Mr. Prang's Defense," *NYDT*, 7 Dec. 1866, 6; see also "Fine-Arts," *NYDT*, 20 Nov. 1866, 6. Cook's concern that artists choose appropriate media to accomplish particular artistic and formal tasks can also be seen in Sea Urchin [CCC], "From Boston," *NYDT*, 25 Nov. 1865, 10.
69. Walter Benjamin, "The Work of Art in the Age of Mechanical Reproduction," in his *Illuminations*, ed. Hannah Arendt, trans. Harry Zohn (New York: Schocken Books, 1969), 221.
70. "Mr. Prang's Defense," 6.
71. [E. L. Godkin], "Chromo-Civilization," *Nation* 482 (24 Sept. 1874): 202.
72. See, for example, Orvell, *The Real Thing*, 37–38; Alan Trachtenberg, *The Incorporation of America: Culture and Society in the Gilded Age* (New York: Hill and Wang, 1982).
73. Charles Sumner, *The Best Portraits in Engraving* (New York: Frederick Keppel, 1875), 26.
74. Charles Sumner, mss. and corrected proof for *The Best Portraits in Engraving*, Charles Sumner Papers, Box 10, Folder 10, AAS.
75. "A Selective Art Museum," 423.
76. "Fine Arts—Mr. Prang's Recent Chromos," *NYDT*, 21 July 1868, 2.
77. CCC, "Leonardo Da Vinci," *SM* 17 (Jan. 1879): 351–52.
78. [CCC], "National Academy of Design: The Thirty-ninth Exhibition, Third Article," *NYDT*, 7 May 1864; "Table Talk," *Putnam's Magazine*, n.s., 3 (Apr. 1869): 513; "Mr. Walters's Collection of Pictures," *NYDT*, 13 Feb. 1864, 12; [CCC], "Exhibition of Pictures at the Sanitary Fair," *NYDT*, 16 Apr. 1864, 12; [CCC], "Art," *AM* 34 (July 1874): 122.
79. "Brady's Photographs of the War," *NYDT*, 24 Feb. 1866, 7; "The Brady Collection of Photographs," *NYDT*, 22 Mar. 1867, 8; "The Fine Arts: Mr. Leutze's Portrait of President Lincoln," *NYDT*, 13 June 1865, 7.
80. Thus he wrote of Rosenberg's *New York Bay* that "the color is not harmonious and the painting is crude, yet the picture is valuable as a transcript of the scene, and we should think would become popular if it could be engraved or chromolithographed" ("Opening of the Exhibition of the Philadelphia Sketch-Club," *NYDT*, 19 Jan. 1866, 8).
81. "Mr. F. B. Carpenter's Picture—'The Emancipation Proclamation before the Cabinet,'" *NYDT*, 2 June 1866, 4.
82. "Art," *AM* 34 (Sept. 1874): 376. See also "Art," *AM* 30 (Aug. 1872): 246–48.
83. [CCC], "National Academy of Design: Fortieth Annual Exhibition (Third Article)," *NYDT*, 31 May 1865, 3; [CCC], "The Fine Arts," *NYDT*, 26 June 1865, 9. Cook's preference for the simplicity of form over detail is also evident in his architectural writings, such as in his

plea that New York "put plain shafts of stone at the terminations of the wall, let these shafts be large, handsome, dignified and with whatever ornaments will most add to their dignity without detracting from their simplicity," instead of building Hunt's highly decorated Central Park gates ("Mr. Hunt's Designs," 8).

84. "Fine Arts," *NYDT*, 28 July 1866, 6.
85. [CCC], "Art," *AM* 34 (Sept. 1874): 376.
86. Dow, "Painting with Wooden Blocks," 86–90.
87. MGVR, *American Etchers*, 8.
88. Ibid., 9, emphasis in original.
89. Ibid., 9, 14.
90. Ibid., 26.
91. Ibid., 9.
92. Ibid., 26.
93. *Transformations and Migrations of Certain Statues in the Cesnola Collection* (New York: Gaston L. Feuardent, [1881?]).
94. The most complete study of Cesnola's life and exploits is Elizabeth McFadden, *The Glitter and the Gold* (New York: The Dial Press, 1971).
95. Hiram Hitchcock, "The Explorations of Di Cesnola in Cyprus," *HM* 45 (July 1872): 188–208; William Prime, "The Golden Treasures of Kurium," *HM* 55 (Aug. 1877): 333–44 and "Some Notes about Pottery and Porcelain," *HM* 48 (Feb. 1874): 320–37; Bayard Taylor, "Ephesus, Cyprus, and Mycenae," *NAR* 126 (Jan.–Feb. 1878): 111–31; "Editor's Scientific Record," *HM* 46 (May 1873): 935; "Editor's Literary Record–Schliemann's Ancient Mycenae," *HM* 56 (Mar. 1878): 626–27; "New English Books," *SM* 15 (Feb. 1878): 601–3; "Recent Literature–Schliemann's Mycenae," *AM* 42 (Oct. 1878): 511–12; "Cesnola's 'Cyprus,'" *SM* 16 (May 1878): 151–52; "Local Miscellany–The Metropolitan Museum," *NYDT*, 14 Jan. 1873, 8; "The Cesnola Collection," *NYDT*, 20 Jan. 1873, 4; "Treasures from Cyprus," *NYDT*, 8 May 1877, 8; "Editor's Literary Record–Di Cesnola's Cyprus," *HM* 56 (Mar. 1877): 626.
96. McFadden, *Glitter*, 211.
97. Ibid., 234.
98. [CCC], "Fine Arts," *NYDT*, 27 Mar. 1874, 5. See also "Fine Arts–The Di Cesnola Collection," *NYDT*, 23 May 1873, 4–5; "Art," *AM* 33 (Apr. 1874): 502–9; "Art," *AM* 33 (June 1874): 756–57.
99. McFadden, *Glitter*, 151.
100. Ibid., 197.
101. "I regret now, that I ever wrote a line in favor of the collection, and so far as I have been able, which has only been in one case, I have endeavored to unsay my saying and cancel what I wrote. Mr. A. J. Johnson has allowed me to expunge from all the articles I wrote for his valuable Cyclopaedia everything that could be construed into a belief in the authenticity of this collection or in the integrity of the objects contained in it, and in the new edition of the Cyclopaedia, the ridiculous myth of Mr. di Cesnola's exploits in our war has been entirely omitted. . . . In my edition of Lubke's *History of Art*, published by Dodd & Mead, the appendix relating to the Cypriote collection was added at the last minute at the pressing demand of the publisher. I cannot, having no copy-right in the book, remove that chapter as I would gladly do. But I counsel every reader of that work to remember that no statement contained in that supplementary chapter is to be relied upon" (CCC, *Transformations*, 13–14).
102. Ibid., 37.
103. CCC, *Transformations*, 11; McFadden, *Glitter*, 191.
104. CCC, *Transformations*, 11.
105. Ibid., 19.
106. McFadden, *Glitter*, 239.
107. Calvin Tomkins, *Merchants and Masterpieces: The Story of the Metropolitan Museum of Art* (New York: H. Holt, 1989), 65.
108. On Barnum and his culture, see Neil Harris, *Humbug: The Art of P. T. Barnum* (Chicago: University of Chicago Press, 1973).
109. Indeed, a sign of just how differently these issues are understood today is the MFA's refusal to grant permission to reproduce the plate from their copy of Cook's *Transformations* (fig. 60) in this book, on the grounds that Cook's image was "copy work" and that only the owner of the "original" art work–in other words, Statue No. 39 itself–could grant such permission without risk of being sued for copyright infringement. Restrictions on the deformation of copyrighted artworks are described in *American Association of Museums, A Museum Guide to Copyright and Trademark* (Washington, D.C.: American Association of Museums, 1999).

Chapter 4
The Armory Show in Critical Perspective

1. For general information on the show, see Milton Brown, *The Story of the Armory Show* (Greenwich, Conn: New York Graphic Society, 1963); Martin Green, *New York 1913: The Armory Show and the Paterson Strike Pageant* (New York: Scribner's, 1988); *1913 Armory Show 50th Anniversary Exhibition* (New York and Utica: Henry Street Settlement and Munson-Williams-Proctor Institute, 1963); *The 1913 Armory Show in Retrospect* (Amherst, Mass.: Amherst College, 1958); and Walt Kuhn's privately printed pamphlet, *The Story of the Armory Show* (New York, 1938).
2. See, for instance, Bernard Bailyn et al., *The Great Republic: A History of the American People* (Lexington, Mass.: D.C. Heath and Co., 1977), 1027–31; or Glen MacLeod's claim that "from that date we can trace the development of modernism in all the arts in America, and more particularly the rapid growth of the New York avant-garde" (*Wallace Stevens and Modern Art: From the Armory Show to Abstract Expressionism* [New Haven, Conn., and London: Yale University Press, 1993], 3).
3. Meyer Schapiro, "Rebellion in Art," in Daniel Aaron, ed., *America in Crisis: Fourteen Crucial Episodes in American History* (New York: Alfred A. Knopf, 1952), 203–42. The Armory Show also determined the chronology of many histories of American art, even those that did not focus on the show itself. See Milton Brown, *American Painting from the Armory Show to the Depression* (Princeton, N.J.: Princeton University Press, 1955); Lloyd Goodrich, *Pioneers of Modern Art in America: The Decade of the Armory Show, 1910–1920* (New York: Praeger/Whitney Museum of American Art, 1963); Bennard Perlman, *The Immortal Eight: American Painting from Eakins to the Armory Show, 1870–1913* (New York: Exposition Press, 1962).
4. See, for example, Robert M. Crunden, *American Salons: Encounters with European Modernism, 1885–1917* (New York: Oxford University Press, 1993); Charles C. Eldredge, "The Arrival of European Modernism," *Art in America* 61 (July–Aug. 1973): 34–41; Judith Zilczer, "The Armory Show and the American Avant-Garde: A Reevaluation," *Arts* 53 (Sept. 1978): 126–30.
5. Zilczer, for instance, argues that "the simultaneous impact on American culture of two such different events as the First World War and the Armory Show undermined the lingering genteel tradition of the late nineteenth century. That tradition could not sustain the byproducts of urban industrialization–global political commitments, immigrant migration, socialism, and feminism" (Zilczer, "The Armory Show," 126).
6. This is true not only of visual artists, but also of literary figures like the young Harvard student John Dos Passos. See Townsend Ludington, *John Dos Passos: A Twentieth-Century Odyssey* (New York: E. P. Dutton, 1980), 55–57.

7. This nostalgia for revolutionary modernism is not limited merely to representations of the Armory Show, but can be found throughout the literature on twentieth-century American art. Even as savvy a post-modernist as Thomas Crow yearned in the bleak 1980s for the "supporting community" of Clement Greenberg's avant-garde or even the "language of morality" within Michael Fried's 1960s criticism, with which "ethical issues could be re-endowed with political meaning" (Crow, "The Birth and Death of the Viewer: On the Public Function of Art," in *DIA Foundation Discussions in Contemporary Culture*, no. 1, ed. Hal Foster [Seattle: Bay Press, 1987], 1–9).
8. Green, *New York 1913*, 7.
9. As Mabel Dodge's letter to Stein suggests, this historical dichotomy derives directly from the interpretations given by participants even before the exhibition took place. What Dodge did not mention was that twenty-one Academy members would exhibit in the Armory Show and twenty-three other American exhibitors were later elected to its membership. The figures are from Lois Marie Fink, *Academy: The Academic Tradition in American Art* (Washington, D.C.: Smithsonian Institution Press, 1975), 235.
10. The relationships between Dodge and both radicals and artists/critics alike, for example, are well known. For a fine study of the complex relationships within the New York art world at the turn of the century, see Crunden, *American Salons*.
11. David Minter, *A Cultural History of the American Novel* (New York: Cambridge University Press, 1994), 50.
12. Not to mention "implacably hostile" and the "rear guard of the nineteenth century" (Rudi Blesh, *Modern Art USA: Men, Rebellion, and Conquest, 1900–1956* [New York: Alfred A. Knopf, 1956], 50–51).
13. Moira McLoughlin, "Negotiating the Critical Discourse: The Armory Show Revisited," in *On the Margins of Art Worlds*, ed. Larry Gross (Boulder, Colo.: Westview Press, 1995), 17–38; Sue Ann Prince, "'Of the Which and the Why of Daub and Smear': Chicago Critics Take on Modernism," in *The Old Guard and the Avant-Garde: Modernism in Chicago, 1910–1940*, ed. Sue Ann Prince (Chicago: University of Chicago Press, 1990), 95–117.
14. The contrast Prince draws between these knowing supporters of modernism and its opponents is instructive, in that it posits the ability to recognize and truthfully represent aesthetic "facts" as the main difference between modernism's defenders and its detractors. Prince constructs the show's detractors as "non-arts writers" motivated by "sensationalism" and "moral outrage" (as opposed to aesthetic concerns) who made "relatively frequent mistakes in names, designations, and historical facts." To this she contrasts Chicago's three early critical defenders of modernism, whom she constructs as "thoughtful, complex, and sophisticated." Lena May McCauley, for example, "discussed the lives of the post-impressionist painters objectively, in contrast to other writers whose accounts twisted the facts into exaggerated, sensationalist stories"; Harriet Monroe's writings demonstrate "her ability to think analytically and independently." In this account, the taste for "academic" aesthetics is motivated by social concerns—the desire for elites to retain power as arbiters of culture—but the taste for modernism is portrayed as free of extra-aesthetic value. This account serves to reproduce participants' own naturalizing accounts of the origins of modernist aesthetics in the guise of historical analysis. Prince, "Of the Which and the Why," 95–101 and passim.
15. Barbara Rose, for example, portrayed the show's detractors as either mouthpieces for the Academy (Cox) or imbeciles capable only of "the honest bewilderment of the man on the street" (Roosevelt); see her essay, "The Armory Show: Success by Scandal," in *Readings in American Art Since 1900: A Documentary Survey*, ed. Barbara Rose (New York and Washington, D.C.: Praeger, 1968), 72–87.
16. Prince, "Of the Which and the Why," 95–98 and passim; Schapiro, "Rebellion in Art," 236–37.
17. Prince, "Of the Which and the Why," 98.
18. Kenyon Cox, "The 'Modern' Spirit in Art: Some Reflections Inspired by the Recent International Exhibition," *Harper's Weekly* 57 (15 Mar. 1913): 10.
19. [Leila Mechlen], "Lawless Art," *Art and Progress* 4 (Apr. 1913): 940–41.
20. Minter, *A Cultural History*, 50.
21. Throughout his career, Mather vacillated between journalism and academia. At the time of the Armory Show, he was a professor at Princeton and a regular contributor to the *Nation*. On Mather, see H. Wayne Morgan, "Frank Jewett Mather, Jr.: The Critic as Humanist," in Morgan, *Keepers of Culture: The Art Thought of Kenyon Cox, Royal Cortissoz, and Frank Jewett Mather, Jr.* (Kent, Ohio: Kent State University Press, 1989), 103–49.
22. Frank Jewett Mather, Jr., "Old and New Art," *Nation* 96 (16 Mar. 1913): 240–41.
23. John W. Alexander, "Is Our Art Distinctively American?" *Century* 87, n.s., 65 (Apr. 1914): 827.
24. Theodore Roosevelt, "A Layman's Views of an Art Exhibition," *Outlook* 103 (29 Mar. 1913): 719.
25. "Lawlessness in Art: The Exploitation of Whimsicality as a Principle," *Century* 86 (May 1913): 150; Adeline Adams, "The Secret of Life," *Art and Progress* 4 (Apr. 1913): 932; "History of Modern Art at the International Exhibition Illustrated by Paintings and Sculpture," *New York Times*, 23 Feb. 1913, sec. 6, 15.
26. Edwin. H. Blashfield, "The Painting of To-Day," *Century* 87, n.s., 65 (Apr. 1914): 837–40.
27. Royal Cortissoz, "The Post-Impressionist Illusion," *Century* 85, n.s., 63 (Apr. 1913): 809. This commentary is not surprising given Cortissoz's background as a defender of Impressionism in America, and particularly of the Ten. See William H. Gerdts, "The Ten: A Critical Chronology," in *Ten American Painters* (New York: Spanierman Gallery, 1990), 11.
28. Mather, "Old and New Art," 240, 241.
29. Mather, "The Academy Exhibition," *Nation* 96 (27 Mar. 1913): 317; see also H. Wayne Morgan, *New Muses: Art in American Culture, 1865–1920* (Norman: University of Oklahoma Press, 1978), 131.
30. Editorial, "The Old and the New," *Outlook* 103 (1 Mar. 1913): 467.
31. Editor, "Bedlam in Art," *co* 54 (Apr. 1913): 316; Editor, "Art Madness Recaptured," *co* 54 (Apr. 1913): 316.
32. "The Greatest Exhibition of Insurgent Art Ever Held," *co* 54 (Mar. 1913): 230.
33. Ibid.
34. Ibid.
35. See also "Art Revolutionists on Exhibition in America," 442.
36. Alexander, "Is Our Art Distinctively American?" 827.
37. Ibid.
38. Ibid., 828.
39. Ibid., 827.
40. Critics self-consciously promoted the capacity of periodicals to effect art-world change. An article praising the artistic potential of billboards and other commercial work praised the Berlin club that published "*Das Plakat*, which is devoted entirely to graphic work," as "the most definite educative movement . . . which aims to place advertizing upon the plane of a true art" ("The New Art of Advertizing—Or the Redemption of the Billboard," *co* 54 [May 1913]: 407).
41. At this time the *Century*, for example, continued to present reproductions of works by Americans or in American collections, as well as originally

commissioned works on paper by American artists. See "The Century's American Artists Series," *Century* 86, n.s., 64 (1913): 44, 110, 264; "Timothy Cole's Wood Engravings of Masterpieces in American Galleries: Une Dame Espagnole by Fortuny," *Century* 86, n.s., 64 (May 1913): frontispiece; "The Grand Cañon of the Colorado: Six Lithographs drawn from nature in 1912 for the *Century* by Joseph Pennell," *Century* 86, n.s., 64 (June 1913): 202–7. See also Ernest Knaufft, "What the Morgan Art Collection Means," *American Review of Reviews* 47 (Mar. 1913): 321–26; "What an Academy Could Do," *co* 54 (Mar. 1913): 227; "Objections to the Academy," *co* 54 (Mar. 1913): 227; Editorial, "The Study of the History of Art," *Outlook* 103 (8 Feb. 1913): 291; Editorial, "How to Popularize Art," *Outlook* 104 (28 June 1913): 411.

42. Editorial, "A Tax on Beauty," *Outlook* 104 (5 July 1913): 491–92; Editorial, "A Tax on Beauty," *Outlook* 104 (2 Aug. 1913): 727–28; Editorial, "Free Art For the People," *Outlook* 105 (27 Sept. 1913): 161–63; Editorial, "Tariff and Art," *Outlook* 105 (4 Oct. 1913): 242; "The American 'Immortals,'" *co* 54 (Mar. 1913): 227.
43. "Art for Life's Sake," *co* 54 (Feb. 1913): 149; "The Greatest Exhibition," 230–32; "Artistic Aspects of the Skyscraper," *co* 54 (Apr. 1913): 321–23; "Matisse and Picabia Compared," *co* 54 (Apr. 1913): 316; "New Tendencies in Art," *American Review of Reviews* 48 (Aug. 1913): 245; "A Sculptress Who Has Caught the American Rhythm," *co* 55 (Aug. 1913): 124–25; "A Great Artistic Interpreter of the Frozen North," *co* 55 (Oct. 1913): 274–75; "Leon Bakst and the Renaissance of Color," *co* 55 (Nov. 1913): 350–51.
44. "History of Modern Art," sec. 6, 15.
45. Blashfield, "Painting of To-Day," 837.
46. Ibid., 837.
47. Ibid., emphasis in original.
48. A writer in *co*, who criticized Edmond De Goncourt's ceaseless promotion of Hokusai, echoed this sentiment. While the critic excused Goncourt's preference as a matter of taste, he condemned the French writer for having caused the European public's failure both to appreciate other Japanese artists and to understand their historical relevance to French art ("Toyokuni: The Japanese Father of French Post-Impressionism," *co* 55 [Dec. 1913]: 435).
49. Cox, "The 'Modern' Spirit in Art," 10.
50. Cortissoz, "Post-Impressionist Illusion," 806.
51. This inability to locate a comprehensible theory of modernism also plagued one of Cortissoz's more sensationalistic peers, who exclaimed that "the exploitation of a theory of discords, puzzles, uglinesses, and clinical details, is to art what anarchy is to society, and the practitioners need not so much a critic as an alienist" ("Lawlessness in Art," 150).
52. Of Émile Bernard's description of the new art as "the manifestation of the eternal idea," for instance, Cortissoz asked, "could anything be more . . . vague?" (Cortissoz, "Post-Impressionist Illusion," 806–7).
53. Ibid., 807.
54. Ibid., 810.
55. Ibid.
56. Ibid., 815.
57. Alexander, "Is Our Art Distinctively American?" 826.
58. Ibid.
59. Roosevelt, "Layman's Views," 718.
60. Ibid., 719. As in much of his correspondence to KBW, WHW signed his post cards from the Armory Show "John."
61. Again, in his or her elevation of the skeptical cop as the authentic voice of American taste, this critic echoed Gilded Age critics' insistence on the safety in a "multitude of counsellors" in deriving opinions about art. Although this comment can be read as a ploy to capitalize on readers' suspicions of European decadence, and it is far from likely that the critic actually spoke for the interests of policemen, the comment is insightful in showing that institution-building critics were at least interested in staking a claim to a wider audience than their opponents, whom they saw as representing the voices only of the French and art-world insiders ("An Opportunity to Study New Art Tendencies," *Outlook* 103 [1 Mar. 1913]: 466).
62. Indeed, critics sometimes suggested that artists had made critics their willing dupes. Cortissoz, for example, wrote that "George Eliot speaks in one of her novels of the credulity in a guard which permits an interloper to get past him on the flimsiest pretexts, and she adds, 'There are some men so stupid that if you say, "I am a buffalo," they will let you pass.' I have thought of this when I have gone hunting for the line and rhythm of Matisse, and have marveled at those critics who have, so to say, let them pass" (Cortissoz, "Post-Impressionist Illusion," 812).
63. Roosevelt, "Layman's Views," 719.
64. See also Adams, "Secret of Life," 926–27.
65. "An Opportunity to Study New Art Tendencies," 466.
66. A similar dynamic was at work in Cortissoz's assessment of the Futurist exhibition at the Bernheim-Jeune gallery. While he had admired Van Gogh's use of color to solve purely technical problems, Cortissoz balked at the Futurists' attempts to combine such problem solving with claims about external reality. He griped, "The Bernheim-Jeune gallery was thronged every day with people who came to see how the trick was done. What they saw was a series of canvases bearing intelligible titles, but otherwise resembling patchworks of color" (Cortissoz, "Post-Impressionist Illusion," 813).
67. The quote is from Eldredge, "Arrival of European Modernism," 35, but similar comments can be found in MacLeod, *Wallace Stevens*, 7; and Prince, "'Of the Which and the Why,'" 97–98.
68. I should note, however, that MacLeod does suggest that the work's title did provoke the lion's share of viewers' anger. Yet, while he mentions the frustrated expectations produced by the work's whimsical title, his brief explanation of why the title caused such consternation is not entirely fulfilling. According to MacLeod, this hostility derived not from thwarted expectations about the relationship between representation, the "real," and interpretation, but from viewers' mainly moral concerns about the place of the nude in painting. Thus, viewers objected not to the fact that they could not recognize a nude in the painting, but to Duchamp's placement of a nude in an inappropriate setting. Although he does not express the connection directly, MacLeod thus portrays the painting as a latter-day version of Manet's *Olympia*. In this case, however, it is not clear why Duchamp's painting created more havoc than Gauguin's depictions of unclothed women of color who had previously been little represented in Western painting, or than Matisse's frank *Blue Nude* (1907; Baltimore Museum of Art), a more direct descendant of Manet's controversial canvas that later caused a public outcry in Chicago.
69. Roosevelt, "Layman's Views," 719.
70. On "representational seeing," see Nicholas Wolterstorff, *Works and Worlds of Art* (New York: Oxford University Press, 1980), 295–96.
71. Adams, "Secret of Life," 931.
72. Ibid.
73. Ibid., 932.
74. Walter Pach, "The Point of View of the Moderns," *Century* 87, n.s., 65 (Apr. 1914): 861.
75. Walter Pach Papers, Archives of American Art, Finding Aid.
76. *One Hundred and Fifty Years of Lithography* (Cincinnati, Ohio: Cincinnati Art Museum, 1948), acknowledgments, n.p.
77. See also Frederick James Gregg, "A Remarkable Art Show," *Harper's Weekly* 57 (15 Feb. 1913): 13, 20.

78. Pach, "The Point of View of the Moderns," 852.
79. W. D. MacColl, "The International Exhibition," *Forum* 50 (July 1913): 32–33.
80. Willard Huntington Wright, "Impressionism to Synchromism," *Forum* 50 (Dec. 1913): 765.
81. Ernest L. Blumenschein, "The Painting of To-Morrow," *Century* 87, n.s., 65 (Apr. 1914): 845–50.
82. Ibid., 847.
83. Ibid., 848.
84. Ibid., 847.
85. MacColl, "The International Exhibition," 25.
86. Wright, "Impressionism to Synchromism," 770.
87. Ibid., 759.
88. Christian Brinton, "Evolution Not Revolution in Art," *International Studio* 49 (Apr. 1913): xxvii.

Chapter 5
Camera Work: Organizing the Avant-Garde

1. Mary Ann Calo, "African American Art and Critical Discourse between World Wars," *American Quarterly* 51, no. 3 (Sept. 1999): 586–87.
2. Bram Dijkstra, *The Hieroglyphics of a New Speech: Cubism, Stieglitz, and the Early Poetry of William Carlos Williams* (Princeton, N. J.: Princeton University Press, 1969); William Innes Homer, *Alfred Stieglitz and the American Avant-Garde* (Boston: New York Graphic Society, 1977); Judith Zilczer, "Alfred Stieglitz and John Quinn: Allies in the American Avant-Garde," *American Art Journal* 17 (summer 1985): 18–33.
3. Robert Haines succinctly describes this as "Stieglitz's success in making truth visible" in *The Inner Eye of Alfred Stieglitz* (Washington, D.C.: University Press of America, 1982), 5; Miles Orvell, *The Real Thing: Imitation and Authenticity in American Culture, 1880–1940* (Chapel Hill: University of North Carolina Press, 1989), 198–99; Robert Crunden, *Ministers of Reform: The Progressives' Achievement in American Civilization, 1889–1920* (New York: Basic Books, 1982), 133–62.
4. Alexandra Arrowsmith and Thomas West, eds., *Two Lives: A Conversation in Paintings and Photographs* (New York: HarperCollins in association with the Phillips Collection, Washington, D.C., 1992); Peter C. Bunnell, *Degrees of Guidance: Essays in Twentieth-Century American Photography* (New York: Cambridge University Press, 1993), 1–38; William Innes Homer, *Alfred Stieglitz and the Photo-Secession* (Boston: Little, Brown, 1983); Christian Peterson, *Alfred Stieglitz's "Camera Notes"* (New York: Minneapolis Institute of Arts in association with W.W. Norton, 1993); Peninah R. Y. Petruck, *American Art Criticism, 1910–1939* (New York: Garland, 1981); Steven Watson, *Strange Bedfellows: The First American Avant-Garde* (New York: Abbeville Press, 1991). There is some disagreement among scholars as to the exact trajectory of American artistic photography in the early decades of the twentieth century. While some authors see Stieglitz's prewar efforts in terms of an antiquated pictorialist style which drew derivatively on the conventions and vision of painting, and others argue that Stieglitz began to see the apprehension and depiction of stripped-down objects as the photographic route to spiritual understanding at a much earlier date, some authors take the position that there was not a sharp break between the painterly pictorialist style of the turn of the century and the hard-edged style which developed in the ensuing decades. *Camera Work* itself is a record of this lengthy transition from the atmospheric to the concrete. See Arrowsmith and West, *Two Lives*; Dijkstra, *Hieroglyphics*, 95–107; Jonathan Green, *Camera Work: A Critical Anthology* (Millerton, N.Y.: Aperture, 1973), "Introduction"; Orvell, *The Real Thing*, chaps. 3 and 6; Bunnell, *Degrees of Guidance*, 8–12.
5. The image of Stieglitz as photographic seer and father of modernism was one which he himself cultivated, and which his contemporaries were unafraid to promote. In a 1934 volume whose contributors included William Carlos Williams, Marsden Hartley, and Gertrude Stein, Harold Clurman wrote that the photographer's "capacity for love has made Stieglitz a seer. Because nothing is too unimportant for him to see, and because everything he sees finally becomes the object of an all-embracing and therefore single love, his very simple, always accessible photographs take on a 'mystic' quality, and Stieglitz is regarded as a 'visionary'! We are unused to such attention in modern times. Stieglitz is incessantly attentive. He is attentive to everything that immediately confronts him. Because he cares for everything, because he loves" (Clurman, in Waldo Frank et al., *America and Alfred Stieglitz: A Collective Portrait* [Garden City, N.Y.: Doubleday, Doran and Co., 1934], 268). See also Dorothy Norman's aptly titled *Alfred Stieglitz: Introduction to an American Seer* (New York: Duell, Sloan and Pearce, 1960).
6. For the most concise expression of the need to reevaluate cultural production in terms of the conditions of practice, as opposed to text- or object-based analysis, see Raymond Williams, *Problems in Materialism and Culture: Selected Essays* (London: Verso, 1980).
7. Much of the literature on Stieglitz is devoted to describing Stieglitz's "good works" within the art world, including his role in the Photo-Secession, *Camera Work*, and the Little Galleries. By and large, however, this literature concerns itself with these institutions only as inert vessels for the presentation of a deracinated aesthetic "message." Peninah Petruck, thus, describes Stieglitz's "passion for innovation and experimentation" as "that of a missionary," locating *Camera Work* and the Little Galleries as the prime outlets for his zeal. In describing the actual impact of these two institutions, however, Petruck merely describes them as venues in which Stieglitz elaborated his ideas or presented previously unknown European modernists to an American audience, without exploring the character of the institutions themselves (Petruck, *American Art Criticism*, 25). On the whole, scholarly descriptions of Stieglitz's projects rely heavily on his own depiction of them as "laboratories," or disinterested spaces for unfettered "experimentation"—terms that themselves drew on the cultural authority and supposed neutrality of science. Matthew Baigell, for instance, writes that "Stieglitz in his various galleries . . . offered something equivalent to Emerson's Concord—a place in which ideals could be considered reasonably free of trade and commerce" (Baigell, "American Landscape Painting and National Identity: The Stieglitz Circle and Emerson," *Art Criticism* 4, no. 1 [1987]: 27–47). To date, the relationship between modernist criticism as discourse and modernist criticism as institution has not been explored in a full and convincing manner.
8. The most thorough examination of this dynamic can be found in the work of Ulrich Keller, who argues that the success of "Art Photography" owed more to Stieglitz's promotional efforts than to the content of his work or the work of his associates. Although his argument is highly suggestive, Keller's central preoccupation with the epistemological ramifications of Stieglitz's institution-building activities renders it ultimately unsatisfying. To Keller, Stieglitz's organizational activities are problematic mainly in that they led to the creation of

"a prestige-oriented pseudo art world" whose components failed to live up to the standards set by "legitimate and functional support institutions" such as the Academy, and which promoted mediocre work as "genuinely innovative." The problem with this line of analysis is that it presumes that the evaluation of artworks can ever take place outside "the manufacture of . . . fame," and that by erasing the "promotional" effects of Stieglitz's organizational activities we can achieve an objective "re-evaluation of the movement" (Keller, "The Myth of Art Photography: A Sociological Analysis," *History of Photography* 4 [Oct.–Dec. 1984]: 249–75).

9. Alan Trachtenberg's account of contemporaries' reception of the work of Lewis Hine provides stunning evidence of Stieglitz's narrowing effect on American definitions of "artistic" photography. According to Trachtenberg, Stieglitz initiated and codified a deep and artificial gulf in American consciousness between "artistic" photographs, made by self-consciously artistic producers and judged solely according to aesthetic qualities, and "documentary" photographs, which neither bore the stamp of artistic intent nor excluded accidental detail. This gulf, Trachtenberg argues, prevented contemporaries from recognizing Hine's socially motivated work as "art" at all. Trachtenberg further interprets Stieglitz's drive for accommodation within the established structures of the art world as a backward-looking, anti-avant-garde strategy (*Reading American Photographs: Images as History, Mathew Brady to Walker Evans* [New York: Hill and Wang, 1989], chap. 4). In contrast, I will argue that the drive for official recognition is itself integral to the American avant-garde.
10. An interesting attempt to relate organizational transformations in the corporate and the cultural sphere, and to examine their effect on modernist production, can be found in Terry Smith, *Making the Modern: Industry, Art, and Design in America* (Chicago: University of Chicago Press, 1993).
11. Weston J. Naef, *The Collection of Alfred Stieglitz: Fifty Pioneers of Modern Photography* (New York: The Metropolitan Museum of Art, 1978), 116–53.
12. Peterson, *Alfred Stieglitz's "Camera Notes,"* 12–16; Homer, *Alfred Stieglitz and the Photo-Secession*, 34–39.
13. Works exhibited by Photo-Secession member George A. Seeley, for example, provoked the editor to comment that "although it was a severe test for these pictures to be hung after the exceptionally imaginative [drawings] of Miss [Pamela Colman] Smith, they well sustained the prestige of the galleries. The exhibition is still open as we go to press" ("Photo-Secession Notes," *CW* 18 [Apr. 1907]: 49). This self-conscious tone of reassurance quickly gave way. By October, the editors had adopted a more matter-of-fact strategy for demonstrating the appropriateness of displaying photography alongside works in more traditional media, breezily mentioning photography, etching, and drawing all in the same breath as if there had never been any dispute as to photography's position among the arts: "Some of the exhibitions planned for the succeeding month are: Drawings by Rodin; Etchings by Willi Geiger, of Munich; Photographs, by Frank Eugene; by Eduard Steichen, in color and monochrome; by Joseph T. Keiley; by F. Holland Day; a series of platinotype studies made by Clarence H. White and Alfred Stieglitz in collaboration [etc.]" ("Exhibitions at the Little Galleries," *CW* 20 [Oct. 1907]: 26).
14. Quoted in Peterson, *Alfred Stieglitz's "Camera Notes,"* 16.
15. "The Rodin Drawings at the Photo-Secession Galleries," *CW* 22 (Apr. 1908): 35–41.
16. "The Photo-Secession," *CW* 3 (July 1903): supplement.
17. Ibid.
18. "An Apology," *CW* 1 (Jan. 1903): 16.
19. Charles Caffin, "Is Herzog Also among the Prophets?" *CW* 17 (Jan. 1907): 27.
20. Current literature reproduces this interpretation, emphasizing the "collective faith" that held Secessionists together. See Watson, *Strange Bedfellows*, 68.
21. "The Editors' Page," *CW* 18 (Apr. 1907): 37–38.
22. Haviland, "The Home of the Golden Disk," *CW* 25 (Jan. 1909): 22.
23. On European Secession movements' self-conscious withdrawal from the market, see Frederick R. Karl, *Modern and Modernism: The Sovereignty of the Artist, 1885–1925* (New York: Atheneum, 1985), 109–10.
24. Stieglitz, "The 'First American Salon at New York,'" *CW* 9 (Jan. 1905): 50–51; Eva Watson-Schutze, "Salon Juries," *CW* 2 (Apr. 1903): 46–47.
25. Charles Caffin (1854–1918), who emigrated from Britain in 1892, was one of the foremost critical defenders of artistic photography in the United States. After doing decorative work at the World's Columbian Exhibition in Chicago, Caffin moved to New York, where he worked as a critic for *Harper's Weekly*, the *Evening Post*, the *New York Sun*, the *Studio*, and the *New York American*, as well as lecturing at the Pennsylvania Academy of Fine Arts and the Yale School of Fine Arts. Although initially hostile to Stieglitz's work, Caffin was convinced of its merit after Stieglitz recommended him to the editor of *Everybody's* to author a series of articles the editor had asked Stieglitz to write. Thereafter, Caffin became committed to demonstrating the artistic merits of photography, both in articles and in his *Photography as a Fine Art* (1901). On Caffin, see Sandra Lee Underwood, *Charles Caffin: A Voice for Modernism, 1897–1918* (Ann Arbor, Mich.: UMI, 1983).
26. Charles Caffin, "Pictorial Photography: The St. Louis Exposition," *CW* 1 (Jan. 1903): 44.
27. Ibid., 37. The editors' firmness on this point is evidenced by their reiteration, in the next issue, that "Mr. Strauss did not represent the spirit or ideas of those 'photographic pictorialists' who have gained the recognition of modern photography in the field of art" ("Exhibition Notes—Re: St. Louis," *CW* 2 [Apr. 1903]: 51. The friction between artistically minded photographers and their commercial/professional associates was not limited to Stieglitz's circle, but was a mainstay of organized amateur photographic "reform" rhetoric during the last two decades of the nineteenth century. For an account of amateurs' attempts to differentiate themselves from commercial photography, see Keller, "Myth of Art Photography," 251–52.
28. Joseph Keiley, "The Photo-Secession Exhibition at the Pennsylvania Academy of Fine Arts—Its Place and Significance in the Progress of Pictorial Photography," *CW* 16 (Oct. 1906): 49–50.
29. Keiley also took a personal interest in photography's readmission into Philadelphia's official art scene; he had been a participant in the first Philadelphia Photographic Salon of 1898 and experienced its subsequent lockout (Peterson, *Alfred Stieglitz's "Camera Notes,"* 169).
30. Keiley, "Photo-Secession Exhibition," 49–50.
31. Keiley's spin on this event was not unique within *Camera Work*. In describing the change from "ridicule to silence and . . . amusement to conviction" that the exhibitions at the Little Galleries had wrought during their first year, the editors wrote that "it comes as a peculiarly gratifying climax to our endeavors that the Pennsylvania Academy of the Fine Arts, one of the foremost and most influential of the American art institutions, has, unasked, requested us to select and hang an exhibition of photographs on its walls" ("Photo-Secession Notes," *CW* 15 [July 1905]: 42).

32. The Editors, "Exhibition Notes—Photo-Secession Notes," *cw* 2 (Apr. 1903): 50.
33. Cheerfully setting the terms of selection for the 1910 photographic exhibition at the Buffalo Fine Arts Academy (Albright-Knox Art Gallery), however, the Secession seemed to have no trouble assessing the works of others, announcing in *Camera Work* that "those desirous of exhibiting in the . . . Open Section are requested to send their prints, unframed, express prepaid, to 291 Fifth Avenue, New York City, where they will be judged by The Photo-Secession. . . . The selection will be governed by the principle of Independent Vision and Quality of Rendering. To eliminate accidental successes, each exhibitor in this section must be represented by at least three examples" ("An Important International Exhibition of Photographs," *cw* 30 [Apr. 1910]: 60).
34. S. L. Willard, "Exhibition Notes—The Third Salon in Chicago," *cw* 2 (Apr. 1903): 49.
35. "Photo-Secession Notes," *cw* 6 (Apr. 1904): 39.
36. Joseph Keiley, "The Buffalo Exhibition," *cw* 33 (Jan. 1911): 23.
37. The Editors, "A Daniel Come to Judgment," *cw* 31 (July 1910): 53.
38. The editors took pains to remind readers that the Little Galleries had nothing in common with art institutions with which they might be familiar, urging potential visitors to "[remember] that the Little Gallery is nothing more than a laboratory, and experimental station, and must not be looked upon as an Art Gallery in the ordinary sense of that term" ("Photo-Secession Notes," *cw* 30 [Apr. 1910]: 47). Haviland also described shows at 291 as "demonstrations of development, rather than either exhibitions of final accomplishment or 'shows' in the popular sense" ("Photo-Secession Notes," *cw* 38 [Apr. 1912]: 36).
39. As Haviland wrote, "If the position of photography among the arts is to be firmly and permanently established, this can be accomplished by proving it capable of standing the test of comparison with the best work in other media and not by isolating it" (Haviland, "Photo-Secession Notes," *cw* 31 [July 1910]: 42).
40. Charles Fitzgerald, "The Pictorial Photographers," *New York Evening Sun*, 9 Dec. 1905, reprinted in "The Photo-Secession Galleries and the Press," *cw* 14 (Apr. 1906): 33.
41. Annette Blaugrund, "The Tenth Street Studio Building" (Ph.D. diss., Columbia University, 1987), 105–7, 143–45, 149–51, 155, and passim; Gerald L. Carr, *Frederic Edwin Church: The Icebergs* (Dallas: Dallas Museum of Fine Arts, 1980).
42. Deanna Marohn Bendix, *Diabolical Designs: Paintings, Interiors, and Exhibitions of James McNeill Whistler* (Washington, D. C.: Smithsonian Institution Press, 1995), 205–68.
43. Trudie A. Grace, "The National Academy of Design and the Society of American Artists: Rivals Viewed by Critics, 1878–1906," in *Rave Reviews: American Art and Its Critics, 1826–1925*, ed. David B. Dearinger (New York: National Academy of Design, 2000), 107.
44. SRK, *USAD*, 136–37.
45. Huneker, "'The Younger American Painters' and the Press," *New York Sun*, reprinted in *cw* 31 (July 1910): 51.
46. Caffin, "The Recent Exhibitions—Some Impressions," *cw* 16 (Oct. 1906): 33, emphasis added.
47. Caffin, "The Exhibition at Buffalo," *cw* 33 (Jan. 1911): 21.
48. SRK, *USAD*, 136–37; "Photo-Secession Notes—St. Louis," *cw* 5 (Jan. 1904): 50.
49. For useful commentary on Stieglitz's recontextualization of his own work, see Trachtenberg, *Reading American Photographs*, chap. 4.
50. The Editors, "America at the London Salon," *cw* 1 (Jan. 1903): 26–27; "Exhibition Notes—The Photo-Secession," *cw* 10 (Apr. 1905): 49–50; "American Photography and the Foreign Annuals," *cw* 14 (Apr. 1906): 63. The Editors, "Photography at Important Art Exhibitions," *cw* 1 (Jan. 1903): 60–61; "Foreign Exhibitions and the Photo-Secession—Notes," *cw* 7 (July 1904): 39–40. The magazine also cited praise from "General di Cesnola, the Director of the Metropolitan Museum of Art" ("The Photo-Secession," *cw* 9 [Jan. 1905]: 56–57).
51. The Editors, "America at the London Salon," 26–27; "Exhibition Notes," *cw* 12 (Oct. 1905): 59; "Calendar of Exhibitions," *cw* 14 (Apr. 1906): advertising section.
52. The Editors, "Exhibition Notes," *cw* 11 (Jul. 1905): 57.
53. The Editors, "An Apology," *cw* 1 (Jan. 1903): 16.
54. The Editors, "Our Articles," *cw* 17 (Jan. 1907): 41.
55. "The trouble with most . . . artists is that they have 'too much ego in their cosmos.' While the majority of men are content to subordinate their ego to the aggregate cosmos, and those whose ego is of superior usefulness or superior audacity reap a material benefit, the artist is not measuring his ego with the world, but hugging it to himself. It is so dear to him that he cherishes it in seclusion, and gives out little scraps of it in charity to the world. This he calls expressing himself; and when the world, full of large preoccupation and in no need of charity, overlooks his scraps, he gives it bad names" (Charles Caffin, "As Others See Us," *cw* 10 [Apr. 1905]: 25–26). See also Caffin, "Tweedledum and Tweedledee," *cw* 19 (July 1907).
56. A useful discussion of metadiscursive editorial strategies in another modernist context can be seen in Charles Briggs and Richard Bauman, "'The Foundation of All Future Researches': Franz Boas, George Hunt, Native American Texts, and the Construction of Modernity," *American Quarterly* 51, no. 3 (Sept. 1999): 479–528.
57. Caffin, "As Others See Us," 25–26.
58. Caffin, "Is Herzog Also among the Prophets?"
59. The Editors, "Our Articles," 41.
60. "The Rodin Drawings at the Photo-Secession Galleries," *cw* 22 (Apr. 1908): 35–41. See also "Photo-Secession Exhibitions," *cw* 29 (Jan. 1910): 51–54.
61. "Rodin Drawings at the Photo-Secession Galleries," 35.
62. Ibid.
63. McCormick, in the *Press*, quoted in ibid., 39.
64. J. N. Laurvik, in the *New York Times*; J. E. Chamberlin, in the *Evening Mail*; Arthur Hoeber, in the *Globe*; all quoted in ibid., 36–39.
65. "The Fight for Recognition," *cw* 30 (Apr. 1910): 22–23.
66. "The Art Season of 1878–9," *SM* 18 (June 1879): 310–13; "Art at the Capitol," *SM* 5 (Feb. 1873): 494.
67. Theodore Child, quoted in *MA* 1, no. 1 (winter 1893): n.p.
68. Sadakichi Hartmann, "The Photo-Secession Exhibition at the Carnegie Art Galleries, Pittsburg [*sic*], Pa.," *cw* 6 (Apr. 1904): 47.
69. Hartmann, "That Toulouse-Lautrec Print!" *cw* 29 (Jan. 1910): 37.
70. Hartmann, "The Esthetic Significance of the Motion Picture," *cw* 38 (Apr. 1912): 19.
71. Recent literature tends to reiterate this, representing Stieglitz's influence as immediate, spellbinding, contextless, and driven purely by his artistic productions. Haines, for example, writes that "Stieglitz's major contribution to writers was in providing contacts" not with other writers, but with "avant-garde aesthetics" (Haines, *Inner Eye*, 7).
72. J. M. Bowles, "Photography, What D'Ye Lack?" *cw* 19 (July 1907): 17.
73. Ibid.
74. Ibid., 17–18.
75. Ibid., 17.
76. Ibid., 17–18.

Chapter 6
Continuity and Rupture

1. See, for example, Ann Douglas, *Terrible Honesty: Mongrel Manhattan in the 1920s* (New York: Farrar, Straus, and Giroux, 1995); Robert Crunden, *American Salons: Encounters with European Modernism, 1885–1917* (New York: Oxford University Press, 1993); Christine Stansell, *American Moderns: Bohemian New York and the Creation of a New Century* (New York: Metropolitan Books, 2000).
2. See Stansell, *American Moderns*; Martin Green, *New York 1913: The Armory Show and the Paterson Strike Pageant* (New York: Scribner's, 1988); Edward Abrahams, *The Lyrical Left: Randolph Bourne, Alfred Stieglitz, and the Origins of Cultural Radicalism in America* (Charlottesville: University Press of Virginia, 1986).
3. The "forefathers" approach can be seen in Crunden, *American Salons* and Douglas, *Terrible Honesty*.
4. Allan Antliff, *Anarchist Modernism: Art, Politics, and the First American Avant-Garde* (Chicago: University of Chicago Press, 2001).
5. Elizabeth McCausland, *Marsden Hartley* (Minneapolis: University of Minnesota Press, 1952), 3.
6. Townsend Ludington, *Marsden Hartley: The Biography of an American Artist* (Boston: Little, Brown, 1992), 29.
7. Ludington, *Marsden Hartley*, chap. 4 and passim.
8. As Hartley wrote about his youth, "I began somehow to have curiosity about art at the time when sex consciousness is fully developed and as I did not incline to concrete escapades, I of course inclined to abstract ones and the collection of objects which is a sex suppression took the upper hand" (Hartley, "Somehow a Past," transcript of autobiography in AAA-EM, Reel D267).
9. Jonathan Weinberg, *Speaking for Vice: Homosexuality in the Art of Charles Demuth, Marsden Hartley, and the First Avant-Garde* (New Haven, Conn., and London: Yale University Press, 1993).
10. Ludington, *Marsden Hartley*, 17.
11. Will South, public lecture on Stanton Macdonald-Wright at Los Angeles County Museum of Art, 5 Aug. 2001.
12. Ludington, *Marsden Hartley*, 18–19.
13. Ibid., 19, 21.
14. Ibid., 21, 22, 26, 47. The quote on Cox is Ludington's.
15. St. Botolph Club Records, MHS MS N-237, Box 21, Folder 16; app. B; app. C.
16. Ludington, *Marsden Hartley*, 52–53; St. Botolph Club Records, MHS MS N-237, "Bound Member Lists 1898–1939," Box 22.
17. Ludington, *Marsden Hartley*, 58–59.
18. Hartley, "Somehow a Past," AAA-EM, Reel D267.
19. SRK, *USAD*, 32.
20. Hartley, "Somehow a Past," AAA-EM, Reel D267.
21. Philip Leslie Hale to Elizabeth Saltonstall, 30 Mar. 1923, Philip Leslie Hale Papers, AAA, Reel 100; Hale to the "Chairman of the House Committee, Algonquin Club," 24 Feb. [no year], Philip Leslie Hale Papers, AAA, Reel 100.
22. Ludington, *Marsden Hartley*, 22, 55.
23. Ibid., 23; Hartley, "Somehow a Past," AAA-EM, Reel D267.
24. Rockwell Kent to Charles Daniel, 22 May 1914; Rockwell Kent to Charles Daniel, 7 Sept. 1914; Rockwell Kent to Charles Daniel, 7 Oct. 1914; Rockwell Kent to Charles Daniel, 2 Nov. 1914; Rockwell Kent to Charles Daniel, 17 Jan. 1915; Rockwell Kent to Charles Daniel, Mar. 1915; all in Papers of Rockwell Kent, UVA.
25. Marsden Hartley to Philip Leslie Hale, n.d., Philip Leslie Hale Papers, AAA, Reel D100; Ludington, *Marsden Hartley*, 54.
26. Hartley, "Somehow a Past," AAA-EM, Reel D267; Ludington, *Marsden Hartley*, 18.
27. Hartley, ibid.
28. Stansell, *American Moderns*, 102; Green, *New York 1913*, 7.
29. WHW, *Modern Painting: Its Tendency and Meaning* (New York, 1915); WHW, *The Future of Painting* (New York: B. W. Huebeh, 1923); "The Forum Exhibition of Modern Painters," announcement card, 13 Mar. 1916, UVA-WHW, Box 3.
30. WHW to Katherine Boynton Wright (KBW), 11 Sept. 1909, UVA-WHW, Box 1; WHW to KBW, Sept 16, 1909, UVA-WHW, Box 1.
31. WHW to KBW, 14 Sept. 1909, UVA-WHW, Box 1; WHW to KBW, 1? [*sic*] Nov. 1909, UVA-WHW, Box 1. Emphasis in original.
32. WHW to KBW, 12 Jan. 1913, UVA-WHW, Box 2.
33. WHW to KBW, 10 Jan. 1913, UVA-WHW, Box 2; WHW to KBW, 1912 n.d., UVA-WHW, Box 2; WHW to KBW, 1 Jan. 1913, UVA-WHW, Box 2; 1911 n.d., UVA-WHW, Box 2; 21 Oct. 1911, UVA-WHW, Box 2; WHW to KBW, 22 Feb. 1913, UVA-WHW, Box 2; WHW to KBW, n.d. (Mar. 1913), UVA-WHW, Box 2; WHW to KBW, 7 Jan. 1913, UVA-WHW, Box 2.
34. Stansell, *American Moderns*, 7.
35. Will South, *Color, Myth, and Music: Stanton Macdonald-Wright and Synchromism* (Raleigh: North Carolina Museum of Art, 2001), 15. WHW to KBW, 10 or 13 Sept. 1909, UVA-WHW, Box 1.
36. WHW, *The Man of Promise* (New York: Charles Scribner's Sons, 1930); WHW to KBW, 7 Aug. 1915 [likely misdated], UVA-WHW, Box 3.
37. WHW to KBW, 31 Mar. 1916, UVA-WHW, Box 3; advertisement and miscellaneous letters, Sept. 1915, Box 3. Beverley Boynton Wright, "Family History," unpublished ms. (n.d.), UVA-WHW, Box 10, p. 15.
38. Mrs. A. D. Wright to KBW, 4 Aug. 1915, UVA-WHW, Box 3. It is worth pointing out that, after he gave up art criticism but before he divorced Katherine, Wright did become a millionaire as mystery writer S. S. Van Dine, a fact that did not ease his meanness toward his family. His daughter recounted that, on her eighteenth birthday, he showed her his closet full of clothes and "a rack with 35 canes," gave her $25, and sent her on her way. Indeed, Katherine and Beverley Wright were not mentioned in Wright's will; they received part of his estate only because his second wife provided for them (Beverley Boynton Wright, "Family History," UVA-WHW, Box 10, pp. 24, 38).
39. Nancy Dustin Wall Moure, "Chronology of Southern California Art," in *Publications in Southern California Art 1, 2 & 3* (Los Angeles: Dustin Publications, 1984), xv.
40. South, *Color, Myth, and Music*, 18.
41. I am not imputing originality to Willard in this instance, only suggesting that, as his brother's intellectual ally and companion and as the movement's most forceful critical proponent, he played an important role in its development.
42. For Wright's own presentation of the theory behind synchromism, see *Les Synchromistes: Morgan Russell et S. Macdonald-Wright*, in Morgan Russell Papers, AAA, Reel 4539; Stanton Macdonald-Wright, *A Treatise on Color* (Los Angeles: S. M. Wright, [1924]).
43. South, *Color, Myth, and Music*.
44. "New Perspectives: Stanton Macdonald-Wright in the Twentieth Century," in South, *Color, Myth, and Music*, 1–2.
45. "Prang's Publications," *PC* 1, no. 4 (Christmas 1868): 7.
46. "Prang's Publications," 7; Pratt, *Baby's Lullaby Book: Mother Songs. Water Colors by W. L. Taylor* (Boston: L. Prang & Co., 1888). The quote is from South, *Color, Myth, and Music*, 16.
47. Nathaniel Currier was originally from Roxbury, Massachusetts. On Currier & Ives, see Sarah Burns, *Pastoral Inventions: Rural Life in Nineteenth-Century American Art and Culture* (Philadelphia: Temple University Press, 1989). The figure of a million images is from http://www.geocities.com/scurrier/history.html.
48. My thanks to Ward McAfee for pointing this out.

49. Robert Hoe, *A Short History of the Printing Press and of the Improvements in Printing Machinery from the Time of Gutenberg up to the Present Day* (New York: R. Hoe, 1902); good examples of color printing in the newspapers of the 1890s can be seen in the *San Francisco Examiner*, which used color for comics and supplements (86). On nineteenth-century color printing, see also William S. Reese, *Stamped with a National Character: Nineteenth Century American Color Plate Books* (New York: Grolier Club, 1999).
50. Wilhelm von Bezold, *The Theory of Color in Its Relation to Art and Art-Industry*, trans. S. R. Koehler (Boston: L. Prang & Co., 1876).
51. William R. Ware, "The Theory of Color," *AAR* 1, div.1 (1880): 36. This was a review of Ogden Rood, *Modern Chromatics, with Applications to Art and Industry* (New York: D. Appleton and Co., 1879).
52. Mary McArthur Tuttle, *Color: Theoretically and Practically Considered* (Cambridge, Mass.: Edward Wheeler, 1898).
53. "Introduction by Henry Lefavor," in Milton Bradley, *Elementary Color* (Springfield, Mass.: Milton Bradley & Co., 1895), 2.
54. Vivian A. C. Henmon, "The Detection of Color-Blindness," *The Journal of Philosophy, Psychology, and Scientific Methods* 3, no. 13 (21 June 1906): 341–44.
55. On the chromatrope, see Philip and Caroline Freeman Sayer, *Victorian Kinetic Toys and How to Make Them* (London: Evans Brothers, 1977), 72–76. On the relationship between modernism and psychology, see Martin Jay, "Modernism and the Specter of Psychologism," *Modernism/Modernity* 3, no. 2 (1996): 93–111.
56. "Color Work," *AAP* 1, no. 1 (Jan.–Feb. 1887): 8.
57. "The Press Room—Working Red Ink," *AAP* 1, no. 4 (July–Aug. 1887): 9–10.
58. [Walter Smith], *The American Text-Books of Art Education. Teachers' Manual. Part I* (Boston: L. Prang & Co., 1880), 5–6.
59. Bradley, *Elementary Color*, 5.
60. Bradley, *Elementary Color*, 6.
61. Dow, "Painting with Wooden Blocks," *MA* 4, no. 3 (summer 1896): 86–90.
62. Mary Dana Hicks, *Art Instruction in Primary Schools: A Manual for Teachers*, illustrated by Edith Clark Chadwick (Boston: L. Prang & Co., 1899).
63. Hicks, *Art Instruction in Primary Schools*, 67; the Prang Color Chart is between pages 66 and 67.
64. Louis Prang, *Catalogue of an Exhibition Illustrative of a Centenary of Artistic Lithography, 1796–1896* (New York: Grolier Club, 1896), 7.
65. "Color Sounds," *AAP* 1, no. 4 (Sept.–Oct. 1887): 11. Galton explored this issue in *Inquiries into Human Faculty and Its Development* (New York: Macmillan, 1883).
66. G. Stanley Hall, "The Contents of Children's Minds," *Princeton Review*, 1883, 249–72; William Krohn, "Pseudo-Chromesthesia or the Association of Colors with Words, Letters, and Sounds," *American Journal of Psychology* 5 (1892): 20–41.
67. Mary Dana Hicks Prang, "Color Hearing," *Science* 58 (1923): 421–22.
68. Hoxie, *Hand Work for Kindergartens and Primary Schools* (Springfield, Mass.: Milton Bradley & Co., 1905), 11.
69. Hoxie, *Hand Work*, 12.
70. A. H. Munsell, *The Munsell Color System: Children's Studies in Measured Colors* (Boston: Wadsworth, Howland & Co., 1910), HEH-KAEE, Box 44, envelope 5, pp. 1, 4.
71. H. G. Maratta, "The Maratta Scales of Artists' Oil Pigments," 1916, AAA-JW, Reel N60-2.
72. Cynthia Jaffee McCabe, *The Golden Door: Artist-Immigrants of America, 1876–1976* (Washington, D.C.: Smithsonian Institution Press, 1976).
73. This is conveyed graphically in the chart on ibid., 104–5.
74. Carl Zuckmayer, quoted in *The Muses Flee Hitler: Cultural Transfer and Adaptation, 1930–1945*, ed. Jarrell C. Jackman and Carla M. Borden (Washington, D.C., 1983), 104.
75. Exhibition catalogue, untitled, AAA-JW, Reel N60-1; People's Art Guild to "Dear Sir," 14 Feb. 1916, AAA-JW, Reel N60-1; Exhibition Catalogue and Invitation by the Trustees of the Hudson Guild to "The Loan Exhibition of the Pictures of John Sloan Being Held under the Auspices of the People's Art Guild," 4 Mar. 1916, AAA-JW, Reel N60-1; Statement of expenses, Jan.–Feb. 1916, AAA-JW, Reel N60-1; "List of Exhibits at the Bronx Y.M.H.A.," AAA-JW, Reel N60-1; "List of Exhibits at the 'Center' Coffee House," AAA-JW, Reel N60-1; "List of Exhibits at the University Settlement," AAA-JW, Reel N60-1; "The Young Men's Hebrew Association, The Bronx," handwritten list of works, AAA-JW, Reel N60-1; "Delivered Nov. 22 1915 to Bronx House, Washington Ave," handwritten list of works by artists including Hartley, Nathan Dolinsky, Ernest Lawson, n.d., AAA-JW, Reel N60-1.
76. The main source of biographical information on Weichsel is in an appendix to a master's thesis written by his grandson, John Weichsel: "The People's Art Guild" (M. A. thesis, Hunter College, City University of New York, 1965), app. D, AAA-JW, Reel 1079. All references from AAA, Reel 1079 are from this work.
77. "Constitution of the People's Art Guild, Organized 1915," AAA-JW, Reel N60-1; *The Forum Exhibition Committee*, "Forum Exhibition of Modern American Painters" (call to artists for entries), AAA-JW, Reel N60-1; WHW to John Weichsel, 31 Jan. 1916 and 26 Jan. 1916, AAA-JW, Reel N60-1; *The Forum Exhibition of Modern American Painters* (New York: Anderson Galleries, 1916); *Collection of the Société Anonyme: Museum of Modern Art 1920* (New Haven, Conn.: Yale University Art Gallery, published for the Associates in Fine Arts, 1950), xxi.
78. S. R. Slavsky to John Weichsel, 19 Mar. 1918, AAA-JW, Reel N60-1. Indeed, this plan resulted in disagreements with artists like Jerome Myers, who objected to what seems to have been a plan on Weichsel's part to sell his engravings through the Guild for a lower price than they would get on the regular market, and with a "Miss Morling," who apparently was very angry to find out that Weichsel had sold the first casting of one of her sculptures (and which he claimed was just like any other casting) (Myers to Weichsel, Nov. 1915, AAA-JW, Reel N60-1; John Weichsel to Elizabeth Stieglitz, 19 Jan. 1918, AAA-JW, Reel N60-2).
79. John Weichsel, "An Outline for a Prospectus. The Society of the Jewish Museum," 28 Dec. 1917, AAA-JW, Reel N60-1.
80. Ibid.
81. Ibid.
82. Statement of expenses, Jan.–Feb. 1916, AAA-JW, Reel N60-1; "Exhibition of Paintings at the Madison House," 28 Nov. to 28 Jan. 1916; AAA-JW, Reel N60-1; receipt for "6,000 catalogues" from the Modra Press, 17 Dec. 1915, AAA-JW, Reel N60-1; receipt from W. S. Budworth & Son, "Removers, Packers & Shippers of Fine Paintings, Furniture, Sculpture, Bric-a-Brac," 6 Dec. 1915, AAA-JW, Reel N60-1; receipt for deliveries, 9 May 1916, AAA-JW, Reel N60-1; receipt from *Novy Mir* for "Ads," 16 Dec. 1915, AAA-JW, Reel N60-1; receipt from *The Day* "for two adds [*sic*]," 6 Dec. 1915, AAA-JW, Reel N60-1; receipt from *[R]usskoye Slovo*, 19 Dec. 1915, AAA-JW, Reel N60-1; Alfred Stieglitz to John Weichsel, 8 Nov. 1915, AAA-JW, Reel N60-1; Maurice B. Prendergast to People's Art Guild, 2 Nov. 1915, AAA-JW, Reel N60-1; People's Art Guild to "Dear Sir," 29 Oct. 1915, AAA-JW, Reel N60-1; "The Library of the People's Art Guild," 12 Jun. 1919, AAA-JW, Reel N60-1.

83. Anna H. Drayton to John Weichsel, 18 Jan. 1916, AAA-JW, Reel N60-1; "The People's Art Guild: A Prospectus," AAA-JW, Reel N60-1; "List of Exhibits at the Bronx Y.M.H.A.," AAA-JW, Reel N60-1; "List of Exhibits at the 'Center' Coffee House," AAA-JW, Reel N60-1; "List of Exhibits at the University Settlement," AAA-JW, Reel N60-1; "The Young Men's Hebrew Association, The Bronx," handwritten list of works, AAA-JW, Reel N60-1; "Delivered Nov. 22 1915 to Bronx House, Washington Ave," handwritten list, n.d., AAA-JW, Reel N60-1; Florence N. Levy to John Weichsel, 13 Oct. 1919, AAA-JW, Reel N60-1.
84. Receipt from W. S. Budworth & Son, "Removers, Packers & Shippers of Fine Paintings, Furniture, Sculpture, Bric-a-Brac," 6 Dec. 1915, AAA-JW, Reel N60-1.
85. John Weichsel, "The People's Art Guild," preface to appendices (n.p.) and app. A, ii–x, AAA-JW, Reel 1079; John Weichsel to Albert J. Kennedy, 19 Oct. 1919, AAA-JW, Reel N60-2; S. R. Slavsky to John Weichsel, 19 Mar. 1918, AAA-JW, Reel N60-1.
86. John Weichsel to Albert J. Kennedy, 19 Oct. 1919, AAA-JW, Reel N60-2.
87. Ibid.
88. Jane Addams, "The Subjective Necessity for Social Settlements," in *Twenty Years at Hull-House* (New York: Macmillan, 1938), 113–27.
89. John Weichsel to Albert J. Kennedy, 19 Oct. 1919, AAA-JW, Reel N60-2.
90. Albert J. Kennedy to John Weichsel, 4 Nov. 1919, AAA-JW, Reel N60-2.
91. Jules Pascin to John Weichsel, 17 Jan. 1920, AAA-JW, Reel N60-2.
92. Invitation, "Committee of Hostesses for the Exhibit of the Work of Polish Jewish Artists for Private View at the Jewish Center," 1921, AAA-JW, Reel N60-2; Weichsel, "People's Art Guild," app. A, vii, AAA-JW, Reel 1079.
93. Receipts from *Novy Mir* from People's Art Guild for "Ads," 16 Dec. 1915, AAA-JW, Reel N60-1; *The Day* from People's Art Guild "for two adds [*sic*]," 6 Dec. 1915, AAA-JW, Reel N60-1; *Russkoye Slovo* from People's Art Guild, 19 Dec. 1915, AAA-JW, Reel N60-1.
94. Thomas Hart Benton to John Weichsel, n.d., AAA-JW, Reel N60-1.
95. Receipt for "Delivery, two boys carfare" for "Glintencamp painting, Dasburg, Walkowitz, Polowetsky," 23 Nov. 1915, AAA-JW, Reel N60-1.
96. M. D. Conway to James Thomas Fields, 24 Jan. n.d. (probably 1866), HEH, FI 850; M. D. Conway to Susan B. Anthony, 13 June 1882, HEH, HM 19582.
97. Louis Prang to Caroline Severance, 11 Jan. 1900 and 13 Nov. 1908, Caroline Maria (Seymour) Severance Collection Box 22, HEH.
98. Biographical information and samples of Wood's writing can be found in Robert Hamburger, *Two Rooms: The Life of Charles Erskine Scott Wood* (Lincoln: University of Nebraska Press, 1998); Erskine Wood, *Life of Charles Erskine Scott Wood: A Renaissance Man* (Portland, Ore.: E. Wood, 1978); Edwin Bingham and Tim Barnes, eds., *Wood Works: The Life and Writings of Charles Erskine Scott Wood* (Corvallis: Oregon State University Press, 1997).
99. CESW, "Autobiographical Notes–1940 c. Jan 13," WD Box 6 (4), HEH-CESW; Wood, "Autobiographical Notes 1912–1916–Biography II," WD Box 6 (1), 4, HEH-CESW; Wood, Diary #3, 1893–1894, WD Box 26 (8), 45–47, 53, 62–65, HEH-CESW; Diary #6, 1895–1896, WD Box 26 (11), 105–7, HEH-CESW. For general information on Wood's activities in this area, see Bingham and Barnes, *Wood Works*, 12–13, 101, 190; Hamburger, *Two Rooms*, 89–93, 105, 350–51; E. Wood, *Life*, 57–62, 64–76.
100. CESW, Diary #6, 1895–1896, WD Box 26 (11), 108, HEH-CESW; Diary 1913, WD Box 28 (1), 27 June 1913, HEH-CESW.
101. CESW, "Autobiographical Notes 1912–1916–Biography II," WD Box 6 (1), 4, HEH-CESW; "Autobiographical notes prepared for Max Hayek [1927?]," WD Box 6 (2), HEH-CESW.
102. CESW, "Autobiographical notes transcribed from dictaphone cylinders," WD Box 6 (9), folder 5, HEH-CESW; Hamburger, *Two Rooms*, 25–26, 69–74.
103. Wood, "Autobiographical Notes 1912–1916 [first biography]," WD Box 6 (1), 6, HEH-CESW; see also Wood, "Autobiographical Notes 1912–1916–Biography II," WD Box 6 (1), 9, HEH-CESW; Wood, "Autobiographical Notes 1912–1916–Biography II," WD Box 6 (1), 1, HEH-CESW; George S. Pappas, *To the Point: The United States Military Academy, 1802–1902* (Westport, Conn.: Praeger, 1993), 250; James L. Morrison Jr., *"The Best School in the World": West Point, the Pre-Civil War Years, 1833–1866* (Kent, Ohio: Kent State University Press, 1986), 55–56.
104. Wood, "Autobiographical notes transcribed from dictaphone cylinders [1942–3]," WD Box 6 (9) folder 18, HEH-CESW.
105. Wood, Diary 1913, WD Box 28 (1), 29 June 1913, HEH-CESW.
106. "In my youth, as an army officer I chased and killed Indians driven to revolt by the oppressions of that vague thing called, 'the government.' Looking deeper I saw that 'government' was in this case a corrupt gang which defrauded the Indian and drove him to open revolt" (CESW to Max Hayek, c. 1927, WD Box 6 [2], HEH-CESW).
107. Before the First World War intervened, Wood specially revised his "Poet in the Desert" at Goldman's request so that it could be sold cheaply "to her audiences of the proletariat" (Charles Erskine Scott Wood to Max Hayek, c. 1927, WD Box 6 [2], HEH-CESW). See also Wood, "Emma Goldman in Oregon," *The Public* 11, no. 534 (26 June 1908): 295–96.
108. Wood, "Prohibition at Its Worst," book review, *New Masses* 2, no. 5 (Mar. 1927): 26; Stanley Burnshaw, "One of the Few," *New Masses* (Oct. 1929): 22.
109. Wood, "Poems," *Poetry* 23, no. 5 (Feb. 1924): 246–49; Wood, "Cradling Wheat," *The Measure, A Journal of Poetry* 42 (Aug. 1924): 3–8.
110. Wood, "Autobiographical Notes 1912–1916–Biography II," WD Box 6 (1), 2, HEH-CESW; see also Wood, "Autobiographical Notes 1912–1916–Biography VIII," WD Box 6 (1), 1, HEH-CESW.
111. Hamburger, *Two Rooms*.
112. Wood, Diary #3, 1893–1894, WD Box 26 (8), 66–71, HEH-CESW; Wood, 15 Nov. 1913, Diary 1913, WD Box 28 (1), HEH-CESW.
113. Will South, public lecture on Stanton Macdonald-Wright at Los Angeles County Museum of Art, 5 Aug. 2001.
114. Wood, "Autobiographical Notes 1912–1916–Biography II," WD Box 6 (1), 1, HEH-CESW.
115. Wood, "Ave! Caesar. Imperator. Morituri te salutant" [anti-WWI pamphlet], n.d., WD Box 302, WD-HEH; Wood, "How Christ Spent His Christmas," WD Box 302, 1914, HEH-CESW; Wood, "Free Speech and the Constitution in the War," reprint of Wood's argument in Case No. 3328, U.S. Court of Appeals, 9th Circuit, WD Box 303, HEH-CESW.
116. Wood, Diary #3, 1893–1894, WD Box 26 (8), 1, HEH-CESW.
117. Sarah Bard Field Wood, "Charles Erskine Scott Wood," obituary, in *Assembly: Association of Graduates, U.S.M.A.* 3, no. 3 (Oct. 1944): 3–4, HEH-CESW.
118. Wood, "Autobiographical notes transcribed from dictaphone cylinders [1942–3]," WD Box 6 (9) folder 9, HEH-CESW. Examples of Wood's explicit allegiance to the abolitionists can be seen in quotes he employed in "Free Speech and the Constitution in the War," reprint of Wood's argument in Case No. 3328, U.S. Court of Appeals, 9th Circuit, WD Box 303, HEH-CESW; Wood, "Ave! Caesar."

Postscript
Pre-Modernism and Postmodernism: Reflections on the *Tilted Arc* Crisis

1. Harriet F. Senie, *The "Tilted Arc" Controversy: Dangerous Precedent?* (Minneapolis: University of Minnesota Press, 2002), 55.
2. As Senie argues, *Tilted Arc* reflected much more than a controversy about one sculpture: "Presented variously as a symbol of the end of modernism, the failure of all or a certain type of public art, the primacy of public opinion in public art matters, and the censorship of art typical of the American 1980s, the sculpture consistently stood for more than itself" (ibid., 136).
3. Or, as Senie described it, "arguments against relocation focused on the primacy of professional opinion over popular taste" (ibid., 37). Blake's arguments can be found in "An Atmosphere of Effrontery: Richard Serra, *Tilted Arc*, and the Crisis of Public Art," in *The Power of Culture: Critical Essays in American History*, ed. Richard Wightman Fox and T. J. Jackson Lears (Chicago: University of Chicago Press, 1993), 246–89.
4. Benjamin H. D. Büchloh, quoted in *The Destruction of "Tilted Arc": Documents*, ed. Clara Weyergraf-Serra and Martha Buskirk (Cambridge, Mass.: MIT Press, 1991), 91–92; and in American Council for the Arts (Sherill Jordan, Lisa Parr, Robert Porter, and Gwen Storey, eds.), *Public Art, Public Controversy: The "Tilted Arc" on Trial* (New York: ACA Books, 1987), 78. Brackets are as printed in *Public Art, Public Controversy*. It is interesting to note that Weyergraf-Serra and Buskirk omitted the adjectives "quacks and vigilantes" from their version of the transcript.
5. The quotes are from Claes Oldenburg, Joel Kovel, Annette Michelson, and Oldenburg; they are all quoted in Weyergraf-Serra and Buskirk, *The Destruction of "Tilted Arc,"* 78, 94, 96, 78.
6. A. Solomon-Godeau, quoted in Weyergraf-Serra and Buskirk, *The Destruction of "Tilted Arc,"* 75–76.
7. The ellipses do not alter the meaning of the original text, which reads: "statements from experts and laymen, from public servants, from museum curators, from public sculpture foundations, from artists, from critics, from doctors, from lawyers" (Solomon-Godeau, quoted in Weyergraf-Serra and Buskirk, *The Destruction of "Tilted Arc,"* 75).
8. "Part III: Selected Testimony," *Public Art, Public Controversy*, 57–154.
9. *Public Art, Public Controversy*, 141–46.
10. Robert Porter, Foreword, *Public Art, Public Controversy*, ix. Maksymowicz is included in the "List of Speakers Arguing for Removal of *Tilted Arc* at the Hearing" in Weyergraf-Serra and Buskirk's book, but her testimony is not included in that volume, either (*The Destruction of "Tilted Arc,"* 64). Maksymowicz summarized her objections as follows: "The issue, as it seemed then and as it still seems now, was not whether the piece was good art or bad art . . . but rather an arrogance on the part of art professionals and government bureaucrats that led to a shutdown in communication. Disdain for the concerns of the people who were to live permanently with the sculpture was not only evident in the selection of the art, but in the hearings as well, where testifying office workers were often jeered by *Tilted Arc*'s defenders" (quoted in Maksymowicz, "Through the Back Door: Alternative Approaches to Public Art," in W. J. T. Mitchell, ed., *Art and the Public Sphere* [Chicago: University of Chicago Press, 1990], 156).
11. CESW, "The Skidmore Fountain," *Oregon Historical Quarterly* 34, no. 2 (June 1933): 101.
12. CESW, Diary #6, 1895–96, WD Box 26 (11), 100, HEH-CESW.
13. Wood, "The Skidmore Fountain," 101.
14. Serra defended his right to keep the sculpture in place in terms of the artist's moral right against the destruction of his or her works. See Vera Zlatarski, "'Moral' Rights and Other Moral Interests: Public Art Law in France, Russia and the United States," *Columbia–VLA Journal of Law and the Arts* 23, no. 2 (1999): 202–40. For more general information on the current status of copyright, *droit moral*, and other relevant issues in American law, see *A Museum Guide to Copyright and Trademark* (Washington, D.C.: American Association of Museums, 1999).
15. See Richard Serra's comments in Weyergraf-Serra and Buskirk, *The Destruction of "Tilted Arc,"* 70, 3.
16. Senie, *"Tilted Arc" Controversy*, 42.
17. Julian Stallabrass, *High Art Lite: British Art in the 1990s* (London: Verso, 1999).
18. See, for example, Robert J. Holton, "Multicultural Citizenship: The Politics and Poetics of Public Space," in *Democracy, Citizenship and the Global City*, ed. Engin F. Isin (London: Routledge, 2002), 189–202.
19. Paul J. DiMaggio, "Constructing an Organizational Field as a Professional Project: U. S. Art Museums, 1920–1940," in *The New Institutionalism in Organizational Analysis*, ed. Walter W. Powell and Paul J. DiMaggio (Chicago: University of Chicago Press, 1991), 275.

Selected Bibliography

Abbott, Andrew D. *The System of Professions: An Essay on the Expert Division of Labor*. Chicago: University of Chicago Press, 1988.

Abrahams, Edward. *The Lyrical Left: Randolph Bourne, Alfred Stieglitz, and the Origins of Cultural Radicalism in America*. Charlottesville: University Press of Virginia, 1986.

Abrams, Ann Uhry. "Catalyst for Change: American Art and Revolution, 1906–1915." Ph.D. diss., Emory University, 1975.

Acton, David. *A Spectrum of Innovation: Color in American Printmaking, 1890–1960*. New York: W. W. Norton and Company, 1990.

Adams, Clinton, ed. *Second Impressions: Modern Prints and Printmakers Reconsidered*. Albuquerque: University of New Mexico Press, 1996.

Agee, William C. "New Perspectives: Stanton Macdonald-Wright in the Twentieth Century." In *Color, Myth, and Music: Stanton Macdonald-Wright and Synchromism*, ed. Will South. Raleigh: North Carolina Museum of Art, 2001.

——. "Willard Huntington Wright and the Synchromists: Notes on the Forum Exhibition." *Archives of American Art Journal* 24, no. 3 (1984): 10–15.

Allaback, Sarah. "'Better than Silver and Gold': Design Schools for Women in America, 1848–1860." *Journal of Women's History* 10, no. 1 (spring 1998): 88–107.

Altshuler, Bruce. *The Avant-Garde in Exhibition: New Art in the Twentieth Century*. Berkeley and Los Angeles: University of California Press, 1998.

Anderson, Benedict. *Imagined Communities*. London: Verso, 1983.

Antliff, Allan. *Anarchist Modernism: Art, Politics, and the First American Avant-Garde*. Chicago: University of Chicago Press, 2001.

Arrowsmith, Alexandra, and Thomas West, eds. *Two Lives: A Conversation in Paintings and Photographs*. New York: HarperCollins in association with the Phillips Collection, Washington, D.C., 1992.

Auther, Elissa. "Materials That Make a Difference: Non-Art, Media, and the Hierarchy of Art and Craft in American Art of the 1960s and '70s." Ph.D. diss., University of Maryland, 2001.

Baigell, Matthew. "American Landscape Painting and National Identity: The Stieglitz Circle and Emerson." *Art Criticism* 4, no. 1 (1987): 27–47.

Bailyn, Bernard. *The Ideological Origins of the American Revolution*. Cambridge, Mass.: Harvard University Press, 1967.

Barnhill, Georgia Brady, Diana Korzenik, and Caroline F. Sloat, eds. *The Cultivation of Artists in Nineteenth-Century America*. Worcester, Mass.: American Antiquarian Society, 1997.

Battersby, Christine. *Gender and Genius: Toward a Feminist Aesthetics*. London: Women's Press, 1989.

Baxandall, Michael. *Painting and Experience in Fifteenth-Century Italy: A Primer in the Social History of Pictorial Style*. New York: Oxford University Press, 1972.

Beard, Rick, and Leslie Cohen Berlowitz, eds. *Greenwich Village: Culture and Counterculture*. New Brunswick, N.J.: Rutgers University Press in association with the Museum of the City of New York, 1993.

Becker, Howard S. *Art Worlds*. Berkeley and Los Angeles: University of California Press, 1982.

Beckert, Sven. *The Monied Metropolis: New York City and the Consolidation of the American Bourgeoisie, 1850–1896*. New York: Cambridge University Press, 2001.

Bender, Thomas. *New York Intellect: A History of Intellectual Life in New York City, from 1750 to the Beginnings of Our Own Time*. New York: Knopf, 1987.

Bendix, Deanna Marohn. *Diabolical Designs: Paintings, Interiors, and Exhibitions of James McNeill Whistler*. Washington, D.C.: Smithsonian Institution Press, 1995.

Benjamin, Walter. *Illuminations*. Ed. Hannah Arendt. Trans. Harry Zohn. New York: Schocken Books, 1969.

Benson, Susan Porter. *Counter Cultures: Saleswomen, Managers, and Customers in American Department Stores, 1890–1940*. Urbana: University of Illinois Press, 1986.

Berger, Klaus. *Japonisme in Western Painting from Whistler to Matisse*. New York: Cambridge University Press, 1980.

Berlant, Jeffrey Lionel. *Profession and Monopoly: A Study of Medicine in the United States and Great Britain*. Berkeley and Los Angeles: University of California Press, 1975.

Bienenstock, Jennifer A. Martin. "The Formation and Early Years of the Society of American Artists, 1877–1884." Ph.D. diss., City University of New York, 1983.

Bing, Samuel. *Artistic America, Tiffany Glass, and Art Nouveau*. Ed. Robert Koch. Cambridge, Mass.: MIT Press, 1970.

Bixler, Paul. "Little Magazine, What Now?" *Antioch Review* 8, no. 1 (spring 1948). Reprinted in "1941–1950: The First Decade." *Antioch Review* 50, nos. 1–2 (winter–spring 1992): 75–88.

Blanchard, Mary W. "Embroidery, Enterprise, and the Modernist Vision in Gilded Age America." *American Quarterly* 54, no. 4 (Dec. 2002): 661–79.

——. "'It Is Surprising That There Are Any Happy Wives': *The Art Interchange*, 1878–1886." *Journal of Women's History* 8, no. 3 (1996): 36–65.

Blaugrund, Annette. "The Tenth Street Studio Building." Ph.D. diss., Columbia University, 1987.

——. "The Tenth Street Studio Building: A Roster, 1857–1895." *American Art Journal* 14, no. 2 (1982): 64–71.

——, ed. *Paris 1889: American Artists at the Universal Exposition*. Philadelphia and New York: Pennsylvania Academy of the Fine Arts and Harry N. Abrams, 1989.

Bledstein, Burton. *The Culture of Professionalism*. New York: W. W. Norton, 1976.

Blesh, Rudi. *Modern Art USA: Men, Rebellion, and Conquest, 1900–1956*. New York: Alfred A. Knopf, 1956.

Bogardus, R. F. "The Reorientation of Paradise: Modern Mass Media and Narratives of Desire in the Making of American Consumer Culture." *American Literary History* 10, no. 3 (1998): 508–23.

Bogart, Michele H. *Advertising, Artists, and the Borders of Art*. Chicago: University of Chicago Press, 1995.

——. *Public Sculpture and the Civic Ideal in New York, 1880–1930*. Chicago: University of Chicago Press, 1989.

Boime, Albert. *The Academy and French Painting in the Nineteenth Century*. New Haven, Conn., and London: Yale University Press, 1986.

Boris, Eileen. *Art and Labor: Ruskin, Morris, and the Craftsman Ideal in America*. Philadelphia: Temple University Press, 1986.

Bourdieu, Pierre. *Distinction: A Social Critique of the Judgment of Taste*. Trans. Richard Nice. Cambridge, Mass.: Harvard University Press, 1984.

Bowman, Leslie Greene. *American Arts and Crafts: Virtue in Design*. Los Angeles: Los Angeles County Museum of Art in association with Bulfinch Press/Little, Brown and Company, 1990.

Brennan, Marcia. "Abstract Passion: Images of Embodiment and Abstraction in the Art and Criticism of the Alfred Stieglitz Circle." Ph.D. diss., Brown University, 1997.

Briggs, Charles, and Richard Bauman. "'The Foundation of All Future Researches': Franz Boas, George Hunt, Native American Texts, and the Construction of Modernity." *American Quarterly* 51, no. 3 (Sept. 1999): 479–528.

Brooks, Van Wyck. *Fenollosa and His Circle*. New York: E. P. Dutton and Co., 1962.

Brown, JoAnne. *The Definition of a Profes-*

sion: The Authority of Metaphor in the History of Intelligence Testing, 1890–1930. Princeton, N. J.: Princeton University Press, 1992.

Brown, Milton. *The Story of the Armory Show*. Greenwich, Conn.: New York Graphic Society, 1963.

——. *American Painting from the Armory Show to the Depression*. Princeton, N.J.: Princeton University Press, 1955.

Bryant, Keith L., Jr. *William Merritt Chase, A Genteel Bohemian*. Columbia: University of Missouri Press, 1991.

Bunnell, Peter C. *Degrees of Guidance: Essays in Twentieth-Century American Photography*. New York: Cambridge University Press, 1993.

——, ed. *A Photographic Vision: Pictorial Photography, 1889–1923*. Salt Lake City: Peregrine Smith, Inc., 1980.

Bürger, Peter. *Theory of the Avant-Garde*. Trans. Michael Shaw. Minneapolis: University of Minnesota Press, 1984.

Burke, Doreen Bolger, ed. *In Pursuit of Beauty: Americans and the Aesthetic Movement*. New York: The Metropolitan Museum of Art and Rizzoli, 1986.

Burns, Sarah. *Inventing the Modern Artist: Art and Culture in Gilded Age America*. New Haven, Conn., and London: Yale University Press, 1996.

——. *Pastoral Inventions: Rural Life in Nineteenth-Century American Art and Culture*. Philadelphia: Temple University Press, 1989.

Burt, Nathaniel. *Palaces for the People: A Social History of the American Art Museum*. Boston: Little, Brown, 1977.

Busby, Ken, and Anne Morand. "Art and the Critic." *Gilcrease Journal* 8, no. 2 (2000–2001): 18–35.

Bushell, S. W. *Oriental Ceramic Art: Illustrated by Examples from the Collection of W. T. Walters, with One Hundred and Sixteen Plates in Colors and Over Four Hundred Reproductions in Black and White*. New York: D. Appleton and Co., 1897.

Calinescu, Matei. *Five Faces of Modernity: Modernism, Avant-Garde, Decadence, Kitsch, Postmodernism*. Durham, N.C.: Duke University Press, 1987.

Calo, Mary Ann. "African American Art and Critical Discourse between World Wars." *American Quarterly* 51, no. 3 (Sept. 1999): 586–87.

——. "Bernard Berenson and America." *Archives of American Art Journal* 36, no. 2 (1996): 8–18.

——. *Bernard Berenson and the Twentieth Century*. Philadelphia: Temple University Press, 1994.

Cary, Richard. *The Genteel Circle: Bayard Taylor and His New York Friends*. Ithaca, N.Y.: Cornell University Press, 1952.

Chen, Constance Jing Shue. "From Passion to Discipline: East Asian Art and the Culture of Modernity in the United States, 1876–1945." Ph.D. diss., University of California, Los Angeles, 2000.

Chesterton, Laura Prieto. "A Cultural History of Professional Women Artists, 1830 to 1930." Ph.D. diss., Brown University, 1998.

Clapper, Michael Roy. "'I Was Once a Barefoot Boy!': Cultural Tensions in a Popular Chromo." *American Art* 16, no. 2 (summer 2002).

——. "Popularizing Art in Boston, 1865–1910: L. Prang and Company and the Museum of Fine Arts." Ph.D. diss., Northwestern University, 1997.

——. "Art, Industry, and Education in Prang's Chromolithograph Company." *Proceedings of the American Antiquarian Society* 105, no. 1 (1995): 145–61.

Clark, Eliot Candee. *History of the National Academy of Design, 1825–1953*. New York: Columbia University Press, 1954.

Clark, Lenore. "Forbes Watson: Independent Revolutionary." Ph.D. diss., University of Oklahoma, 1995.

Clark, T. J. *The Painting of Modern Life: Paris in the Art of Manet and His Followers*. Princeton, N. J.: Princeton University Press, 1984.

Clarke, Robert Judson, ed. *The Arts and Crafts Movement in America, 1876–1916*. Princeton, N.J.: Princeton University Press, 1972.

Cole, Jr., David Allen. "The Rhetoric of Degeneracy and Evolutionism in the American Critical Response to Modern Art, 1908–1921." Ph.D. diss., University of Texas-Austin, 1996.

Coleman, Laurence Vail. *The Museum in America: A Critical Study*. Washington, D.C.: American Association of Museums, 1939.

Conn, Steven. *Museums and American Intellectual Life, 1876–1926*. Chicago: University of Chicago Press, 1998.

Conrads, Margaret C. *Winslow Homer and the Critics: Forging a National Art in the 1870s*. Princeton, N.J.: Princeton University Press in association with the Nelson-Atkins Museum of Art, 2001.

Cook, Clarence Chatham. *Transformations and Migrations of Certain Statues in the Cesnola Collection*. New York: Gaston L. Feuardent, 1881(?).

Corn, Wanda. *The Great American Thing: Modern Art and National Identity, 1915–1935*. Berkeley and Los Angeles: University of California Press, 1999.

——. "Coming of Age: Historical Scholarship in American Art." *Art Bulletin* 70, no. 2 (June 1988): 188–207.

——. *The Color of Mood: American Tonalism, 1880–1920*. San Francisco: M. H. de Young Memorial Museum and the California Palace of the Legion of Honor, 1972.

Cornell, Alice M., ed. *Art as Image: Prints and Promotion in Cincinnati, Ohio*. Athens: Ohio University Press in association with the University of Cincinnati Digital Press, 2001.

Cowdrey, Mary Bartlett, et al. *American Academy of Fine Arts and American Art-Union*. New York: New York Historical Society, 1953.

Crary, Jonathan. *Techniques of the Observer: On Vision and Modernity in the Nineteenth Century*. New York: Cambridge University Press, 1990.

Crosby, Everett U. *Chromos*. Nantucket, Mass.: Tetaukimmo Press, 1954.

Crow, Thomas. "The Birth and Death of the Viewer: On the Public Function of Art." In *DIA Foundation Discussions in Contemporary Culture*, no. 1, ed. Hal Foster, 1–9. Seattle: Bay Press, 1987.

Crunden, Robert. *American Salons: Encounters with European Modernism, 1885–1917*. New York: Oxford University Press, 1993.

——. *Ministers of Reform: The Progressives' Achievement in American Civilization, 1889–1920*. New York: Basic Books, 1982.

Currie, Gregory. *An Ontology of Art*. Basingstoke, United Kingdom: Macmillan in association with the Scots Philosophical Club, 1989.

Danto, Arthur C., ed. *The Wake of Art: Criticism, Philosophy, and the Ends of Taste*. Amsterdam: G + B Arts International, 1998.

Davidson, Abraham. *Early American Modernist Painting, 1910–1935*. New York: Harper and Row, 1981.

Davidson, Cathy N. *Revolution and the Word: The Rise of the Novel in America*. New York: Oxford University Press, 1986.

Deardourff, Elisabeth Griffith. "The New Spirit: The Armory Show and Its Impact on Modern Art in America, 1913–1929." M.A. thesis, Johns Hopkins University, 1973.

Dearinger, David B., ed. *Rave Reviews: American Art and Its Critics, 1826–1925*. New York: National Academy of Design, 2000.

Dijkstra, Bram. *The Hieroglyphics of a New Speech: Cubism, Stieglitz, and the Early Poetry of William Carlos Williams*. Princeton, N.J.: Princeton University Press, 1969.

DiMaggio, Paul J. "Cultural Entrepreneurship in Nineteenth-Century Boston: The Creation of an Organizational Base for High Culture in America." In *Rethinking Popular Culture: Contemporary Perspectives in Cultural Studies*, ed. Chandra Mukerji and Michael Schudson, 374–97. Berkeley and Los Angeles: University of California Press, 1991.

Dinnerstein, Lois. "Opulence and Ocular Delight, Splendor and Squalor: Critical Writings in Art and Architecture by Mariana Griswold Van Rensselaer."

Ph.D. diss., City University of New York, 1979.
Docherty, Linda Jones. "A Search for Identity: American Art Criticism and the Concept of the Native School, 1876–1893." Ph.D. diss., University of North Carolina at Chapel Hill, 1985.
Doss, Erika. *Benton, Pollock, and the Politics of Modernism: From Regionalism to Abstract Expressionism*. Chicago: University of Chicago Press, 1991.
Douglas, Ann. *Terrible Honesty: Mongrel Manhattan in the 1920s*. New York: Farrar, Straus, and Giroux, 1995.
——. *The Feminization of American Culture*. New York: Knopf, 1977.
Drucker, Johanna. *Theorizing Modernism: Visual Art and the Critical Tradition*. New York: Columbia University Press, 1994.
——. *The Visible Word: Experimental Typography and Modern Art, 1909–1923*. Chicago: University of Chicago Press, 1994.
Duncan, Carol, and Alan Wallach. "The Universal Survey Museum." *Art History* 3, no. 4 (Dec. 1980): 448–74.
Dunlop, Ian. *The Shock of the New: Seven Historic Exhibitions of Modern Art*. London: Weidenfeld and Nicolson, 1972.
Edsforth, Ronald, and Larry Bennett, eds. *Popular Culture and Political Change in Modern America*. Albany: State University of New York Press, 1991.
Egbert, Donald D. "The Idea of 'Avant-Garde' in Art and Politics." *American Historical Review* 73 (Dec. 1967): 339–66.
Einreinhofer, Nancy. *The American Art Museum: Elitism and Democracy*. London and Washington, D.C.: Leicester University Press, 1997.
Eisenman, Stephen F., et al. *Nineteenth-Century Art: A Critical History*. London: Thames and Hudson, 1994.
Eldredge, Charles C. "The Arrival of European Modernism." *Art in America* 61 (July–Aug. 1973): 34–41.
Evans, Paul. *Art Pottery of the United States*. New York: Feingold and Lewis Publishing, 1987.
Everdell, William. *The First Moderns: Profiles in the Origins of Twentieth-Century Thought*. Chicago: University of Chicago Press, 1997.
Ewen, Stuart. *All Consuming Images: The Politics of Style in Contemporary Culture*. New York: Basic Books, 1988.
Fanning, Kathryn. "American Temples: Presidential Memorials of the American Renaissance." Ph.D. diss., University of Virginia, 1996.
Faulkner, Peter. *Modernism*. New York: Routledge, 1977.
Fay, Stephanie Wasielewski. "American Pictorial Rhetoric: Describing Works of Art in Fiction and Art Criticism, 1820–1875." Ph.D. diss., University of California at Berkeley, 1982.
Ferber, Linda S., and William H. Gerdts, eds. *The New Path: Ruskin and the American Pre-Raphaelites*. New York: Schocken Books and the Brooklyn Museum, 1985.
Fidler, Patricia. *Art with a Mission: Objects of the Arts and Crafts Movement*. Lawrence, Kan.: Spencer Museum of Art, 1991.
Fink, Lois Marie. *Academy: The Academic Tradition in American Art*. Washington, D.C.: Smithsonian Institution Press, 1975.
Finlay, Nancy. "Some Influences on the Color Woodcuts of Arthur Wesley Dow." *Harvard Library Bulletin* 35, no. 2 (1987): 184–200.
——. *Artists of the Book in Boston, 1890–1910*. Boston: Houghton Library, 1985.
Fiske, John. *Understanding Popular Culture*. Boston: Unwin Hyman, 1989.
Floyd, Margaret Henderson. "A Terra-Cotta Cornerstone for Copley Square: Museum of Fine Arts, Boston, 1870–1876, by Sturgis and Brigham." *Journal of the Society of Architectural Historians* 32, no. 2 (May 1973): 83–103.
Fox, Richard Wightman, and T. J. Jackson Lears, eds. *The Power of Culture: Critical Essays in American History*. Chicago: University of Chicago Press, 1993.
——. *The Culture of Consumption: Critical Essays in American History, 1880–1980*. New York: Pantheon Books, 1983.
Frank, Waldo, et. al. *America and Alfred Stieglitz: A Collective Portrait*. Garden City, N.Y.: Doubleday, Doran and Co., 1934.
Frederickson, George. *The Inner Civil War: Northern Intellectuals and the Crisis of the Union*. New York: Harper and Row, 1965.
Freeman, Larry. *Louis Prang: Color Lithographer, Giant of a Man*. Watkins Glen, N. Y.: Century House, 1971.
Fried, Michael. *Art and Objecthood: Essays and Reviews*. Chicago: University of Chicago Press, 1998.
Garvey, Ellen Gruber. *The Adman in the Parlor: Magazines and the Gendering of Consumer Culture, 1880s to 1910s*. New York: Oxford University Press, 1996.
Gee, Malcolm, ed. *Art Criticism since 1900*. Manchester, England: Manchester University Press, 1993.
Gerdts, William H., et al. *Ten American Painters*. New York: Spanierman Gallery, 1990.
Goldwater, Robert. "Problems of Criticism, I: Varieties of Critical Experience." *Artforum* (Sept. 1967).
Goodrich, Lloyd. *Pioneers of Modern Art in America: The Decade of the Armory Show, 1910–1920*. New York: Praeger/Whitney Museum of American Art, 1963.
Green, Jonathan. *Camera Work: A Critical Anthology*. Millerton, N.Y.: Aperture, 1973.
Green, Martin. *New York 1913: The Armory Show and the Paterson Strike Pageant*. New York: Scribner's, 1988.
Green, Nancy E. *Arthur Wesley Dow and His Influence*. Ithaca, N.Y.: Herbert F. Johnson Museum of Art, 1990.
Green, Nancy E., and Jessie Poesch. *Arthur Wesley Dow and American Arts and Crafts*. New York: American Federation of Arts in association with Harry N. Abrams, 1999.
Greenberg, Clement. "Avant-Garde and Kitsch." In *Clement Greenberg: The Collected Essays and Criticism*, vol. 1., ed. John O'Brien. Chicago: University of Chicago Press, 1986.
Greene, Theodore P. *America's Heroes: The Changing Models of Success in American Magazines*. New York: Oxford University Press, 1970.
Gross, Larry, ed. *On the Margins of Art Worlds*. Boulder, Colo.: Westview Press, 1995.
Guilbaut, Serge. *How New York Stole the Idea of Modern Art: Abstract Expressionism, Freedom, and the Cold War*. Trans. Arthur Goldhammer. Chicago: University of Chicago Press, 1983.
Haber, Samuel. *The Quest for Authority and Honor in the American Professions, 1750–1900*. Chicago: University of Chicago Press, 1991.
Haines, Robert. *The Inner Eye of Alfred Stieglitz*. Washington, D.C.: University Press of America, 1982.
Hall, Peter Dobkin. *The Organization of American Culture, 1700–1900: Private Institutions, Elites, and the Origins of American Nationality*. New York: New York University Press, 1982.
Halle, David. *Inside Culture: Art and Class in the American Home*. Chicago: University of Chicago Press, 1993.
Halligan, Emily Julia. "Art Criticism in America before *The Crayon*: Perceptions of Landscape Painting, 1825–1855." Ph.D. diss., University of Delaware, 2000.
Haltunnen, Karen. *Confidence Men and Painted Women: A Study of Middle-Class Culture in America, 1830–1870*. New Haven, Conn., and London: Yale University Press, 1982.
Hamburger, Robert. *Two Rooms: The Life of Charles Erskine Scott Wood*. Lincoln: University of Nebraska Press, 1998.
Harbert, Earl, and Ellen Harbert. "Art Criticism in America, 1865–1880: The Early Voices of Dissent." *Journal of American Studies* 8 (Aug. 1974): 203–10.
Harris, Neil. *Cultural Excursions: Marketing Appetites and Cultural Tastes in Modern America*. Chicago: University of Chicago Press, 1990.
——. *The Artist in American Society: The Formative Years, 1790–1860*. Chicago: University of Chicago Press, 1982.

——. *Humbug: The Art of P. T. Barnum*. Chicago: University of Chicago Press, 1973.
——. "The Gilded Age Revisited: Boston and the Museum Movement." *American Quarterly* 14 (winter 1962): 545–66.
Haskell, Thomas. *The Emergence of Professional Social Science: The American Social Science Association and the Nineteenth-Century Crisis of Authority*. Urbana: University of Illinois Press, 1977.
——, ed. *The Authority of Experts: Studies in History and Theory*. Bloomington: Indiana University Press, 1984.
Hatch, Nathan O., ed. *The Professions in American History*. Notre Dame, Ind.: University of Notre Dame Press, 1988.
Herwitz, Daniel. *Making Theory/Constructing Art: On the Authority of the Avant-Garde*. Chicago: University of Chicago Press, 1993.
Hiesinger, Ulrich W. *Impressionism in America: The Ten American Painters*. Munich: Prestel, 1991.
Hills, Patricia. *Turn-of-the-Century America: Paintings, Graphics, Photographs, 1890–1910*. New York: Whitney Museum of Art, 1977.
Holton, Robert J. "Multicultural Citizenship: The Politics and Poetics of Public Space." In *Democracy, Citizenship, and the Global City*, ed. Engin F. Isin, 189–202. London: Routledge, 2002.
Homer, William Innes. *Alfred Stieglitz and the Photo-Secession*. Boston: Little, Brown, 1983.
——. *Alfred Stieglitz and the American Avant-Garde*. Boston: New York Graphic Society, 1977.
——. *Robert Henri and His Circle*. Ithaca, N.Y.: Cornell University Press, 1969.
——, ed. *Avant-Garde Painting and Sculpture in America 1910–1925*. Wilmington: Delaware Art Museum, 1975.
Hook, Dorothy Jean. "Fenollosa and Dow: The Effect of an Eastern and Western Dialogue on American Art Education." Ph.D. diss., Pennsylvania State University, 1998.
Horowitz, Helen Lefkowitz. *Culture and the City: Cultural Philanthropy in Chicago from the 1880s to 1917*. Lexington: University Press of Kentucky, 1976.
Howe, Winifred. *A History of the Metropolitan Museum of Art*. New York: Metropolitan Museum of Art, 1913.
Hughes, Edan Milton. *Artists in California, 1786–1940*. Ann Arbor, Mich.: Braun-Brumfield, 1989.
Jay, Martin. "Modernism and the Specter of Psychologism." *Modernism/Modernity* 3, no. 2 (1996): 93–111.
Johns, Elizabeth. *Thomas Eakins: The Heroism of Modern Life*. Princeton, N. J.: Princeton University Press, 1983.
Kaplan, Wendy. *The Art That Is Life: The Arts and Crafts Movement in America, 1875–1920*. Boston: Museum of Fine Arts, 1987.
Karl, Frederick R. *Modern and Modernism: The Sovereignty of the Artist, 1885–1925*. New York: Atheneum, 1985.
Karp, Ivan, and Steven D. Lavine, eds. *Exhibiting Cultures: The Poetics and Politics of Museum Display*. Washington, D.C.: Smithsonian Institution Press, 1991.
Kaufmann, Edgar, Jr. "Frank Lloyd Wright's Mementos of Childhood." *Journal of the Society of Architectural Historians* 41, no. 3 (1982): 232–37.
——. "*Form* Became *Feeling*: A New View of Froebel and Wright." *Journal of the Society of Architectural Historians* 40, no. 2 (1981): 130–37.
Keen, Kirsten Hoving. *American Art Pottery, 1875–1930*. Wilmington: Delaware Art Museum, 1978.
Keller, Ulrich F. "The Myth of Art Photography: A Sociological Analysis." *History of Photography* 4 (Oct.–Dec. 1984): 249–75.
Kern, Stephen. *The Culture of Time and Space, 1880–1918*. Cambridge, Mass.: Harvard University Press, 1983.
Kiefer, Geraldine Wojno. "Alfred Stieglitz, *Camera Work*, and Cultural Radicalism." *Art Criticism* 7, no. 2 (1992): 1–20.
Kimball, Bruce A. *The "True Professional Ideal" in America: A History*. Cambridge, Mass.: Blackwell, 1992.
Kinnard, Cynthia D. "Mariana Griswold Van Rensselaer, 1851–1934: America's First Professional Woman Art Critic." In *Women as Interpreters of the Visual Arts, 1820–1979*, ed. Claire Richter Sherman with Adele Holcomb, 181–205. Westport, Conn.: Greenwood Press, 1981.
——. "The Life and Works of Mariana Griswold Van Rensselaer, American Art Critic." Ph.D. diss., Johns Hopkins University, 1977.
Kinsey, Joni Louise. *Thomas Moran and the Surveying of the American West*. Washington, D.C., and London: Smithsonian Institution Press, 1992.
Korzenik, Diana. *Drawn to Art: A Nineteenth-Century American Dream*. Hanover, N.H.: University Press of New England, 1985.
Krauss, Rosalind. *The Originality of the Avant-Garde and Other Modernist Myths*. Cambridge, Mass.: MIT Press, 1985.
Kuspit, Donald. *The Cult of the Avant-Garde Artist*. New York: Cambridge University Press, 1993.
Landgren, Marchal E. *Years of Art: The Story of the Art Students' League of New York*. New York: R. M. McBride & Company, 1940.
Lang, Gladys Engel, and Kurt Lang. *Etched in Memory: The Building and Survival of Artistic Reputation*. Chapel Hill: University of North Carolina Press, 1990.
Larkin, Oliver. *Art and Life in America*. New York: Holt, Rinehart, and Winston, 1960.
Larson, Magali Sarfatti. *The Rise of Professionalism*. Berkeley and Los Angeles: University of California Press, 1977.
Lears, T. J. Jackson. "The Concept of Cultural Hegemony." *American Historical Review* 90 (June 1985): 567–93.
——. *No Place of Grace: Antimodernism and the Transformation of American Culture, 1880–1920*. New York: Pantheon Books, 1981.
Leja, Michael. "Modernism's Subjects in the United States." *Art Journal* 55, no. 2 (summer 1996): 65–72.
——. *Reframing Abstract Expressionism: Painting and Subjectivity in the 1940s*. New Haven, Conn., and London: Yale University Press, 1993.
Levine, Lawrence. *Highbrow/Lowbrow: The Emergence of Cultural Hierarchy in America*. Cambridge, Mass.: Harvard University Press, 1988.
Livingston, James. *Pragmatism and the Political Economy of Cultural Revolution, 1850–1940*. Chapel Hill: University of North Carolina Press, 1994.
Longwell, Dennis. *Steichen: The Master Prints, 1895–1914*. Boston: New York Graphic Society, 1978.
Loughery, John. "Charles Caffin and Willard Huntington Wright, Advocates of Modern Art." *Arts* 59, no. 5 (1985): 103–9.
Lowe, Sue Davidson. *Stieglitz: A Memoir/Biography*. New York: Farrar, Straus, and Giroux, 1983.
Ludington, Townsend. *Marsden Hartley: The Biography of an American Artist*. Boston: Little, Brown, 1992.
Lynes, Barbara Buhler. *O'Keeffe, Stieglitz, and the Critics, 1916–1929*. Chicago: University of Chicago Press, 1989.
Lynes, Russell. *The Tastemakers*. New York: Harper, 1954.
Macbeth Gallery. *Fiftieth Anniversary Exhibition, 1892–1942*. New York: Macbeth Gallery, 1942.
MacDonald, Stuart. *The History and Philosophy of Art Education*. New York: American Elsevier Publishing, 1970.
Macleod, Dianne Sachko. *Art and the Victorian Middle Class: Money and the Making of Cultural Identity*. Cambridge: Cambridge University Press, 1996.
MacLeod, Glen. *Wallace Stevens and Modern Art: From the Armory Show to Abstract Expressionism*. New Haven, Conn., and London: Yale University Press, 1993.
Mansfield, Elizabeth, ed. *Art History and Its Institutions: Foundations of a Discipline*. London: Routledge, 2002.
Marchand, Roland. *Advertising the American Dream: Making Way for*

Modernity, 1920–1940. Berkeley and Los Angeles: University of California Press, 1985.
Marzio, Peter. *The Democratic Art: Pictures for a 19th-Century America*. Boston: David R. Godine, 1979.
Masten, April F. "The Work of Art: American Women Artists and Market Democracy, 1820–1880." Ph.D. diss., Rutgers University, 1999.
——. "Art, Money, and Cultural Power in America." *Reviews in American History* 21 (1993): 69–74.
McCabe, Cynthia Jaffee. *The Golden Door: Artist-Immigrants of America, 1876–1976*. Washington, D.C.: Smithsonian Institution Press, 1976.
McCarthy, Kathleen D. *Women's Culture: American Philanthrophy and Art, 1830–1930*. Chicago: University of Chicago Press, 1991.
McCarthy, Laurette Eileen. "Walter Pach: Artist, Critic, Historian and Agent of Modernism." Ph.D. diss., University of Delaware, 1996.
McCausland, Elizabeth. *Marsden Hartley*. Minneapolis: University of Minnesota Press, 1952.
McClinton, Katharine Morrison. "L. Prang and Company." *Connoisseur*, Feb. 1976, 97–105.
——. *The Chromolithographs of Louis Prang*. New York: Clarkson N. Potter, 1973.
McCormick, Richard L. *The Party Period and Public Policy*. New York: Oxford University Press, 1986.
McFadden, Elizabeth. *The Glitter and the Gold*. New York: The Dial Press, 1971.
Mecklenburg, Virginia McCord. "American Aesthetic Theory, 1908–1917: Issues in Conservative and Avant-Garde Thought." Ph.D. diss., University of Maryland, 1983.
Meech, Julia, and Gabriel P. Weisberg. *Japonisme Comes to America*. New York: Harry N. Abrams, 1990.
Merrill, Linda. *A Pot of Paint: Aesthetics on Trial in Whistler v. Ruskin*. Washington, D.C.: Smithsonian Institution Press, 1992.
Meyer, Marilee Boyd, et al. *Inspiring Reform: Boston's Arts and Crafts Movement*. Wellesley, Mass.: Davis Museum and Cultural Center, in association with Bulfinch Press/Little, Brown and Company, 1997.
Michaels, Barbara L. *Gertrude Käsebier*. New York: Harry N. Abrams, 1992.
Miley, Randolph Benton. "A Critical Examination of Henry Turner Bailey's Method of Pedagogical Art Criticism in Context." Ph.D. diss., Florida State University, 1994.
Miller, Angela. *The Empire of the Eye: Landscape Representation and American Cultural Politics, 1825–1875*. Ithaca, N.Y.: Cornell University Press, 1993.
Miller, David, ed. *American Iconology: New Approaches to Nineteenth-Century Art and Literature*. New Haven, Conn., and London: Yale University Press, 1993.
Miller, Lillian B. *Patrons and Patriotism: The Encouragement of the Fine Arts in the United States, 1790–1860*. Chicago: University of Chicago Press, 1966.
Mills, Sally. *Japanese Influences in American Art, 1853–1900*. Williamstown, Mass.: Sterling and Francine Clark Art Institute, 1981.
Milroy, Elizabeth. *Painters of a New Century: The Eight and American Art*. Milwaukee, Wis.: Milwaukee Art Museum, 1991.
Minter, David. *A Cultural History of the American Novel*. New York: Cambridge University Press, 1994.
Mitchell, W. J. T., ed. *Art and the Public Sphere*. Chicago: University of Chicago Press, 1990.
Moffatt, Frederick C. *Arthur Wesley Dow, 1857–1922*. Washington, D. C.: Smithsonian Institution Press, 1977.
——. "Arthur Wesley Dow and the Ipswich School of Art." *New England Quarterly* 49, no. 3 (1976): 339–55.
——. "The Education of the New England Artist: The Early Years of Arthur Wesley Dow." *Essex Institute Historical Collections* 112, no. 4 (1976): 275–89.
Moore, Eudora M., et al. *California Design 1910*. Pasadena: California Design Publications, 1974.
Moore, Sarah J. "John White Alexander (1856–1915): In Search of the Decorative." Ph.D. diss., City University of New York, 1992.
Morgan, H. Wayne. *Keepers of Culture: The Art Thought of Kenyon Cox, Royal Cortissoz, and Frank Jewett Mather, Jr.* Kent, Ohio: Kent State University Press, 1989.
——. *New Muses: Art in American Culture, 1865–1920*. Norman: University of Oklahoma Press, 1978.
Morrison, James L., Jr. *"The Best School in the World": West Point, the Pre-Civil War Years, 1833–1866*. Kent, Ohio: Kent State University Press, 1986.
Mott, Frank Luther. *A History of American Magazines*. Cambridge, Mass.: Harvard University Press, 1938.
Moure, Nancy Dustin Wall. *Publications in Southern California Art*. 3 vols. in 1. Los Angeles: Dustin Publications, 1984.
Naef, Weston J. *The Collection of Alfred Stieglitz: Fifty Pioneers of Modern Photography*. New York: The Metropolitan Museum of Art, 1978.
Nemerov, Alexander. *Frederick Remington and Turn-of-the-Century America*. New Haven, Conn., and London: Yale University Press, 1995.
Nicholls, Peter. *Modernisms: A Literary Guide*. Basingstoke, Hampshire, United Kingdom: Macmillan, 1995.
1913 Armory Show 50th Anniversary Exhibition. New York and Utica: Henry Street Settlement and Munson-Williams-Proctor Institute, 1963.
The 1913 Armory Show in Retrospect. Amherst, Mass.: Amherst College, 1958.
Norman, Dorothy. *Alfred Stieglitz: Introduction to an American Seer*. New York: Duell, Sloan, and Pearce, 1960.
Ohmann, Richard Malin. *Selling Culture: Magazines, Markets, and Class at the Turn of the Century*. London: Verso, 1996.
Olson, Arlene Rita. *Art Critics and the Avant-Garde: New York, 1900–1913*. Ann Arbor, Mich.: UMI, 1980.
Orosz, Joel. *Curators and Culture: The Museum Movement in America, 1740–1870*. Tuscaloosa: University of Alabama Press, 1990.
Orvell, Miles. *The Real Thing: Imitation and Authenticity in American Culture, 1880–1940*. Chapel Hill: University of North Carolina Press, 1989.
Pancza-Graham, Arleen. "Charles Kurtz and the Glasgow School: An American Critical Response." *Archives of American Art Journal* 31, no. 3 (1991): 14–25.
Pappas, George S. *To the Point: The United States Military Academy, 1802–1902*. Westport, Conn.: Praeger, 1993.
Parker, Roszika, and Griselda Pollock. *Old Mistresses: Women, Art, and Ideology*. London: Routledge, 1981.
Peck, Amelia, and Carol Irish. *Candace Wheeler: The Art and Enterprise of American Design, 1875–1900*. New Haven, Conn., and London: Yale University Press, 2001.
Peet, Phyllis. *American Women of the Etching Revival*. Atlanta: High Museum of Art, 1988.
Perlman, Bennard. *The Immortal Eight: American Painting from Eakins to the Armory Show, 1870–1913*. New York: Exposition Press, 1962.
Peters, Harry T. *America on Stone: The Other Printmakers to the American People, A Chronicle of American Lithography other than Currier & Ives*. Garden City, N.Y.: Doubleday, Doran, and Company, 1931.
Peterson, Christian. *Alfred Stieglitz's "Camera Notes."* New York: Minneapolis Institute of Arts in association with W. W. Norton, 1993.
Peterson, Richard A., and Roger M. Kern. "Changing Highbrow Taste: From Snob to Omnivore." *American Sociological Review* 61, no. 5 (1996): 900–907.
Petruck, Peninah R. Y. *American Art Criticism, 1910–1939*. New York: Garland, 1981.
Phillips, David Clayton. "Art for Industry's Sake: Halftone Technology, Mass Photography, and the Social Transformation of American Print Culture, 1880–1920." Ph.D. diss., Yale University, 1996.
Pisano, Ronald G. *One Hundred Years: A*

Centennial Celebration of the National Association of Women Artists. Roslyn Harbor, N.Y.: Nassau County Museum of Fine Art, 1988.
Plagens, Peter. "The Critics: Hartmann, Huneker, de Casseres." *Art in America* 61 (July–Aug. 1973): 66–71.
Pocock, J. G. A. *The Machiavellian Moment: Florentine Political Thought and the Atlantic Republican Tradition*. Princeton, N.J.: Princeton University Press, 1975.
Poesch, Jessie. *Newcomb Pottery: An Enterprise for Southern Women, 1895–1940*. West Chester, Penn.: Schiffer Publishing Limited, 1984.
Poggioli, Renato. *The Theory of the Avant-Garde*. Trans. Gerald Fitzgerald. New York: Icon Editions, 1971.
Pollitzer, Anita. *A Woman on Paper: Georgia O'Keeffe*. New York: Simon and Schuster, 1988.
Postle, Kathleen. *The Chronicle of the Overbeck Pottery*. Indianapolis: Indianapolis Historical Society, 1978.
Powell, Walter W., and Paul J. DiMaggio, eds. *The New Institutionalism in Organizational Analysis*. Chicago: University of Chicago Press, 1991.
Prebus, Cynthia H. "Transitions in American Art and Criticism: The Formative Years of Early American Modernism, 1895–1905." Ph.D. diss., Rutgers University, 1994.
Prince, Sue Ann, ed. *The Old Guard and the Avant-Garde: Modernism in Chicago, 1910–1940*. Chicago: University of Chicago Press, 1990.
Radway, Janice A. *Reading the Romance: Women, Patriarchy, and Popular Literature*. Chapel Hill: University of North Carolina Press, 1984.
Ratcliff, Carter. "Art Criticism: Other Minds, Other Eyes, Part IV: 1913–25." *Art International* 18 (20 Sept. 1974).
Rebora, Carrie J. "The American Academy of the Fine Arts, New York, 1802–1842." Ph.D. diss., City University of New York, 1990.
Reese, William S. *Stamped with a National Character: Nineteenth-Century American Color Plate Books*. New York: Grolier Club, 1999.
Rewald, John. *Cézanne and America*. Princeton, N.J.: Princeton University Press, 1989.
Richardson, Edgar P., Brooke Hindle, and Lillian Miller. *Charles Willson Peale and His World*. New York: Harry N. Abrams, 1983.
Risatti, Howard Anthony. "American Critical Reaction to European Modernism, 1908 to 1917." Ph.D. diss., University of Illinois, 1978.
Roeder, George. "What Have Modernists Looked At? Experiential Roots of Twentieth-Century American Painting." *American Quarterly* 39, no. 1 (spring 1987): 56–83.
Rose, Barbara, ed. *Readings in American Art since 1900: A Documentary Survey*. New York and Washington, D.C.: Praeger, 1968.
Rosenzweig, Roy. *Eight Hours for What We Will: Workers and Leisure in an Industrial City, 1870–1920*. New York: Cambridge University Press, 1983.
Ross, Dorothy. "A Sampler of Modernisms." *Reviews in American History* 21, no. 1. (Mar. 1993): 121–25.
Rubin, Jeanne S. "The Froebel-Wright Kindergarten Connection: A New Perspective." *Journal of the Society of Architectural Historians* 48, no. 1 (1989): 24–37.
Samuels, Ernest. *Bernard Berenson: The Making of a Legend*. Cambridge, Mass.: Harvard University Press, 1987.
———. *Bernard Berenson: The Making of a Connoisseur*. Cambridge, Mass.: Harvard University Press, 1979.
Sander, Kathleen Waters. *The Business of Charity: The Woman's Exchange Movement, 1832–1900*. Urbana: University of Illinois Press, 1998.
Sayer, Philip, and Caroline Freeman Sayer. *Victorian Kinetic Toys and How to Make Them*. London: Evans Brothers, 1977.
Schapiro, Meyer. "Rebellion in Art." In *America in Crisis: Fourteen Crucial Episodes in American History*, ed. Daniel Aron, 203–42. New York: Alfred A. Knopf, 1952.
Scheele, Carl H. *A Short History of the Mail Service*. Washington, D.C.: Smithsonian Institution Press, 1970.
Schmidt, Leigh Eric. "The Commercialization of the Calendar: American Holidays and the Culture of Consumption, 1870–1930." *Journal of American History* 78, no. 3 (Dec. 1991): 887–916.
Schudson, Michael. *Discovering the News: A Social History of American Newspapers*. New York: Basic Books, 1978.
Schwab, Arnold T. *James Gibbons Huneker: Critic of the Seven Arts*. Stanford, Calif.: Stanford University Press, 1963.
Sellers, Charles Coleman. *Mr. Peale's Museum: Charles Willson Peale and the First Popular Museum of Natural History*. New York: W. W. Norton, 1980.
Senie, Harriet F. *The "Tilted Arc" Controversy: Dangerous Precedent?* Minneapolis: University of Minnesota Press, 2002.
———. *Contemporary Public Sculpture: Tradition, Transformation, and Controversy*. New York: Oxford University Press, 1992.
Senie, Harriet F., and Sally Webster, eds. *Critical Issues in Public Art: Content, Context, and Controversy*. Washington, D.C.: Smithsonian Institution Press, 1998.
Shea, James J. *It's All in the Game*. New York: G. P. Putnam's Sons, 1960.
Shifman, Barry. *The Arts and Crafts Metalwork of Janet Payne Bowles*. Indianapolis: Indianapolis Museum of Art in cooperation with Indiana University Press, 1993.
Shipp, Steve. *American Art Colonies, 1850–1930: A Historical Guide to America's Original Art Colonies and Their Artists*. Westport, Conn.: Greenwood Press, 1996.
Siedell, Daniel Andrew. "An Excavation of Tenth Street: The Failure of Modernism and the Politics of Postwar Historiography." Ph.D. diss., University of Iowa, 1995.
Simon, Janice. "*The Crayon*, 1855–1861: The Voice of Nature in Criticism, Poetry, and the Fine Arts." Ph.D. diss., University of Michigan, 1990.
Simoni, John Peter. "Art Critics and Criticism in Nineteenth-Century America." Ph.D. diss., Ohio State University, 1952.
Singal, Daniel Joseph. "Towards a Definition of American Modernism." *American Quarterly* 39, no. 1 (spring 1987): 7–26.
Skalet, Linda Henefield. "The Market for American Painting in New York, 1870–1915." Ph.D. diss., Johns Hopkins University, 1980.
Smith, Joel. *Edward Steichen: The Early Years*. Princeton, N.J.: Princeton University Press with The Metropolitan Museum of Art, 1999.
Smith, Peter. *The History of American Art Education: Learning about Art in American Schools*. Westport, Conn.: Greenwood Press, 1996.
Smith, Terry. *Making the Modern: Industry, Art, and Design in America*. Chicago: University of Chicago Press, 1993.
Smyth, Craig Hugh, and Peter M. Lukehart, eds. *The Early Years of Art History in the United States*. Princeton, N.J.: Princeton University Press, 1993.
South, Will, ed. *Color, Myth, and Music: Stanton Macdonald-Wright and Synchromism*. Raleigh: North Carolina Museum of Art, 2001.
Stallabrass, Julian. *High Art Lite: British Art in the 1990s*. London: Verso, 1999.
Stansell, Christine. *American Moderns: Bohemian New York and the Creation of a New Century*. New York: Metropolitan Books, 2000.
Starr, Paul. *The Social Transformation of American Medicine*. New York: Basic Books, 1982.
Stein, Roger. *John Ruskin and Aesthetic Thought in America, 1840–1900*. Cambridge, Mass.: Harvard University Press, 1967.
Stephanic, Barbara Jean. "Clarence Cook's Role as Art Critic, Advocate for Professionalism, Educator, and Arbiter of Taste in America." Ph.D. diss., University of Maryland, 1997.

Stewart, Patrick. "The European Art Invasion: American Art and the Arensberg Circle, 1914–1918." *Arts* 51 (May 1977): 108–12.

Tebbel, John. *The American Magazine: A Compact History*. New York: Hawthorn Books, 1969.

Tomkins, Calvin. *Merchants and Masterpieces: The Story of the Metropolitan Museum of Art*. New York: H. Holt, 1989.

Trachtenberg, Alan. *Reading American Photographs: Images as History, Mathew Brady to Walker Evans*. New York: Hill and Wang, 1989.

——. *The Incorporation of America: Culture and Society in the Gilded Age*. New York: Hill and Wang, 1982.

Trapp, Kenneth R. *American Art Pottery*. New York: Cooper-Hewitt Museum, 1987.

Trapp, Kenneth R., et al. *The Arts and Crafts Movement in California: Living the Good Life*. New York: Abbeville Press, 1993.

Underwood, Sandra Lee. *Charles Caffin: A Voice for Modernism, 1897–1918*. Ann Arbor, Mich.: UMI, 1983.

Wallach, Alan. *Exhibiting Contradiction: Essays on the Art Museum in the United States*. Amherst: University of Massachusetts Press, 1998.

Walls, Nina de Angeli. "Art and Industry in Philadelphia: Origins of the Philadelphia School of Design for Women, 1848–1876." *Pennsylvania Magazine of History and Biography* 117, no. 3 (1993): 177–99.

Warner, Michael. *The Letters of the Republic: Publication and the Public Sphere in Eighteenth-Century America*. Cambridge, Mass.: Harvard University Press, 1990.

Watson, Peter. *From Manet to Manhattan: The Rise of the Modern Art Market*. New York: Random House, 1992.

Watson, Steven. *Strange Bedfellows: The First American Avant-Garde*. New York: Abbeville Press, 1991.

Weaver, Jane Calhoun, ed. *Sadakichi Hartmann, Critical Modernist: Collected Art Writings*. Berkeley and Los Angeles: University of California Press, 1991.

Weichsel, John. "The People's Art Guild." M.A. thesis, Hunter College, City University of New York, 1965.

Weinberg, H. Barbara. *The Lure of Paris: Nineteenth-Century American Painters and Their French Teachers*. New York: Abbeville Press, 1991.

Weinberg, Jonathan. *Speaking for Vice: Homosexuality in the Art of Charles Demuth, Marsden Hartley, and the First Avant-Garde*. New Haven, Conn., and London: Yale University Press, 1993.

Weiss, Joann W. "Clarence Cook: His Critical Writings." Ph.D. diss., Johns Hopkins University, 1976.

Weiss, Peg, ed. *Adelaide Alsop Robineau: Glory in Porcelain*. Syracuse, N.Y.: Syracuse University Press, 1981.

Wertheim, Arthur Frank. *The New York Little Renaissance*. New York: New York University Press, 1976.

Weyergraf-Serra, Clara, and Martha Buskirk, eds. *The Destruction of "Tilted Arc": Documents*. Cambridge, Mass.: MIT Press, 1991.

Whelan, Richard. *Alfred Stieglitz: A Biography*. New York: Da Capo Press, 1997.

White, Maynard. *Clarence H. White*. New York: Aperture, 1979.

Whitehill, Walter Muir. *The Museum of Fine Arts, Boston: A Centennial History*. Cambridge, Mass.: Belknap Press, 1970.

Wiebe, Robert. *The Search for Order, 1877–1920*. New York: Hill and Wang, 1967.

Williams, Raymond. *Problems in Materialism and Culture: Selected Essays*. London: Verso, 1980.

Wilson, James Grant, and John Fiske, eds. *Appleton's Cyclopaedia of American Biography*. New York: D. Appleton and Co., 1888.

Wilson, Richard Guy, Diane H. Pilgrim, and Richard R. Murray. *The American Renaissance, 1876–1917*. New York: Brooklyn Museum in association with Pantheon Books, 1979.

Wolff, Janet. *The Social Production of Art*. New York: St. Martin's Press, 1981.

Wolterstorff, Nicholas. *Works and Worlds of Art*. New York: Oxford University Press, 1980.

Wood, Gordon S. *The Creation of the American Republic, 1776–1787*. New York: W. W. Norton, 1972.

Wygant, Foster. *School Art in American Culture, 1820–1970*. Cincinnati, Ohio: Interwood Press, 1993.

Ziff, Larzer. *The American 1890s: Life and Times of a Lost Generation*. New York: Viking Press, 1966.

Zilczer, Judith Katy. "Alfred Stieglitz and John Quinn: Allies in the American Avant-Garde." *American Art Journal* 17 (summer 1985): 18–33.

——. "The Armory Show and the American Avant-Garde: A Reevaluation." *Arts* 53 (Sept. 1978): 126–30.

——. "The Aesthetic Struggle in America, 1913–1918: Abstract Art and Theory in the Stieglitz Circle." Ph.D. diss., University of Delaware, 1975.

Zlatarski, Vera. "'Moral' Rights and Other Moral Interests: Public Art Law in France, Russia and the United States." *Columbia–VLA Journal of Law and the Arts* 23, no. 2 (1999): 201–40.

Zolberg, Vera L. *Constructing a Sociology of the Arts*. New York: Cambridge University Press, 1990.

Index